Certified Professional Secretary® Examin

Betty L. Schroeder, *Series Editor*

Schroeder, Lauer, and Stricklin *Certified Professional Secretary®* Review for Behavioral Science in Business, *Module I, Second Edition*

Cherry *Self-Study Guide to CPS®* Review for Behavioral Science, Module I

Schroeder, Clark, and DiMarzio *Certified Professional Secretary®* Review for Business Law, Module II, Second Edition

Cherry *Self-Study Guide to CPS®* Review for Business Law, Module II

Schroeder, Lewis, and Stricklin *Certified Professional Secretary®* Review for Economics and Management, Module III, Second Edition

Cherry *Self-Study Guide to CPS®* Review for Economics and Management, Module III

Schroeder and Webber *Certified Professional Secretary®* Review for Accounting, Module IV, Second Edition

Cherry *Self-Study Guide to CPS®* Review for Accounting, Module IV

Schroeder and Graf *Certified Professional Secretary®* Review for Office Administration and Communication, Module V, Second Edition

Cherry *Self-Study Guide to CPS®* Review for Office Administration and Communication, Module V

Schroeder and Graf *Certified Professional Secretary®* Review for Office Technology, Module VI, Second Edition

Cherry *Self-Study Guide to CPS®* Review for Office Technology, Module VI

Certified Professional Secretary® Examination
Review Series

Module V
Office Administration and Communication

Second Edition

Betty L. Schroeder, Ph.D., *Editor*
Northern Illinois University

Authors

Betty L. Schroeder, Ph.D.
Northern Illinois University

Diane Routhier Graf, CPS, Ed.D.
Saint Xavier University / Chicago

A joint publication of
PSI Professional Secretary International and

Regents/Prentice Hall
Englewood Cliffs, New Jersey 07632

```
Library of Congress Cataloging-in-Publication Data
Schroeder, Betty L.
    Office administration and communication, Module V / Betty L.
  Schroeder, Diane Routhier Graf.
         p.   cm. -- (Certified professional secretary examination
  review series)
    ISBN 0-13-188574-X
    1. Office management--Handbooks, manuals, etc.  2. Business
  communication--Handbooks, manuals, etc.    I. Routhier Graf, Diane,
          II. Title.  III. Title: Module V.  IV. Series: CPS
  examination review series.
  HF5547.S39  1993
  651--dc20                                                 92-35683
                                                                 CIP
```

Acquisition editor: *Elizabeth Kendall*
Production editor: *Penelope Linskey*
Copy editor: *Patty Boyd*
Cover designer: *Marianne Frasco*
Prepress buyer: *Ilene Levy*
Manufacturing buyer: *Ed O'Dougherty*
Editorial Assistant: *Jane Avery*

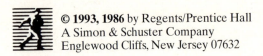 © **1993, 1986** by Regents/Prentice Hall
A Simon & Schuster Company
Englewood Cliffs, New Jersey 07632

The following are registered marks owned by Professional Secretaries International:
Trademarks and Registered Service Marks
PSI®
Professional Secretaries International®
Since 1942 known as The National Secretaries Association (International)
10502 N.W. Ambassador Drive, Kansas City, MO 64153, 816-891-6600
A.I.S.P (French equivalent of PSI®)
l'Association Internationale des Secretaries Professionalles
CPS®
Certified Professional Secretary®
Professional Secretaries Week®
Professional Secretaries Day
The Secretary®
FSA®
Future Secretaries Association®
International Secretary of the Year®

All rights reserved. No part of this book may be
reproduced, in any form or by any means,
without permission in writing from the publisher.

Printed in the United States of America
10 9 8 7 6 5 4 3 2 1

ISBN 0-13-188574-X

Prentice-Hall International (UK) Limited, *London*
Prentice-Hall of Australia Pty. Limited, *Sydney*
Prentice-Hall Canada Inc., *Toronto*
Prentice-Hall Hispanoamericana, S.A., *Mexico*
Prentice-Hall of India Private Limited, *New Delhi*
Prentice-Hall of Japan, Inc., *Tokyo*
Simon & Schuster Asia Pte. Ltd., *Singapore*
Editora Prentice-Hall do Brasil, Ltda., *Rio de Janeiro*

Contents

Preface xxi

Acknowledgments xxv

PART I OFFICE ADMINISTRATION 1

CHAPTER 1 Business Travel 1

Overview **1**

Definition of Terms **1**

A. Organization Policies and Procedures for Travel **2**
  1. Approval for Business Travel **3**
  2. Approval for Transportation **3**
B. Preparation of Itinerary **3**
  1. Determination of Travel Needs **4**
     a. Organizational requirements for travel **4**
     b. Personal preferences of traveler **4**
  2. Source Books **4**
     a. Transportation guides **4**
     b. Hotel and motel indexes **5**
     c. Timetables **6**
     d. Atlases **6**
  3. Travel Agencies and In-House Transportation Departments **6**
     a. Commercial travel agency **6**
     b. In-house transportation department or agency **7**
  4. Online Reservation Systems **7**
     a. Airline schedules **7**
     b. Hotel/motel reservations **7**
  5. Travel Reservations **8**
     a. Transportation reservations **8**
     b. Hotel or motel reservations **8**
     c. Reservations for special facilities **9**

6. Organization of Materials for Trip **9**
   a. Trip file **9**
   b. Confirmed reservations **9**
   c. Travel funds **10**
   d. Travel advances **10**
   e. Credit cards **10**
   f. Debit card **11**
   g. Itinerary **11**
   h. Traveler's quick reference file **11**
C. Types of Travel **11**
   1. Domestic Travel **14**
      a. Air travel **14**
      b. Railway travel **14**
      c. Bus travel **14**
   2. International Travel **14**
      a. Air transportation **14**
      b. Ship transportation **14**
      c. Foreign railway service **14**
      d. Automobile travel **14**
      e. Hotel accommodations **15**
   3. Ground Transportation **15**
   4. Company Transportation and Lodging **15**
D. Documents and Credentials **15**
   1. Passport **15**
   2. Visa **15**
   3. Special Requirements **16**
E. The Executive Assistant's Role in Executive's Absence **16**
   1. Understanding Limits of Authority **16**
      a. Decisions **16**
      b. Judgments **16**
   2. Communicating with Traveler **17**
      a. Communicating before the trip **17**
      b. Communicating during the trip **17**
   3. Preparing Materials to be Handled on the Traveler's Return **18**
      a. For–your–information file **18**
      b. For–your–attention file **18**
F. Follow-up Activities **18**
   1. Expense Reports **18**
      a. Receipts **18**
      b. Travel advances **19**
   2. Special Reports **19**
   3. Correspondence **19**
   4. File Materials **19**
   5. Travel Notes **19**

Review Questions **21**

Solutions **29**

CHAPTER 2 Office Management   31

Overview **31**

Definition of Terms **31**

A. Planning **33**

1. Types of Planning 33
    a. Strategic planning 33
    b. Tactical planning 33
    c. Operational planning 34
2. Establishing Priorities 34
    a. Guidelines for prioritizing work 34
    b. Identifying office tasks 35
    c. Analyzing the tasks 35
    d. Adjusting priorities when interruptions occur 36
3. Managing Time and Work Completion Effectively 36
    a. Scheduling of time 37
    b. Simplifying office assignments 40
    c. Completing tasks 40
4. Coordinating with Other Office Personnel 41
    a. Coordinating with superiors 41
    b. Coordinating with co-workers 42

B. Organizing 43
  1. Organizing Support Personnel 43
      a. Centralization 43
      b. Decentralization 44
      c. Matrix 44
  2. Organizing Work 45
      a. Leffingwell's principles of effective work 45
      b. Analysis of work 46
  3. Establishing Work Procedures 47
      a. Planning and organizing specific tasks 47
      b. Developing office manuals 49

C. Supervising 51
  1. Staffing 51
      a. Human resource planning 51
      b. Recruiting office employees 51
      c. Selecting office employees 51
      d. Orienting new employees to the job 52
      e. Providing special on-the-job training 52
      f. Employee training for different positions 52
      g. Providing guidance and counseling through special programs 52
  2. Controlling 52
      a. Delegating office assignments 53
      b. Conducting performance appraisals 53

Review Questions 55

Solutions 63

CHAPTER 3 Work Simplification 67

Overview 67

Definition of Terms 67

A. Analyzing Functions and Processes 68
   1. Selecting Work Process for Analysis 69

2. Identifying Components of Work Process **69**
   a. Work patterns **69**
   b. Work volume **69**
3. Analyzing Operations in Work Process **69**
4. Improving the Present Work Process **69**
   a. Eliminating nonessential steps **69**
   b. Combining steps **69**
   c. Inserting new steps **69**
   d. Sequencing steps **69**
   e. Redesigning forms **70**
   f. Eliminating problems **70**
5. Considering Alternative Methods **70**
6. Trying Out the Revised or New Process **70**
   a. Employee training or retraining **70**
   b. User feedback **70**
7. Implementing the Revised Process **70**
8. Evaluation of Entire Process **70**

B. Designing Systems **71**
1. Characteristics of Systems **71**
   a. Acceptability **71**
   b. Dependability **71**
   c. Effectiveness **71**
   d. Efficiency **71**
   e. Flexibility **71**
   f. Resourcefulness **71**
   g. Simplicity **71**
   h. Systematic operation **71**
2. Phases of Systems Design **71**
   a. Systems planning **71**
   b. Systems analysis **72**
   c. Systems development **73**
3. Systems Implementation **74**
   a. Phasing in the implementation **74**
   b. Refining the system **74**
   c. Communicating to employees **74**
4. Systems Evaluation **74**
   a. Measurement of results **74**
   b. Comparison with objectives **74**
5. Systems Cessation **74**

C. Tools of Systems Analysis and Design **75**
1. The Task Analysis **75**
   a. Establishing procedures for the task analyses **75**
   b. Interviewing employees **75**
   c. Interviewing supervisors and managers **76**
   d. Using a questionnaire **76**
2. Procedures Analysis **76**
   a. Flow process chart **76**
   b. Procedure flow chart **78**
   c. Office layout chart **78**
   d. Work distribution charts **79**
3. Motion Study **79**
   a. Right-hand and left-hand analysis **80**
   b. Person-equipment process chart **80**
4. Time Plans **80**
   a. Gantt chart **80**

Contents

   b. PERT and CPM **80**

Review Questions **83**

Solutions **89**

CHAPTER 4 Records Management   91

Overview **91**

Definition of Terms **91**

 A. Analyzing Records and Records Systems **95**
  1. Classifying Records **95**
   a. Record activity or use **95**
   b. Importance of records **95**
  2. The Records Cycle **96**
   a. Creation of records **97**
   b. Utilization of records **97**
   c. Retention of records **98**
   d. Transfer of records **98**
   e. Disposal of records **98**
 B. Designing and Controlling Records **98**
  1. Forms Development **99**
   a. Conventional formats **99**
   b. Nonconventional formats **105**
  2. Forms Management **108**
   a. Key factors in forms management **108**
   b. Forms management program **109**
 C. Filing Procedures for Manual and Automated Systems **110**
  1. Designing Basic Procedures for Records Storage **110**
   a. Accessing files **110**
   b. Inspecting, indexing, and coding records **111**
   c. Cross-referencing records **112**
   d. Charging out records **112**
  2. Designing Filing Classification Systems **113**
   a. Alphabetic classification systems **113**
   b. Numeric classification systems **115**
   c. Alphanumeric classification systems **118**
  3. Storing Records **119**
   a. Selecting records storage equipment **119**
   b. Storing correspondence **120**
   c. Storing noncorrespondence records **123**
  4. Retaining and Disposing of Records **124**
   a. Appraisal of records **124**
   b. Records transfer **126**
   c. Records purging and destruction **126**
  5. Maintaining Records Centers **127**
   a. On-site storage **127**
   b. Off-site storage **127**
  6. Maintaining Archives **127**

Review Questions **129**

Solutions **135**

CHAPTER 5 Reference Materials 137

    Overview 137

    Definition of Terms 138

    A. Research Procedures 138
        1. Understanding the Purpose of the Research 139
        2. Listing Possible Sources of Information 139
            a. Facilities 139
            b. Types of references 139
            c. Personal contacts 139
            d. Computer searches 139
        3. Determining Special Research Costs 139
        4. Making Appointments for Research 139
        5. Keeping Complete Records of Research Information 139
            a. Preparing a bibliography 140
            b. Taking appropriate reading notes 140
            c. Duplicating materials for later reference 141
            d. Recording interview information 141

    B. Research Facilities 142
        1. Libraries 142
            a. Classification systems 142
            b. Vertical file service 143
            c. Reference collections 143
            d. Interlibrary networks 143
            e. Computer information banks 143
            f. Library micrographics centers 143
        2. In-House Research Services 144
            a. Research department 144
            b. Computer information banks 144
            c. Business archives 144
        3. Business and Professional Associations 144
        4. Community Organizations 144

    C. Reference Materials 144
        1. Almanacs 144
        2. Biographical Indexes and Directories 145
        3. Book and Periodical Directories 145
        4. Business, Governmental, and Professional Directories and Publications 146
            a. Professional associations 146
            b. Governmental directories and records 146
            c. Business directories and publications 146
        5. Business Newspapers and Periodicals 147
        6. Dictionaries 148
        7. Encyclopedias 148
        8. Etiquette References 149
        9. Financial Services 149
      10. Newsletters and Reports 150
      11. Newspaper Indexes 150
      12. Office Administration Reference Books 150
      13. Parliamentary Procedures 151
      14. Mailing and Shipping Publications 151
      15. Quotations 151

Contents   xi

      16. Thesauri **151**
      17. Travel and Transportation Guides **152**
      18. Word Books **152**

Review Questions **153**

Solutions **157**

CHAPTER 6 Conferences and Meetings   **159**

Overview **159**

Definition of Terms **159**

A. Conferences **161**
    1. Types of Conferences **161**
      a. Company-sponsored conferences **161**
      b. Association-sponsored conventions **162**
    2. Planning a Convention **163**
      a. Before the convention **163**
      b. During the convention **164**
      c. After the convention **164**
B. Meetings **165**
    1. Planning and Organizing Meetings **165**
      a. Informal meetings **165**
      b. Formal meetings **166**
    2. Arranging Meetings **168**
      a. Selecting convenient date and time **168**
      b. Notifying participants of meeting date/time **168**
      c. Notifying executive of those attending **169**
      d. Preparing materials for meeting **169**
      e. Preparing an agenda **169**
      f. Taking notes at meeting **169**
      g. Noting important dates on executive's calendar **170**
      h. Getting room ready for next meeting **170**
      i. Transcribing notes **170**
      j. Sending minutes or meeting report **170**
    3. Conducting Meetings **170**
      a. Using meeting time effectively **170**
      b. Using proper parliamentary procedures **172**
    4. Preparing and Using Visual Aids **174**
      a. Overhead transparencies **174**
      b. 35 mm slides **176**
      c. Electronic blackboards **177**
    5. Preparing Resolutions and Petitions **177**
      a. Resolution **177**
      b. Petition **177**
    6. Preparing Minutes of Meetings **178**
      a. Preliminary writing **178**
      b. Approval by presiding officer **179**
      c. Distribution of minutes **179**

Review Questions **181**

Solutions 187

CHAPTER 7 Reprographics Management 189

Overview 189

Definition of Terms 189

A. Determining Reprographic Needs 190
  1. Original Documents 190
  2. Production Requirements 190
  3. Copies Needed 190
  4. Quality Required for Copies 191
  5. Turnaround Time 191
B. Organizing Reprographic Systems 191
  1. Decentralized vs. Centralized Control 191
     a. Advantages of decentralized control 191
     b. Advantages of centralized control 192
  2. In-House Reprographics Services vs. Commercial Printing 193
     a. In-house services 193
     b. Use of commercial services 193
C. Controlling Reprographics Systems 194
  1. Selecting Reprographics Equipment 194
     a. Specific applications 194
     b. Basic equipment operation 194
     c. Training needed by operators 194
     d. Equipment cost 195
     e. Estimated delivery time 195
  2. Matching Production with the Process 195
     a. Copy quality desired 195
     b. Number of copies needed 195
     c. Copy costs 196
     d. Preparation time 196
  3. Establishing Operations Procedures and Controls 196
     a. Operations procedures 196
     b. Operations controls 197
  4. Controlling Reprographics Costs 198
     a. Selecting most appropriate reprographics process 198
     b. Standardizing equipment and supply usage 199
     c. Conducting departmental surveys 199
D. Innovations and Trends in Reprographic Systems 199
  1. Integration of Reprographics with Other Systems 199
  2. Increased Use of In-House Facilities 200
  3. Laser Printing 200
  4. Facsimile Transmission (FAX) 200
  5. Voice Pressing 200
  6. Visual Information Display 200
  7. Optical Character Recognition (OCR) 200

Review Questions 201

Solutions 207

PART II: COMMUNICATION 209

CHAPTER 8 Composing Communications 209

Overview 209

Definition of Terms 210

A. Fundamentals of Writing 212
   1. Effective Word Selection 213
      a. Positive language 213
      b. Tone 213
      c. Familiar words 214
      d. Concrete language 214
      e. Active words 215
      f. Contemporary words and expressions 216
      g. Unbiased language 216
   2. Effective Sentence and Paragraph Construction 219
      a. Constructing effective sentences 219
      b. Developing organized paragraphs 220
      c. Criteria for effective sentence and paragraph construction 221
      d. Development of goodwill 225
B. Business Letters 227
   1. Positive Letters 227
      a. Types of positive letters 227
      b. Writing approach 228
   2. Routine or Neutral Letter 229
      a. Types of routine letters 229
      b. Writing approach 230
   3. Negative Letter 231
      a. Types of negative letters 231
      b. Writing approach 232
   4. Combination Letter 234
      a. Types of combination letters 234
      b. Writing approach 235
   5. Persuasive Letter 236
      a. Types of persuasive letters 236
      b. Writing approach 237
   6. Form Letters 238
      a. Personalized repetitive letters 238
      b. Letters with variable information 240
      c. Letters from form paragraphs 242
C. Interoffice Communication 243
   1. Memorandums 243
      a. Favorable memorandums 244
      b. Unfavorable memorandums 245
      c. Persuasive memorandums 246
   2. Informal or Short Reports 247
      a. Types of informal or short reports 247
      b. Acceptable formats 248
      c. Writing approach 248
D. Business Reports 248
   1. Types of Reports 248
      a. Material 248
      b. Time interval 249

c. Informational flow **249**
d. Context **249**
e. Function **249**
f. Message style **249**
2. Planning, Designing, and Conducting Research **249**
a. Definition of problem **250**
b. Collecting data **250**
c. Analyzing data **256**
d. Reporting findings and drawing conclusions **257**
e. Organizing the report **258**
f. Writing the report **259**
E. Dictation Skills **261**
1. Interpreting Dictation **261**
a. Numeric data **261**
b. Grammar and punctuation **261**
2. Dictating Messages **261**
a. Dictation machine **261**
b. Voice mail **263**
c. Answering machine **263**
F. Listening and Oral Communication Skills **264**
1. Suggestions for Better Listening **264**
a. Avoid distractions **264**
b. Identify a purpose **264**
c. Understand the main ideas **264**
d. Control emotions **264**
e. Stay alert **264**
2. Listening Techniques **264**
a. Taking directions **265**
b. Taking instructions **265**
c. Taking orders **265**
d. Sharing ideas **265**

Review Questions **267**

Solutions **275**

CHAPTER 9 Editing Communications 277

Overview **277**

Definition of Terms **277**

A. Proofreading **278**
1. Proofreading Methods **278**
a. Proofreading for typographical errors **278**
b. Proofreading for content **278**
c. Proofreading by other personnel **278**
2. Proofreading Techniques **278**
a. Reading the copy **279**
b. Aligning copy **279**
c. Proofreading vertically **279**
d. Counting entries **279**
e. Delaying final proofreading **279**
3. Proofreading Symbols **279**
4. Proofreading Software **279**

Contents

        a. Activating the spell-check feature **279**
        b. Adding unrecognized words to dictionary **279**
        c. Checking grammar **279**
  B. Editing for Technical Correctness **281**
    1. Grammar and Word Usage **281**
        a. Elements of a sentence **281**
        b. Secondary elements of a sentence **284**
    2. Punctuation **286**
        a. Apostrophe **286**
        b. Colon **287**
        c. Comma **288**
        d. Dash **291**
        e. Exclamation point **291**
        f. Ellipsis **291**
        g. Hyphen **292**
        h. Parentheses **293**
        i. Period **294**
        j. Question mark **295**
        k. Quotation mark **295**
        l. Semicolon **296**
        m. Underscore **297**
    3. Capitalization **297**
        a. Beginning a sentence **298**
        b. A sentence within parentheses **298**
        c. Beginning a quotation **298**
        d. Pronoun I
        e. Titles of people **298**
        f. Books and articles **298**
        g. Academic courses **299**
        h. Geographic locations **299**
        i. Organizations **299**
        j. Institutions **299**
        k. Groups **300**
        l. Objects **300**
        m. Elements of time **300**
    4. Format and Appearance **300**
        a. Format **300**
        b. Appearance **301**
    5. Consistent Style **305**
        a. Format patterns **305**
        b. Word Usage **306**
        c. Tone **306**
        d. Punctuation **306**
    6. Spelling and Keyboarding Accuracy **306**
        a. *ie* and *ei* **307**
        b. *ie* ending **307**
        c. Silent *e* ending **307**
        d. Silent *e* with compounds **307**
        e. *ee* ending **307**
        f. *cle* and *cal* **308**
        g. *ph, gh, ch, i* **308**
        h. *cede, ceed, sede* **308**
        i. *y* ending preceded by a vowel **308**
        j. *y* ending preceded by a consonant **308**
        k. *ful* **308**
        l. Doubling the ending consonant **309**

            m. Compounds **309**
    7. Guidelines for Proper Use of Numbers **309**
        a. Numbers from one through ten **309**
        b. Specific numbers ten or under **309**
        c. Sets of numbers within sentence **310**
        d. Money **310**
        e. Percentages **310**
        f. Mixed numbers **310**
        g. Beginning sentence with number **311**
        h. Hyphens in numbers **311**
        i. Two numbers for one item **311**
        j. Dates **311**
        k. Time **311**
        l. Grouping of numbers **311**
        m. Expressing large numbers **312**
        n. Spelling out other forms of numbers **312**
        o. Numbers in legal copy **312**
        p. Descriptive numbers **312**
        q. Age **312**
        r. Street names **312**
        s. Plurals **313**
    8. Guidelines for Word Division and Hyphenation **313**
        a. General suggestions for word division **313**
        b. Rules for word division **313**
        c. Hyphenation with word processing **317**
    9. Use of Editing Software **317**
C. Copy Editing for Application of Writing Fundamentals **317**
    1. Guidelines for Preparing Copy for Editing **318**
        a. Side margins **318**
        b. Spacing **318**
        c. Paragraphs **318**
        d. Readability of copy **318**
    2. Basic Skills for Editing **318**
        a. Grammar skills **318**
        b. Punctuation skills **318**
        c. Spelling skills **318**
        d. Composition skills **319**
    3. Effective Word Selection **319**
        a. Accept and except **319**
        b. Advise and advice **319**
        c. All ready and already **319**
        d. Among and between **320**
        e. Awhile and a while **320**
        f. Bad and badly **320**
        g. Complement and compliment **320**
        h. Effect and affect **320**
        i. Good and well **321**
        j. Lay and lie **321**
        k. Lose and loose **321**
        l. Most and almost **321**
        m. Proceed and precede **322**
        n. Principal and principle **322**
        o. Real and really **322**
        p. Set and sit **322**
        q. Site, cite, and sight **322**

r. Their, there, and they're **322**
s. Then and than **323**
t. To, too, and two **323**
u. Who, which, and that **323**
4. Effective Sentence and Paragraph Construction **323**
    a. Incomplete sentence **323**
    b. Run-on sentences **324**
    c. Paragraph construction **324**
5. Tone, Goodwill, Considerateness, and Writing Style **325**
6. Editing for Organization **325**
    a. Communication between writer and copy editor **325**
    b. Approach used **326**
    c. Outline **326**
7. Editing for Completeness and Content Accuracy **326**
    a. Looking it up **327**
    b. Checking and double-checking **327**
    c. Being consistent **327**
    d. Maintaining the author's writing style **327**
8. Copy Editing Style Sheet **328**
9. Copy Editing Symbols **328**
10. Word Processing and Copy Editing **328**
    a. Using word processing **328**
    b. Using a typewriter **329**

Review Questions **331**

Solutions **341**

CHAPTER 10 Abstracting Communications 345

Overview **345**

Definition of Terms **345**

A. Techniques **345**
    1. Photocopying **346**
        a. Efficient use of the photocopier **346**
        b. Legal use of the copier **347**
    2. Highlighting Key Points **348**
        a. Underlining **348**
        b. Overmarking **348**
        c. Colored marker, pen, or pencil **348**
    3. Summarizing Key Points **348**
        a. Abstract **349**
        b. Précis **349**
    4. Computerized Services **349**
        a. Subscription **349**
        b. Database search **349**
B. Effective Abstracts and Précis **350**
    1. Concise Summary of Key Points **350**
        a. Abstract **350**
        b. Précis **350**
    2. Relevant Information **350**
        a. Facts **350**

    b. Listings **350**
    c. Headings **350**
    d. Topic sentences **350**
  3. Reporting Major Conclusions **351**
  4. Complete Documentation **351**
    a. Bibliographical information **351**
    b. Placement of bibliographical information **351**
  5. Level of Language Consistent with Original **351**
    a. Summaries within original **352**
    b. First reading **352**
    c. Second reading **352**
    d. Taking notes **352**
    e. Rough copy **352**
    f. Edit **352**
    g. Final copy **352**
  6. Easy-to-read Format **352**
    a. Abstract format **352**
    b. Précis format **352**
  7. Distinguishing Abstracts from Précis **352**
  8. Using the Abstract or Précis **355**

Review Questions **357**

Solutions **361**

CHAPTER 11 Preparing Communications in Final Format 363

Overview **363**

Definition of Terms **363**

A. Business Letter Format **365**
  1. Format of Business Letter **365**
    a. Date **365**
    b. Inside address **366**
    c. Attention line (optional) **367**
    d. Salutation **367**
    e. Subject line (optional) **367**
    f. Body of the letter **368**
    g. Complimentary closing **368**
    h. Typed signature line **368**
    i. Reference initials **369**
    j. Enclosure notation **369**
    k. Copy notation **369**
    l. Spacing summary **370**
    m. Special notations **370**
  2. Letter Styles **371**
    a. Blocked letter style **371**
    b. Modified block letter style **371**
    c. Simplified letter style **371**
  3. Punctuation Styles **371**
    a. Open punctuation **372**
    b. Mixed punctuation **372**
  4. Second Page of a Letter **373**
    a. Blocked style **373**
    b. Modified blocked style **374**
    c. Word processing headings **374**

- B. Envelopes **374**
    1. Conventional Style **376**
    2. OCR Requirements **376**
    3. Label/Plate **379**
    4. Computer Generated Addresses **379**
        a. Database management software **380**
        b. Word processing software with mail-merge **380**
        c. Word processing software with no mail-merge function **381**
- C. Memorandum Format **381**
    1. Format of Interoffice Memorandum **381**
        a. Top margin and heading **381**
        b. Side margins **381**
        c. Notation lines **382**
        d. Reference initials **383**
    2. Style for Interoffice Memorandum **383**
- D. Business Report Format **383**
    1. Physical Layout **383**
        a. Margins **383**
        b. Title of report **385**
        c. Spacing of paragraphs **385**
    2. Headings **386**
        a. Hierarchy of divisions **386**
        b. Spacing for headings **386**
    3. Pagination **386**
        a. Numbering the first page **386**
        b. Numbering succeeding pages **387**
    4. Automatic Generation of Supplements **387**
    5. Word Processing Format for Printing Reports **387**
        a. Plan **387**
        b. Create **387**
        c. Edit **387**
        d. Format **387**
        e. Save/Print **388**
    6. Margin Guide **389**
        a. Preparing the margin guide **389**
        b. Using the margin guide **389**
    7. Documentation **389**
        a. Types of citations **389**
        b. Formats for citations **392**
        c. Later references to same citation **392**
        d. Placement of citations **393**
        e. Bibliography **394**
        f. Format for bibliography **394**
    8. Graphics **396**
        a. Purposes of business graphics **396**
        b. Placement of graphic illustrations within text **397**
        c. Types of graphic illustrations **399**
        d. Preparation of graphic illustrations **401**
    9. Statistical Data Format **402**
        a. Word Processing table feature **402**
        b. Placement of table **403**
- E. Disk Storage Notations **408**
    1. Naming Files **408**

a. Characters in file name **409**
b. File contents **409**
c. Unique file names within applications **409**
2. Naming Storage Medium **410**
a. External label **410**
b. Disk label **410**
c. Disk organization **410**
F. Other Forms of Business Communications **411**
1. Minutes **411**
a. Heading **411**
b. Attendance **411**
c. Body **412**
d. Motions **413**
e. Closing **413**
2. News Release **413**
a. Heading **414**
b. Body **414**
c. Closing symbols **414**
d. Spacing the news release **414**
3. Itinerary **415**
a. Types of information **415**
b. Parts of the itinerary **415**
c. Format of itinerary **417**
4. Outline **417**
a. Coding the outline **417**
b. Spacing an outline **419**
5. Speech **419**
a. Typed outline of speech **420**
b. The actual speech **420**
c. Handout materials **421**
d. Visual aids **421**

Review Questions **423**

Solutions **433**

Glossary **435**

PREFACE

The PRENTICE HALL CERTIFIED PROFESSIONAL SECRETARY® EXAMINATION REVIEW SERIES consists of six review manuals, jointly published by Prentice Hall and Professional Secretaries International (PSI), designed as review materials for the Certified Professional Secretary (CPS) Examination. The content of each module is based on the current CPS Study Outline published in CAPSTONE, the publication of the Institute for Certifying Secretaries publicizing application and requirements for the CPS Examination.

Module V—Office Administration and Communication is meant to be a *review* for those secretaries who already have completed one or more courses in office administration or business communication or an *introduction* for those secretaries who have never before enrolled in an office administration or business communications course. A thorough study of this module, of course, does not guarantee passage of Part V of the CPS Examination. Using this review manual, however, should provide valuable assistance for self-study or group review sessions. In addition to using this review manual for study, it will probably be necessary for secretaries to enroll in at least one office management course as a more thorough review.

The format used for each of the six modules in the series is identical. The current CPS Study Outline and Bibliography were used initially to define exactly what the content of the module should be and the types of references that the Institute was recommending for study. Then, this outline was expanded so that more comprehensive coverage of the topics could be planned and included in the manual. Each chapter includes:

- An **overview** introducing the reader to the chapter and its content.
- The **definition of terms** to be found within the chapter.

- A complete **sentence/paragraph outline**, with examples highlighted in italic type to enhance the sentence outline.
- **Review questions** at the end of the chapter, developed in similar format to those found on the CPS Examination.
- **Solutions** to the review questions, with the identification of the correct answer, and reference to the sentence/paragraph outline.

Module V—Office Administration and Communication is divided into two parts—the first part emphasizing basic content in office administration and the second part emphasizing basic content in communications, as outlined in the current CPS Study Outline. The question formats used for the review questions at the end of each chapter include multiple-choice questions, matching sets, and problem situations with multiple-choice questions pertaining to them. The current CPS Examination presents questions primarily as multiple-choice questions, alone or in problem situations. For review of technical terms as well as developing an understanding of basic concepts and principles, the authors believe that other question formats can also be helpful tools. Therefore, some matching sets are included with each set of review questions to provide adequate practice in studying terms, definitions, and other basic principles included in the chapter. Past CPS examinations have sometimes included these questions in this format as well.

The solutions to the review questions are presented in a format that should be particularly helpful for review. These solutions include the correct answer, a reference to the section of the chapter content that has a more complete explanation, and any additional explanation that the authors believe may be necessary in understanding the correct response to the question. Here is an example:

        Answer   *Refer to Chapter Section*
10. (b)   {B-6-d} A travel advance enables the
                          business traveler to pay ...
The content reference {B-6-d} refers to:
    Section B, Point 6, Subpoint d of the chapter

When a solution seems unclear, it is an excellent idea to return to the sentence/paragraph outline and review the material included under that topic. Review questions have been included to give candidates further review and practice with questions similar to those found on the exam before going on to the next chapter.

At the end of this module, a complete Glossary of terms and definitions included in each chapter of *Module V—Office Administration and Communication* is presented as a quick guide to terms. The Glossary is divided into two parts—Office Administration and Communication. A reference is included to the chapter where the term may be found in context.

The question arises as to why this review manual and the other review manuals in the series are formatted in this particular way. The response is simple: we want you to have a thorough, but rather quick, review of the content that may appear on the CPS Examination this year. You should still refer to other office management, office administration, and business communications references, especially those referred to in the CPS Study Outline and Bibliography, for more detailed explanations and/or a variety of learning materials to test your knowledge and competence in these topical areas.

The INSTRUCTOR'S MANUAL is a separate publication, correlated to accompany *Module V—Office Administration and Communication*. This manual is available to instructors of CPS review courses and includes the following helpful materials:

- **Teaching Suggestions:** Suggested teaching ideas for office administration and communication review sessions; learning activities to incorporate into classroom or seminar instruction.
- **Test Bank:** A sample test for office administration and communication; solutions for each test, with outline references correlated with the review manual.
- **Reading References:** Bibliography of books, periodical, and special references that may be helpful to secretaries as well as instructors.

We hope that the contents of this INSTRUCTOR'S MANUAL will help instructors provide a successful CPS review program in office administration and communication.

Betty L. Schroeder, Ph.D.
Series Editor

ACKNOWLEDGMENTS

The development of the second edition of *Module V—Office Administration and Communication* of the PRENTICE HALL CERTIFIED PROFESSIONAL SECRETARY® EXAMINATION REVIEW SERIES was possible only because of the sincere and dedicated efforts of a number of individuals who are committed to helping secretaries, office administration students, and business educators become Certified Professional Secretaries. Like the other review manuals in the series, *Module V—Office Administration and Communication* has become a successful review tool because of the contributions of a number of people who have given of their time and expertise to assist in the review process to be sure that the content of the review manuals is appropriate for this particular examination.

We gratefully acknowledge the contributions of Virginia Melvin CPS, Shelley J. Stoeckl CPS, Susan C. Bauer, and Jean M. Mills for their extremely helpful reviews and critiques of the manuscript.

Professional Secretaries International, through the Institute for Certifying Secretaries, has provided not only the incentive for the development of the second edition of this review manual but also valuable input during the review process. We sincerely thank the following individuals for their continued interest in and enthusiasm for the development and revision of the series:

Mrs. Jean Mills, Dean, Institute for Certifying Secretaries

Jerome Heitman, Executive Director, Professional Secretaries International

Dr. Susan Fenner, Education/Professional Development Manager, Professional Secretaries International

Mrs. Janet Heat, Operations/CPS/Membership, Professional Secretaries International

A very special thank you is given to the members of the Illinois Division of Professional Secretaries International and, in particular, those members of Kishwaukee Chapter, DeKalb, Illinois, who have pursued or have received their professional certification over the past several years. They have continued to be extremely supportive and positive about the use of these review manuals, and their friendship is very much appreciated.

Lastly, we are most appreciative of the leadership and assistance given by Elizabeth Kendall of Prentice Hall, Inc., and her staff for their continued strong support of this series. It is a joy to work with individuals so professional in their judgment of what secretaries need in preparation for the CPS Examination.

And, of course, thank you to anyone else who helped along the way!

We hope that all of the input provided by professionals throughout the review and revision process will continue to make this review manual (and the other five in the series) the "leaders" in providing an excellent review for the CPS Examination in the future.

Betty L. Schroeder, Ph.D.
Diane Routhier Graf, Ed.D., CPS

PART I Office Administration

CHAPTER 1
Business Travel

OVERVIEW

A very important business procedure that office personnel are often required to handle is travel. Company policy will dictate how business travel should be arranged. Some companies with large travel budgets make special agreements with travel agencies, hotels, or transportation companies. The executive assistant or secretary needs to be aware of the procedures to use (a) when the organization has its own travel department, (b) when it is necessary to use the services of a local travel agency, or (c) when office personnel must make all travel arrangements for business travel.

The person who assists the executive in making business travel arrangements must be familiar with various types of services and conditions of travel facilities that may be available as well as personal preferences with regard to dates, times, and types of travel. After the trip, the traveler's satisfaction with the arrangements made for the trip needs to be checked.

It will be especially important for the secretary to recognize and be familiar with terms associated with business travel as well as procedures for preparing an itinerary, using source books and the services of agencies, making reservations, and assembling trip folders for the executive.

DEFINITION OF TERMS

COMMERCIAL TRAVEL AGENCY. A business firm specializing in making travel arrangements for individuals and organizations requesting travel services.

CONFIRMED RESERVATION. Notification from a transportation carrier or a hotel that a reservation is being held for a given individual.

DEBIT CARD. A card issued by a bank, similar to a credit card, which allows the cardholder to charge the purchases of merchandise or services and have that charge come directly out of the cardholder's bank account.

DOMESTIC TRAVEL. Transportation services provided for travel within the boundaries of a country.

IN-HOUSE TRANSPORTATION DEPARTMENT. A department within a firm organized to provide travel services for all departments within the organization, sometimes organized as an in-house travel agency.

INTERNATIONAL TRAVEL. Transportation services provided for travel in, to, and from other countries.

ITINERARY. A business traveler's plan which includes departure and arrival information, confirmed transportation and hotel/motel reservations, and scheduled appointments and meetings.

LETTER OF CREDIT. A letter from a bank or other financial institution stating the maximum amount of money available through that bank or institution to the individual carrying the letter.

OFFICIAL AIRLINE GUIDE (OAG). A published guide with detailed information on airline schedules and fares for both domestic and international flights.

ONLINE RESERVATION SYSTEM. A computer system connecting the travel department or agency directly with the transportation companies or with the Official Airline Guide (OAG) reservation system in order to make travel reservations directly with the carriers.

PASSPORT. A formal document that is proof of citizenship and identity, valid for ten years, issued by the citizen's own government granting permission to the citizen to leave the country and travel in foreign countries.

SOURCE BOOK. A reference with specific travel information useful in making appropriate transportation, hotel, and motel reservations.

TRAVEL ADVANCE. An amount of money received from the organization to be used for payment of out-of-pocket expenses incurred while on business travel.

TRAVELERS' CHECKS. Drafts purchased through local banks, credit unions, the American Automobile Association, and savings and loan associations that can be cashed *only* by the purchaser.

TRIP FILE. A folder (or series of folders) containing all business materials the business traveler needs to carry on a business trip.

VISA. An endorsement stamped or written on a passport, showing examination by appropriate officials of a foreign country, which grants the bearer entry into that country for a specified period of time. In many foreign countries, a visa is not required.

A. Organization Policies and Procedures for Travel

Before any travel arrangements can be made, the executive assistant or secretary needs to be familiar with organization policies and procedures concerning approved business travel. Travel policies and procedures are very important for the individual traveler to be aware of and follow. They specify coverage for work duties usually performed or eligibility for business insurance coverage during the trip. Business travelers need to follow specific procedures established by the organization in arranging authorized travel.

1. *Approval for Business Travel:* Any employee—executive, manager, or other office professional—must receive supervisory approval for business travel. Typically, a form requesting authorization to travel must be completed, signed by the traveler, and approved by the immediate supervisor. Sometimes an estimate of business expenses to be incurred on the trip will be required on the form. Typical procedures such as these must be followed:

    a. Acquiring needed travel advances prior to the trip.
    b. Following company policies regarding hotel or motel reservations.
    c. Using business credit cards and other forms of charging expenses directly to the organization.
    d. Reporting business expenses once the business trip is over.

2. *Approval for Transportation:* If company-owned vehicles or airplanes are being used for business travel, the traveler will need to complete an appropriate form requesting permission to schedule these forms of transportation. In addition to the traveler's name and driver's license number, other types of information requested on the form may include

    - the date(s) of the business travel.
    - the time of departure.
    - the date and time of return.
    - the destination city or cities.
    - the purpose of the trip.
    - the approximate number of miles driven or flown.

    Once this approval has been granted, the traveler is able to make appropriate arrangements with the transportation department for pickup of the automobile or boarding the airplane. Many organizations issue credit cards to be used only for gasoline and other transportation expenses during such business travel.

Appropriate approval for business travel and/or the use of company-owned vehicles and carriers is very important for the business traveler. There should be no question that the traveler is traveling on organizational business so that business insurance policies will cover the individual in case of accident or emergency.

B. **Preparation of Itinerary**

An itinerary is a business travel plan usually prepared in typewritten or computerized form with copies prepared for the office, the traveler's file, and the traveler's family. The office assistant or secretary should keep a copy in the office for reference, too. Before the itinerary can be finalized with accurate and complete travel information, source books and/or travel services need to be consulted in order to determine the types of transportation services available, the costs, and the types of travel documents and currency needed.

1. *Determination of Travel Needs:* In assisting with the arrangements needed for business travel, the executive assistant or secretary must be prepared to determine what the exact travel needs will be. These needs range from organizational requirements to personal preferences of the business traveler.

    a. *Organizational requirements for travel:* The business traveler represents the organization in conducting business for the organization in various parts of the country and the world. Some of the requirements placed on the traveler by the organization include

    (1) Specific meetings to attend in destination city(ies), with names and titles of company executives, addresses, and telephone numbers of companies involved.
    (2) Dates and times scheduled for certain cities with appropriate travel information.
    (3) Customers or clients with whom the business traveler must meet.

    b. *Personal preferences of traveler:* The business traveler may have certain preferences for the way in which the travel is arranged. Here are some preferences that the executive assistant or secretary must be aware of.

    (1) Preferred modes of transportation, that is, automobile, airplane.
    (2) The class of service that is preferred.
    (3) Hotel or motel accommodations.
    (4) Scheduling of appointments during the trip.

2. *Source Books*: In assisting with travel arrangements, the office assistant or secretary should know how to use source books for specific types of travel information. Guides and indexes commonly called *source books* assist the secretary in making appropriate travel arrangements. Those source books used most often are transportation guides, hotel and motel indexes, timetables, and atlases.

    a. *Transportation guides:* Detailed information on travel accommodations, airline schedules, railway schedules, and bus schedules is included in various types of transportation guides. Here are brief descriptions of some of the most commonly used guides:

(1) *The Official Airline Guides:* Travel agencies and transportation departments subscribe to these guides in order to have up-to-date information on airline schedules and fares. Here are some of the specific OAG publications available from Official Airline Guide, Oak Brook, Illinois, that are particularly useful in finalizing travel plans.

   (a) *The Official Airline Guide (North American Edition):* This guide gives detailed information on airline schedules and fares for the North American area (flights, flight times, carriers, classes of service, connecting flights, fares).
   (b) *The Official Airline Guide (Worldwide Edition):* This edition of the OAG gives detailed information on flights outside North America.
   (c) *The OAG Pocket Flight Guide:* This guide is a condensed version of the OAG and is a pocket-sized book of information on airline travel (flight schedules, flight numbers, classes of service, meal service). Several editions are available including North American, Pacific-Asia, Latin American, Worldwide, and European editions.
   (d) *The OAG Desktop Flight Guide:* North American and Worldwide editions of this flight guide are available.

   In addition, an electronic edition of the OAG is available for users who wish to have online service through a computer and modem. Flight disks are also available, with all OAG books in computer disk form. *Travel Age* and *Frequent Flyer* magazines are also available by subscription.
(2) *World Cruise and Shipline Guide:* This guide, published by OAG, shows all cruise and ferry schedules worldwide.
(3) *The Official Guide of the Railways:* This guide includes detailed information on all railway schedules and fares within the United States and in foreign countries.
(4) *Russell's Official National Motor Coach Guide:* Complete bus schedules and fares are included in this guide for motor coach transportation.

b. *Hotel and motel indexes:* These indexes are primarily used by travel agencies to access information on hotel and motel accommodations available throughout the United States and foreign countries. Some of the more commonly used hotel and motel indexes are:

(1) *The Hotel & Motel Red Book:* This source book is the official lodging directory published by the American Hotel & Motel Association.
(2) *Business Travel Planner (North American and Worldwide Editions):* This is another OAG publication that includes hotel and motel rates, maps, dining and sightseeing information about destination cities.
(3) *Hotel and Travel Index:* This source book, published quarterly by the Reed Travel Group, 500 Plaza Drive, Secaucus, NJ 07096, includes hotel and motel rates, maps, and sightseeing information for the traveler.

c. *Timetables:* Information on railway and bus schedules for all scheduled runs is included in the most commonly used timetables:
(1) *The Official Guide of the Railways* [see Section B-2-a(3)].
(2) Bus schedules for Greyhound, Trailways, and other private bus companies.

d. *Atlases:* Road maps for the United States as well as other locations within the North American continent or foreign countries are included in many published atlases, such as *Rand McNally Road Atlas for United States, Canada, and Mexico,* published by Rand McNally & Company, Chicago, Illinois.

3. *Travel Agencies and In-House Transportation Departments:* The services offered through travel agencies or transportation departments to obtain the types of transportation services desired are extremely important in planning and arranging business travel. The preparation of travel schedules and reservations for accommodations represent primary purposes of travel agencies and in-house transportation departments. These organizational units assist office personnel in making appropriate plans for business travelers.

a. *Commercial travel agency:* A business firm specializing in making travel arrangements for individuals and companies requesting their services operates as a *commercial travel agency.* In addition to handling commercial accounts, such travel agencies serve the public, scheduling leisure travel as well.

(1) *Services provided:* Services provided by the travel agency include hotel and transportation reservations (air, car rentals, railroad, bus, ground transportation) and other types of travel information.
(2) *Cost of services:* The agency receives a commission (percentage) normally based on ticket sales or room rates from those hotels, airlines, and other transportation companies that indicate their willingness to pay the agency a

commission on bookings. The traveler who uses the services of an agency pays no additional surcharge for such service.

Sometimes an agency is not eligible to receive a commission from a particular hotel, airline, or transportation company. In these situations, reservations would need to be made directly with the appropriate transportation companies, hotels, or motels.

    b. *In-house transportation department or agency:* Travel services provided by an in-house transportation department or agency are similar to those of a commercial travel agency, with the exception that these services are provided only to personnel and departments within the company.

        (1) *Services provided:* The transportation department or in-house agency makes all necessary transportation arrangements and reservations directly with carriers. Some in-house departments may be large enough to warrant online computer networking directly with the airlines.

        (2) *Cost of services:* Operational costs may be charged to individual departments using in-house transportation services.

4. *Online Reservation Systems:* Commercial travel agencies and transportation departments utilize online reservation systems in order to provide quick, efficient service to clients. Travel information is available through a computer network rather than looking through books, guides, and other publications.

    a. *Airline schedules:* Online systems permit the viewer to access all airline schedules and make appropriate flight reservations. The air fares shown on an online system are the same as those quoted by the airlines' reservation systems.

    b. *Hotel/motel reservations:* Online systems may be used to make hotel, motel, or automobile rental reservations directly with the provider.

An online network will sometimes permit the operator to pull up an airport map on the screen or access additional information about luggage requirements, ground transportation available, or actual distances involved in traveling from city to city.

EXAMPLE: Philip Morrison is the chief executive officer for Morrison Plastics, a firm with plants in Germany and Japan. Phyllis Johnson, his executive assistant, must be sure that appropriate travel arrangements are made for his semimonthly flights to these locations. She works closely with the Royale Travel Agency whenever tickets and reservations are needed. If she needs additional information, such as the number of bags allowed on a flight, she calls the agency to get the information.

5. *Travel Reservations:* As indicated previously, one of the executive assistant's responsibilities may be to make appropriate travel reservations for transportation, lodging, or conference facilities. The business traveler learns to rely upon the assistant's judgment in handling these types of arrangements.

    a. *Transportation reservations:* Whether made directly with the airlines or other transportation companies, reservations should be confirmed and complete information included on the travel itinerary:

    - Flight numbers or schedule numbers.
    - Departure and arrival times/dates.
    - Type of service reserved.
    - Name of carrier.
    - Meals furnished on flights (breakfast, lunch, snacks, dinner).

    b. *Hotel or motel reservations:* Business information about needed hotel or motel arrangements needs to be compared with what is available for the business traveler. The following types of information need to be considered in making appropriate reservations:

    (1) *Information supplied by the secretary:*

    - A brief description of the room or suite to be reserved.
    - The traveler's preference for specific accommodations (bed, shower, whirlpool bath).
    - The number of persons for whom the reservation will be made.
    - Arrival date/time (guaranteed, if after 6:00 P.M.). [*Note:* The term *late arrival* refers to arrival after 6:00 P.M.]
    - An estimate of the length of stay.

    (2) *Information supplied by hotel or motel:*

    - Availability of rooms.
    - The rate to be charged.
    - Official confirmation of the reservation made.

    Once the information supplied on behalf of the business traveler and that supplied by the hotel or motel have been compared, appropriate reservations can be made. Normally, reservations are held for check-in by 6 P.M. unless the hotel is notified prior to that time and the reservation is guaranteed with a credit card.

c. *Reservations for Special Facilities:* Sometimes reservations must be made for meeting rooms or conference facilities. Special information needed to reserve these types of facilities includes:

   (1) The number of meeting rooms that will be needed (if the number of people attending can be determined).
   (2) The agreed-upon rates for the use of these rooms.
   (3) Specifications of rooms needed for special functions such as convention exhibits, meals, or banquet (if the number of people attending can be determined).
   (4) Audio-visual equipment needed for meeting rooms.
   (5) Telecommunications equipment needed for meeting rooms.
   (6) Special room arrangements: furniture, lectern, blackboard.
   (7) Availability of electrical outlets and/or special conditions required for computerized equipment and communications networks.
   (8) Special arrangements for special tours or transportation to other local sites.

6. *Organization of Materials for Trip:* The business traveler will need specific materials organized for the trip. Before the trip takes place, the office assistant must make sure that these materials are organized in a trip file.

   a. *Trip file:* Setting up a trip file is essential in tracking all information and procedures involved in business travel. Maintenance of a folder in which all notes on errands to run, materials to collect, and other arrangements needed prior to the trip is essential. Other folders, to be carried by the traveler, might contain:

      (1) Background information pertaining to the purpose of the trip, for example, a file containing records of previous transactions with a company.
      (2) Confirmations of all travel reservations.
      (3) Confirmations for hotel accommodations reserved, including the confirmation numbers sometimes quoted over the telephone.
      (4) Copies of computer disks with needed information stored on them, properly marked so airport security personnel will not put them through electronic sensors.

   b. *Confirmed reservations:* Confirmations should be received for all reservations made for travel and hotel accommodations, if time permits.

      (1) *Competitive fares/rates:* In making appropriate decisions concerning transportation and hotel accommodations,

attention needs to be paid to competitive fares or rates. These fares or rates need to be compared with travel budget allowances if organization policy dictates.

(2) *Receipt of tickets:* To ensure that the traveler has the desired travel accommodations and is able to conduct business efficiently, tickets should be purchased and obtained in advance of the traveler's scheduled departure. In this way possible errors can more easily be detected and corrections made prior to the departure date.

c. *Travel funds:* For business purposes, traveler's checks or letters of credit are convenient and safe ways of carrying funds.

(1) *Traveler's checks:* A safer way to carry funds in a form other than cash is through sequentially numbered traveler's checks available in denominations of $10, $20, $50, and $100. Traveler's checks are available for a small fee from local banks, credit unions, savings and loan associations, and the American Automobile Association. The traveler must purchase these in person and must sign each traveler's check immediately. When the traveler's check is cashed, it must be signed by the same person in a second place on the check in the presence of the sales agent.

(2) *Letter of credit:* A letter of credit allows a traveler to draw funds on a specific bank or financial institution up to a predetermined amount while on trips.

Additional funds may be transferred to individuals who are traveling in foreign countries through international services such as American Express, international telegraph services, or local bank services.

d. *Travel advances:* For authorized travel, an individual may request a travel advance from the organization to be applied to the business expenses to be reimbursed. A travel advance enables the traveler to use company funds rather than personal funds for business expenses incurred during the trip (taxi fares, meal expenses).

e. *Credit cards:* Sometimes business travelers are expected to pay for travel expenses out of personal funds and receive reimbursement from the company after an expense report has been filed. A record of expenses incurred must be kept by the traveler for accounting, reimbursement, or income tax purposes. Out-of-pocket expenses may best be handled through the use of business or personal credit cards. Here are some of the benefits derived from using credit cards for keeping accurate records of travel expenses for business purposes:

(1) *Ready purchase of goods and services:* Use of credit cards enables the traveler to purchase goods and services from

businesses which accept credit cards up to a predetermined credit limit.

(2) *Receipts for purchases:* Credit card receipts will verify business expenditures for tax purposes and for preparing company expense reports.

(3) *Monthly expense statement:* The monthly billing for charges itemizes all charges and services and can serve as a cumulative record of all business-related charges incurred during the month. When credit cards are used overseas, the rate of exchange cannot be determined until the traveler returns home. The rate of exchange used is that of the date of posting and not the date of purchase. Therefore, one must wait until receipt of the invoice from the credit card company to find out the rate of exchange.

f. *Debit card:* A card issued by a bank, similar to a credit card, enables the cardholder to charge the purchase of merchandise and services directly to his/her bank account. As soon as the transaction is completed, a deduction is made from the cardholder's bank account.

g. *Itinerary:* Once all arrangements for the trip have been approved, final copies of the itinerary need to be prepared (see Figure 1-1 for sample itinerary.) The itinerary is a travel plan that typically includes the following types of information:

- Departure date, time, and place.
- Type of transportation (including the type of airplane).
- Arrival date, time, and place.
- Meals provided by transportation company (breakfast, lunch, snacks, dinner).
- Hotel and motel reservation(s) for each date or segment of the trip (addresses and telephone numbers included).
- Scheduled appointments and meetings (including dinner meetings as well as other functions, if known).
- Complete travel information for return trip.

Copies of the itinerary need to be prepared for the traveler, the office, and the traveler's family.

h. *Traveler's quick reference form*: Sometimes a synopsis of the information contained in a complete itinerary can be prepared as a quick reference for the traveler to carry in a wallet, purse, or briefcase. Figure 1-2 shows what such a quick reference might look like. More complete information would be contained in the itinerary.

C. Types of Travel

In preplanning the arrangements necessary for business travel, the executive assistant or secretary must have a knowledge of the types of

ITINERARY
Marlene Bailey
January 10-12, 199-

MONDAY, JANUARY 10 (Chicago to New York City)

8:20 a.m. (CST)	Leave Chicago O'Hare Airport on United Airlines Flight 208; 747; breakfast served.
9:33 a.m. (EST)	Arrive at New York LaGuardia Airport. Take limousine to Waldorf Hotel, 2021 Second Avenue, New York (212-542-6000); guaranteed hotel reservation; confirmation in trip file.
1:00 p.m.	Meeting with Roger C. Harper, Jr., President, ACF Corporation, 994 Third Avenue, New York (212-776-1420).
7:00 p.m.	Dinner-Meeting at Stewart's Restaurant, 727 Avenue of the Americas, New York, with Joyce L. Rohrson, Consultant, American Business Systems (212-325-4692).

TUESDAY, JANUARY 11 (New York City)

9:30 a.m.	The National Office Systems Conference, City Conference Center, 1004 Central Parkway, New York (212-554-4200).
9:45 a.m.	Presentation: "The Office Environment--Networking and Today's Automated Office"
1:00 p.m.	Luncheon with Raymond L. Bernard, Vice-President and General Manager, Wilson Automation, Inc., at the Oakdale City Club, 9250 Fifth Avenue, New York (212-347-3300).
3:00 p.m.	Tour of Advanced Business Systems, Inc., 125 Seventh Avenue, New York. Contact Person: Helen Adams, Office Automation Consultant (212-774-1550).

WEDNESDAY, JANUARY 12 (New York City to Chicago)

9:45 a.m.	Leave Waldorf Hotel by limousine for John F. Kennedy Airport.
11:55 a.m. (EST)	Leave Kennedy Airport on United Flight 648, business class; lunch served.
2:10 p.m. (CST)	Arrive at Chicago O'Hare Airport. Company limousine will meet you at baggage claim.

Figure 1-1
Sample Itinerary

Quick Reference		
Name	Company	Number
Roger Harper	ACF Corp.	(212) 776-1420
Joyce Robinson	Am. Bus.	(212) 325-4692
NOS Conference	City Center	(212) 554-4800
*R.L. Bernard	Wilson Auto	(212) 347-3300
Helen Adams	Adv. Bus. Sys.	(212) 774-1550

Notes:
* Luncheon 1/11 at 1:00 p.m. at Oakdale City Club.
** Company limo pickup

Frequent Flier Information	
Airline/Club	Account Number
United	101-45-1984-B

Itinerary				
Date 1/10/9-	Airline	Flight	Seat	6E
	United	208	Departure Time	8:20 am (CST)
	From	To	Arrival time	
	Chicago O'Hare	NYC		9:33 am (EST)
Date 1/12/9-	Airline	Flight	Seat	4C
	United	648	Departure Time	11:55 am (EST)
	From	To	Arrival time	
	NYC	** Chicago O'Hare		2:10 pm (CST)
Date	Airline	Flight	Seat	
			Departure Time	
	From	To	Arrival time	
Date	Airline	Flight	Seat	
			Departure Time	
	From	To	Arrival time	

Travel Arrangements

Marlene Bailey

Prepared by	Date	Trip
BLS	03/02/92	

Figure 1-2
Quick Reference Form

transportation services available, the classes of service available for the type of transportation preferred, baggage allowances, and transportation available to and from airports. In addition, alternative modes of travel may have to be considered in case of bad weather. Depending on the nature of the business travel, even combination modes of travel (auto-ship, auto-air) may have to be considered.

1. *Domestic Travel:* Domestic transportation services (air, railroad, bus, and automobile) provide a variety of options for travel within a country. Selection of those services to be utilized depends on time allotted for travel, cost, and destination.

    a. *Air travel:* Accommodations include first-class, business-class, coach-class, and economy seating. Fares depend upon the class of seating selected and special plans established by the airline, for example, excursion rates. Air shuttle service is also available between some of the larger U.S. cities within short distances of each other.
    b. *Railway travel:* Amtrak and Conrail are national railway systems that connect metropolitan areas throughout the country. Commuter railway services are available between large cities and suburban areas. Passenger accommodations include first class or coach class or may provide the option of auto-train facilities.
    c. *Bus travel:* For some business trips, bus travel may be preferred, especially for short distances. Interstate highways and toll roads make this type of travel very acceptable.

2. *International Travel:* Travel in and to other countries may necessitate the utilization of various modes of travel.

    a. *Air transportation:* Of course, the fastest way to travel is to fly. The 24-hour clock is used in the timetables for foreign transportation. Scheduling information is included in the *Official Airline Guide (Worldwide Edition)* [see Section B-2-a(1)(b) of this chapter].
    b. *Ship transportation:* Transatlantic liners do provide the option of more leisurely travel, perhaps to combine a business trip with a vacation. Time may be an important factor inasmuch as there may be appointments already scheduled in one of the countries to be visited. A combination air-ship plan might be used.
    c. *Foreign railway service:* Schedules for first-class and second-class train service need to be examined when railway service is required in foreign countries.
    d. *Automobile travel:* Car rentals are available through airlines, travel agencies, or car rental firms. A U.S. driver's license is accepted in most countries, but an international traveler may wish to obtain an American International Driving Permit

available through the American Automobile Association prior to the trip.

  e. *Hotel accommodations:* Local travel agencies can be very helpful in making hotel reservations. The travel agent will need a complete description of the kind of accommodations preferred. It is important to receive from the travel agent a complete description of the reservations actually made and written confirmations if time permits. Following the trip, a list of the most appropriate accommodations should be kept for future reference.

3. *Ground Transportation:* When travel is by air, it may be necessary to reserve ground transportation (auto rental or limousine service) to reach local destinations. Taxi or bus service is generally available at every airport. A check should be made in the *Official Airline Guide* for available ground transportation. This information is also entered on the traveler's itinerary.

4. *Company Transportation and Lodging:* Company-owned airplanes, ships, automobiles, and lodging may be available for use during business travel. Appropriate reservations for use of these carriers and facilities must be made within a reasonable period of time prior to the planned travel to ensure availability.

D. Documents and Credentials

When traveling to a foreign country, a business traveler must have appropriate documents and credentials in order to be allowed to leave any country and also to enter a specific foreign country. A traveler needs to provide proof of citizenship in order to enter Mexico or one of the Caribbean countries. Such proof would be a passport or a notarized copy of a birth certificate.

1. *Passport:* A *passport* is a formal document, valid for ten years, issued by the citizen's government granting permission to the citizen to travel in certain foreign countries. A passport also certifies citizenship and protection for the traveler. A passport may be obtained by:

  a. Completing an application and paying a fee for the passport.
  b. Including two identical, recent, and signed black-and-white photographs with the application.
  c. Showing a valid driver's license that contains the applicant's signature.
  d. Presenting proof of citizenship, such as an original birth certificate, baptismal certificate, or naturalization papers.

2. *Visa:* A *visa* is an endorsement stamped or written on a passport, showing examination by the proper officials of a country and granting the bearer entry into that country. A visa is in effect for a

specified period of time. Sometimes a visa is issued as a separate document which must be surrendered upon departure from the country.

EXAMPLE: You may be taking several weeks of vacation for a trip to China, and you apply for a visitor's visa, which is usually valid for six months. The visa will be in effect only for six months unless you make application to have it renewed.

In many foreign countries, a visa is not required. A list of countries requiring a visa should be kept in the office.

EXAMPLE: France does not require a visa from a person with U.S. citizenship.

3. *Special Requirements:* A check should be made to determine if any inoculations are required to travel in the foreign countries to be visited. In some instances this requires a series of either inoculations or medication which must be completed before the commencement of a trip. Travelers may be required to carry official International Certificates of Vaccination verifying immunization against specified diseases that could be threatening to the U.S. and other countries. [See *Health Information for International Travelers,* a government document published by the Superintendent of Documents, Washington, D.C.]

E. **The Executive Assistant's Role in Executive's Absence**

The executive assistant must be able to function so as to minimize the executive's absence. There are many tasks that may be handled without the executive being present, but there may be others that require the executive's attention. The executive assistant must be prepared to work within the limits of authority, to communicate with the executive as needed during the travel period, and to prepare materials that can be handled upon the executive's return.

1. *Understanding Limits of Authority:* Decision making in the absence of the executive requires the exercise of careful judgment and clear understanding of the consequences of any action taken. The limits of the executive assistant's authority in handling office functions should be clearly understood before the executive leaves the office. Questions like, "What can I approve while you are gone?" are typical queries the alert executive assistant or secretary would make prior to the executive's departure.

   a. *Decisions:* Usually decisions can be made about office procedures for which there is a precedent, that is, a similar decision made in the past.
   b. *Judgments:* In cases where an exception to the standard procedure has not occurred before, the executive assistant will

need to be a bit more cautious in making an appropriate judgment. If the situation parallels one that has previously been handled, the past situation can be used as an example to determine how to handle the present one. If, in fact, the situation has not occurred before, perhaps the secretary should either inform the executive immediately and ask for a judgment (in the case of a high priority) or hold the item until the executive returns.

At any rate, the executive assistant or secretary must be careful to work within the limits of authority already imposed upon the position. Any time decisions or judgments are required, the person making those decisions or judgments must be prepared to face the consequences (positive or negative) of action taken.

2. *Communicating with Traveler:* An executive assistant must maintain constant communication with the executive prior to business travel as well as during the trip. In this way the office will continue to function effectively during the executive's absence.

   a. *Communicating before the trip:* There are certain decisions that must be made prior to a business trip, and some of these can only be taken care of by the executive. The executive assistant or secretary can assist with some of these decisions and also in making preparations for the planned absence from the office. Here are some of the questions that will need to be answered:

   (1) Who will make major decisions while the business traveler is away from the office?
   (2) Are there any additional materials or mail that should be forwarded during the trip? If so, where are these materials located? When should they be forwarded and by what means?
   (3) Are there parcels or packages of materials that will need to be shipped ahead of time? When do they need to arrive at the destination? How should they be shipped?
   (4) Are all appointments on the itinerary confirmed?
   (5) Is there any correspondence to be sent to firms being visited or to individuals with whom the traveler plans to meet during the upcoming trip?
   (6) Should a time be arranged for communicating by telephone, for example, each morning at 8:30 A.M.?

   b. *Communicating during the trip:* Equally important is communication with the traveler as needed during the trip. There may be additional materials that need to be sent or important business that needs attention.

   (1) If necessary for extended trips, copies of mail or other information needed must be forwarded during the trip.

(Express mail, FAX, or other fast-delivery services will be particularly helpful in this regard.)

(2) If there are changes in the itinerary such as reservations or flight departure times, the traveler must be notified immediately.

(3) A log of correspondence, folders, or other business matters to be handled upon the executive's return must be kept. Prioritizing these items will help, too.

(4) A log of correspondence that has been handled by the secretary may be kept as an update for the executive.

(5) Dictation may be received from the traveler either through the mail or received via the telephone to a central recorder. Transcription of this dictation should be completed as soon as possible; some items may be urgent.

3. *Preparing Materials to be Handled on the Traveler's Return:* When the traveler returns from a business trip, the executive assistant or secretary needs to review any business that has transpired during the absence. Two types of files will be extremely helpful:

   a. *For-your-information file:* This file should contain all matters that have already been taken care of but which need to be reviewed only for informational purposes (copies of letters mailed).

   b. *For-your-attention file:* This file should contain correspondence and other business materials related to those matters that had to wait to be handled until the traveler's return.

   A complete report of office events or business activities that have taken place which are of significance to the activities of the business or office needs to be available.

F. Follow-up Activities

It is customary to handle follow-up activities as soon as possible. Business expenses incurred during the travel need to be itemized and appropriate reports completed and approved. Any special reports and correspondence need to be prepared, too, while the factual information is readily available. Sometimes the executive assistant or secretary has to remind the traveler of deadlines for completing any of these follow-up activities.

1. *Expense Reports:* Appropriate business expense reports must be prepared and submitted in order to obtain reimbursement if indicated.

   a. *Receipts:* All of the traveler's receipts must be accumulated and itemized on the expense report.

   b. *Travel advances:* If a travel advance was received prior to the trip, the amount must be deducted from the expenses incurred during the trip. There are appropriate entries that can be made on the expense report.

Once all receipts and travel advances have been accounted for, the typed business expense report may be prepared. This report must be signed by the traveler and approved by a supervisor before being submitted for reimbursement. Usually the receipts (or copies) must be attached to the form.

2. *Special Reports:* One of the assistant's most important follow-up activities will be to assist in the writing of any special reports that need to be submitted to superiors concerning the trip and the reporting of business transacted during the trip. The preparation of these types of reports should take place within a short time while the information is still readily available.

3. *Correspondence:* Follow-up letters to those people with whom the traveler met during the business trip represent a courtesy that is expected. Thank-you letters or confirmation letters are perhaps the most typical. The secretary should reserve adequate time to take dictation, transcribe, and write follow-up letters as soon as possible.

EXAMPLE: Marian Ellenberg just returned from a business trip to New York. On the return trip her luggage was lost by the airline. Peter Fehrly, her secretary, needs to contact the airlines to see if the luggage has been located and, if not, to make the appropriate claim.

EXAMPLE: While she was in New York, Marian met with Paul R. Thompson, the president of one of the leading advertising agencies. She contracted with Mr. Thompson for the development of a new advertising campaign that Marian will present to her superiors for approval. Marian dictates a letter to Mr. Thompson, confirming some of the provisions of the new contract.

4. *File Materials:* A check to see if all files taken on the trip have been returned is important. These materials need to be refiled as soon as possible in case others in the organization must refer to them. In addition, any other materials collected during the trip need to be filed.

5. *Travel Notes:* Because there will be future business travel to arrange, comments regarding hotel, motel, or transportation preferences should be noted for the next trip. Sometimes meeting notes need to be typed and filed for future reference.

Chapter 1: Review Questions

Part A: Multiple-Choice Questions

DIRECTIONS: Select the best answer from the four alternatives. Write your answer in the blank to the left of the number.

_____ 1. Before any business travel arrangements are made, the secretary needs to

   a. acquire a travel advance for the business traveler.
   b. be aware of the business traveler's preferences for transportation and hotel accommodations.
   c. know the organization's policies governing approved business travel.
   d. complete the necessary authorization forms.

_____ 2. Organization travel policies require a business traveler to

   a. secure a travel advance prior to the departure date.
   b. make reservations only at company-owned hotels.
   c. submit a request for authorization to travel for approval.
   d. prepare a detailed itinerary for the business trip.

_____ 3. Business insurance policies

   a. protect the organization only in case of unexpected emergency.
   b. cover the business traveler who has approval to travel.
   c. cover only the business traveler who uses company-owned transportation.
   d. cover only executives who have authorization to travel.

_____ 4. An itinerary is

   a. a listing of all confirmed hotel reservations for the business trip.
   b. a travel plan containing a list of all reservations, scheduled appointments, and meetings.
   c. a list of all items of business to be discussed during a business meeting.
   d. a document giving permission for a citizen to enter a foreign country.

_____ 5. Which of the following would be considered a source book for making appropriate domestic transportation arrangements?

a. The Official Airline Guide, Worldwide Edition
b. Hotel & Motel Red Book
c. The Official Airline Guide, North American Edition
d. Travel Age magazine

_____ 6. In-house transportation departments or agencies assist in planning travel services for

a. individual employees in any of the firm's departments who are approved for business travel.
b. clients of the firm.
c. any employee who requests assistance in making travel reservations.
d. individual employees who seek assistance with personal travel plans.

_____ 7. Which of the following is considered a safe way to carry travel funds?

a. Cash (in U.S. dollars or foreign currency)
b. Letter of credit
c. Travel advance
d. International credit card

_____ 8. A complete flight reservation includes the following types of information:

a. flight number, departure time, and fare.
b. flight number, name of carrier, and departure time.
c. name of carrier, flight number, departure and arrival times, fare, and class of service.
d. name of carrier, flight number, fare, class of service, and arrival time.

_____ 9. A confirmed travel reservation means that

a. the business travel has been approved.
b. the transportation carrier has notified the business traveler of the arrangements made.
c. the business traveler will have to pick up the reservation tickets on the day of departure.
d. the reservation cannot be canceled or changed.

_____ 10. Business travelers may prefer to receive a travel advance from the company so that

a. all expenses incurred for hotel, meals, and miscellaneous items are prepaid by the company.

b. sufficient funds are available for "out-of-pocket" expenses, thus avoiding the use of personal funds.
c. all transportation costs will be prepaid by the company.
d. rental of ground transportation can be secured more easily.

_____ 11. One benefit of using a business or personal credit card for out-of-pocket expenses is that it

a. enables the traveler to purchase goods and services, no matter what the cost.
b. provides a complete expense report for the entire trip.
c. substitutes readily for cash.
d. provides a receipt for each transaction.

_____ 12. The selection of the mode of transportation to be used for domestic business travel will depend most upon

a. how many individuals from the organization will be traveling at one time.
b. the availability of ground transportation at the destination city.
c. the distance to be traveled in relation to the transportation cost and time allotment.
d. the primary purpose of the business trip.

_____ 13. A government document issued by the U.S. Department of State that grants permission to a U.S. citizen to travel in certain foreign countries is called

a. a visa.
b. a travel permit.
c. a passport.
d. an itinerary.

_____ 14. An endorsement which grants a U.S. citizen entry into a foreign country for a specified period of time is known as

a. a visa.
b. a passport.
c. an itinerary.
d. a travel permit.

_____ 15. Before the business traveler leaves on a business trip, the secretary needs to

a. set up a "for-your-information" file for trip information.
b. prepare a detailed expense report for the trip.
c. respond to incoming correspondence on behalf of the executive who is on a business trip.
d. find out who is designated to make major decisions while the business traveler is away from the office.

_____ 16. A technique often used to update the business traveler on office events that occurred during an absence is to

a. keep a log of hard copies of correspondence and other items that were handled by the secretary during the absence.
b. write reminders on the traveler's desk calendar.
c. keep a journal with a detailed day-to-day account.
d. reserve at least two hours on the traveler's first day back in the office to discuss office operations during the absence.

_____ 17. A for-your-attention file contains items that

a. must wait to be handled until the business traveler returns.
b. have already been taken care of by the secretary prior to the traveler's return.
c. give a complete report of office events during the absence.
d. pertain to the detailed expense report to be prepared.

_____ 18. Follow-up activities to business travel include

a. writing summary reports to be submitted to management.
b. preparation of expense reports.
c. writing correspondence to people with whom the business traveler had appointments during the trip.
d. all of the above.

Part B: Matching Sets

Matching Set 1

Match each of the kinds of travel services (A-B) with the correct operation (19-24). Write the letter of your response in the blank to the left of the number.

Travel Services

A. Commercial Travel Agency
B. In-house Transportation Department

Business Travel

OPERATIONS

_____ 19. Specialized in making business and leisure travel arrangements.

_____ 20. Charges no surcharge to the traveler for reservation services rendered.

_____ 21. Provides travel services for business travel only within an organization.

_____ 22. Receives a commission directly from hotels and transportation carriers.

_____ 23. Serves the public in reserving hotel and transportation accommodations.

_____ 24. Charges operational costs to individual department.

Matching Set 2

Match each of the types of travel funds (A-E) with the appropriate descriptive phrase (25-31). Write the letter of your response in the blank to the left of the number.

Travel Funds

A. Traveler's Checks
B. Letter of Credit
C. Credit Card
D. Debit Card
E. Travel Advance

DESCRIPTIVE PHRASES

_____ 25. Receipt of designated funds from the organization prior to business travel.

_____ 26. Purchased by business traveler as a safeguard to carrying cash.

_____ 27. Amount received will be applied to business expenses to be reimbursed.

_____ **28.** Used primarily for miscellaneous expenses during business travel, which is paid after monthly statement is received.

_____ **29.** Permits withdrawal of funds from a bank account to a certain limit.

_____ **30.** The amount charged for a given purchase is immediately deducted from the balance in a bank account.

_____ **31.** Two signatures are required when cashed.

Part C: Problem Situations

DIRECTIONS: For each of the following problem situations, select the best answer from the four alternatives. Write the letter of your response in the blank to the left of the question.

Problem 1

As the secretary for John Charles, Executive Vice-President for Motor Wheels, Inc., you have the option of obtaining all travel reservations through transportation companies and hotels yourself or using the services of a commercial travel agency.

_____ **32.** You decide to use the services of the Acme Travel Agency, a commercial agency, who will
   a. bill Motor Wheels, Inc. directly for the commission for providing travel services.
   b. affix (add) a commission to the total cost of travel reservations.
   c. receive a commission based only on transportation costs.
   d. receive a commission directly from hotels, airlines, and other transportation companies based on ticket sales and/or room rates.

Problem 2

Janette Bradford, Vice President of Steeps, Inc., has a hotel reservation but finds that she will not be able to arrive at the Blackstone Hotel in Washington, D.C., until 8 P.M.

_____ **33.** In this case, the hotel will
   a. hold the reservation since the reservation had been made two weeks ahead of time.
   b. cancel the room reservation.
   c. hold the reservation if Ms. Bradford telephones the hotel prior to 6 p.m. and guarantees payment for the room with a credit card.
   d. arrange for her to stay at another hotel if there is no room left when she arrives.

_____

34. While she is in Washington, D.C., Ms. Bradford is making preliminary arrangements for a two-day conference to be held next March entitled "Office Technology Systems for the Year 2000." Which of the following facts will she need in order to make a decision about what hotel facilities to reserve for this meeting?
    a. Confirmed hotel rates to be charged for the meeting rooms.
    b. Estimated number of people attending who will need hotel reservations.
    c. Ground transportation available from the airport.
    d. Guest speakers involved in the conference.

Problem 3

Helen Snyder, Vice President of Operations, needs to travel to New York next week. She asked Steve Williams, an executive assistant, to help with the final preparations.

_____

35. Before the final itinerary is prepared, Steve needs to consult with Helen to determine
    a. the class of air transportation preferred.
    b. her appointment schedule in New York.
    c. ground transportation preferred.
    d. all of the above.

Chapter 1: Solutions

Part A: Multiple-Choice Questions

	Answer	Refer to Chapter Section
1.	(c)	[A] The secretary needs to be very knowledgeable about business travel policies and procedures within the organization.
2.	(c)	[A-1] First, a business traveler must receive authorization to travel on company business.
3.	(b)	[A-2] One of the primary reasons the business traveler wants prior approval for business travel is the insurance coverage in case of unexpected emergency.
4.	(b)	[B] This is the definition of an itinerary. See Figure 1-1 for a sample itinerary.
5.	(c)	[B-2-a(1)] The North American Edition of the OAG would have all domestic flights that should be considered.
6.	(a)	[B-3-b] In-house transportation departments are established to schedule only business travel for employees.
7.	(b)	[B-6-c] A letter of credit permits the traveler to draw funds from a bank account up to a maximum limit.
8.	(c)	[B-5-a] The business traveler needs complete information about the flight.
9.	(b)	[B-6-b] Confirmation is proof that the carrier has actually made the reservation.
10.	(b)	[B-6-d] A travel advance enables the business traveler to pay miscellaneous business expenses during the trip with company funds rather than personal funds.
11.	(d)	[B-6-e(2)] A credit card receipt is a record of a specific purchase made.
12.	(c)	[C-1] Selection of mode of transportation will depend most upon the destination, cost, and time allotted.
13.	(c)	[D-1] A passport, valid for ten years, permits a U.S. citizen to leave the United States and travel abroad.
14.	(a)	[D-2] A visa is an endorsement from a foreign country permitting a U.S. citizen to travel in that country. Not all foreign countries require visas any more.
15.	(d)	[E-1] The limits of the secretary's authority in handling office functions during an executive's absence must be clearly understood.
16.	(a)	[E-3] A complete report of office events needs to be available for the executive's review after returning from a business trip.
17.	(a)	[E-3-b] These are items which still need to be completed or handled by the executive.
18.	(d)	[F] All of the items listed refer to follow-up activities to business travel.

Part B: Matching Sets

Matching Set 1

19.	(A)	[B-3-a]
20.	(A)	[B-3-a(2)]
21.	(B)	[B-3-b(1)]
22.	(A)	[B-3-a(2)]
23.	(A)	[B-3-a]
24.	(B)	[B-3-b(2)]

Matching Set 2

25.	(E)	[B-6-d]
26.	(A)	[B-6-c(1)]
27.	(E)	[B-6-d]
28.	(C)	[B-6-e(3)]
29.	(B)	[B-6-c(2)]
30.	(D)	[B-6-f]
31.	(A)	[B-6-c(1)]

Part C: Problem Situations

32.	(d)	[B-3-a(2)]
33.	(c)	[B-5-b]
34.	(a)	[B-5-c]
35.	(d)	[B-1]

CHAPTER 2
Office Management

OVERVIEW

Office administration includes those office management functions that provide support to individuals throughout the organization through the use of specialized office systems. A recent trend is toward networking information processing (data processing, word processing, communications), reprographics, and records administration. Much attention is being given to the establishment of local area networks (LANs) throughout the organization. Another trend is toward the increased use of office automation wherever possible so that more production can be realized in the day-to-day operations of the organization.

Specific secretarial responsibilities require executive assistants and secretaries to make appropriate application of the functions of management: to *plan* aspects of their work assignments very carefully; to *organize* materials, supplies, and work areas for specific office tasks; and to *supervise* other office personnel effectively. The process of planning and organizing office tasks in order to perform tasks efficiently, complete them on time, and supervise office personnel who are performing these functions is called *managing*.

In this chapter secretaries will become more familiar with tools and techniques used for developing office procedures that will result in work simplification and the improvement of work patterns.

DEFINITION OF TERMS

AUTHOR. An executive, manager, supervisor, or other individual who originates work to be completed by professional secretaries or word processing personnel; may also be called an end user.

CALENDARING. Making appropriate notations on office calendars of upcoming appointments, meetings, or other events; appointments may be entered on a computer so that a printout of appointments and meetings can be obtained each morning.

CENTRALIZATION. The plan of operation that organizes support personnel in work centers with easy access to and from all departments in the company.

CONTROLLING. One of the functions of supervising that involves comparing actual productivity and results with those that were anticipated during a specific period of time.

CROSS TRAINING. The process of being trained on more than one job in the office.

DECENTRALIZATION. The plan of operation in which clerical support personnel are housed within individual departments and perform office functions needed by that department only.

EDITING. The procedure used by an author to revise the original document.

EMPLOYEE MANUAL. A handbook that provides specific information needed to be a functional worker within the company; includes work schedules, hours, salaries, schedules for salary reviews, dress codes, vacations, benefits, and other types of employee information.

HORIZONTAL COMMUNICATION. Communication from one supervisor to another supervisor or from one subordinate to another subordinate, in other words, communication on the same level.

HUMAN RESOURCE PLANNING. The process of determining personnel needs for the future and developing strategies for meeting these needs.

JOB SHARING. The formal arrangement whereby two office employees share the same job; one full-time job is shared part time by two people on either a temporary or permanent basis.

LEFFINGWELL, WILLIAM H. The father of office management; applied the principles of scientific management to office work in his book, *Scientific Office Management*, in 1917.

LOGGING FORM. The record that indicates the date/time the job is received, the number/name of the job, the name of the person for whom the work is being done, the deadline for the job, the name of the person to whom the task is assigned, and any special instructions.

MANAGEMENT-BY-OBJECTIVES (MBO) APPRAISAL. With the help of the supervisor/manager, the employee establishes job objectives, both for individual performance and for personal development, against which his/her performance is measured.

MATRIX PLAN. The combination plan of operation which permits some office operations to be centralized and others to be decentralized, depending upon the needs of the firm.

ORGANIZATIONAL MANUAL. An office handbook that shows the formal relationship of divisions or departments, including duties and responsibilities, within the company; includes statement of company objectives, basic philosophy, and organizational structure.

ORGANIZING. The managerial function that permits the office administrator to establish specific goals that are to be accomplished through office services.

PERFORMANCE STANDARDS. Criteria for evaluating the behavior, personal traits, and results of office production.

TICKLER SYSTEM. A reminder system that includes project or task deadlines on a daily, weekly, and monthly basis.

TURNAROUND TIME. The elapsed time between the receiving of a task and its completion; or the elapsed time that results when the author sends the task to word processing and waits for its return; or the elapsed time between the time the word processing supervisor receives the document from the author and the time it is received back from the word processing specialist.

A. Planning

Planning is the visualization and formulation of proposed activities designed to achieve certain results. In office administration, planning is essential in setting initial objectives, analyzing present situations, determining various alternatives to meet the objectives, analyzing the cost-benefit of each alternative solution, and finally selecting the most appropriate alternative and putting it into action. The secretary is always involved in planning; but three aspects of planning are perhaps the most crucial: establishing priorities, managing time, and coordinating office activities with other office personnel.

1. *Types of Planning:* Planning activities focus primarily on three types of planning: strategic planning, tactical planning, and operational planning.

   a. *Strategic planning:* The long-term goals and major targets of an organization are the primary focus of strategic planning. This type of planning affects all major divisions within the organization as well as the external environment, for example, attention to international or global developments. *Strategy* is defined as a pattern of actions and investment of resources to attain organizational goals. Top-level executives are typically involved in developing strategic plans.

   EXAMPLES:
   Organization's contribution to society
   Return to shareholders
   Quantity of outputs
   Quality of outputs

   b. *Tactical planning:* Specific goals and plans are developed that are relevant to a definite unit within the organization, such as human resource development or marketing. Tactical plans outline the actions required of that work unit to achieve its part of the total strategic plan. These plans are developed by managers of those particular work units or divisions within the company.

    c. *Operational planning:* Operational managers develop short-term plans for routine tasks within their work units (delivery schedules, production schedules, personnel requirements for specific tasks). Operational planning identifies procedures required at lower levels within the organization.

Strategic, tactical, and operational planning within an organization must network to show consistent and supportive sets of objectives for the entire organization.

2. *Establishing Priorities:* One of the most critical office duties is the organizing of tasks for efficient completion. Deadlines for the work and coordination of employee work schedules need to be considered as decisions are made concerning the work to be done, when it will be done, and by whom.

    a. *Guidelines for prioritizing work:* One of the best ways to manage the work process, both in terms of specific tasks and the time required, is to learn how to set work priorities. Many individuals complete tasks in the order in which these tasks are presented for completion, without any consideration for those items which are of the highest priority. Priority of work should not be based on "likes" and "dislikes" but rather on factors such as these:

        (1) *The due date for the job:* Deadlines established for specific jobs must be considered in establishing a work priority.

            EXAMPLE: A letter that must be in the mail today obviously will take priority over one requesting information for a meeting that will take place a month from now.

        (2) *Consultation with supervisor(s):* There must be appropriate time to discuss and review work orders with the supervisor and sometimes the end user. It is important that all questions concerning production be answered *before* an office worker begins work on that task.

        (3) *Involvement of other people:* Other people's schedules must be considered. Any deadline for the job must be coordinated with others' time schedules so last-minute-crisis work can be avoided.

        (4) *Delegation of work:* Often an executive, manager, or departmental secretary will be in a position to delegate work to other office workers. If there is a rush for the work, then a higher priority should be assigned to it. However, if there is no particular rush or there is more lead time for the work to be done, then a lower priority

could be assigned. Having the assistance of other office workers relieves some of the secretary's workload but still requires a degree of supervision so that the work does get out on time.

(5) *Length of the task:* Completion time for a given work assignment is often difficult to judge. With experience, however, the secretary should be able to determine approximately how long a particular task should take. *Turnaround time* is defined as the elapsed time between the receiving of a task and its completion. This can mean the elapsed time that results when the end user sends the task to information processing and waits for its return; or the elapsed time between the time the information-processing supervisor receives the document from the end user and the time it is received back from the information-processing specialist.

EXAMPLE: Sally sends a request to the information-processing center for the creation of a standard letter to be mailed to 350 clients. Her request reached the center on Monday at 9:30 A.M. The 350 letters and envelopes were ready for pickup at 3:30 P.M. the same day. The turnaround time may be computed as six hours.

b. *Identifying office tasks:* Each day those tasks or jobs left in the in-tray, in-basket, or on the electronic mail network must be examined to see what work needs to be done. In addition, every secretary receives additional tasks at various times during the day in the form of directives and/or dictation. It is essential to identify *all* tasks that superiors need to have completed.

EXAMPLE: Beth's early-morning routine includes scanning any items deposited in her in-basket in order to see what is required to complete these tasks. In addition, she must access voice mail to obtain telephone messages that have been recorded as well as electronic mail on the computer network in order to be certain that she has accessed all messages left for her on the telephone and computer systems.

c. *Analyzing the tasks:* Each task must be examined carefully to determine if there are specific directions or requirements. Additional information such as "needed by 8/31" or "special meeting at 4 P.M. today" are clues that are helpful in setting priorities.

(1) *Making priority decisions:* The efficient executive assistant or secretary must decide exactly how to categorize (or group) tasks for completion. One of the easiest ways

to categorize tasks is, first, to group the tasks into three primary categories:

Priority 1: Those tasks that need to be done immediately.
Priority 2: Those tasks that need to be done within the next one to two working days.
Priority 3: Those tasks that can be delayed until time permits or can be scheduled within a few days.

(2) *Arranging the tasks:* Within each priority category, the tasks need to be arranged in sequence from the most important to the least important. It is critical that tasks be completed in the order of priority so that documents needed for an important meeting, a telephone call confirming a speaking engagement, or transcription of a letter going out in the day's mail will be completed in time.

Another way that tasks need to be arranged relates to those items that require use of the computer and those which do not. Perhaps those tasks that require use of the computer can be grouped together for more efficient operation of the computer and software. People lose valuable work time when switching from one software package to another. Sometimes the secretary will have to gauge how much time to spend on the computer at any one time. Some experts estimate that the secretary needs a break from computer work every hour; others say every two hours.

d. *Adjusting priorities when interruptions occur:* Receiving another item to handle in the middle of the day or an urgent FAX message requesting information on an order received last week will cause the office professional to adjust priority categories to include these new items.

EXAMPLE: You are transcribing a letter to be signed by your supervisor, Mary Schumacher, before she leaves at 4 P.M. (This is a Priority 1 item.) Ben Johnson, one of the marketing representatives, comes into the office and asks to see Mary immediately. The telephone rings just as you begin to respond to his request. How should your priorities be instantly adjusted? The telephone call will take first priority now, then Mr. Johnson's request to see your supervisor will be the next priority item, and finally you may return to your transcription.

3. *Managing Time and Work Completion Effectively:* Every secretary should be concerned about efficient use of time, especially since the 7½- or 8-hour day provides a limited time frame in which to handle all types of tasks. In managing time for the completion of tasks, the secretary needs to utilize the assistance of other office personnel,

Office Management

including office managers or supervisors, in the process of completing required job assignments.

a. *Scheduling of time:* The development of personal techniques for appropriate scheduling of time should be a high priority in the office. Here are some of the more common scheduling techniques frequently used.

(1) *Identifying daily office tasks:* An excellent scheduling technique is to develop a *daily* list of office tasks that must be taken care of that day. Specially printed memos like the one in Figure 2-1 may be used to prepare such a list.

(2) *Designing reminder systems:* So that enough time can be set aside for upcoming tasks, create reminder systems that will prompt you as you work toward project/task deadlines on a daily, weekly, and monthly basis.

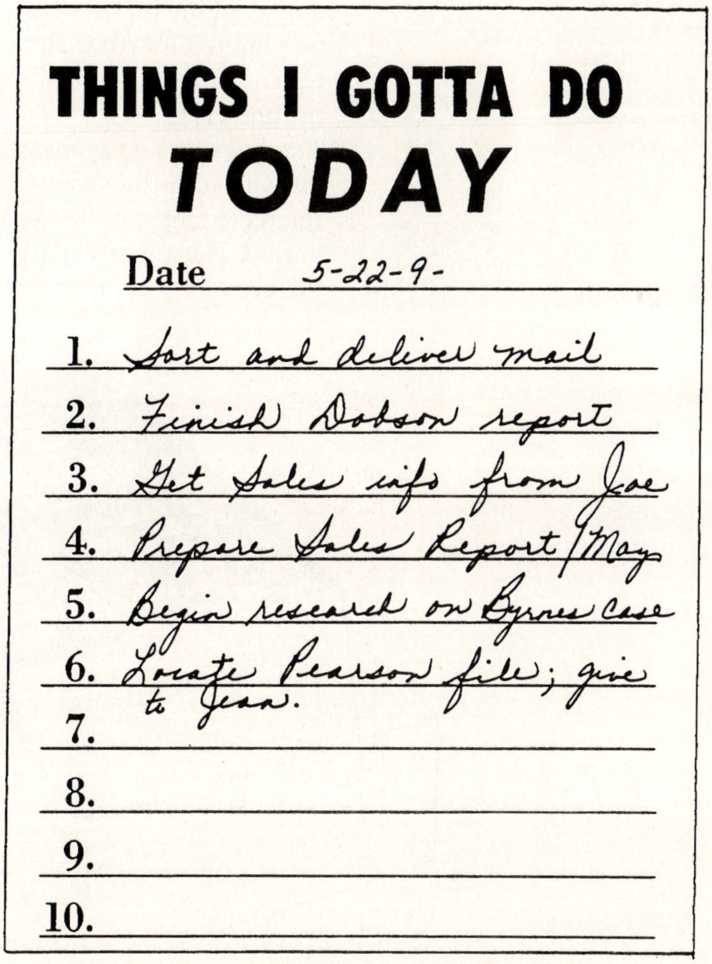

THINGS I GOTTA DO TODAY

Date 5-22-9-

1. Sort and deliver mail
2. Finish Dobson report
3. Get Sales info from Joe
4. Prepare Sales Report/May
5. Begin research on Byrnes case
6. Locate Pearson file; give to Jean.
7.
8.
9.
10.

Figure 2-1
Daily List of Office Tasks

(a) *Tickler system:* Usually a manual reminder system consists of a set of folders or cards for each day of the month (1-31) and folders or cards for each month in the calendar year. These folders are used to file materials or notes about specific work assignments to be done by particular deadlines and prompt the secretary to begin working on them by certain dates. See Figure 2-2 for an example of a tickler system.

(b) *Automated reminder system:* An electronic calendar can be generated easily with an automated calendaring system installed on either a personal computer or a networked system. This system reminds the user of appointments or project due dates for today, tomorrow, this month, on up to a year from now. A daily schedule can be printed out each morning to serve as a reminder list for the day.

(3) *Planning daily/weekly routine tasks:* Such tasks as handling routine reports, correspondence, and filing need to be planned for, too. Time should be set aside each day, week, or month (depending on the need) to perform such routine tasks.

(4) *Batch processing of tasks:* To save valuable time, similar tasks need to be grouped together in "batches" so that related items can be completed during a specific time period. This is particularly helpful with tasks that involve the use of the computer and various software packages.

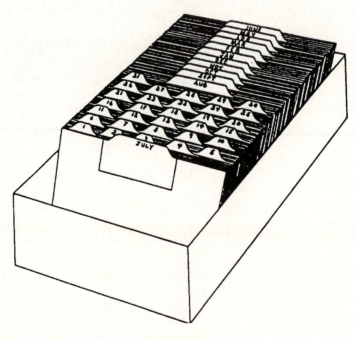

Figure 2-2
Tickler System

Office Management 39

EXAMPLE: *Mary's primary responsibilities include transcription of dictation (which comes from both recorded machine dictation and shorthand dictation), filing copies of correspondence appropriately in the files, answering the telephone (especially to take sales orders over the phone), and preparing a daily report each morning showing all company sales for the previous day. She finds that "batching" helps her to manage her time more efficiently. She finds that correspondence can be handled more easily early in the day, between 8:30 and 11:00 A.M. Preparation of the daily sales report is usually scheduled for 11:00 A.M. each day after the input has been received. The time from 1:00 to 3:00 P.M. seems best for preparing the sales orders received during the day. She usually catches up on the filing late in the day to be ready for the next day's tasks.*

Another way that Mary uses batch processing is to group all tasks that involve word processing together so that she will complete word processing tasks that require the use of the same software. She also uses a spreadsheet package, primarily for the daily sales report. If she can perform word processing functions at one time and spreadsheet functions at another time, she finds that she saves much time in making smooth transitions between these two types of work.

(5) *Calendaring:* Keeping an up-to-date calendar proves to be one of the secretary's most important time-savers. By keeping accurate notations for upcoming appointments, meetings, or other events, time will be saved in locating needed information. The secretary also needs to coordinate calendar entries with those on the executive's calendar so that both will be complete records of appointments and other events.

Electronic calendaring enables the secretary to maintain a complete schedule of appointments and meetings, along with any special notes, on the computer—on an individual disk, a hard drive, or a network.

EXAMPLE: *Networked use of a calendaring system helps the secretary to schedule internal meetings and appointments more easily. Quick access to others' appointment schedules is available, and entries can be inserted into the calendar to be viewed and responded to by those receiving the message.*

Appointments may be entered on a busy executive's calendar as well as conferences, meetings, or reminders. The schedule may be accessed at any time (with the appropriate password, of course) to see what commitments have already been made. A printout of the daily calendar may take the place of the traditional appointment book on the desk.

(6) *Simplifying tasks by utilizing office tools:* Electric letter openers, collating racks and/or small electric collators, electric pencil sharpeners, electric staplers, shredders, and other small pieces of automated office equipment simplify various work assignments and speed the production process.

b. *Simplifying office assignments:* A close look at work assignments is necessary to analyze these tasks in terms of ways of simplifying procedures to save personal time and energy.

(1) *Analyzing routine office tasks:* One basic goal should be to eliminate unnecessary tasks, steps, or motions in performing office work. Routine tasks should be examined to see if procedures can be modified to save valuable office time.

EXAMPLE: Shirley is an executive assistant for three vice presidents in the firm. Her work load includes many routine functions throughout the day (running errands, making copies, updating mailing lists) as well as specialized tasks only she can handle (making travel arrangements, assisting in the writing of research reports). She delegates many of the routine tasks to Nancy, a part-time employee, in order to free her own time for working on more specialized work tasks.

(2) *Analyzing time requirements for specific tasks:* How much time is being spent on specific tasks? Keeping a log for at least one week (be sure it is a fairly typical week) of the tasks performed and the amount of time required results in a listing of tasks as well as basic time requirements. A two-week log would be even better. Procedures used in completing the tasks should be scrutinized carefully to see how time can be saved during the entire process.

(3) *Planning schedules:* Three types of planning schedules can be extremely helpful in office work: daily schedules, weekly (or monthly) schedules, and long-range schedules. Planning, a function that is often overlooked, is the real key to more efficient office schedules.

c. *Completing tasks:* What really gives a secretary or executive assistant a high degree of satisfaction is the ability to actually complete both routine tasks as well as more difficult, complex tasks. Too often one task gets started, only to be left unfinished to respond to another urgent request. With the multitude of demands placed on the secretary from home, family, and the workplace, it is essential that the secretary's primary focus in the workplace be: What tasks *can* be completed today? Focusing on the completion of needed tasks may give the secretary a greater sense of accomplishment at the end of the workday, with the beginning of a fresh start the following day.

4. *Coordinating with Other Office Personnel:* Most office tasks require interaction with supervisors and/or co-workers. Communication (both vertical and horizontal) is very important in maintaining productive working relationships among office personnel. Vertical communication refers to communication from supervisor to employee or from employee to supervisor. Horizontal communication refers to communication from one supervisor to another supervisor or from one employee to another employee, in other words, communication on the same level.

   a. *Coordinating with superiors:* Two-way communication with superiors is essential in order to coordinate office tasks to be completed.

      (1) *Understanding preferences:* Executives and managers have personal preferences as to how the telephone should be answered, messages will be handled, or appointments will be made. The secretary has an obligation to find out preferences for the handling of these routine office procedures and then to manage office functions accordingly.

      (2) *Following directions carefully:* Basic and special instructions for doing a particular task must be considered carefully. More directions appear in written form today, perhaps because of the use of more technology in the office.

      EXAMPLE: There is a special meeting of the Board of Directors scheduled for Friday at 10 A.M., and Ronald Young, the chairman of the board, has asked Mary, his executive assistant, to notify each member by telephone and letter. Mary knows from experience that she will need to set aside time to review with Mr. Young what materials will be needed for the meeting. She enters a note on her calendar to ask about the meeting during the next dictation session.

      (3) *Questioning directives:* When a problem arises relating to the completion of a particular task, the alert secretary should analyze the problem or question first to determine possible solutions. Very often problems arise be-

cause the directives for completing the task are unclear and ambiguous. By asking the right questions early in the process, errors in judgment or performance may be eliminated. (Personal problems should be kept out of the office except when they affect particular work assignments.)

b. *Coordinating with co-workers:* Establishing a spirit of teamwork in the office is important for building rapport among the members of the office staff. Secretaries and other office professionals need to feel that they play vital roles in the success of the business.

(1) *Sharing the work load:* When there is a larger-than-normal project to be completed, is there a way to share the work load?

EXAMPLE: If you offer to help Bill with that annual report which he must complete by next Tuesday, he should be willing to help you when you need an extra hand with one of your projects.

(a) *Job sharing:* The formal arrangement whereby office personnel are actually sharing job responsibilities is called *job sharing*. This means that one full-time job is shared part time by two people on a permanent basis.

EXAMPLE: Joan Smythe and Steve Lockwood are information systems specialists, each employed part time and sharing one full-time position. Because she has children in school, it is easier for Joan to work the morning hours; and Steve, who is attending college in the mornings, prefers to work the afternoon hours.

(b) *Cross training:* Another means of sharing the work load occurs through cross training. Co-workers who are prepared to perform the job functions of more than one position are invaluable as vacations or emergencies arise. *Cross training* is the process of being trained to handle the responsibilities for more than one job in the office.

(2) *Using others' suggestions:* Encouraging office personnel to make suggestions fosters more cooperation among workers in the office. A secretary must be an attentive listener to ideas posed by others; it could be that improvements in current office procedures will result.

(3) *Taking responsibility for personal actions:* The secretary

who makes decisions about work priorities, delegates work assignments to other office personnel, or evaluates work performance must take individual responsibility for these types of decisions. Consequences of action taken must be an initial consideration in deciding a particular action to be taken.

EXAMPLE: Larry forgot to schedule an appointment for Stephanie Clark, his supervisor, with the president this morning at 10:00 A.M. When Stephanie returns from the president's office with the information that the president was not available, Larry must be ready to account for his action (or nonaction in this case).

EXAMPLE: Gladys fired Susie, a new part-time clerical worker, for insubordination. Gladys will need to be ready to present her supervisor with documentation that will present the situation clearly and objectively, especially since Susie has approached the Equal Employment Opportunity Commission about the incident.

B. Organizing

The second managerial function, *organizing,* permits the office administrator to establish specific goals that are to be accomplished through office support services. Today's business firm is especially concerned that all resources (people, supplies, equipment, space) needed for the successful completion of a project be organized for efficient utilization in the performance of office duties. The application of organizational principles, that is, span of control, delegation, among others, provides the basis for the organization of personnel and the work itself for the particular assignment.

1. *Organizing Support Personnel:* To the busy executive or manager, adequate office support is a "must" in order to complete the myriad of communication necessary in the day-to-day routine of the office. Such support responsibilities range from receptionist duties to general office duties (such as light typing, filing/records, copying, or keying information into the computer system), depending on the specific needs of the office staff. Support personnel may be organized according to a centralized plan, a decentralized plan, or a matrix plan of operation.

    a. *Centralization:* Centers are established for specific purposes such as word/information processing, data processing, or records management in locations providing easy access to and from all departments within the company. Each center requires a supervisor who reports to the administrative office manager. Management of centralized office support services usually rests with one administrator, whose primary responsibility may include the supervision of all office personnel throughout the organization.

EXAMPLE: The XYZ Corporation has centralized office support services under the management of Alan Olson, the administrative office manager. Alan has responsibility for several centralized operations: (a) the Information Processing Center, with 15 word-processing specialists who perform word processing functions, one desktop publishing specialist, two proofreaders/editors, and one supervisor; (b) the Data Processing Center, with 12 system operators, programmers, and analysts, and one supervisor; (c) the In-House Printing Center with 11 press operators, design personnel, and one supervisor; and (d) the Records Center, with eight records specialists and one supervisor. Each of the supervisors reports directly to Alan.

(1) *Physical location:* Related office operations for an entire organization are concentrated at one location.
(2) *Functions:* Similar office activities are located within one work group or department.
(3) *Authority:* A few individuals at the top managerial and executive levels have the authority to make all major decisions.

b. *Decentralization:* Office support personnel are housed within individual departments, for example, Sales Department, Finance Department, Personnel Department. Their responsibilities generally include office functions needed only by that department. Each department has its own administration, for example, the Sales Department is managed by the sales manager.

(1) *Physical location:* Related office operations for an organization are concentrated at several locations throughout the organization, typically within specific departments or divisions of the organization.
(2) *Functions:* The supervisor of each work group or the department manager is responsible for seeing that office activities are performed at a quality level and supervises the office employees within that department.
(3) *Authority:* Managers at middle-management levels (department or division) are delegated the authority to make decisions.

c. *Matrix:* Sometimes a combination plan which involves both centralization and decentralization occurs which permits some office operations to be centralized and others to be decentralized, depending upon the needs of the firm. This combination plan is known as a *matrix plan.* Those activities that are centralized are typically managed by one individual within the firm, and those activities that are decentralized are usually managed within specific departments or divisions of the organization.

EXAMPLE: The ABC Company established a centralized information processing center to prepare documents for various departments in the firm. This center accepts work orders from any department and currently has a turnaround time of eight hours. The Legal Department has such a profound quantity of document preparation that a satellite center with identical equipment has been established within the Legal Department to handle only the documents produced for that department. Not only does this alleviate the strain on the centralized information processing center, but it enables the Legal Department to supervise the intricate detail that is required in law.

EXAMPLE: The XYZ Corporation utilizes the satellite concept to enhance the operation of the Sales Department. Within the firm, each department is organized with its own administrative support and secretarial support personnel. The Sales Department has an executive secretary whose primary responsibility is to serve as the secretary for Marilyn Adkins, the Sales Manager, and supervise the other five office support people. The department produces so much correspondence that it became necessary six months ago to update the computer system and purchase more sophisticated word processing software. Two additional operators were hired.

2. *Organizing Work:* Work assignments need to be organized, too, so that they may be effectively handled within the timelines established by principals (end users) throughout the organization. It is important that the work be analyzed to determine the difficulty level, the priority, and the sequencing needed in order to complete the assignment.

   a. *Leffingwell's principles of effective work:* Known as the father of office management, William H. Leffingwell applied the principles of scientific management to office work in his book, *Scientific Office Management,* in 1917. These principles are still important today for secretaries and other office personnel to apply in daily office routines, even though procedures and technology have changed over the years.

      (1) *Planning the work:* The work to be done must be identified and how, when, and where it will be done must be determined. The deadline for its completion is also important in the planning stages.
      (2) *Scheduling the work:* A definite schedule needs to be established for the completion of work even though the

work may appear to be difficult to accomplish. Schedules should be established with the intention that they will be kept.
- (3) *Execution of the work:* The work must be performed with skill, accuracy, and speed, without unnecessary effort or delay.
- (4) *Measurement of the work:* Work must be measured according to quantity produced, quality of the work produced, and individual performance.
- (5) *Rewards:* If the work is completed effectively, the office worker should be rewarded with money, opportunities for self-development, and good working conditions, among others.

b. *Analysis of work:* A preliminary analysis of the work to be done will indicate how difficult the work is, what the priority should be, and the sequence in which the work should be done.

- (1) *Difficulty level of work:* Whether to work from the simple to the complex or the complex to the simple depends upon the individual and how important the work is perceived to be. Some secretaries like to handle a difficult task early in the day and then proceed to less complex tasks. Others work better from simple, relatively easy tasks to more complex ones as the day progresses. At any rate, the difficulty level of the work should be determined and compared with the human resources available to work on that particular assignment.
- (2) *Priority of work:* Work needs to be prioritized from the most important to the least important. If the task is very important and the deadline is approaching, then it should be handled very soon (possibly today or tomorrow). If the task is less important, it may serve as a "filler item" and can be done at any time within the next few days.
- (3) *Sequence of work:* Completion of a work assignment many times depends on the sequencing of the steps in the process. Before a task is begun, the steps in the process need to be identified so that the individual worker can proceed without any further direction. Especially in working with office technology, the employee who forgets one of the steps will probably have difficulty in completing the task.

   EXAMPLE: Sally uses word processing in her position as a legal secretary for the Porter Law Firm. Legal forms, with only a few exceptions, are stored on disks so that when she must prepare a new document, she can retrieve

Office Management 47

the form and fill in the new variable information. If she does not follow the sequence of the process carefully, she may fill in variable information in the wrong locations within the document or may not have the variable information needed to complete the form.

3. *Establishing Work Procedures:* In any office environment, appropriate procedures need to be established for accepting work orders from executives, supervisors, and others who originate work (authors) and for completing it according to company policies and procedures. *Procedures manuals* assist secretaries in following the steps required for certain processes, for example, receiving telephone orders for merchandise.

   a. *Planning and organizing specific tasks:* Each assigned task must be examined carefully to be sure that all requirements and instructions are understood.

      (1) *Logging in the task:* Especially if the secretary works for more than one person, it is imperative to log in each work assignment. This involves using a *logging form* to indicate the date/time the job is received, the number/name of the job, for whom the work is being done, the deadline, the name of the person to whom the task is assigned, and any special instructions. Logging in each task is especially important in centers where production is being handled for the various departments within the firm, for example, a reprographics center.

      (2) *Reviewing job requirements:* Before assigning the task to someone else (or deciding to do it yourself), the instructions need to be reviewed carefully. Here are other checkpoints that need to be considered:

         (a) Files and other needed reference materials should be gathered and assembled.
         (b) Formats to be used in the preparation of documents need to be checked for accuracy.
         (c) The work assignment must be made: who will complete this particular task?
         (d) If the work is assigned to another person, *all* the details and special instructions need to be reviewed with that person.

      (3) *Accepting responsibility for meeting deadlines:* Meeting deadlines is crucial in document preparation. The secretary's ability to meet these deadlines will be enhanced if:

         (a) Production logs are set up so that office personnel

who are assigned specific tasks will be more accountable for completion by given deadlines.

(b) Proofreading, editing, and revision procedures are established.

(4) *Proofreading and editing:* Just as important as keying in input for documents are the proofreading and editing necessary in checking the accuracy and content of a document.

   (a) *Proofreading:* Proofreading is the process of reading through the material that has been typed or keyed in to detect corrections needed.

   EXAMPLE: As part of the proofreading strategy, Ruth Graham runs an initial spelling check of the text that is recorded on disk. With this procedure, she finds most of the obvious errors that had been made in keying in the material. Then, she reads a hard copy (printout) of the material so that she can see precisely how it printed out.

   Proofreading facilitates the detection of errors in keying in the written text as well as errors in word processing commands (bold, underline, indent) that may be needed within the text. Software packages with grammar checks may also be used to advantage.

   (b) *Editing:* Editing is the procedure used by an author to make content revisions in the original document.

   EXAMPLE: Larry has just delivered a draft copy of a report to Mary Stone, the author, for approval. If Mary wishes to make further revisions, Larry will also be responsible for making any necessary revisions since he was also involved in the preparation of the document.

(5) *Completing the job:* Every office requires work assignments to be completed on time and accurately. Accuracy should be a crucial element in each secretary's work.

EXAMPLE: Suzanne is a legal secretary in a law firm which specializes in probate. When she prepares a will, she must be extremely careful that absolutely no errors in the text go unnoticed or uncorrected. Typing $100,000 instead of $10,000 in a specific bequest would be a very costly (and embarrassing) error to make.

Office Management 49

(6) *Logging the job out:* When the job has been completed to the satisfaction of the author, the job should be logged out, in other words, the completion of the job is recorded on a log sheet. The amount of time to do the job, the number of revisions needed, and the production count (lines, pages, or documents) need to be recorded along with any other required information.

b. *Developing office manuals:* Basic office procedures used in offices organized with a traditional principal-secretary structure tend to be "carried around in people's heads." Perhaps this once-common practice served as a security measure, protecting the knowledge base of the organization. However, with the entry of word processing, data processing, and other office automation systems into the office, more emphasis has been placed in recent years on the use and development of functional office manuals that include written documentation of company policies and procedures.

(1) *Features of office manuals:* Typically, office manuals may include the following types of information:

(a) Job descriptions for specific office positions (or clusters of positions).
(b) Standardized formats used in preparing documents.
(c) Individual positions and tasks to be performed.
(d) The time schedule for completing specific jobs.
(e) Policies related to specific office operations.
(f) General goals and objectives of the organization relating to specific procedures or functions.
(g) Measurement standards, if applicable.

(2) *Specific types of office manuals:* Not everyone within a particular organization needs the same kind of operational information. Therefore, different types of manuals may be needed for individuals at different levels and in different departments within the organization—and for different purposes.

(a) *Organizational manual:* This type of office manual shows the formal relationship of divisions or departments within the organization and includes a statement of objectives, basic philosophy, organizational structure, change strategies, and other pertinent historical facts and futuristic plans.
(b) *Policy manual:* Courses of action relating to company objectives, day-to-day operations, and departmental conduct of business in effect for the organization are included in a policy manual.
(c) *Employee manual or handbook:* Specific informa-

tion needed to be a functional worker within the company is summarized in an employee manual or handbook. Included are such information as work schedules and hours, salaries, schedule for salary reviews, dress codes, vacations, benefits, profit-sharing plans available, and retirement plans.

(d) *Procedures or operations manual:* The procedures manual outlines detailed instructions for processing specific tasks or jobs: what is to be done, formats to use, who will do it, when it is to be done, and why it must be done in this way.

EXAMPLE: Word processing supervisors have found procedures manuals extremely useful in assuring that different word processing operators will perform specific jobs using identical document formats and procedures.

(e) *Specialty guide or handbook:* Specialized handbooks are sometimes prepared to give assistance to specific employee groups.

EXAMPLES: Secretarial manuals or handbooks; guides for marketing representatives; established guides for records retention within the company; forms manuals.

(3) *Standardizing procedures for developing office manuals:* Office employees need to follow the same or similar procedures in performing office tasks. Standardizing the procedures for writing and developing manuals helps to coordinate the efforts of different departments or divisions within the company. Here are a few suggestions that could make manuals easier for employees to use:

(a) The use of action words will communicate more clearly to employees.
(b) A general pattern of "who does what-why-how-when-where" should be followed so that definite procedures and steps result.
(c) Procedures should be briefly and concisely written. The important thing is for the employee to be able to use the manual for quick reference and get to the task at hand.
(d) Any manual should be written to the employee. The "you" approach often used will necessitate the application of language, sentence structure, and illustrations to enable the employee to understand and follow the policy or procedure.

C. Supervising

Individuals whose primary responsibility is to supervise and manage other people in the work environment must be able to understand human behavior in order to assist in motivating and leading office personnel to be more productive. The typical office supervisor/manager is responsible for a major unit or department within the organization or is a lead coordinator within a major unit with responsibility for both operations and supervision. Although all of the major functions of management (planning, organizing, staffing, directing, and controlling) are important to the supervisor, the two functions of *staffing* and *controlling* are especially unique to the supervision of office personnel.

1. *Staffing:* Building a staff of office employees who can work cooperatively with each other and with the supervisor is a major supervisory responsibility. From initial human resource planning to the point at which employees become productive workers, the office supervisor/manager is responsible for working with people through orientation, staff development and training, and special guidance and assistance programs. Here are some of the major staffing responsibilities of the office supervisor:

    a. *Human resource planning:* Human resource planning is the process of determining personnel needs for the future and developing strategies for meeting these needs. There are severe shortages of qualified secretaries in many organizations throughout the country, and this may be because too little human resource planning has taken place in office management. These plans should include both short-term (one to three years) and long-term goals (five years or more).

    b. *Recruiting office employees:* Job specifications developed for positions that are vacant in the organization serve as the basis for the development of appropriate recruitment strategies. These job specifications include the skill and knowledge requirements that an applicant must possess in order to meet the requirements of the job. Applicants may be recruited from either internal or external sources.

    EXAMPLES OF INTERNAL SOURCES:
    Employee referrals
    Employee promotions

    EXAMPLES OF EXTERNAL SOURCES:
    Public and private employment agencies
    Professional organizations
    Placement offices within educational institutions
    Advertising in local newspapers
    Temporary employment agencies

    c. *Selecting office employees:* One of the primary responsibilities of the supervisor/manager is to see that qualified, competent office personnel are hired, either internally or externally, to fill job vacancies as they occur. Application and interview processes need to be monitored carefully in order that the company follows affirmative action guidelines in conducting hiring procedures.

    d. *Orienting new employees to the job:* A planned orientation program for new office employees provides the new person with valuable information on the background of the company, the organization and structure of the business, and policies and procedures in effect. Such a program may be scheduled for the first day or two of full-time employment and is often conducted by either the administrative office manager or an individual within the company designated to direct the orientation program for new employees.

    e. *Providing special on-the-job training:* The immediate supervisor is usually the individual responsible for coordinating the on-the-job training (OJT) needed for an office employee to take on new, changed, or additional responsibility.

EXAMPLE: Jeanne is an information systems specialist for Smith Corporation, with particular responsibility for maintaining the CT-1000 computer system. She has been employed in this capacity for three years. The system is being replaced this month by the latest model, the CT-5000, which has many new software applications available. Her supervisor, Sam Little, has approved Jeanne as a participant in a special three-day training program sponsored by the CT Corporation at the CT training center.

    f. *Employee training for different positions:* Cross training is becoming increasingly important in business; there is a great need for more than one employee to know a particular job or task. When employees go on vacation or sick leave, there needs to be a backup individual who is trained to perform the duties of the position.

    g. *Providing guidance and counseling through special programs:* Many organizations have initiated programs to help individual employees combat problems with alcohol and drug abuse. In addition, personal problems of employees and how these may affect them on the job have received attention, also. Many companies provide staff counselors to work individually with these types of problems. A rather new development is the initiation of stress management programs, especially with office employees who are working with high technology. Office workers face more stress, too, because of the necessity to try to balance the pressures of family, home, and workplace responsibilities.

2. *Controlling:* An essential phase of office supervision and management involves comparing actual productivity and results with those that were anticipated. In other words, were the actual goals and objectives of the department and the organization achieved? What was actually accomplished? In addition to monitoring and evaluating work processes, the supervisor/manager has the responsibility of evaluating the performance of individual office employees.

a. *Delegating office assignments:* Perhaps one of the most difficult tasks is delegating to another person the responsibility for completing a specific office assignment. Here are some steps to keep in mind when delegating work to others:

(1) All input (handwritten copy, cassettes, computer disks) needed for the task must be organized and ready for use.
(2) The supervisor should discuss all instructions with the individual who will be doing the work. These instructions should be in writing.
(3) The supervisor should encourage the worker to ask questions if any of the instructions need clarification.
(4) The completed work needs to be reviewed by the supervisor prior to its transmittal to the user (author). In this way needed changes or revisions may be made effectively before submitting the completed work for final approval or signature.

b. *Conducting performance appraisals:* Office personnel are evaluated in terms of specific jobs assigned and total performance over a period of time, that is, six months, one year. The responsibility for performance appraisals is usually delegated to the office manager and/or department manager. A performance appraisal is an evaluation of the performance of an individual office employee over a designated period of time.

(1) *Procedures for performance appraisal:* In order for performance appraisal to take place, definite procedures must be established. Here are some of the primary considerations in implementing a performance appraisal system:

(a) *Performance standards:* Each job is analyzed in terms of behaviors, personal traits, and results required to perform the job. From these requirements, performance standards are specified as criteria for evaluating each employee.
(b) *Employee performance:* Various appraisal methods are used to observe and measure employee performance. Such performance can then be described in terms of what is observed and measured.
(c) *Appraisal data:* The supervisor and the employee need to discuss the appraisal and establish performance standards for the next appraisal period.

General progress should be discussed as well as the determination of future goals or objectives.
(d) *Decision making:* The appraisal data can be used as input for other types of decision making related to employee appraisal (selection, training, promotion, salary).

(2) *Performance appraisal methods:* The office manager needs to be aware of the various performance appraisal methods in use today that may be applied to performance appraisal in the office. There are three primary groups of methods: comparative methods, absolute methods, and objective-setting methods. Here are some examples of each of these three methods:

(a) *Rank comparison:* The supervisor ranks employees from the best to the worst (Comparative Method). This method does not take into consideration the fact that the job responsibilities of the employees will differ.
(b) *Paired comparison:* The supervisor compares each employee to be ranked with every other one in the group, one at a time (Comparative Method).
(c) *Checklist:* The supervisor selects from a list those statements judged to be descriptive of the employee's job performance (Absolute Method).
(d) *Graphic rating scale:* Each individual is evaluated on the basis of factors identified as essential to job performance (Absolute Method).
(e) *Management-by-objectives (MBO) appraisal:* With the help of the supervisor/manager, the employee establishes job objectives, both for individual performance and for personal development, against which his/her performance will be measured during the next appraisal period (Objective-setting Method).

(3) *Performance interview:* Once the written evaluation has been prepared, a performance appraisal interview is typically conducted privately with each employee. The primary purpose is to review positive aspects of the employee's performance. In addition, those areas needing improvement during the next evaluation period must be identified. Such a procedure presents the supervisor with the opportunity to provide feedback to each individual being evaluated. The emphasis should be on personal growth and needed improvement related to the job. Positive reinforcement of preferred behaviors that have been observed during the evaluation period should be stressed.

Chapter 2: Review Questions

Part A: Multiple-Choice Questions

DIRECTIONS: Select the best answer from the four alternatives. Write your answer in the blank to the left of the number.

_____ 1. A primary difference between strategic planning and tactical planning is

   a. strategic planning focuses primarily on the internal environment of the organization, and tactical planning emphasizes the external environment.
   b. tactical planning is developed at the executive level, and strategic planning is developed at the division (department) level.
   c. strategic planning focuses on the development of long-term goals for the organization, and tactical planning focuses on actions required of a specific work unit.
   d. tactical planning focuses on the achievement of organizational goals, while strategic planning focuses on the achievement of division (department) goals.

_____ 2. The secretary's ability to set appropriate work priorities is most dependent upon

   a. whether it is an enjoyable task.
   b. the proofreading necessary to check the completed work.
   c. whether there are frequent interruptions during the work process.
   d. how long the task will take.

_____ 3. The time required from the moment a work order is received until the completed work is returned to the originator (author) is referred to as

   a. turnaround time.
   b. logging time.
   c. planning time.
   d. work in process.

_____ 4. One thing a secretary can do to become more efficient in scheduling time is to

   a. use a manual or automated tickler system.
   b. assign another secretary the responsibility of scheduling specific tasks.
   c. complete tasks in the order they are presented by superiors.
   d. ask superiors to keep their own calendars up to date.

5. Batch processing is the term that would apply to which of the following?

   a. Getting input ready for data processing.
   b. Grouping those tasks requiring the use of word processing software and doing the high-priority items first.
   c. Delegating office tasks to other support personnel.
   d. Scheduling time for the high-priority items first.

6. Keying appointments, meetings, and other commitments directly into the computer for scheduling purposes by secretaries, managers, and executives is known as

   a. batch processing.
   b. coordination of work assignment.
   c. calendaring.
   d. priority scheduling.

7. Which of the following types of communication is most needed to maintain good rapport between the supervisor and employees in a work unit?

   a. Interpersonal communication
   b. Both vertical and horizontal communication
   c. Vertical communication
   d. Horizontal communication

8. The arrangement whereby one full-time position is held by two people, each one working part time, is known as

   a. job rotation.
   b. fringe benefit.
   c. participative management.
   d. job sharing.

9. The management function that permits the office administrator to monitor the information processing center's progress in meeting objectives for the year is

   a. planning.
   b. organizing.
   c. controlling.
   d. directing.

10. When records services are provided in a location with easy access to and from all departments within the firm, we say that the records function is

a. centralized.
b. decentralized.
c. matrix.
d. departmentalized.

11. When all office support personnel are housed within individual departments, the organizational plan is

    a. matrix.
    b. centralized.
    c. decentralized.
    d. shared.

12. Some companies organize word/information processing support for a particular department which produces a large quantity of correspondence so the work load can be handled by

    a. word/information processing specialists.
    b. the information processing center for the organization.
    c. a satellite center established within that department.
    d. administrative support personnel.

13. Information about a specific work order, namely, the name of the job, the department for whom the work will be done, the deadline, should be placed on

    a. a procedure form.
    b. an assignment form.
    c. a priority form.
    d. a logging form.

14. The process of reading through text in order to detect necessary corrections is called

    a. editing.
    b. proofreading.
    c. checking accuracy.
    d. production.

15. Information relating to the organizational objectives and structure will most likely be included in

    a. an operations manual.
    b. an employee manual.

c. a policy manual.
d. an organizational manual.

_____ 16. Detailed instructions for processing specific tasks will most likely be included in

a. a procedures manual.
b. an organizational manual.
c. a specialty guide.
d. an employee manual.

_____ 17. Which one of the following relates to a supervisor's staffing responsibilities?

a. Evaluating a secretary's performance on the job.
b. Orienting a new office employee to tasks performed on the job.
c. Identifying the competencies needed for a particular office position.
d. Analyzing a computer system for possible lease/purchase.

_____ 18. One of the secretary's responsibilities involves the delegation of work assignments to other support personnel. Which of the following examples indicates effectiveness in delegating a work assignment?

a. "Sue, Muriel Johnson needs this report for her meeting with the president tomorrow morning at 10 o'clock. Would you please type this right away?"
b. "Sue, use any format that will give Muriel Johnson time to revise the report before her meeting with the president tomorrow morning."
c. "Sue, this report needs to be typed this afternoon and delivered before 9 o'clock tomorrow morning to the people I have listed on the attached sheet. I'll be glad to help you proofread the report before you make copies for these people."
d. "Sue, please put everything else aside and work on this report. It is very important—Muriel Johnson needs it right away!"

_____ 19. Comparing actual productivity of employees through the results of their work performance with those results which were anticipated is an important part of which of the following functions of management?

a. Planning
b. Organizing
c. Supervising
d. Controlling

Office Management 59

_____ 20. Criteria that are established for evaluating each employee in terms of job behaviors, personal characteristics, and productivity results are known as

   a. performance appraisals.
   b. performance standards.
   c. performance assignments.
   d. performance interviews.

_____ 21. The supervisor ranks each employee so that a list from the best to the worst employees results. This comparative method of performance appraisal is called

   a. the paired-comparison method.
   b. a graphic-rating scale.
   c. the rank-comparison method.
   d. management by objectives.

_____ 22. The performance-appraisal method that requires the employee and the office supervisor to establish job objectives from which performance objectives will be derived is known as

   a. the rank-comparison method.
   b. management by objectives.
   c. the performance-standards method.
   d. the paired-comparison method.

Part B: Matching Sets

Matching Set 1

Match the types of planning (A-C) with the descriptive examples (23-27). Write the letter of your answer in the blank to the left of each number.

Types of Planning

   A. Strategic Planning
   B. Tactical Planning
   C. Operational Planning

DESCRIPTIVE EXAMPLES

_____ 23. A major promotion planned for a new product.

_____ 24. Regional sales representatives scheduled for personal visits to major accounts.

_____ 25. The marketing department's plan for sales of new product with prizes (travel packages) for sales representatives selling the most each month of the coming year.

_____ 26. Increase in quantity of outputs of organization during specific period of time.

_____ 27. The organization's involvement in recycling effort.

Matching Set 2

Match each type of office manual (A-D) with the descriptive examples (28-33). Write the letter of your answer in the blank to the left of each number.

Types of Office Manuals
- A. Policy Manual
- B. Employee Handbook
- C. Procedures Manual
- D. Specialty Guide

DESCRIPTIVE EXAMPLES

_____ 28. Document formats for letters, memos, and reports.

_____ 29. Information on dress codes, work schedules, hours, and employee salaries.

_____ 30. Samples of all business forms used in the organization.

_____ 31. Specific directions relating to an office task and the individual (position) responsible for its completion.

_____ 32. Detailed instructions for specific office tasks.

_____ 33. Management's expectations for departmental conduct of business on a day-to-day basis.

Office Management   61

Part C: Problem Situations

DIRECTIONS: For each of the following questions relating to problem situations, select the best answer from the four alternatives. Write the letter of your response in the blank to the left of the question.

Problem 1

It is a few minutes before two o'clock on Tuesday afternoon. Joe Swain, the office manager, hands you a draft of a report to be prepared. He tells you, "I need this report for my meeting with the president at ten o'clock on Thursday."

_____ 34. Which priority would you assign this task?

    a. Priority 1
    b. Priority 2
    c. Priority 3
    d. No priority necessary

Problem 2

Yesterday you were assigned a rather complex research report to be formatted in final form and ready for the author by this afternoon. It is now 4 P.M., and you are still working on it. You realize that there is no way the report will be done by the time you must leave the office.

_____ 35. Which of the following would be the best thing to do?

    a. Finish the report no matter what time you get through.
    b. Say nothing to the author this afternoon about not completing it, but plan to finish it first thing in the morning.
    c. Explain the problem briefly to the author.
    d. Tell your manager the status of the report, explaining the amount of time required to complete it.

Problem 3

Mary Simmons, the administrative secretary for the Marketing Department, is responsible for the accuracy of the sales report that is sent to all of the sales representatives each morning. In yesterday's report a $100,000 error was made in the total sales for the previous week.

_____ 36. Which of the following would be the most satisfactory response when Nancy Hughes, the vice president of marketing, confronts her with the error?

    a. "I don't know how this error could have been made. I checked the data very carefully."
    b. "Shirley was the person who prepared the report."

c. "I'm sorry this happened, but I'll see that a revised report goes out to all of the representatives this afternoon."
d. "Perhaps the best thing to do is just wait and see if any of the representatives notice the error."

Problem 4

The XYZ Company established an information processing center as support for all departments except the Personnel Department which has its own word/information processing operation.

37. The company is utilizing which of the following organizational plans?

a. Matrix
b. Decentralized
c. Centralized
d. Departmentalized

Chapter 2: Solutions

Part A: Multiple-Choice Questions

	Answer	Refer to Chapter Section
1.	(c)	[A-1-a and A-1-b] Strategic planning involves the development of long-term plans and goals affecting the entire organization, whereas tactical planning involves the development of plans and goals that are more departmentalized or for a particular work unit but will contribute to the overall goals of the organization.
2.	(d)	[A-2-a(5)] The turnaround time for the task is an extremely important consideration in determining the priority for the task.
3.	(a)	[A-2-a(5)] This is the definition of turnaround time.
4.	(a)	[A-3-a(2)] A tickler system is a reminder system. Either a manual card-based system or an automated calendaring system may be used to prompt the secretary of project due dates.
5.	(b)	[A-3-a(4)] When performing tasks using computer software, the secretary will find it advantageous to group tasks according to type of software needed first, for example, word processing tasks, and then complete the high-priority items first. It is sometimes difficult to switch from one type of software to another and then back again.
6.	(c)	[A-3-a(5)] Answers (a), (b), and (d) refer to completely different kinds of procedures for the secretary to use.
7.	(b)	[A-4] Both vertical and horizontal communication are needed for a supervisor and employees within a work unit.
8.	(d)	[A-4-b(1)] Job sharing permits two part-time employees to share a full-time position, but they each are typically eligible for employee benefits.
9.	(c)	[C-2] Answers (a), (b), and (d) refer to management functions the secretary may be involved in besides controlling.
10.	(a)	[B-1-a] When there exists one records center that serves the entire organization, the organizational structure is centralized for the records management function.
11.	(c)	[B-1-b] Decentralization means that the individual work units or departments take responsibility for the specific function, in this case, the office support function.
12.	(c)	[B-1-c] Such a satellite center would perform operations required of that particular department.
13.	(d)	[B-3-a(1)] Managing office support services requires the tracking of work orders from the time they are received until the moment they are delivered back to the user.
14.	(b)	[B-3-a(4)] Proofreading must take place so that *all* errors

64 Office Management

15. (d) [B-3-b(2)(a)] There are many different types of company manuals that can be developed. One manual should obviously deal primarily with organizational objectives and structure.

16. (a) [B-3-b(2)(d)] Procedures manuals present complete descriptions and step-by-step directions for completing specific tasks.

17. (b) [C-1-d] Staffing responsibilities include human resource planning, recruiting and selecting new office employees, and orienting new employees to the job.

18. (c) [C-2-a] The deadline is identified and directions given, and a willingness to assist is evident since the situation appears to be a rush job.

19. (d) [C-2] Answers (a), (b), and (c) refer to other management functions the secretary may be involved in besides controlling.

20. (b) [C-2-b(1)(a)] Performance standards do reflect supervisors' expectations of employees in terms of job behaviors, personal characteristics, and output.

21. (c) [C-2-b(2)(a)] The rank-comparison method results in a list of the employees ranked from best to worst, according to the evaluation.

22. (b) [C-2-b(2)(e)] The management-by-objectives (MBO) approach to performance appraisal does give the employee more involvement in setting personal goals for the appraisal period that also coordinate with department and organizational goals.

are detected and corrected before the final draft is prepared.

Part B: Matching Sets

Matching Set 1

23. (B) [A-1-b]
24. (C) [A-1-c]
25. (B) [A-1-b]
26. (A) [A-1-a]
27. (A) [A-1-a]

Matching Set 2

28. (C) [B-3-b(2)(d)]
29. (B) [B-3-b(2)(c)]
30. (D) [B-3-b(2)(e)]
31. (C) [B-3-b(2)(d)]
32. (C) [B-3-b(2)(d)]
33. (A) [B-3-b(2)(b)]

Office Management

PART C: Problem Situations

34. (b) [A-2-c(1)] A time limit is indicated, but the work does not have to be done immediately.

35. (c) [A-4-a] By giving the author an idea of the project's status, you shift the decision back to the author. The author can then judge how much additional time is needed for completion; this should help you better plan the completion of the project, too.

36. (c) [A-4-b(3)] This response indicates that Mary is accepting the necessary responsibility to see that the job is getting done correctly.

37. (a) [B-1-c] The XYZ Company is utilizing a matrix organization which consists of some centralized functions as well as some decentralized functions, depending on the needs of the organization and specific departments.

CHAPTER 3
Work Simplification

OVERVIEW

From an economic standpoint, office administrators need to control office costs (personnel costs as well as operations costs) for all phases of the work process from the moment work is originated by a user (author) until it is ready for final distribution. Approximately 80 percent of the total operating costs for an office is spent on salaries for office personnel. Therefore, the office manager needs to be concerned with the ways in which office personnel are being utilized in work processes within the total system.

In today's automated office it is especially important that office systems and procedures be analyzed to see if work methods can be improved to eliminate unnecessary waste. Office personnel need to be able to do *more* work in *less* time at *reduced* costs using technology. *Work simplification* is the process of improving work performance by determining how people, resources, technology, time, and space can be utilized more effectively and efficiently.

DEFINITION OF TERMS

CRITICAL PATH METHOD (CPM). An outgrowth of the Gantt chart which is a more precise method of examining the breakdown of a project into procedures and an associated time plan.

DOCUMENTATION. The development of written procedures that identify user requirements, functions, workflows, reports, files, and other information needed.

FLOW PROCESS CHART. The most widely used tool of procedures analysis; each step in a specific work process is identified and classified into an operation, a transportation, an inspection, a delay, or a storage step.

GANTT CHART. A bar chart developed by Henry L. Gantt in the early 1900s for scheduling work; depicts work in progress over a period of time—day, week, or month.

MOTION STUDY. The analysis of bodily motions to determine the efficiency of manual operations within certain types of office activities.

OFFICE LAYOUT CHART. A flow diagram that shows the flow of work through the office as an overlay on a scale drawing of the present office layout.

PROCEDURE FLOW CHART. A diagram of the entire work flow in a procedure which involves more than one department in order for the procedure to be completed.

PROCEDURES ANALYSIS. The study of specific office processes to determine the steps involved, the time involved in each step, the distance involved in each step, and the departments involved in the procedure.

PROGRAM EVALUATION AND REVIEW TECHNIQUE (PERT). A time plan that is an outgrowth of the Gantt chart; PERT uses a time-event network so that activities needed to complete a project by a certain deadline can be presented in a flow-chart diagram.

SYSTEM. A network of interrelated procedures, personnel, and technology working together within the business environment to achieve well-defined goals.

SYSTEMS ANALYSIS. The step-by-step investigation of a system in order to define what it does and determine how it can best continue to perform these operations.

SYSTEMS DESIGN. The determination of the actual inputs needed in order to achieve the desired outputs.

SYSTEMS PLANNING. The process of recognizing the need for a change in the present system and conducting a preliminary investigation to determine the feasibility of further development of the idea.

TASK ANALYSIS. The study of all office tasks performed by an office worker in a specific assignment over a specified period of time.

WORK DISTRIBUTION CHART. A technique used to identify the major work activities performed within a specific work group and the amount of time the work group as a whole spends on each activity.

WORK SIMPLIFICATION. The process of improving work performance by finding out how people, resources, technology, time, and space can be utilized more effectively and efficiently.

A. Analyzing Functions and Processes

First of all, it is necessary to examine the work process as it presently exists in the office. Next, improvements in the process must be identified to eliminate, combine, or add steps for simplifying the procedures used.

Perhaps the most important key to work simplification is active participation by those performing the particular work process in question.

1. *Selecting Work Process for Analysis:* The work process to be analyzed and possibly simplified should be selected. Reasons for selection of the work process may be based on criteria such as these:

    a. The process is a relatively expensive and time-consuming work process.
    b. The process affects an organization-wide process.
    c. The process is plagued by apparent "bottlenecks" identified by people involved in the process.

2. *Identifying Components of Work Process:* Each step of the work process needs to be examined in detail.

    a. *Work patterns:* Graphic illustrations and charts may be used to portray present work patterns.
    b. *Work volume:* Any fluctuations in the work volume should be identified and noted.

3. *Analyzing Operations in Work Process:* Each operation in the work process must be analyzed to determine specific aspects of the process. Key questions which need to be answered include these:

    - Why is this operation necessary?
    - What is the actual step-by-step procedure involved in the work process?
    - How is each step performed?
    - Which of these steps are manual operations? Which are automated operations?
    - When is this operation performed? What is the time frame?
    - Are work schedules rigid or flexible?
    - Where is this operation performed?
    - Who performs this operation?

4. *Improving the Present Work Process:* The primary reason for conducting an in-depth analysis of the work process is to derive some ways to improve the way the process currently functions.

    a. *Eliminating nonessential steps:* Those steps in the process which are deemed unnecessary and nonessential need to be identified and eliminated from the process.
    b. *Combining steps:* Steps which overlap with others should be simplified and sometimes combined.
    c. *Inserting new steps:* The addition of new steps will smooth out work patterns at appropriate points in the process.
    d. *Sequencing steps:* All steps need to be properly sequenced within the new work pattern.

    e. *Redesigning forms:* Business forms used in the work process must be redesigned to reflect new requirements in the process. The automation of forms design and management is a "must" in order to simplify the design procedure.
    f. *Eliminating problems:* Any problems imposed by peak loads should be reduced through the new procedure.

5. *Considering Alternative Methods:* All possible alternative methods should be considered in terms of cost, time, feasibility, and effort expended. "What if" scenarios should be developed for each different set of circumstances.
6. *Trying Out the Revised or New Process:* Once a work process has been revised or a new work process has been developed, a tryout of the process is essential in order to test it in a realistic business situation. A segment of the organization (a department or a work group) must be selected for the tryout.

    a. *Employee training or retraining:* Employees within that department or work group must receive appropriate training or retraining in the new work process before they are required to use it for the tryout. This is a crucial time within the process because employee acceptance of the new process and commitment to the change will depend on individual ability to perform the new functions.
    b. *User feedback:* Users need to provide feedback as to the ease and efficiency of using the simplified or new process.

7. *Implementing the Revised Process:* As a result of the tryout, additional changes or revisions in the process may be made. Then the revised process is ready to be implemented (put into operation) within the organization on a larger scale.
8. *Evaluation of Entire Process:* Every work process needs to be evaluated, especially if it has been simplified or is a new process. A regular schedule for evaluation should be established within the company so that every work process is analyzed and evaluated at regular intervals.

EXAMPLE: Ajax Office Systems Co. has been in operation for twelve years, specializing in the marketing of microcomputer systems and software. With the volume of business increasing this year, Bob McIntyre, the president, decided that the time was right for the installation of a new business computer for processing business transactions. This will necessitate a complete analysis of various work processes, for example, payroll, purchase order requisitions, accounting procedures for sales, among others. The best time to perform such an analysis is now, before the new computer is selected, not after the selection and installation. The president as well as division managers will want to be sure that the new system can handle all applications for which it is being purchased.

B. **Designing Systems**

A *system* is defined as a network of interrelated procedures, personnel, and technology working together within the business environment to achieve well-defined goals. *Systems design* is really a "backward" approach to development. Beginning with goals or output desired, data files are examined to determine the actual inputs needed to achieve the desired results.

1. *Characteristics of Systems:* In order to operationalize a system, a number of characteristics (or features) must be present.

   a. *Acceptability:* People who are involved with the system accept it rather than reject it, primarily because of special consideration for the human element during the design stages.
   b. *Dependability:* The system produces consistent results, has reliable output, and operates with a minimum of downtime.
   c. *Effectiveness:* The system accomplishes the purpose for which it was designed, depending on any constraints imposed on the system.
   d. *Efficiency:* The system achieves the purpose at a low enough cost to allow the organization to make a profit.
   e. *Flexibility:* The system has the ability to adjust to changes in input, environment, or procedures and to accommodate exception processing without disruption of system operation.
   f. *Resourcefulness:* The system utilizes organizational resources (people, equipment, materials, other assets) in order to produce a product and make a profit.
   g. *Simplicity:* Dependable operation stems from simplified procedures; the system facilitates learning on the part of the users.
   h. *Systematic operation:* The system performs logical, step-by-step operations.

2. *Phases of Systems Design:* Primary phases of systems design include systems planning, systems analysis, systems development, and systems evaluation. Once the system has been developed, the implementation of the system is the next step.

   a. *Systems planning:* The first step in designing a system is to recognize the need for a change in the present system and to conduct a preliminary investigation to determine the feasibility of further development of the idea. Some of the considerations involved in this phase include:

      (1) *Defining major systems:* In addition to describing the business systems involved, all input and output must be defined. The sources of all input and output must also be identified.
      (2) *Identifying the specific need:* The actual need to improve

service must be identified, especially in terms of future requirements, to provide better service at lower costs. Also important at this time are evaluating the initial request from the user, screening user requests, and determining exactly what further study and analysis will be required.

(3) *Investigating the present system:* A feasibility study will determine the characteristics or features of the present system that relate to the achievement of objectives and those that do not. Users or vendors can be helpful in assisting in the development of ideas for proposed system changes. Organizational factors, such as the organizational culture, employee resistance to change, or organizational politics, need to be examined. Of course, the resources required to make a change must be considered as well.

(4) *Involving the user:* The impact of the new system on the organization and individual departments must be determined. Potential users need to be involved so that specific operations of the present system might be compared with proposed new systems. The user will be an important ally in assuring the success of the new system if involved during the early developmental stages.

(5) *Securing top management support:* In the early stages of systems design, it is important that top management show support for the project, both in terms of dollars and in terms of human resources needed for the analytical work.

b. *Systems analysis:* The second phase of systems design, systems analysis, is the step-by-step investigation of a system to define what the system does and determine how it can best continue to perform these operations. Primary focus is on objectives, organization, and detailed procedures currently involved in the system. An examination of the requirements of the new system is vital at this point, also, because the foundation for the new or revised system needs to be developed. Some of the aspects of determining the new or revised systems requirements include:

(1) *Operations analysis:* An analysis is needed to determine current user objectives, operations, and information flows. This analysis should also show what information and data files need to be maintained.

(2) *Identifying existing problems:* Any problems that exist with the present system should be identified and noted so that as the system design continues, these problems can be addressed.

(3) *Defining user objectives:* The impact of the system on

user operations must be identified, and the objectives of primary users must be developed.

(4) *Determining documentation needed:* The new system will require new documentation in terms of the user requirements, functions, workflows, reports, or files needed. The best methods for processing data will also need to be determined at this point.

(5) *Identifying technical support needed:* The hardware, software, data-base-management system, control programs, communications, and other technical support must be identified for the new system.

c. *Systems development:* In this phase the conceptual design of the system (developed during the systems analysis phase) is utilized to develop a completely new system. Here are some of the steps in the process that are among the most important:

(1) *Developing preliminary design:* Requests for proposals must be prepared to send to potential vendors, and evaluative criteria are developed to use when these proposals are received. A preliminary evaluation of the entire project needs to be conducted.

(2) *Preparing technical specifications:* Detailed specifications are required for both new applications and technical software support. Technical procedures and programming are finalized.

(3) *Preparing applications specifications:* The technical specifications must be converted into detailed programming specifications for specific business applications.

(4) *Completing program documentation:* Applications specifications are converted into computer instructions. These instructions are tested, completing the program documentation.

(5) *Developing user procedures:* Detailed user procedures are developed for the new system. Such procedures as normal operation of the system, manual backup, error correction, the use of reports, and terminal operations are included.

(6) *Planning the implementation:* Final plans for implementation of the new system are prepared as well as plans for systems testing and conversion to the new system.

(7) *Performing systems test:* A complete test must be run on all new system components to see if the new system indeed meets the user requirements.

EXAMPLE: The time frame for systems development within many organizations today is being reduced. One of the procedures being used to enhance new systems development is to physically place all members of the development team involved in the creation of the new system in close proximity within the office structure. This means that members of the work group, though they come from different departments (engineering, marketing, production), are physically situated next to each other day after day as they work on the new system. Though some may be reluctant to leave their departments, most find that the change permits higher levels of communication and cooperation necessary to speed up the process, decreasing development time by months and even years.

3. *Systems Implementation:* The months and years of hard work in developing the new system begins to pay off when the system is finally implemented and put into operation. The primary objectives during this phase include:

   a. *Phasing in the implementation:* Rather than trying to change the entire system at once, it may be better to implement the new system in phases, such as:

      - Introduction of hardware and software.
      - Conversion to the new system.
      - User training.
      - Training for operations personnel.

   b. *Refining the system:* Areas that still need to be changed or refined must be identified. In addition, any errors that seem to recur must be analyzed and the problems causing the errors must be solved.

   c. *Communicating to employees:* One of the primary needs during systems implementation is the involvement of employees. They need to know and understand the purposes of the new system and the advantages that will accrue to the organization as a result of using the new system. Even though employees may have been involved somewhat during previous phases, employee involvement during implementation is crucial—the systems analyst will leave, but the employee will remain to carry on. A commitment to the change is imperative.

4. *Systems Evaluation:* There needs to be an ongoing evaluative process to determine efficiency, accuracy, timeliness, economy, and productivity of the system.

   a. *Measurement of results:* As the system begins to be used, the results need to be measured over a period of time. Productivity levels need to be determined.

   b. *Comparison with objectives:* The efficiency and effectiveness of the new system need to be evaluated in terms of the outputs (goals) identified in the early systems planning stages.

5. *Systems Cessation:* All systems have a "life" and need to be replaced or modified as the operations within the organization

change. System cessation may be planned as part of the implementation process.

EXAMPLE: The Qwik-Computer Company, a manufacturer of computer systems, halts the production system for one month, in June of each year, so that the entire company can gear up for the changeover to the new model for the following year. When production starts up during July, the new model will be produced.

Systems cessation could be temporary (as in the foregoing example) or permanent (the system is obsolete and will never be used again).

C. Tools of Systems Analysis and Design

A number of different types of analytical tools are used in analyzing and designing systems. The more prominent ones used for task, procedure, and motion analyses are included here.

1. *The Task Analysis:* Task analyses are conducted to find out what skills, knowledges, and behaviors are required within specific positions, for example, secretary, information processing specialist, accountant, computer programmer. The *task analysis* is the study of all tasks performed by an individual in a specific work assignment over a specified period of time. Task analyses may be conducted in-house by managers, supervisors, or special teams of company personnel; or an organization may find it more feasible to hire an outside consultant to conduct the research.

    a. *Establishing procedures for the task analyses:* First of all, a definite set of procedures needs to be developed for conducting task analyses. The support of top-level management is imperative for people within the organization to want to be involved in helping with this type of research. Typical procedures include the steps involved in gathering information from various levels and departments within the organization.

    b. *Interviewing employees:* In performing a task analysis, an employee is asked to share information relating to the day-to-day performance of routine as well as specialized tasks. One method that has been quite successful in obtaining this information is the direct interview. Typical questions asked during the task analysis are:

- What tasks are you expected to perform in this position?
- What specific skills, knowledge, and behaviors are an essential part of your duties and responsibilities?
- How frequently is each task performed: daily, weekly, monthly, longer?
- How important do you think each task is: very important, important, nonessential?

c. *Interviewing supervisors and managers:* It is important to interview supervisors and managers as well to get their perspective of the work that is done in particular kinds of positions. A comparison might be made of what the supervisor or manager thinks is done in a particular position and what the employee says is actually done.

d. *Using a questionnaire:* Another way to gather the information is through the use of a survey or questionnaire. If this method is used, care must be used in developing the specific questions so that the respondent will be able to provide the information easily. Sometimes sensitive information relating to specific problems can best be gathered through this method. Anonymity should be maintained so that names of people are not readily associated with problems that are identified.

EXAMPLE: JoAnn Martin, the office manager for Republic Corporation, identified the rewriting of all office job descriptions as a high priority for this year, since this had not been done for about five years. In order to ascertain exactly what tasks are currently being performed in each position, she is conducting a task analysis of each position by using a written questionnaire. She then plans to follow up with an in-depth interview to clarify certain responses to the questions asked. She plans to encourage employees in these positions to make suggestions for improvement of work processes.

2. *Procedures Analysis:* The study of specific office processes to determine the steps involved, the time involved in each step, the distance involved in each step (if applicable), and the departments involved in the procedure is called *procedures analysis*. The most widely used types of procedures analysis are the flow process chart, the procedure flow chart, the flow diagram, and the work distribution chart.

   a. *Flow process chart:* The flow process chart is the most widely used tool of procedures analysis (see Figure 3-1). Each step in a specific work process is identified and classified into one of these five categories: operation, transportation, inspection, delay, or storage.

      (1) *Operation (O):* Something is actually being created, revised, added, or completed.
      (2) *Transportation (⇒):* Something is being moved from one place to another.
      (3) *Inspection (□):* Something is being checked or verified.
      (4) *Delay (D):* An interruption or delay in the work flow is occurring.
      (5) *Storage (▽):* Something is being stored for later retrieval only by authorized persons.

FLOW PROCESS CHART			No.		Page No. **32**		No. of Pages **1**			
Process **Prepare merged letter**			SUMMARY							
☐ Man or ☐ Material			ACTIONS		Present		Proposed		Difference	
					No.	Time	No.	Time	No.	Time
			○ operations		8					
Chart Begins		Chart Ends	⇨ transportations		2					
			☐ inspections		1					
Charted By **CRA**		Date **9/10/9-**	D delays		0					
			▽ storages							
Organization **ABC Communications**			Distance Traveled (Feet)		**155'**					

Step No.	DETAILS OF METHOD ☒ Present ☐ Proposed	operation / transportation / inspection / delay / storages	Distance (in Feet)	Quantity	Time	analysis (why?) what? where? when? who? how?	NOTES	analysis chart
1	Key in primary file	○⇨☐D▽						
2	Key in secondary file	○⇨☐D▽						
3	Run spelling check	○⇨☐D▽						
4	Print master copies	○⇨☐D▽						
5	Send masters to user	○⇨☐D▽						
6	Revise files	○⇨☐D▽						
7	Store revised files	○⇨☐D▽						
8	Prepare merged letters	○⇨☐D▽						
9	Prepare merged envelope	○⇨☐D▽						
10	Check entire job	○⇨☐D▽						
11	Deliver to user	○⇨☐D▽						
12		○⇨☐D▽						
13		○⇨☐D▽						
14		○⇨☐D▽						
15		○⇨☐D▽						
16		○⇨☐D▽						
17		○⇨☐D▽						
18		○⇨☐D▽						
19		○⇨☐D▽						
20		○⇨☐D▽						
21		○⇨☐D▽						

Figure 3-1
Flow Process Chart

b. *Procedure flow chart:* The procedure flow chart depicts the entire work flow in a procedure which involves more than one department in the process of completion (see Figure 3-2).
c. *Office layout chart:* The flow of work through the office may be studied. The office layout chart, sometimes referred to as a flow diagram, applies the flow chart to a scale drawing of the present office layout. The purpose of this type of analysis is to see if there are any faults in the office arrangement that need to be corrected to smooth out the procedure. Sometimes

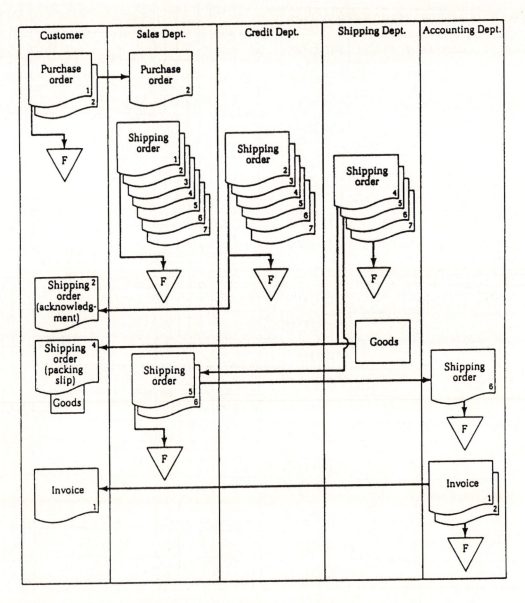

Figure 3-2 Procedure Flow Chart (Source: Eleanor Hollis Tedesco and Robert B. Mitchell, *Administrative Office Systems Management,* Second Edition, New York: John Wiley & Sons, Inc., 1987, p. 60.)

work flow is inefficient, creating a situation in which there is too much backtracking or crisscrossing of documents or people. Software is now available so that the flow of work through the office and the physical layout of the office can be analyzed and alternative layouts studied.

d. *Work distribution charts:* Sometimes it is necessary to identify the major work activities performed within a specific work group. Using the work distribution chart helps to determine the amount of time the work group as a whole (or individuals within the work group) spends on each activity (See Figure 3-3).

EXAMPLE: Relating to the previous task analysis example, JoAnn plans to study the activities of each person involved in the information processing center's operations. She especially wants to be sure that any realignment of individual responsibilities is supported by a work distribution analysis first. In this way, she will be able to identify all tasks performed by each employee and the amount of time each employee spends during the course of a typical day performing each activity. At the same time she will be able to see how efficiently the entire work group, consisting of nine people, functions.

3. *Motion Study:* When analysts study office procedures, they may want to study physical motion to determine the efficiency of neces-

WORK DISTRIBUTION CHART FOR ONE WEEK

Major Activity	Total Work Hours	Name/Title	Work Hours	Name/Title	Work Hours	Name/Title	Work Hours
Purchases	32	B. Johnson	12	J. Ackley	10	H. Browne	10
Billing	27	B. Johnson	10	J. Ackley	6	H. Browne	11
Ordering	18	B. Johnson	11	J. Ackley	—	H. Browne	7

WORK DISTRIBUTION SUMMARY SHEET

Organizational Unit/Charted: Accounting
Date 3/1/9-

Number	Activities	Hours	Tasks (in hours)					
			1	2	3	4	5	6
1	Purchases	32	6	7	5	8	4	2
2	Billing	27	5	3	4	4	10	1

Figure 3-3
Work Distribution Chart

sary manual operations when performed alone or in combination with office automation systems. In this way, barriers to efficient performance may be determined and suggestions made to improve the person-task and person-equipment interfaces that exist with many office procedures.

    a. *Right-hand and left-hand analysis:* A specific office procedure, like using the telephone and taking messages, may be studied to see what motions are performed by each hand. A right-hand and left-hand analysis chart may be used to depict the steps in the procedure, with the steps performed by the left hand listed down the left side of the sheet and those steps performed by the right hand listed down the right side of the sheet. After the present work process has been carefully outlined, the importance of each step in the process is decided. Unnecessary motions are eliminated, and the proposed process is developed and outlined on a second right-hand and left-hand chart.

    b. *Person-equipment process chart:* Sometimes referred to as a multiple activity chart, a person-equipment process chart provides a detailed analysis of the activity of one person with one machine, one person with several machines, or several people with several machines. Usually this type of analysis is conducted with high-volume, repetitive work processes to show the interaction of people with equipment and possible delays created by either the people or the equipment.

4. *Time Plans:* Time in relationship to specific tasks that need to be performed is a vital element. In the early 1900s, Henry L. Gantt developed a bar chart for scheduling work. Two of the newer techniques are PERT (Program Evaluation and Review Technique) and CPM (Critical Path Method).

    a. *Gantt chart:* The Gantt chart depicts work in progress over a period of time—day, week, or month. Variations of the Gantt chart include progress charts, work load charts, and machine record charts. The Gantt chart identifies when different jobs must be completed so that managers can check the work in process and make adjustments as needed in the work schedules.

    b. *PERT and CPM:* Both PERT (Program Evaluation and Review Technique) and CPM (Critical Path Method) are outgrowths of the Gantt chart, but each offers a more precise method of examining the breakdown of a project into procedures and associated times. PERT uses a time-event network so that activities needed to complete a project by a certain deadline can be presented in a flow-chart diagram. In order for projects to be charted in this way, they must have the following characteristics:

(1) The project must have a definite starting point and an ending point.
(2) The activities must be performed in a precise sequence.
(3) Each activity requires the expenditure of time. Times must be assigned to each activity.

The manager who uses a time plan to chart the progress of a given project over time will probably feel more committed to meeting specified deadlines than one who does not. Projects that involve numerous steps or phases require a keen analysis of time in order to assure completion according to schedule.

Chapter 3: Review Questions

Part A: Multiple-Choice Questions

DIRECTIONS: Select the best answer from the four alternatives. Write your answer in the blank to the left of the number.

_____ 1. The process of improving work performance by analyzing how people, resources, technology, time, and space can be utilized more effectively is

　　a. procedures analysis.
　　b. work simplification.
　　c. systems analysis.
　　d. task analysis.

_____ 2. Perhaps the most important key to work simplification is

　　a. selecting the work process that will be analyzed.
　　b. analyzing each operation in the work process.
　　c. active participation by those employees who are currently involved in performing the work process.
　　d. elimination of unnecessary steps in the work process.

_____ 3. A specific work process should be selected for analysis for the reason that

　　a. charts can be developed to portray accurately the present work pattern.
　　b. the work process is a relatively expensive one.
　　c. the time frame for performing the work is definite.
　　d. there are fluctuations in the work volume that need to be identified.

_____ 4. Once a work process has been revised or developed

　　a. the new or revised process needs a tryout to detect any faults.
　　b. steps which overlap with others should be combined.
　　c. business forms need to be redesigned to reflect the changes.
　　d. the specific need for the work process should be identified.

_____ 5. A system is resourceful if

　　a. the system is based on logical, step-by-step operations.
　　b. the system accomplishes the purpose for which it was designed.

c. people who are involved with the system accept it rather than reject it.
d. the system utilizes organizational assets in order to produce a product and make a profit.

_____ 6. The primary purpose of a feasibility study is to

a. recognize the need for a change in the present system.
b. determine the actual inputs needed in order to achieve the desired outputs.
c. determine the features of the present system that are or are not meeting objectives.
d. identify the step-by-step operations of a new system.

_____ 7. In designing and implementing a new system, it is imperative that top management show support during which phase?

a. Systems planning
b. Systems analysis
c. Systems development
d. Systems implementation

_____ 8. A task analysis is conducted to discover

a. the training or retraining needed by an office worker.
b. how well an office worker is functioning on the job.
c. the skills, knowledge, and behaviors needed for a specific office position.
d. the steps involved in performing specific office procedures.

_____ 9. The study of a specific office process in order to determine the steps involved, the time and distances involved in each step, and the departments involved is called

a. task analysis.
b. work simplification.
c. systems analysis.
d. procedures analysis.

_____ 10. An analytical tool that is used to identify the major work activities performed within a specific work group and the amount of time spent on each activity is the

a. work distribution chart.
b. office layout chart.

Work Simplification

c. PERT chart.
d. flow process chart.

_____ **11.** A study of the efficiency of manual operations in an office activity may involve the use of

a. a work distribution chart.
b. a flow process chart.
c. motion study.
d. time plan.

_____ **12.** A Gantt chart is an example of
a. motion study to detect efficiency of manual operations.
b. a time plan that depicts work in progress.
c. procedures analysis to determine steps involved in a process.
d. task analysis of all tasks performed by an individual in a particular position.

_____ **13.** Which of the following types of analyses uses a time-event network to show the activities needed to complete a project by a given deadline?

a. Flow process chart
b. PERT chart
c. Gantt chart
d. Motion study

Part B: Matching Sets

Matching Set 1

Match each of the phases of systems design (A-C) with the correct characteristic or feature (14-20). Write the letter of your response in the blank to the left of the number.

Phases of Systems Design
A. Systems Planning
B. Systems Analysis
C. Systems Development

CHARACTERISTICS/FEATURES

_____ **14.** An investigation to determine what information and data files need to be maintained.

_____ 15. Recognition of need for a change in present system.

_____ 16. Evaluative criteria are developed to use when proposals for systems equipment are received from vendors.

_____ 17. Development of objectives of primary users.

_____ 18. A feasibility study to determine the features of the present system.

_____ 19. Detailed user procedures developed for system.

_____ 20. Identification of hardware, software, or other technical support needed for new system.

Part C: Problem Situations

DIRECTIONS: For each of the following problem situations, select the best answer from the four alternatives. Write the letter of your response in the blank to the left of the question.

Problem 1

Prior to preliminary planning for the purchase of a new computer system, the XYZ Company has contracted with Bonnie Bradford, a private consultant, to conduct task analyses for every office-support position. She wants to use the information gathered to see how the work assignments might change as employers become more versatile with the new system.

_____ 21. Which of the following would be the best means of examining the work load assigned to each office position?

a. Examining the business forms associated with each office function.
b. Interviewing each employee to determine the basic requirements of the position.
c. Having all office employees complete a questionnaire, with several questions pertaining to the work load.
d. Interviewing only the office supervisor to obtain an overall perspective of the various work processes being supervised.

_____ 22. As Bonnie approaches her first interview, she is questioned by the employee (the interviewee) in this way: "How do you plan to use the information I give you about my job?" Which of the following replies would be the most appropriate?

a. "We're going to use the data to determine better productivity standards."
b. "We want to find out how satisfied you are in working here."
c. "We are in the process of evaluating how well you perform your job."
d. "We want to find out exactly what you do on your job and how you spend your time."

Chapter 3: Solutions

Part A: Multiple-Choice Questions

	Answer	Refer to Chapter Section
1.	(b)	Overview
2.	(c)	[A]
3.	(b)	[A-1-a]
4.	(a)	[A-6] The tryout of the new procedure will enable the developers to determine any defects in the new or revised process.
5.	(d)	[B-1-f]
6.	(c)	[B-2-a(3)]
7.	(a)	[B-2-a(5)] Top management needs to show support right from the beginning of the project during the systems planning phase.
8.	(c)	[C-1]
9.	(d)	[C-2]
10.	(a)	[C-2-d]
11.	(c)	[C-3]
12.	(b)	[C-4-a]
13.	(b)	[C-4-b]

Part B: Matching Sets

Matching Set 1

14.	(B)	[B-2-b(1)]
15.	(A)	[B-2-a]
16.	(C)	[B-2-c(1)]
17.	(B)	[B-2-b(3)]
18.	(A)	[B-2-a(3)]
19.	(C)	[B-2-c(5)]
20.	(B)	[B-2-b(5)]

Part C: Problem Situations

21.	(b)	[C-1-b] The employee is the one individual who knows the day-to-day routine of the particular position.
22.	(d)	[C-1-b] The task analysis is primarily designed to find out exactly what an employee does in his/her job.

CHAPTER 4
Records Management

OVERVIEW

The management of records has become an extremely important office support function. Records such as letters, memorandums, invoices, and financial statements must be managed so that they continue to serve their purposes effectively within an organization. Records are the products of office work, and they serve as the "memory" of the organization. The average cost of each misfiled record or filing error is between $80 and $100.

Records management is the systematic control of recorded information required for the operation of the organization from the moment of creation through the use, storage, transfer, and disposal phases of the records cycle. Managing records within an organization must provide a planned approach to records retention as well as easy use and access to stored records by authorized individuals.

Any successful records management program must have top management support and a knowledgeable staff to direct and control records systems within the organization. A working knowledge of both manual and electronic methods of records management is essential for today's secretaries, administrative assistants, records technicians and analysts, and office managers.

DEFINITION OF TERMS

ACTIVE RECORDS. Those records that are consulted in the current administration of the business.

ALPHABETIC CLASSIFICATION SYSTEM. A set of filing procedures that is based on the use of the alphabet as a means of organizing the records.

APERTURE CARD. A punched card that contains a slot into which a microimage (or microimages) can be inserted; text may be punched into the card or interpreted on the card.

APPRAISAL OF RECORDS. The examination of company records to determine the value of the records.

ARCHIVE. A facility that houses records that are being retained for research or historical value.

BLOCK CODES. Groups of numbers reserved for records that have a common feature or characteristic.

BUSINESS FORM. A record that is designed with constant information preprinted or appearing on it and space provided for variable information to be inserted later.

BUSINESS REPORT. The final output of some information-gathering activity within the business, summarizing the methods, procedures, and results of a business project or research.

CHRONOLOGICAL SYSTEM. A set of filing procedures used when records are filed according to date, either most recent date first or oldest date first.

CLASSIFICATION SYSTEM. A set of procedures used in a filing system based on alphabetic, numeric, or alphanumeric rules.

CODING. Making notations on the record itself as to exactly how the record will be stored (under what names or numbers).

COLOR CODING. An identification system that uses colored strips on the side of file folders to represent numeric or alphanumeric codes.

CONSTANT INFORMATION. Descriptors, key words, or phrases preprinted or appearing on a business form that remain the same on all forms of a particular kind.

CONVENTIONAL FORMAT. A design for correspondence, business forms, or business reports that results in paper (or hard) copies.

CORRESPONDENCE. Business letters created primarily as external communication and memorandums created as internal communication.

CROSS-REFERENCING. A notation in the file that indicates where the original document or complete file can be located; used whenever a record could possibly be filed in more than one place in the files.

DATA. Information items that describe a person, place, event, or object.

DATABASE. An electronic method of organizing facts or data that involves the creation of one or more computer data files.

DIRECT-ACCESS PROCEDURES. Procedures that permit an individual to go directly to the file cabinet and locate the file, without any intermediate steps.

DISPERSAL. The duplication of hard copies of documents and their storage in other locations.

DUPLEX-NUMERIC SYSTEM. Two or more sets of code numbers are assigned to files; sets of numbers are separated by a dash, comma, period, or space.

FIELD. A location reserved for a specific type of information.

FILE. A set of related records that are stored together or under the same filename.

FILE FOLDER. An individual container used to store the documents pertaining to one correspondent, case, or account.

FORMS MANAGEMENT. A system designed to provide an organization with forms that are both necessary and efficient and that can be produced at the lowest printing and processing costs.

GEOGRAPHIC FILING. A system in which records are arranged alphabetically according to geographic locations.

GUIDES. Dividers for groups of records which indicate the sections of the file.

IMPORTANT RECORDS. Documents that contribute to the continued smooth operation of a company and can be replaced or duplicated (at considerable expense of time and money) if lost or destroyed in a disaster.

INACTIVE RECORDS. Those records no longer referred to on a regular basis.

INDEX RECORD. A record containing only reference information that may be part of a relative index for files based upon either a numeric or alphanumeric classification system.

INDEXING. The decision making that is necessary in deciding what names or numbers to use in filing.

INDIRECT-ACCESS PROCEDURES. A filing system that requires an individual to consult a relative index in order to locate the name, subject, or number under which the file is stored.

INSPECTING. Examining a record to be sure that it has been released for filing by an appropriate authority within the firm.

JACKET. A plastic unitized record the same size as a microfiche that has single or multiple channels in which the film is inserted.

MICROFICHE. A 6" x 4" sheet of film on which microimages are placed in rows from left to right and from top to bottom; holds approximately 60 to 70 microimages.

MICROFILM. The oldest type of microform; stores page images side by side on a roll of 16mm, 35mm, 70mm, and 105mm film.

MICROFORM. Any record that contains reduced images on film.

MIDDLE-DIGIT FILING. A numeric system that uses the middle digits of a number as the primary indexing units.

MNEMONIC CODE. A code used for an item that takes on additional meaning about the item.

NONESSENTIAL RECORDS. Records that are not necessary to the restoration of business, have no predictable value, and probably should be destroyed once their usefulness is over.

NONRECORDS. Documents made for the organization's convenience or temporary need in some operation, but normally disposed of after use.

NUMERIC CLASSIFICATION SYSTEM. An indirect-access filing system that consists of numeric codes assigned to names of individuals, businesses, or subjects.

OUT GUIDE. A special guide that is substituted for a folder or a record that has been temporarily removed from the file.

PERIODIC TRANSFER. The physical movement of records from active status within a particular department or office to a centralized records center as of a specific date each year.

PERPETUAL TRANSFER. The physical movement of records from active to inactive status at any time that the event has been completed or the case closed and future referral to the records will be infrequent and limited.

POSTED RECORD. A card record that is used to record information to bring the record up to date; information may be updated, changed, deleted, or added to.

PRIMARY GUIDE. A guide which highlights a major division or subdivision of records stored in a file drawer or on a shelf.

PURGING. The process of automatically deleting the contents of a record that has been electronically stored on a magnetic medium.

RECORD. A document that contains information about a set of related data items.

RECORDS. Official documents of the company or organization valuable enough to be retained, using a format for storing information to be used and distributed later.

RECORDS CYCLE. A series of steps from the time the record is created until its final disposition.

RECORDS MANAGEMENT. The systematic control of recorded information required for the operation of the business from the time of creation through the use, storage, transfer, and disposal phases of the records cycle.

RECORDS TRANSFER. The physical movement of records from active status within a particular department or office to a centralized records center.

RELATIVE INDEX. A card file that identifies the numeric or alphanumeric codes that have been assigned to files.

RETENTION SCHEDULE. An agreement between the department creating the record, the user (if not the department of creation), and the records manager specifying how long each active record is to be held in active storage, inactive storage, and when the record may be destroyed, if ever.

SECONDARY GUIDE. A special guide that is used to highlight frequently referenced sections of the records.

STRAIGHT-NUMERIC FILES. The arrangement of files in consecutive order, from the lowest number to the highest number; also known as sequential or serial files.

SUBJECT FILING. A classification system that uses the alphabetic system as a base to arrange records by topics or categories.

TAB. A projection on a file folder that contains a label with a typed caption.

TERMINAL-DIGIT FILING. A numeric system that uses the last digits of a number as the primary indexing units.

ULTRAFICHE. A 6" x 4" sheet of film on which hundreds of microimages can be stored in a similar pattern to that used on a microfiche, from left to right in rows and from top to bottom on the sheet.

Records Management

USEFUL RECORDS. Records used in the operation of the organization that can be easily replaced.

VARIABLE INFORMATION. Information that is inserted on the original document and will change each time the document is prepared.

VITAL RECORDS. Records essential for the effective continuous operation of the firm.

A. Analyzing Records and Records Systems

In any business organization there are *records* and *nonrecords*. *Records* refer to official documents of the company or organization valuable enough to be retained, using a format for storing information to be used and distributed later. *Nonrecords* refer to documents made for the organization's convenience or temporary need in some operation, but normally disposed of after use. Records need to be analyzed in order to determine what the nature of the present records system is in the business. The two primary aspects of records analysis include examining the types of records in use and the records cycle.

1. *Classifying Records:* Individual records are classified according to either the record activity (use) or the importance of particular records used within the business or both.

  a. *Record activity or use:* Records are either active records or inactive records.

   (1) *Active records:* Those records that are consulted in the current administration of business functions are known as *active records*. They are often used to generate more business or to follow up on current transactions of the organization.

   (2) *Inactive records:* Those records no longer referred to on a regular basis, but still of some importance, are called *inactive records*. They do not relate to current business activities of the organization and are usually transferred to inactive status in a central records storage facility. The storage facility could have computer storage as well as physical storage space for files, boxes, and other media.

  b. *Importance of records:* Typically, records are classified as vital, important, useful, or nonessential records.

   (1) *Vital records:* Records classified as *vital* are those records *essential* for the effective, continuous operation of the firm. Vital records are irreplaceable records.

   EXAMPLES:
   Insurance policies
   Property deeds

Copyrights
Leases
Accounts payable
Accounts receivable
Legal documents

(2) *Important records:* Records classified as *important* records contribute to the continued smooth operation of an organization and can be replaced or duplicated (with considerable expenditure of time and money) if lost or destroyed in a disaster. Copies of important records are usually available, but there may be extra time needed to request and locate them, causing a delay in their use.

EXAMPLES:
Tax records
Financial records
Microforms
Magnetic tapes
Computer disks or tapes

(3) *Useful records:* Records used in the operation of the organization that can be easily replaced are called *useful records.* In case of a disaster, the loss of useful records would not prevent any routine operation of the business, only temporary delay or inconvenience.

EXAMPLES:
Letters
Business reports
Customer requests

(4) *Nonessential records:* Records that are not essential to the restoration of business, have no predictable value, and probably should be destroyed once their usefulness is over are known as *nonessential* records.

EXAMPLES:
Interoffice memorandums
Correspondence
Customer order letters
Telephone messages

2. *The Records Cycle:* A record's life cycle includes a series of steps from the moment the record is created until its final disposition. An initial decision is made when a record is created as to its life, that is, how long the record must be retained. Decisions are made at various times during the records cycle as to the continued use of the record, the procedure to be used in filing the record, and its retention or disposal. Figure 4-1 highlights the key steps in the records

Records Management

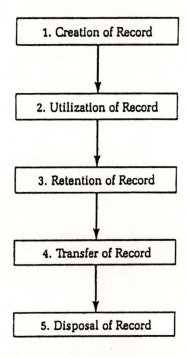

Figure 4-1
The Records Cycle

cycle: creation of the record, utilization of the record, retention of the record, transfer of the record, and disposal of the record. Manual filing *and* electronic filing form the basis for a total records cycle since both manual and electronic procedures must be applied to the information and documents involved.

a. *Creation of records:* Only people having the authority to create records within an organization should be permitted to do so. Central control of records stems from careful monitoring of the creation of all records. Basic considerations in the creation of new records should include:

(1) The format of the new record.
(2) Procedures established for creating the record.
(3) Justification (rationale) for the new record and its purpose.
(4) The cost of producing the record.
(5) The increased office productivity that is likely to result.
(6) The estimated life of the record.

b. *Utilization of records:* Efficient procedures must be developed in order that the record that has been created may be used, stored, and retrieved for the purpose(s) intended. A records inventory might be conducted to determine the actual use to which the record will be put as well as the cost of using the record.

c. *Retention of records:* An important concern in records management is the determination of the life of a particular record on the basis of administrative, legal, fiscal, or research value. Included in this phase of the records cycle are:

   (1) *Development of retention schedules:* A records retention schedule estimates the period of time each type of record is to be held in office storage for active (day-to-day) reference, the period of time each record should be kept in semi-active or inactive storage, and if and when it may be destroyed. A retention schedule approved for use within the organization helps to assure that the importance of records will be considered in deciding how long to keep records on file.

   (2) *Appraisal of records:* In the process of establishing retention schedules, records are also evaluated in terms of their administrative, legal, fiscal, or research value. Once their value has been determined, a set number of years for their retention can be established.

d. *Transfer of records:* During its life, a record may be transferred from active to semiactive to inactive storage, depending upon the record activity. A record may be physically removed from the office and transmitted to remote storage in a computer facility or an off-premises records facility.

e. *Disposal of records:* When the record is no longer needed, it may be purged or destroyed.

   (1) *Purging of records: Purging* is the process of automatically deleting the contents of a record that has been electronically stored on a magnetic medium. As purging takes place, each record is examined to determine if it still has value or can be eliminated.

   EXAMPLE: Grace stores correspondence prepared with word processing each week on diskettes. After a one-week period, she reviews the contents of each disk to see if any of the records can be purged (deleted) from the disk. She labels each disk carefully and keeps all correspondence relating to a particular project on the same disk.

   (2) *Destruction of records:* The method of destruction is very important since many records, even though ready to be destroyed, contain confidential information. Special equipment may be used in the destruction of documents, such as shredders and incinerators.

B. Designing and Controlling Records

Business records must be controlled throughout the records cycle in order to assure efficient handling. The design of the record enhances the ability of the records manager to control the use of that record within the organization. Once the form of the record is designed, appropriate steps must be taken to be sure that the record will be used as intended. Forms management programs are established for ordering, designing, procuring, storing, distributing, reviewing, and disposing of each type of form used within the organization. In an effective forms control program, forms should be used only when the need is clear and justified.

1. *Forms Development:* An office form consists of a format that contains constant information (information that remains the same on each document) and variable information (information that changes on each document). A form may be a paper copy (in typewritten or printed copy) or displayed on a computer screen in the form of a template (electronic copy) stored on a disk. Conventional formats as well as unconventional formats are used for the design of business records.

    a. *Conventional formats:* Correspondence, business forms, and business reports typically appear in conventional formats which result in paper copies (hard copies). Appropriate formatting of these types of records makes control of these records within the business an easier task.

        (1) *Correspondence:* Written messages in the form of business letters created primarily as external communication and memorandums created as internal communication are referred to as *correspondence*.

            (a) *Letter design:* Many companies use logos, standardized formats, and letter styles to create a positive image as well as to reduce letterwriting costs. The use of word processing in merging form paragraphs and form letters with mailing lists of addresses reduces the average cost of correspondence, but still permits personalization of the correspondence.

            EXAMPLE: Since 1930, when the cost of a business letter was estimated at 30 cents, the Dartnell Corporation's Institute of Business Research has continued its annual research into the cost of producing a business letter.

            In 1983, the average cost of producing a business letter was estimated at well over $7 per letter. This figure included all labor costs (executive and secretary), overhead costs, and indirect costs.

            Dartnell's 1991 estimate ranges from $12 to $18, depending on the process used for producing the letter. For a one-page, 185-word letter, the letter that is machine dictated and transcribed on a personal *computer costs $11.77. The same letter transcribed on an electric typewriter costs $17.71.*

(b) *Memorandum design:* Standardized formats are also used for memorandum designs that speed up production and cut costs. Decisions are made within departments on whether memos, the telephone, or electronic mail will be used for internal communication. Electronic mail is becoming an even more popular means of transmitting information among departments as well as keeping a record of memos sent and received. The sender also knows if the message has been received and viewed. The receiver can respond immediately to the memo if desired.

(c) *Maintaining document flow:* Control of the movement of correspondence through the organization is very important. In some large firms, a central distribution area (a mail center) controls all incoming and outgoing correspondence.

(d) *Development of correspondence manuals:* With so much more information being communicated through various means of correspondence, many firms develop manuals to outline recommended procedures for the preparation and handling of correspondence. This enables a more concerted effort to standardize procedures throughout the organization.

(2) *Business forms:* Forms used in business procedures need to be analyzed on a regular basis to determine if they are still in use, need to be revised, or can be eliminated. A *business form* is a record that contains *constant* information appearing on it (printed or electronically imaged on a computer screen) and space provided for *variable* information to be inserted.

EXAMPLE: Some offices have sets of forms stored on word processing or graphics media so that templates can be brought up on the computer screen to be filled in with variable information and completed forms stored under an appropriate file name.

Before a form is redesigned, any problems resulting from either its design or its use should be analyzed.

(a) *Classifications of forms:* Business forms may be classified in two ways: according to specific business functions for which they are intended (external or internal) and the physical way in which they are constructed (single copy, multiple copy, or view copy).

EXAMPLES: Business forms designed for specific business functions include personnel forms (application for employment, interview evaluation form); accounting forms (purchase requisition, purchase order, invoice, check); and sales forms (customer order form, sales order).

The physical construction of a business form includes such things as its physical size (8½" x 5"), paper stock used, and type styles used for constant information.

(b) *Types of business forms:* Forms may be referred to by the type of form, either a flat form (a single sheet of paper which may be interleaved with other forms to produce carbon copies) or a specialty form (requires special equipment to manufacture or use).

(c) *Forms design:* The process of designing a business form depends on what information needs to appear on the form and the sequence of that information. Sound forms design should be based on the actual use of the form and the standardization of the form in relation to others used in the business. Forms may be designed for manual or automated completion.

EXAMPLES OF MANUAL FORMS:
Snap-out or unit-set forms: *A form used when several copies of the same form are needed; used with carbon paper.*
Spot-carbon forms: *Only certain areas on each copy of the form are carbonized so that only that information that needs to be transferred to other copies will be.*
Carbonless (NCR) forms: *Specially treated (coated) paper that permits the pressure of a pen or pencil on the original to create the same images on the copies.*

EXAMPLES OF AUTOMATED FORMS:
Continuous forms: *Forms used with automated printers to produce multiple numbers of forms. After printing, these forms will have to be separated on the perforations between forms.*
Unit-record forms: *Forms that are used as input and output records in automated systems; may be continuous form or in tab-card sets.*
Magnetic ink character recognition (MICR) form:

Coded information on the form can be read by automated equipment and transmitted to a computer for processing. (MICR numbers on checks)

Optical character recognition (OCR) forms: *Data typed or written on the form can be interpreted by OCR readers and scanners for automatic processing.*

View forms or templates: *Forms or templates that have been stored on the computer (hard disk or floppy disk) and are retrieved as needed for fill in and processing; may be created with word processing, spreadsheet, or graphics software.*

(3) *Business reports:* A business report is the final outcome of a specific information-gathering activity within the organization, summarizing the problem, background, procedures, and results of a business project or research. A business report conveys information to top-level management for decision-making purposes or to external sources who need the information to further their own work. The report tends to be the most expensive type of record created within most organizations because of its originality and time and other costs involved in doing the research.

   (a) *Content of reports:* A formal report or an informal report may be created. A formal report usually follows a standard format or structure for content, and the style of writing is more formal in nature. Such a report would most likely include the following sections:

   Abstract
   Introduction to the Problem
   Rationale for the Study
   Body of the Report
       Methods and Procedures
       Statistical Analysis of Data
   Findings
   Conclusions
   Recommendations and/or Implications
   Summary

   Typically, an informal report is needed for a single purpose within the organization: to provide additional information on a specific topic. The informal report is rather short, perhaps only two to three pages. The informal report, prepared in a memorandum format, may be used primarily for internal communication.

Records Management

(b) *Reports design*: As with correspondence, standardized formats are very important in the preparation of business reports. Most reports will be generated through the use of computer systems and word processing software. In these instances particularly, the more standardized the format, the easier it is to control the actual preparation of the report. Only that information absolutely needed should be included in the report.

EXAMPLE: Word processing software permits format decisions to be made prior to printing drafts of the report. These format decisions include line length, page format, right justification of text, placement of headers and footers, location of page numbers, and margins.

(c) *Preparation costs:* Costs incurred as a result of preparing a business report include the research involved in gathering the information and data for the report, the salary of the writer, the time involved in doing the research and writing the report, the length and involvement of the report, fixed costs, and secretarial/word processing costs.

(4) *Card systems:* In records management, cards (3"x 5", 4"x 6", 5"x 8") are used as a means of filing information or referencing information filed elsewhere. Card systems are used for two primary purposes: to create index records and to create posted records.

(a) *Index records:* Cards may be used as a *relative index* for files using a numeric or alphanumeric classification system. As an index record, the card contains only *reference* information. An individual would examine the index record to find out where the original file or document is located.

EXAMPLES OF INDEX RECORDS:
Name and addresses of clients or customers
Employee lists
Membership lists
Stockroom item locations
Price lists
Telephone numbers frequently used
Subscription lists

EXAMPLE: The Burton & Smith Law Firm uses a numeric system for filing. Each client or case is as-

signed a separate file number. A relative index is kept on cards in a special card drawer, in alphabetical order, so that if a file needs to be located, the first step is to look in the index under the client's name or the case name to see what number has been assigned to the file. Once the number is located, the file can be located easily in the file.

Such a system may also be computerized, creating a database to organize or manage facts or data electronically. A database may be accessed by keying in the name of the file desired or conducting a search for that name and/or file number. [See Section B-1-b(3) of this chapter.]

(b) *Posted records:* Card records may be used to record or *post* information (update, change, delete, add to) to bring the record up to date. New information posted on the card form may be entered by hand or computer. Since a source document (an original record) is used to obtain the information to be posted, the posted record is sometimes called a *secondary record.*

EXAMPLES OF POSTED RECORDS:
Stock control cards
Payroll cards
Repair and maintenance cards for office equipment
Auto service records
Hospital records
Student permanent record cards
Dental and medical cards

EXAMPLE: The Jones Veterinary Hospital kept all of its animal records on individual owner cards. Whenever a pet received some type of treatment, medication, or examination, an entry was posted on the card form, indicating what treatment or medication was prescribed, the charge, the date, and any other relevant information. In this way a perpetual record was kept of the medical history of the pet.

Recently Dr. Jones decided that the records should be converted to the computer system. Now, when a pet owner enters the office, the name is keyed in and a copy of the record for that pet is printed. As Dr. Jones examines the pet, she can refer to the previous medical history of the pet in making appropriate decisions on medication or treatment. The billing is immediate, too, with the pet owner presented with a statement for payment before leaving the office.

(c) *Design of card forms:* Many card forms are preprinted with descriptors (key words), horizontal and vertical rulings, and directions for completion. Preprinted card forms are designed so that the user will be able to locate information easily. The descriptors, key words, or phrases preprinted on the form are called *constant information,* since that information remains the same on all forms of a particular kind. Information that is inserted on the card form by a user is called *variable information* and will change for each user. Card forms must be created on card stock that will be durable, compact, and easy to handle.

(5) *Other conventional records:* In addition to correspondence, business forms, reports, and cards, other types of conventional records include engineering documents, maps, charts, drawings, technical catalogs, and manuals (policies, procedures, operations). The design and use of any of these types of records need to be controlled as well.

b. *Nonconventional formats:* In recent years, with more automation being utilized in offices, a greater variety of unconventional formats have been used for business records. Microforms, audiovisual media, videotapes, and information processing media are becoming more versatile in substituting for paper documents.

(1) *Microforms:* Any record that contains reduced images on film is known as a *microform.* The saving of space in the storage of microform records seems to be the greatest advantage for their use. Microforms also appear to be advantageous in preserving records over time.

(a) *Microfilm:* The oldest type of microform is *microfilm,* which stores page images side by side on a roll of 16mm, 35mm, 70mm, and 105mm film. Each roll has a standard size of 100 feet and can hold up to 2,500 letter-size images or up to 30,000 smaller-size images.

(b) *Microfiche:* A standard size for microfiche is a 6" x 4" sheet of film on which the page images are placed in rows from left to right and from top to bottom. A fiche can hold approximately 60 to 70 microimages and is coded to identify its contents.

(c) *Ultrafiche:* An ultrafiche is like a microfiche except that the page images are reduced even more. On a standard 6" x 4" sheet of film hundreds of images can be stored in a similar pattern to that used on a microfiche, from left to right in rows and from top to bottom on the sheet. Ultrafiche stores the largest number of microimages of any microform.

(d) *Aperture card:* An aperture card is a punched card that contains a slot into which a microimage (or microimages) can be inserted. A limited amount of text can be punched into the card or interpreted on the card. Aperture cards can be duplicated if more than one set is needed.

(e) *Jacket:* A jacket is a plastic unitized record the same size as a microfiche. There are single or multiple channels on the jacket in which film is inserted. As many as 60 images can be inserted into a 6" x 4" jacket. Its primary advantage is ease in updating microforms. Each jacket is coded for retrieval and storage purposes.

(2) *Audiovisual media:* Another category of nonconventional records is audiovisual media. Photographs, slides, cassette tape recordings, video disks, videotapes, and transparencies are included in this group. Special attention must be given to the indexing, coding, and storing of these types of records since many times special filing cabinets are required for adequate protection. Special equipment is needed also in order to view or listen to the information contained in these kinds of records.

EXAMPLES: Cassette tapes require the use of cassette players for listening; slides, a slide projector and a screen; videotapes, a video cassette recorder (VCR) with a television screen; transparencies, an overhead projector; video disks, a video disk player with a television screen.

(3) *Electronic media:* Word processing and data processing media are receiving more attention from records managers. Information recorded on magnetic disks and tapes (soft copies) is extremely sensitive and must be handled with extreme care. Appropriate techniques must be used to protect these types of records from excessive handling and damage. Backup copies are routinely prepared for important documents or for an individual day's or week's work so that an extra set of information is always available for the most recent business transactions. Electronic media are especially helpful in planning and creating databases of information for application throughout the organization. A *database* is an electronic method of organizing facts and data in one or more computer data files.

(a) *Preliminary planning:* The following types of questions will be helpful in deciding what types of information will be essential or useful as the creation of a database is being planned.

- What types of information will be included in the database?
- Who will be the database users?
- How often will specific types of data and information be accessed?
- Will the information be used to process transactions such as sales?
- Will the information be used as part of a decision support system?

(b) *Database creation:* The creation of an electronic database expedites the efficient use of information and data. Typically a database consists of one or more computer data files. Here are some brief definitions of terms used in the development of databases:

- *Data:* Information items that describe a person, place, event, or object.

    EXAMPLES:
    Employee Name
    Social Security Number
    Home Address
    Home Telephone Number

- *Field:* Each field of data has a specific type of information (character, data, numeric, logical, memo).

    EXAMPLES:
    Last Name   First Name   Initial
    Area Code   Telephone Number

- *Record:* A document that contains information about a set of related data items.

    EXAMPLES:
    An application form with employee data written on it
    An index card with employee data recorded on it

- *File:* A set of related records that are stored together or under the same filename.

(c) *Database procedures:* A set of logical, step-by-step procedures is necessary in creating and maintaining a data base.

- Plan a database structure.
- Create a database file.
- Add records to the database file.
- Delete records from the database file.
- Combine database files.
- Combine fields within the database file.
- Produce a complete printout of all information stored in the database file.
- Produce a report consisting of selected information from the database arranged in a planned format.
- Backup a database file (create an extra stored copy).

The use of database files and/or a computer database management system (DBMS) should be related to the overall efficiency of systems used within the entire organization. Individuals throughout the organization should be aware of the availability of information through the use of computer databases.

2. *Forms Management:* Forms management is a system designed to provide an organization with forms that are both necessary and efficient and that can be produced at the lowest printing and processing costs. Forms management is considered a primary area for improvement in the administrative system, especially in overall reduction of administrative costs.

    a. *Key factors in forms management:* In some organizations forms management is controlled through one individual, the records manager or administrator, or one work unit. These units control the organization's forms—analysis, design, production, and use. Other organizations contract with firms offering commercial services in forms management. Many companies, however, do not view forms as a vital element in the records management process and have not initiated any kind of forms management program. Some key factors in developing a forms management program include:

    (1) *Top management support:* Any office support service must have the support of top management in actively promoting the program.

    (2) *Forms control:* A forms control program, to be efficient, must go into effect as soon as possible. Time must be devoted to the proper administration and design of forms.

(3) *Training for employees:* Office personnel must be trained so that they can assist with updating procedures for the organization's forms management program. A training plan must be developed and implemented as a part of the program.

b. *Forms management program:* Forms management is one of the most important elements of a total records management program. Here are some of the primary components of a successful program:

(1) *Forms management policy:* Policies for managing forms must be developed and supported by top management. Procedures for creating, reviewing, and producing forms must be identified as well as personnel who will be responsible for forms management.

(2) *Forms analysis:* Analysis to determine the importance of forms and how they should be designed is extremely important. Those forms that receive high usage need to be analyzed first, hopefully resulting in improvements that will decrease the costs of producing and using the form.

(3) *Forms specifications:* Decisions must be made on how the forms are to be produced: the type of paper stock to use, the treatment of these materials, automation required to produce the form, and the method used to produce copies or templates of the form.

(4) *Forms design:* The layout of the form is another very important forms management function. Forms may be designed by professional forms designers or people within the organization who have expertise in forms design. The use of forms design software enables the creation of forms on a computer. Laser printing permits the creation of a form with a variety of type styles and design features.

(5) *Forms production:* Forms may be produced and printed either in an in-house reprographics center or by an outside commercial printer. The decision can also be made about using forms that are stored on disk and accessed for fill-in and completion purposes.

(6) *Forms recording and filing:* As forms are created for use within the organization, sets of samples of these forms should be maintained, recorded, and filed by the forms manager. For each form, printing specifications, information as to its use within the firm, and the department for whom it is produced should be recorded. When the form is created, a decision also needs to be made relative to its retention, that is, how long this type of record will be kept on file.

(7) *Forms storage and distribution:* Storage and distribution of forms are also very important. Because of high storage costs, estimating the quantities of forms to have on hand is very important. Users must be provided with forms as needed, where needed, and in sufficient quantity. Storage may be in hard copy form (paper) or soft copy form (disk).

(8) *Forms control:* Forms control procedures assure that the objectives of the forms management program are being achieved effectively. No system is effective without some types of controls in effect.

C. Filing Procedures for Manual and Automated Systems

If records that have been stored in the records system cannot be found, then the records system in use, whether it is a manual or an automated system, is probably inadequate to handle the organization's records. Records must be stored so that they can be located easily and quickly as needed. If records have been stored according to a basic set of procedures and a classification system, any of these records should be retrievable at any time.

1. *Designing Basic Procedures for Records Storage:* Before records can be retrieved, they must be stored (filed) according to a prescribed set of procedures and rules. An organization will adopt a set of procedures and filing rules to be used in storing manual records as well as procedures to be followed for electronic filing. Each person coming into direct contact with records is expected to use the same filing procedures and rules as those used elsewhere in the organization.

    EXAMPLE: A set of filing rules necessary for proper records management procedures to be used is similar in nature to a set of golfing rules prescribed for playing a good game of golf. If you know how to index and code a name alphabetically, you can proceed from one name to another. In the game of golf, you move from hole to hole in a systematic manner as you follow the rules of the game.

    a. *Accessing files:* Records may be accessed through either direct-access procedures or indirect-access procedures.

        (1) *Direct-access procedures:* A direct-access file permits an individual to go directly to the storage system (file cabinet or computer storage) and locate the file.

            EXAMPLE: An alphabetic filing system is a direct-access system. Without referring to any other information, you can go directly to the file cabinet and try to locate the file. If a file folder is labeled Smith, John, all you need to do is to look under S in order to find the file.

(2) *Indirect-access procedures:* An indirect-access filing system requires an individual to consult a *relative index* in order to locate the name, subject, or number under which the file is stored.

(a) *Manual procedures:* A relative index serves as a backup for numeric and alphanumeric systems. The index consists of cards filed alphabetically, providing a complete list of names or subjects already included in the filing system.

EXAMPLE: In a numeric filing system, you would consult the relative index first to see what number has been assigned to the file you are looking for. If you are looking for a file under Smith, John, you would look in the relative index under S to locate the card for Smith, John (filed alphabetically). This card will indicate something like this:

Smith, John	1028

This means that the file for John Smith is File No. 1028. You can proceed to the file drawer containing File No. 1028, and the file should be there in sequential order.

(b) *Automated procedures:* Electronic systems permit quick storage of records as well as retrieval. As a record is being created or keyed into the system, the operator is prompted to provide the name to be given to the document. Later access to the document requires the operator to view an index or a directory listing first in order to select the correct record, or if the filename is known, that name can be keyed into the computer and the document should appear on the screen in a matter of seconds. Random access allows direct access to the document without having to view all documents stored on the disk or tape.

b. *Inspecting, indexing, and coding records:* Before a record can be filed, it must be *inspected* to be sure that it has been released for filing by an appropriate authority within the firm. Usually, an inspection mark or initials are written on the document to indicate that inspection has taken place. *Indexing* is the term used to indicate the decision making that is necessary in deciding what names or numbers to use in filing. *Coding* refers to making notations on the record itself as to exactly how the record will be stored (under what names or numbers).

EXAMPLE: You have the responsibility of examining each record to be sure that it has been released for filing and is ready to be indexed and coded. Once you have decided the name under which a record will be filed, you will need to code the name in this way:

  2   3   1   4
James G. <u>Blair</u>, Jr.

The first filing unit should be underlined and the number (1) written above it. Then the numbers 2, 3, and 4 (in this case) can be written above the subsequent filing units.

c. *Cross-referencing records:* Whenever a record could be filed in more than one place in the files, a cross-reference is needed. The cross-reference indicates where the original document or complete file can be located. In a card file, the cross-reference is another card coded as a cross-reference card. The cross-reference in a document file is indicated on a cross-reference sheet or folder.

EXAMPLE: Sarah Lou Masterson is married to John L. Masterson. In an alphabetic file, the caption for her file would read:

MASTERSON, SARAH LOU (Mrs.)

If Sarah prefers to keep her maiden name as part of her married name, she may want her name to appear as:

HUGHES-MASTERSON, SARAH LOU (Mrs.)

In this case, there could be a cross-reference under Masterson, Sarah Lou (Mrs.) and under her husband's name. Because some people might recognize her only by her husband's name, a cross-reference should appear under:

MASTERSON, JOHN L. (Mrs.)
See MASTERSON, SARAH LOU (Mrs.)
 or HUGHES-MASTERSON, SARAH LOU (Mrs.)
(depending on where the original file is.)

In this way, if someone only knew her husband's name, her file could still be located.

d. *Charging out records:* There must be a tracking system for any records that have been borrowed from the files. While these records are temporarily removed from the files, a record must be kept identifying the following types of information:

- The name of the person or department borrowing the record or file.
- The date the record or file was borrowed.
- The probable return date of the record or file.

A set of charge-out forms should be maintained for use with the files. Whenever an individual wishes to charge out a particular record, a *charge-out request form* should be completed and presented to the records clerk in charge. Whenever an individual record is removed from a file, an *out guide* should take its place in the file. If an entire file folder is borrowed, an *out folder* should be substituted in the file for that particular folder.

Note: Files that are electronically filed can only be accessed by individuals who have authorization to do so. Therefore, security procedures that are established include the use of log-in numbers and passwords in order to gain access to specific files.

2. *Designing Filing Classification Systems:* There are three primary classification systems for filing: alphabetic, numeric, and alphanumeric. Alphabetic systems use the 26 letters of the alphabet as the primary divisions within the system, whereas numeric systems vary combinations of numeric codes. Alphanumeric systems are combination alphabetic and numeric systems. Sets of rules are contained in all standard office procedures or records management references. No attempt is made here to explain all of the specific rules that might be used with these classification systems. Some examples are used for clarity and basic understanding.

   a. *Alphabetic classification systems:* The alphabetic system is the oldest form of classification system and is the basis for all other types of classification systems. Even a numeric system must have a relative index that is in alphabetic order. The Association of Records Managers and Administrators (ARMA) is a professional organization that has developed a set of standardized alphabetic rules.

   (1) *Name filing:* Names of individuals, companies, organizations, and government agencies are filed according to a set of alphabetic rules.

   (a) *Personal names:* Personal names are filed with surname considered as the first indexing unit, followed by first name and middle name.

   EXAMPLE:
   JoAnn Smith Robinson
   indexed as
   <u>Robinson</u>, JoAnn Smith
   (3 indexing units)

(b) *Organization names:* Company names are filed according to the most prominent words in the name.

EXAMPLE:
The Royale Corporation
indexed as
Royale Corporation (The)
(2 indexing units)

Words such as *the* and *of* might not be used as indexing units, depending on the specific rules being followed.

(c) *Governmental agencies:* Governmental organizations are filed first under *United States Government*, then under name of agency.

EXAMPLE:
Internal Revenue Service
U.S. Treasury Department
indexed as
United States Government
Treasury Department
Internal Revenue Service
(8 indexing units)

(2) *Subject filing:* Another classification system that uses the alphabetic system as a base is subject filing. Instead of arranging records by names of individuals or business names, records are arranged in alphabetical order according to topics or categories.

EXAMPLES:
Administration
  Budgets
  Business Travel
  Costs—Administrative
  Costs—Operating
  Personnel
  Research

(3) *Geographic filing:* In a geographic system, records are arranged alphabetically according to geographic locations. Filing by geographic locations may be particularly useful in a company or organization with branch offices or divisions in different parts of the country or the world.

EXAMPLES:
United States
  Central Region

North-Central Region
Northeastern Region
Northwestern Region
Southeastern Region
Southwestern Region
Western Region

b. *Numeric classification systems:* A numeric filing system is an indirect-access system that consists of numeric codes assigned to names of individuals, businesses, or subjects. An *accession book* (list of names to which numbers have been assigned) and a *relative index* (cards or listing of all names to which numbers have been assigned in alphabetic order) are necessary elements of the system. Computerized files tend to be numeric systems. When numeric files are used within a business, correspondents are usually encouraged to put the numeric code (file number) on each piece of correspondence relating to a business transaction. There are many different types of numeric systems. Those presented here arc examples of some of the more commonly used numeric systems.

(1) *Straight-numeric:* Files are arranged in consecutive order, from the lowest number to the highest number. *Sequential* or *serial files* are other terms used for this type of system.

(2) *Duplex-numeric:* File numbers have two or more sets of code numbers separated by a dash, comma, period, or space. A relative index is needed so that there is a complete list of the primary numbers assigned to the major categories within the system.

EXAMPLES:
Administration	*20*
Budgets	*20*
Business Travel	*20-11*
Costs	*20-12*
Administrative	*20-12-01*
Operating	*20-12-02*
Personnel	*20-13*
Research	*20-14*

(3) *Block codes:* Blocks of numbers are reserved for records that have a common feature or characteristic.

EXAMPLES:
Administration	*201-299*
Production	*301-399*
Sales and Marketing	*401-499*

(4) *Middle-digit:* Records are filed numerically by the *middle digits,* not necessarily according to the number as it ap-

pears on the record. The file numbers in the accession book are still listed in straight-numeric sequence.

EXAMPLE:
File No. 482311
Indexing Units:
   48   *23*   *11*
Secondary Primary Tertiary
   (2)   *(1)*   *(3)*

The record will be filed under 23 first, then 48 within the 23 section, and finally in folder 11.

Drawer:	*23*
Guide:	*48*
Folder:	*11*

The middle-digit system is a very effective one to use if file numbers have six digits or less. When file numbers are more than six digits, other numeric systems would probably be more effective.

(5) *Terminal-digit:* Records are filed by the *last digits* (the terminal digits) in the terminal-digit system, which tends to be a more efficient system than middle-digit. The code number is divided into sets of two or three digits as a general rule. File numbers are listed consecutively in the accession book so that a record is kept of the file numbers already assigned in the system. A primary advantage of the terminal-digit system is security in the handling of confidential files or information.

EXAMPLE:
File No. 482311
Indexing Units:
   48   *23*   *11*
Tertiary Secondary Primary
   (3)   *(2)*   *(1)*

The record will be filed under 11 first, then 23 within the 11 section, and finally in folder 48.

Drawer:	*11*
Guide:	*23*
Folder:	*48*

If the same number is grouped in sets of three digits, the coding would be like this:

   482   *311*
Secondary Primary

EXAMPLE: The catalog stores for Sears, Roebuck and Company use a very simple terminal-digit system to file the orders waiting for customer pickup. When a customer orders merchandise at the catalog store, the customer's telephone number is written on the order form along with other information such as name, address, account number, and items ordered. When the customer returns to pick up the merchandise, the clerk asks for the last two digits of the telephone number. These two digits (the terminal digits) are used to locate the order.

(6) *Dewey decimal system:* The Dewey decimal system is perhaps the most widely known numeric filing system. Developed in 1873 primarily for cataloging library books, the system includes ten general categories:

000	General Works
100	Philosophy
200	Religion
300	Social Science
400	Philology
500	Pure Science
600	Applied Science or Useful Arts
700	Arts Recreation
800	Literature
900	History

Each of these ten categories is then divided into ten parts, with a further subdivision into ten more subdivisions. A typical decimal used in cataloging a book would look like this:

650.231 (a book within the Applied Science or Useful Arts category)

(7) *Coded numeric system:* Sometimes records are given numeric codes where the codes are really numbers telling something about the person or item. When the codes used take on additional meaning about the item, we say that a *mnemonic code* is being used.

(a) *ZIP codes:* The ZIP codes used by the U.S. Postal Service for mail delivery are an example of a coded numeric system. The ZIP + 4 codes (9-digit numbers), the expanded code established in 1981, are an extension of the original system.

EXAMPLE:
60115-2623
6 = area within United States

01 = sectional center
15 = local delivery area
26 = geographic portion of a zone; or a portion of a rural route, part of a box section, or official designation.
23 = a specific block face, apartment house, bank of boxes, firm, building, or other specific delivery locations.

(b) *Area codes:* Telephone networks across the country are divided into geographic zones called area codes. The area code serves as a prefix so that a telephone number can be dialed directly (without intervention by an operator) anywhere in the United States.

EXAMPLE:
(312) 445-2189
312 = the area code for the City of Chicago
445-2189 = telephone number

(c) *Catalog numbers:* Product numbers included in catalogs and on bar codes for merchandise represent information about the items.

EXAMPLE:
110 22 1260-8   110 Item Category
22 Catalog
1260 Item Style
8 Color

(8) *Chronological system:* Many times records need to be filed according to *date*. A filing system that utilizes calendar dates as the significant divisions of the system is known as a chronological system.

EXAMPLE: A tickler file is arranged according to dates, with the most recent date first. Reminder notes are recorded/entered on cards or files for particular dates.

EXAMPLE: A business calendar is arranged by chronological dates (and times). If appointments are entered onto a small handheld computerized calendar system, the calendar can be accessed by entering an appropriate code. The appointments will appear in chronological order according to times on a small screen.

c. *Alphanumeric classification systems:* Whenever a combination of alphabetic characters and numbers are used in a code, the code is *alphanumeric*. In a system like this, it is possible to have the alphanumeric designations on primary guides as well as individual folders. A relative index lists the codes assigned to each letter of the alphabet and any subdivisions.

EXAMPLE: The Soundex code is an alphanumeric code that includes an alphabetic letter (the first letter of the name being coded) and numbers representing the consonant sounds in the name. Vowel sounds and silent letters are omitted. This code is commonly found on drivers' licenses.

S636 = S - r - d - r Schrader
The letters c-h-a-e are omitted in the rules for the code.

3. *Storing Records:* In addition to procedures for filing records for future use, records storage equipment and supplies must be used to guarantee safety of records during their useful life. The costs of maintaining adequate floor space for paper records is encouraging businesses to investigate other methods of records storage such as micrographics and computer storage. The actual cost of records storage equipment and supplies is approximately 20 percent of the overall cost of maintaining a records storage and retrieval system.

   a. *Selecting records storage equipment:* First and foremost, care should be exercised in selecting records storage equipment that will be appropriate for the kinds of records to be stored and for the time period the records will be stored. Here are some of the main concerns to be considered in selecting equipment:

      (1) *Protection of records:* The value of records to the ongoing operation of the business is important to consider in deciding exactly how records should be protected. There needs to be adequate protection against fire, theft, or other disasters.
      (2) *Frequency of record use:* The type of equipment purchased for use with records storage will depend on the frequency with which records will be used and accessed by users.
      (3) *Space requirements:* The volume of records currently housed in records storage as well as the anticipated future volume of records will influence the storage space required.
      (4) *Cost of records storage:* The costs per square foot of office space, compared with the costs incurred in maintaining records storage facilities, are important data to consider in making decisions as to where records will be stored—within the office or at a remote location. Sometimes remote storage can be found at a lower cost in low-rent city districts.
      (5) *Efficient use of the system:* Records storage equipment should alleviate the amount of time spent filing or searching for documents. Easy access to records and accuracy in finding them should be strong considerations in deciding what equipment is needed.

b. *Storing correspondence:* Correspondence may be stored on paper, magnetic media, or computer disks. Correspondence may be filed alphabetically, numerically, or alphanumerically, depending upon the filing system preferred.

(1) *Filing equipment for paper storage:* Conventional storage systems are used in many offices where paper is the primary medium for storage. File cabinets, usually three-drawer or four-drawer models, are generally the most common filing equipment used.

(a) *Vertical file cabinet:* Paper documents are stored in vertical files on end in a vertical fashion. These file cabinets may hold letter-size documents or legal-size documents. Each filing unit may contain anywhere from two to six drawers, and each drawer may be 24, 26, or 28 inches in length. A standard 26-inch drawer can hold up to 5,000 sheets of paper plus guides and folders. Often suspension folders are used within these files so that the file folders and their contents can be readily viewed. Generally, file cabinets such as these are easy to use, and it is not difficult to set up a filing system using this type of equipment.

(b) *Lateral file cabinet:* Lateral files are available in two-drawer (usually placed by the side of a desk) up to five-drawer capacity. Folders can be stored in two ways: facing the front of the file or facing the side of the cabinet. Each drawer pulls out from the wall to a maximum of 16 inches. Less aisle space is needed to accommodate the lateral file. One of its advantages is that the lateral file is flush with the wall and most materials will be filed sideways rather than frontwise as is true of vertical files. Lateral files can house legal-size documents as well as letter-size documents.

(c) *Open-shelf unit:* Open-shelf units are a form of lateral file characterized by the "open" view of all the files in the system. The equipment may be completely open shelf, without door enclosures, or there may be doors that pull down over each shelf for overnight security. Up to 50 percent savings of floor space usage can easily result from using this system, and labor costs may be reduced, too, because of the increased efficiency of the records personnel in working with this type of equipment. Numeric filing with color coding is the most common classification system used with open-shelf units.

(d) *Mobile-aisle unit:* The mobile-aisle unit is a form of open-shelf filing. Sets of file shelves slide, either manually or power-driven, on tracks installed in the floor. The sets of shelves can be moved together when not in use or can be moved apart to create an aisle space when an individual needs to locate a file. Only the last and first sets of file shelves are stationary.

(e) *Carousel or rotary file:* The greatest advantage of the carousel file is that the operator can bring the file to the point of use by turning or rotating the file horizontally. The entire file rotates like a lazy Susan around a central hub. Large rotary files may be power driven, which permits the operator to control the movement of the file with a push button.

(f) *Automated conveyor system:* With an automated conveyor system, the operator must dial a code number in order to let the system know which file is desired. The conveyor revolves around its track and automatically stops at the desired code. A system such as this may use carriers (Lektriever) or actually bring the file folders to the point of use (White's "No-Walk" Mechanized File System).

(g) *Identification aids and supplies:* Proper techniques must be used to index, code, and store documents so that they can be retrieved easily. Otherwise, the storage system, whether manual or automated, will be very ineffective. Correspondence filed in conventional file cabinets requires an identification system consisting of guides and folders prearranged in a sequential manner, depending on the classification system used. Here is a quick review of some of the identification aids that are needed for storage systems for paper documents:

- *Guides:* These key components of the system form an outline of the classification system used. Guides indicate the sections of the file and serve as dividers for groups of records.
- *Primary guides:* These guides highlight the major divisions and subdivisions of records stored in a file drawer or on a shelf.
- *Secondary guides:* These special guides are used to highlight frequently referenced sections of the records, such as "Applications for Employment."
- *Out guide:* This special guide substitutes for a folder or a record that has been temporarily removed from the file.
- *File folder:* An individual folder is used to store the documents pertaining to one correspondent,

case, or account. Each file folder has a projection *(tab)* on which is placed a *label* with a typed *caption.*

- *Color coding:* Colored strips are placed on the side of file folders to represent numeric or alphanumeric codes. This identification system is of particular value in an open-shelf filing system.

See Figure 4-2 for an example of the arrangement of guides and folders in a correspondence file.

(2) *Filing equipment for card storage:* The size of the cards used for storage will help to determine the type of filing equipment that can be used. The most common types of

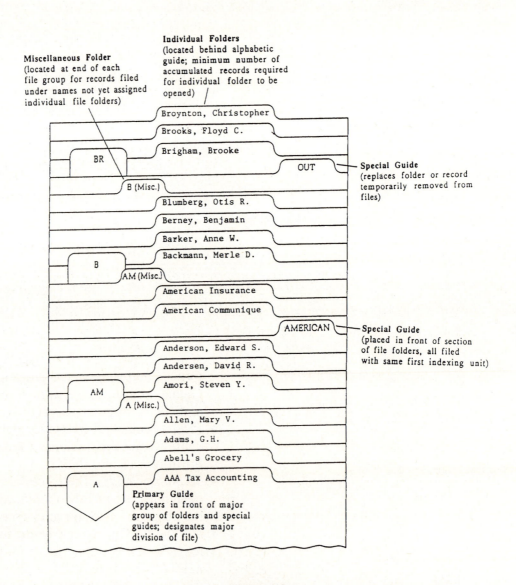

Figure 4-2
The Arrangement of Guides and Folders in a Correspondence System

equipment are vertical, visible, wheel, and rotary card file equipment.

(a) *Vertical card files:* Vertical card files, like vertical correspondence files, allow the cards to stand upright and to be compressed tightly within the file drawer. These files may be individual card file drawers or special card file drawers that are part of a vertical correspondence file. The size of the drawer will determine the size of the cards to be used with that drawer, for example, 3"x 5" cards use a file drawer for cards of that size.

(b) *Visible card files:* With visible files, cards are positioned so that one line of information appears in the *visible margin* that overlaps at the front edge of the files. Visible files are stored in flat drawers, trays, or suspended on panels so that the operator has ready access to the card records at any time. Color coding may be used so that the cards may reflect different groups of records. The biggest advantage is that the visible card files may be updated at any time simply by removing the "old" card or adding "new" cards.

(c) *Wheel card files:* Information that needs to be accessible for quick reference may be kept on cards inserted into a wheel card file. The wheel card file looks like a miniature Ferris wheel with the cards inserted in a particular order, alphabetic or numeric. Usually these are small cards up to 5"x 8" and take up very little space on a work surface.

EXAMPLE: A Rolodex wheel file is a very handy reference to use for names and addresses or telephone numbers used frequently. A card that needs to be removed can just be pulled out of the file, and new cards can be added easily because they contain a slot at the bottom that fits right on the wheel of the file— in whatever location on the wheel—without the need to remove any of the other cards.

(d) *Rotary card files:* Rotary files which move horizontally around a central hub may be used for correspondence or cards, or both, depending upon the particular office needs.

c. *Storing noncorrespondence records:* In addition to business documents recorded on paper and magnetic media, there are numerous other types of noncorrespondence items that also need to be stored in the office. Each item needs to be examined to see what kind of storage system would provide the protection and durability needed. Some typical kinds of noncorrespondence items might include plans, drawings, blueprints, maps, photographs, cassette tapes, videotapes, slides, and computer printouts. Here are some types of storage equipment that might be used for some of these applications:

(1) *File cabinets with horizontal drawers:* Flat storage must be provided for blueprints, maps, and photographs.

(2) *Suspension open-shelf files:* Computer printouts are inserted into plastic binders so that they can be suspended in a "hanging" storage area until needed.

(3) *Rolled files:* Maps, blueprints, or posters may be encased in rolls for easier filing and storage.

(4) *Tape drawers:* Videotapes and cassette tapes can be stored in filing order within special drawers designed just for tapes. The drawers are sectioned with small ridges so that individual tapes can fit vertically inside each drawer. Labels with appropriate filing designations need to be attached to each tape and tape cover.

4. *Retaining and Disposing of Records:* Decisions are needed on a predetermined basis as to the retention (keeping), protection, and disposal of a company's *vital* records. A records retention schedule should be developed that identifies the records of the organization that are being kept in active, semiactive, and inactive storage, the period of time they will be retained in storage, and the value of the record to the organization. A *retention schedule* is an agreement between the department creating the record, the user (if not the department of creation), and the records manager specifying how long each active record is to be held in active storage, semiactive storage, or inactive storage, and when the record may be destroyed, if ever.

a. *Appraisal of records:* In order for an accurate retention schedule to be developed, the organization's records must be appraised to determine the value of the records. *Value* of records depends upon the utilization of the records in ongoing operations. *Primary value* refers to the value of records in active storage, and *secondary value* refers to those records held in semiactive or inactive storage.

(1) *Primary value:* Records that are of primary value are active in nature and are needed for current operations. Primary value may mean administrative, legal, fiscal, or research value.

(a) *Administrative value:* Records that have administrative value are needed for a business to conduct current operations.

EXAMPLES:
Policies and procedures

Executive directives
Purchase requisitions
Inventory records
Personnel records

(b) *Legal value:* Those documents that have legal value contain provisions or agreements that relate to the legal rights and obligations of the business.

EXAMPLES:
Contracts
Agreements to purchase new property or equipment
Leases for business property

(c) *Fiscal value:* Records of fiscal value usually refer to those documents that relate to the financial transactions of the organization.

EXAMPLES:
Budgets
Vouchers
Tax returns
Sales reports

(d) *Research value:* Records that consist of technical information that results from scientific research will have research value to the organization.

EXAMPLES:
Records of procedures used in conducting a research project
Records of step-by-step procedures in analyzing the historical development in word processing equipment over the past ten years

(3) *Secondary value:* Records that are in relatively inactive storage may have historical or archival importance.

(a) *Information value:* Over a period of years, any organization will accumulate records that contain information relating to people, places, events, and other phenomena.

EXAMPLES:
Copyrights
Patents
Blueprints
Photographs
Maps

(b) *Evidence value:* Records that trace the development of an organization from its beginning to the present may have evidentiary value in order to provide proof of policies, procedures, and practices during the organization's lifetime.

EXAMPLES:
Organizational charts
Policies and procedures manuals
Articles of incorporation
Minutes books

b. *Records transfer:* The physical movement of records from active status within a particular department or office to a centralized records center is known as *records transfer*. Two methods of records transfer are the *perpetual* and *periodic* transfer methods.

(1) *Perpetual transfer method:* Using the perpetual method, records can be transferred at any time that the event has been completed or the case closed and future referral to the records will be infrequent and limited.

EXAMPLE: A perpetual method of records transfer is used in the Lawrence & Brown Law Firm. Once a court case has been closed, the file is moved immediately to inactive storage. With this method, a case sometimes remains open for two to three years before it can be closed and becomes inactive.

(2) *Periodic transfer method:* Records are transferred as of a specific date each year. All files for a specific period of time are transferred at that time.

EXAMPLE: The Powell Seed Company uses a periodic transfer method because this particular type of business lends itself to a periodic rather than a perpetual method. On July 1 and December 31 of each year, the files are transferred from active to inactive storage. Of course, on those particular dates all records are perused to see if they are needed for future reference or can be destroyed.

c. *Records purging and destruction:* Before any records are purged or destroyed at the end of a specified retention period, the department which created and/or used the records is contacted to determine if the records indeed can be deleted or destroyed. The records retention schedule specifies the period of time a given record should be retained before disposal.

(1) *Destruction of paper records:* Common ways of destroying paper records include shredding, pulverizing, and incinerating.
(2) *Destruction of microform and magnetic records:* Com-

mon ways of destroying microform or magnetic records include incinerating, shredding, and pulverizing.

(3) *Purging of electronic records:* Periodically, records that are stored electronically on computer disks should be examined to see if they can be purged (deleted) from computer storage. Depending on the particular records in question, purging can take place on a weekly, monthly, or annual basis.

Most organizations are now recycling paper, cardboard, and shredded or pulverized paper.

5. *Maintaining Records Centers:* The records center is the depository for the organization's vital, inactive, and/or active records. Vital records may be classified as active or inactive, depending on the current use. Many times sets of duplicate records exist in the form of electronic tapes, hard copies (paper copies), or microforms. *Dispersal* is the term used to indicate the duplication of hard copies and their storage in other locations.

   a. *On-site storage:* In-house records centers, file rooms, or vaults provide records storage on the company's premises. Vital records are sometimes stored in highly protected vaults or in underground storage for even greater security.
   b. *Off-site storage:* Records storage in off-premises locations may be space owned by the organization or rented from other commercial firms. Usually, off-site storage is in a lower-rent area and, therefore, will result in a lower records storage cost. A higher degree of security exists in off-site facilities primarily because these locations are not public knowledge.

6. *Maintaining Archives:* A *business archive* is a facility that houses records being retained for research or historical value. Archives may be *public* (may be accessed by the general public) or *private* (may be used only by members of the organization). An *accession register* identifies the records in the archive and controls access to documents and retrieval of documents from the archive. Here are some of the basic reasons for the maintenance of archives by organizations:

   a. The organization's history can be preserved for posterity.
   b. The public image of an organization may be enhanced by permitting the public to use its archives.
   c. Relevant administrative, fiscal, or legal information may be maintained for later research and reference.

   Documents maintained in an archive are preserved in special storage containers to deter further deterioration. Access to an archive is limited to those individuals whose reasons for using the archive are approved by appropriate officials of the organization.

Chapter 4: Review Questions

Part A: Multiple-Choice Questions

DIRECTIONS: Select the best answer from the four alternatives. Write your answer in the blank to the left of the number.

_____ 1. The systematic control of recorded information required for the operation of the business is called

    a. word processing.
    b. communications.
    c. data processing.
    d. records management.

_____ 2. Individual business records are classified according to

    a. the record cycle.
    b. the record activity.
    c. the method used for creating the record.
    d. the design of the record.

_____ 3. Records that contribute to the continued smooth operation of an organization and can be replaced if lost or destroyed in a disaster are referred to as

    a. vital records.
    b. important records.
    c. useful records.
    d. nonessential records.

_____ 4. The records cycle refers to

    a. the creation of all types of records within the organization.
    b. the way in which records will be utilized within the firm.
    c. a series of steps from the time the record is created until its final disposition.
    d. the transferring of records from active to inactive storage.

_____ 5. Which of the following records is designed in what would be termed a conventional format?

    a. An invoice
    b. One sheet of microfiche

c. A 35mm slide
d. A computer disk

_____ 6. One of the cards in the card catalog of a library is an example of

a. a relative index.
b. an index record.
c. a posted record.
d. constant information.

_____ 7. Which of the following records is designed in a nonconventional format?

a. A copy of a business letter
b. A 3" x 5" card for equipment repair
c. An aperture card
d. A 3-page business report

_____ 8. Any record that contains reduced images on film is known as

a. a magnetic disk.
b. a cassette tape.
c. an OCR process.
d. a microform.

_____ 9. Before a business record can be retrieved from central files

a. an index must be consulted to see where the record is located.
b. it must be stored according to a prescribed set of rules.
c. approval to retrieve the record must be obtained from the supervisor.
d. the record needs to be inspected and indexed correctly.

_____ 10. Which of the following classification systems assumes that direct-access procedures will be used to retrieve records?

a. An alphabetic system
b. A numeric system
c. An alphanumeric system
d. A subject system

_____ 11. Making notations on the record itself indicating exactly how the record will be stored is referred to as

a. inspecting.
b. coding.
c. indexing.
d. classifying.

Records Management

_____ 12. Whenever a record could be filed in more than one place in the files

    a. a duplicate copy of the record should be filed in each place.
    b. a cross-reference to the original record should be prepared.
    c. a cross-reference should be noted on the original record.
    d. the record should be filed in a special location within the file.

_____ 13. The primary purpose for using a relative index with a filing classification system is so that

    a. cross-references can be located easily.
    b. the record can be retrieved using a direct-access procedure.
    c. a particular record or file can be located quickly.
    d. blocks of numbers can be reserved for certain record categories.

_____ 14. If you were filing the following numbered records using a middle-digit filing system that divides the numbers into two-digit groups, which of the following numbers would be filed *first*?

    a. 204573
    b. 134591
    c. 105424
    d. 115429

_____ 15. If you were filing the following numbered records under a terminal-digit system, again using two-digit groupings of numbers, which record would be filed *second*?

    a. 115119
    b. 154517
    c. 225891
    d. 334717

_____ 16. The length of time each active record is to be held in active storage, inactive storage, or destroyed is specified in the

    a. records appraisal.
    b. relative index.
    c. retention schedule.
    d. records transfer method.

_____ 17. Which of the following types of records would be appraised as having fiscal value?

    a. Company policy on business travel.
    b. The administrative budget for the year.

c. Contract for lease of records-storage space.
d. Inventory records.

_____ **18.** The physical movement of records from active departmental status to a centralized records center is known as

a. records retention.
b. records appraisal.
c. records transfer.
d. records storage.

_____ **19.** Hard-copy storage of a duplicate set of records at a different location is referred to as

a. retention.
b. transfer.
c. dispersal.
d. destruction.

_____ **20.** A facility that houses records retained for their research or historical value is called

a. a historical center.
b. an archive.
c. a records center.
d. a micrographics center.

Part B: Matching Sets

Matching Set 1

Match the classification of records (A-D) with the kinds of records (21-27). Write the letter of your answer in the blank to the left of each number.

Classification of Records

A. Vital Records
B. Important Records
C. Useful Records
D. Nonessential Records

KINDS OF RECORDS

_____ **21.** Computer disks

_____ **22.** Interoffice memorandums

Records Management

_____ 23. Lease

_____ 24. Letters

_____ 25. Tax records

_____ 26. Property deed

_____ 27. Customer requests

Matching Set 2

Match the steps in the records cycle (A-E) with the appropriate statements (28-32). Write the letter of your answer in the blank to the left of each number.

Steps in the Record Cycle

- A. Creation of Records
- B. Utilization of Records
- C. Retention of Records
- D. Transfer of Records
- E. Disposal of Records

STATEMENTS

_____ 28. Justification for the record and its primary purpose are determined.

_____ 29. A decision is made about the life of a record.

_____ 30. A record that is electronically stored on a computer disk is deleted.

_____ 31. A records inventory is conducted to determine the costs involved in using records.

_____ 32. A record is moved from active storage to inactive storage.

Part C: Problem Situations

DIRECTIONS: For each of the following questions about the problem situation, select the best answer from the four alternatives. Write the letter of your response in the blank to the left of the question.

Problem 1

In her office Jane Hoffman uses an alphabetic classification system based on the ARMA rules. Correspondence is filed alphabetically with all correspondence for a particular client filed chronologically by date with most recent date first.

_____ 33. Which of the following names would be filed *first*?

    a. Roberta L. Bernard
    b. Bernarde Robot Company
    c. Robert Louis Bernard
    d. The Bernard Recreation Association

_____ 34. Which of the following names would be filed *last*?

    a. U.S. Department of Labor
    b. United Airlines
    c. U.S. Dept. of Education
    d. United States of America

_____ 35. Which of the following pieces of correspondence will be filed *first* in the file?

    a. A letter from George R. Johnson dated February 4, 1991.
    b. A letter from G. R. Johnson dated January 3, 1991.
    c. A letter to George R. Johnson dated March 14, 1991.
    d. A letter to G. R. Johnson dated December 28, 1990.

_____ 36. In each file drawer Jane arranges guides and folders. In which of the following would the correspondence indicated in #35 be filed?

    a. Primary guide for J
    b. Special guide for Johnson
    c. Miscellaneous folder for J
    d. Individual folder for Johnson

Chapter 4: Solutions

Part A: Multiple-Choice Questions

          Answer   **Refer to Chapter Section**

1. (d)   [Overview]
2. (b)   [A-1] Individual records are classified according to either the record activity (use) or the importance of the particular record to the business.
3. (b)   [A-1-b(2)]
4. (c)   [A-2]
5. (a)   [B-1-a] The other examples are all unconventional formats.
6. (b)   [B-1-a(4)(a)]
7. (c)   [B-1-b(1)(d)] The other choices all have conventional formats.
8. (d)   [B-1-b(1)]
9. (b)   [C-1] Before any record can be retrieved, it must be stored according to an established set of procedures.
10. (a)   [C-1-a(1)] The other choices require indirect-access procedures.
11. (b)   [C-1-b]
12. (b)   [C-1-c]
13. (c)   [C-2-b] A relative index consists of cards or a listing of all names to which numbers have been assigned in alphabetic order.
14. (b)   [C-2-b(4)] In a middle-digit system, the numbers given in the choices would be filed in the following order: 134591, 204573, 105424, and 115429.
15. (d)   [C-2-b(5)] In a terminal-digit system, the numbers given in the choices would be filed in the following order: 154517, 334717, 115119, and 225891.
16. (c)   [C-4] The retention schedule identifies the life of a record.
17. (b)   [C-4-a(1)(c)] Fiscal value means that the record relates to financial transactions.
18. (c)   [C-4-b]
19. (c)   [C-5]
20. (b)   [C-6]

Part B: Matching Sets

Matching Set 1

21. (B)   [A-1-b(2)]
22. (D)   [A-1-b(4)]
23. (A)   [A-1-b(1)]
24. (C)   [A-1-b(3)]

25. (B) [A-1-b(2)]
26. (A) [A-1-b(1)]
27. (C) [A-1-b(3)]

Matching Set 2

28. (A) [A-2-a(3)]
29. (C) [A-2-c]
30. (E) [A-2-e]
31. (B) [A-2-b]
32. (D) [A-2-d]

Part C: Problem Situations

33. (d) [C-2-a(1)(a) and (b)] The names would be filed correctly in this order:
Bernard Recreation Association (The)
Bernard, Robert Louis
Bernard, Roberta Louise
Bernarde Robot Company

34. (a) [C-2-a(1)(b) and (c)] The names would be filed correctly in this order:
United Airlines
United States (of) America
United States Government
   Education Department
United States Government
   Labor Department

35. (b) [C-2-a(1) and C-2-b(8)] The correspondence would be filed correctly in this order:
Johnson, G. R. — January 3, 1991
Johnson, G. R. — December 28, 1990
Johnson, George R. — March 14, 1991
Johnson, George R. — February 4, 1991

36. (d) [C-3-b(1)(g)] The guides and folders shown in the choices would be sequenced in this way:
Primary Guide — J
Special Guide — Johnson
Individual Folder — Johnson
Miscellaneous Folder — J

CHAPTER 5
Reference Materials

OVERVIEW

As more administrative responsibilities are assigned to the executive assistant or secretary, the process of researching information needed by the busy executive is becoming more important. Researching information takes time, a degree of knowledge about the subject or topic, and organizational skills. Sometimes it is difficult to know exactly where to go to find adequate and accurate information for a research report or speech. The secretary must be prepared to spend considerable time "digging" for sources of information.

Research procedures that have proved helpful include discussing the purpose of the research with the person for whom the work is being done *before* actually beginning to search for information. In this way, the secretary will have the basic objectives of the research in mind before embarking on the project. Sometimes it will be necessary to interview people; at other times, book references will be helpful. No matter what procedures are used, it is vital that a detailed record be kept of all persons interviewed, references read and consulted, and other useful reference materials in order to develop a complete bibliography of works consulted.

Research facilities such as libraries, in-house research services, and computer search and information services are among the facilities and services that should be utilized in performing the research function. In addition, business and professional associations as well as community organizations can also be very helpful.

Although the list of reference materials included in this chapter is in no way all-inclusive, it will serve as a starting point for researching information under particular headings. As new publications relating to the categories included in this chapter are discovered, it would be a good idea to add these to the list so that an up-to-date reference list can be maintained.

DEFINITION OF TERMS

ALMANAC. A book or publication, usually published on an annual basis, that includes factual information about the events of the year.

ARCHIVE. A collection of business documents of historical value maintained by a business, government agency, or university.

BIBLIOGRAPHY. A record of each reference used in researching information which includes author's name, title of book or reference, publisher, place of publication, and date of publication.

BIOGRAPHICAL DIRECTORY. A publication that highlights the achievements of noted individuals who contributed to their professions, to government, or the country.

COMPUTER DATA BANK. An information bank to which a company may subscribe in order to have access, through the computer, to a data bank available within a particular profession or field.

DEWEY DECIMAL CLASSIFICATION SYSTEM. A library cataloging system that is based on the premise that all knowledge can be classified into ten primary groupings.

INTERLIBRARY LOAN. A networking system that has been established between libraries for references located in one library to be loaned to an individual through another library for a specific period of time.

LIBRARY OF CONGRESS CLASSIFICATION SYSTEM. A library cataloging system with a larger number of major classifications than the Dewey Decimal System.

MICROGRAPHICS CENTER. A centralized service within a library where research studies, dissertations, and other references are stored on microforms (microfiche and microfilm); access to these materials is typically available only within the center because of the equipment involved.

PARLIAMENTARY PROCEDURE. A set of rules established for the appropriate conduct of business meetings.

THESAURUS. A lexicon (dictionary) or similar book of words or information that focuses on synonyms and antonyms.

VERTICAL FILE SERVICE. Pamphlets, booklets, leaflets, and other loose-leaf materials stored in a file cabinet for easy access.

A. Research Procedures

The secretary's role is changing to include more administrative responsibility in assisting the busy executive with the challenging task of researching information. Such a task demands a high level of organizational skill and ingenuity in gathering accurate information for reports, speeches, and other types of written materials. The kinds of procedures used in collecting the information needed will, of course, have a direct reflection on the quality of the report or speech produced. Here are some handy guidelines for developing a set of procedures for researching business information.

1. *Understanding the Purpose of the Research:* Before you can embark on any type of research, you must know the purpose of the research. Know exactly what the outcome will be and who will make use of the results of the research. Here are some questions that need to be answered before proceeding with the research.

    - Will a speech be written with this information?
    - If so, who will be the audience?
    - What kind of information do you need to find?

2. *Listing Possible Sources of Information:* Your investigation should begin by listing all the possible sources of information you might use.

    a. *Facilities:* Identify facilities, such as libraries, business associations, or community organizations, where you might find the kinds of information you seek.
    b. *Types of references:* Identify specific books, documents, or other types of information that are desired.
    c. *Personal contacts:* List the names of people you need to interview with their addresses and telephone numbers so that it will be easier for you to contact them by letter and phone as you proceed with the research.
    d. *Computer searches:* Investigate the possibility of a computer search for some of the types of information you need. Such a search may take place in a library or research center that has access to the data base(s) you are interested in accessing.

3. *Determining Special Research Costs:* It is very important to estimate the cost of doing the background research. Costs include travel to and from research facilities, telephone expense, computer searches, and additional secretarial assistance.

4. *Making Appointments for Research:* A timesaver in performing research functions is to make appointments ahead of time with individuals (inside or outside the organization) who are in a position to help you obtain the kinds of information you seek. Other people (librarians, business executives, research specialists, community leaders) may be busy on their jobs, just as you are, and a formal appointment will assure you of an hour or two of their undivided attention to your questions.

5. *Keeping Complete Records of Research Information:* As you proceed with the research, it is vital that you keep a recorded or written record of everything you do: sources of information, complete sets of notes, interview schedule, transcribed interview tapes. You will need this information later when you are ready to develop the information you collected into the final draft of the speech or report.

a. *Preparing a bibliography:* Keep a record of each reference you use, manually on a 3"x 5" card or electronically in a computer data base. Include the following kinds of information:

- Author's name (if any)
- Title of book, article, or other reference
- Name of publishing company or agency
- Place of publication
- Date of publication
- Exact page reference(s)
- Library classification number
- ISBN number for ordering copies

File these bibliography cards in a card file according to a specific filing system. You might consider alphabetical order by author name or subject (topic) if your speech or report lends itself to that filing system.

If you key entries (with the preceding categories of information) into a data base, you must be sure to set up the fields of information in the same order for the entire data base. *Fields* of information are the labels you use in the creation of a data base to identify the kinds of information you will include in the data base.

EXAMPLE: In planning the bibliographic entries, you would establish fields like:
Author name
Title of article or book
Title of publication
Place of publication
Date of publication
Publisher

The software will prompt you to identify the fields of information *before* you begin to key in the variable information for each bibliographic entry. Once you have told the system you are using these fields, the system will prompt you each time you need to enter a particular kind of information.

b. *Taking appropriate reading notes:* Reading notes should be complete so that you will not have to return to the original reference later as you begin your writing.

(1) *Manual procedures for taking notes:* Here are some specific procedures to follow in taking accurate notes as you read various references.

- Use only one side of a note card (preferably a 6"x 9" card so you have more writing room).

- If one particular reference refers to more than one subject, place the notes pertaining to each subject on a separate card. Identify the source of the material on each card (a code number or author's last name). The complete bibliographic information is in your bibliography file.
- File your note cards in a card file alphabetically by author name or subject (topic) so that they will not become lost.

(2) *Electronic procedures for taking notes:* You may be using word processing or database software to record your notes. Follow the procedures given in the operating instructions for the software you are using so that you will be clear as to the correct procedures to use. Word processing software permits you to key in your notes and also store these notes on disk for later access.

c. *Duplicating materials for later reference:* You may be using microfilm or microfiche to locate needed materials. It is sometimes an advantage to print copies of those pages with data that you may need to refer to later. Be careful to observe copyright laws carefully when copying copyrighted articles, theses, and other research information.

d. *Recording interview information:* If you find it necessary to conduct an interview with either company personnel or people in outside organizations, follow these steps so that your interview will be conducted in a concise, but complete, fashion.

(1) Develop the questions you wish to ask prior to the interview. In some cases it is an excellent idea to send a copy of these questions to the person you are interviewing ahead of time so that he/she will have an opportunity to think about them and perhaps have some of the information ready for you.

(2) During the interview, take notes in a manner that will not be distracting for the interviewee. If you use a written form of shorthand, you should be able to take the notes quickly as the interviewee responds to specific questions.

(3) If you wish to tape an interview for later replay, transcription, and analysis, be sure to ask the interviewee before you begin for permission to tape the interview. Sometimes people do not wish to be taped, especially if the topic tends to be a sensitive one.

(4) A typed transcript of the interview (questions and answers) prepared from a recorded tape needs to be reviewed by the interviewee to ensure accuracy of the information that has been transcribed.

B. Research Facilities

One of the first items on your list is to identify the types of facilities that may have information relevant to your topic. Libraries, local chamber-of-commerce organizations, business and professional associations, and local businesses may be helpful to you. In addition, various United States Government departments have excellent libraries, with qualified professional librarians in charge. Some have law libraries as well.

1. *Libraries:* Library services are primarily available through public, company, government, and university libraries. If you are looking for rather general information, a public library may be an excellent source. Many companies, however, have established their own libraries so that library references specific to their own industry may be collected and used more easily. Of course, a university library may be one of the most extensive libraries in your vicinity. Private collections are often housed in a university library and would provide very valuable information for your research. Many public and university libraries are part of library consortiums today so that there are online services available linking one library with many others in the network. References that are part of one library's holdings may be borrowed by someone at another library.

   a. *Classification systems:* Libraries use two standardized classification systems: the Dewey Decimal classification system and the Library of Congress classification system.

      (1) *Dewey Decimal classification system:* This system is based upon the premise that all knowledge can be classified into ten primary groupings:

000	General Works
100	Philosophy
200	Religion
300	Social Science
400	Philology
500	Pure Science
600	Applied Science or Useful Arts
700	Arts Recreation
800	Literature
900	History

      Main subjects are identified by the hundreds 000 to 900. Subgroups are assigned numbers 00 to 99 or 0 to 9, if there are two subgroups.

      EXAMPLE:
      347.97 Courts (within 300 Social Science)

      (2) *Library of Congress classification system:* This system provides a larger number of major classifications. The number assigned consists of an alphanumeric code, with

the first two letters representing the major classification group.

EXAMPLE:
KF889.3.R68

b. *Vertical file service:* A valuable library reference is the list of pamphlets, booklets, and leaflets that are available in vertical files but are not indexed in the card catalog.

c. *Reference collections:* Libraries house special collections, either publicly owned or owned by individuals. Information contained in such collections may be accessed, but often all research work must be done on the premises. All books and documents in the collection are kept in the library at all times. Collections such as these give the researcher an opportunity to view manuscripts, reports, and other materials that might not otherwise be available for access. With special permission, it may be possible for the researcher to make photocopies of some of the materials.

d. *Interlibrary networks:* Interlibrary communication networks or consortiums have been established in many areas to enable people to access information stored in more than one library. With a computer system, it is possible to inquire on a terminal in one library about specific books or references that are available in other libraries cooperating in the library consortium. Within two to four days, if the reference is available, any books not available in the local library can be received as a loan from another library.

e. *Computer information banks:* Many organizations subscribe to computerized information banks available within a particular profession or field. In the company library, a terminal is available to access the data bank in order to obtain abstracts of research studies, court cases, or other materials available through the data bank. (See *Module VI—Office Technology*, Chapter 3, Data Processing, and Chapter 4, Records Management, of this module.)

EXAMPLE: The Information Bank is the actual name of one such data bank which is one of the most comprehensive current affairs data banks in the world. The system's database includes several million items accumulated from more than 80 publications.

f. *Library micrographics centers:* Libraries have research studies, dissertations, and other references stored on microfiche and microfilm that may be accessed on the premises only. If copies are needed of particular pages or charts, a reader-printer may be used to produce copies needed. Other types of audiovisual materials may be available on cassettes and videotapes, too, such as a copy of a speech made by the president of a university.

2. *In-House Research Services:* Within the organization, several in-house research services may be maintained. Each of these research operations would provide personal as well as telephone service in locating factual information.

   a. *Research department:* Organizations that are involved heavily in researching information find it valuable to form a research department to assist business personnel in finding needed information.
   b. *Computer information banks:* As mentioned in B-1-e, many organizations subscribe to information services within a particular profession or field. Terminals connect the company to the source of the information so that individuals can access abstracts of information needed or copies of entire documents.
   c. *Business archives:* An *archive* is a collection of business documents of historical value. Businesses, government, and universities have established archives so that researchers will be able to access information that is protected through a high level of security. The research would need to be done on premises since the research materials are so valuable.

3. *Business and Professional Associations:* Specific information relating to a particular profession may be available through a recognized professional organization. By writing directly to the association, much valuable information can be obtained; or by examining the publications of the professional group, you may be brought up to date on the latest happenings in the field. Such sources are particularly helpful if you are researching technological developments in the field.

4. *Community Organizations:* Business information may be obtained from organizations such as the local chamber of commerce or the city government. Service clubs, such as Kiwanis or Lions Club, may also be able to help, depending on the subject of the research. In preparing a speech to be given before a community organization, the executive may ask the secretary to research the group to find out more about the audience.

C. **Reference Materials**

Depending on the topic being researched, many different types of reference materials are available for researching various types of business information. The following list represents samples of different kinds of reference materials available. However, the sources that are included are considered major ones that the professional secretary should be aware of and be able to use in conducting needed research.

1. *Almanacs:* An almanac is a book or publication, usually published on an annual basis, that includes factual information about international and national events of the year.

Almanac of American Politics: 1990 Edition (Macmillan Publishing Company)

The Guinness Book of World Records, published annually (Bantam Books)

Information Please Almanac, Atlas and Yearbook, published annually (Simon & Schuster, Inc., New York)

The Official Associated Press Almanac (Hammond Almanac, Inc.)

Reader's Digest Almanac and Yearbook (W. W. Norton & Company, Inc.)

The World Almanac and Book of Facts, published annually (Newspaper Enterprise Association, Inc., New York)

2. *Biographical Indexes and Directories:* These publications highlight the achievements of noted individuals who contributed to their professions, to government, or the country.

Biography Index, published annually (The H.W. Wilson Company, New York)

Webster's Biographical Dictionary (G. & C. Merriam Company, Springfield, Massachusetts)

Who Was Who in America, published annually (Marquis Who's Who, Inc., Chicago)

Who's Who, published annually (St. Martin's Press, Inc., New York)

Who's Who in America, published biennially (Marquis Who's Who, Inc., Chicago)

3. *Book and Periodical Directories:* Directories provide listings of companies, associations, organizations, individuals, or products in a systematic way—alphabetically, geographically, or in subject arrangements.

N.W. Ayer and Son's Directory of Newspapers and Publications, published annually (N. W. Ayer & Son, Inc., Philadelphia): *Ayer's* lists over 22,000 newspapers and periodicals published in the United States. The listing includes name, place of publication, frequency of publication, circulation, price, and editor's name. There is both a geographical and an alphabetical listing.

Business Periodicals Index, published annually (The H. W. Wilson Company, New York): This index has a subject index to over 200 periodicals in finance, insurance, banking, accounting, marketing, data processing, and other business-related subjects.

Cumulative Book Index, published monthly (The H. W. Wilson Company, New York): This index lists most of the books published in the United States from 1928 to date. The books are arranged by author, title, and subject under one alphabetical listing.

Index to Legal Periodicals, published annually (The H. W. Wilson Company, New York): This index includes references to articles on various topics of law and law-related matters. Both subject and specific case name indexes to articles are given.

Reader's Guide to Periodical Literature, published semimonthly (The H. W. Wilson Company, New York): The *Reader's Guide* is a subject and author index to several hundred popular, nontechnical magazines. It is published twice a month and accumulated into annual volumes.

Other book and periodical directories include:

Book Review Digest, published monthly (The H. W. Wilson Company, New York)

Books in Print, published annually (R. R. Bowker Company, New York)

McRae's Blue Book, a buying guide published annually (McRae's Blue Book Company)

4. *Business, Governmental, and Professional Directories and Publications:* In addition to book and periodical directories, listings of members of professional associations governmental directories and records, and business directories and publications are extremely helpful in locating appropriate sources of information.

   a. *Professional associations:*

   American Dental Directory, published annually (American Dental Association, Chicago)

   American Medical Directory, published annually (American Medical Association, Chicago)

   b. *Governmental directories and records:*

   The Congressional Information Service Index to Publications, Congressional Information Service, Washington, D.C.: This monthly index to congressional publications is indexed by subject, witness names, popular law names, report numbers, document numbers, and bill and public law numbers.

   The Congressional Record, U.S. Government Printing Office, Washington, D.C.: The *Congressional Record* is a daily report of the Senate and the House activity and debates. In this publication, the bill debate transcripts are published.

   Congressional Index, Commerce Clearing House: This index is published weekly and presents all the legislation covered by Congress during that week.

   The Federal Register, U.S. Government Printing Office, Washington, D.C. (published daily, Monday-Friday): All regulations and notices issued by federal agencies are published in the *Federal Register.* This includes Presidential Proclamations and Executive Orders.

   United States Government Manual, Office of the Federal Register, General Services Administration, Washington, D.C. (published annually): This manual is a directory of governmental agencies and key personnel with addresses and telephone numbers.

   c. *Business directories and publications:*

   Directory of Directories (Gale Research Company)

   Standard & Poor's Register of Corporations, Directors, and

Executives, United States and Canada, Standard and Poor's, New York: Directors and executives of nearly 35,000 corporations are listed in the *S & P Register*. Full biographical information is given for all corporations and their executives. The index is arranged alphabetically by corporate name and executive's name.

Thomas' Register of American Manufacturers (12 Volumes), Thomas Publication Company, New York: The Thomas' Register features a listing of over 100,000 manufacturers, giving product lines and addresses. Information is listed by manufacturer's name and product(s) and serves as a buyer's guide.

5. *Business Newspapers and Periodicals:* Current business information is available in numerous newspapers and periodicals published in the United States. Here is an annotated list of some of the more important ones.

Barron's, Dow Jones & Company, Inc., New York (published weekly): National business and financial news is presented in articles on investments, industries, trends, and other business topics; stock and bond prices are included.

Business Week, McGraw-Hill Book Company, New York (published weekly): Articles on specialized business topics present the important business indicators, the investment outlook, and articles on business developments.

Dun's Review and Modern Industry, Dun and Bradstreet, Inc., New York (published monthly): This publication presents reports on industrial development statistics.

Forbes, Forbes, Inc., New York (published semimonthly): The first issue each year contains the "Annual Report on American Industry." The publication includes articles on business administration, new developments in business, and business outlooks.

Fortune, Time, Inc., New York (published monthly): This publication is known for the famous *Fortune* list of the largest corporations (the Fortune 500). Recently *Fortune* has included special sections on business automation, communications, and computer technology two or three times per year.

Harvard Business Review, Graduate School of Business Administration, Harvard University, Boston (published bimonthly): This periodical is one of the outstanding business administration journals published today. The articles are written primarily for the practitioner in the field.

The New York Times, The New York Times Company, Inc., New York (published daily): This newspaper is very well known for its current business news and coverage of daily business events.

Wall Street Journal, Dow Jones & Company, Inc., New York (published daily, Monday-Friday): This newspaper features business and financial news, articles on corporate strategies and events, and stock and bond prices on the various exchanges.

6. *Dictionaries:* As reference books, dictionaries serve a very important function. Secretaries find dictionaries helpful in finding the correct spelling of a term, the correct meaning and usage of a word or expression, and the correct syllabication of the word. Unabridged dictionaries can be especially helpful since they are the most complete dictionaries and not based on a larger work. Some professional dictionaries include the terminology most pertinent to that profession. Here are some of the more commonly used dictionaries:

    The American Heritage Dictionary of the English Language (Houghton-Mifflin Publishing Co., Inc.)
    Black's Law Dictionary (Charles Scribner's Sons)
    The Dictionary of Occupational Titles (U.S. Government Printing Office, Washington, D.C.)
    Encyclopedic Dictionary of English Usage (Prentice Hall)
    Funk & Wagnall's
    Oxford English Dictionary (Oxford Press)
    The Random House College Dictionary (Random House)
    Webster's New Collegiate Dictionary (Merriam-Webster)
    Webster's New Geographical Dictionary (Merriam-Webster)
    Webster's New International Dictionary, Unabridged (Merriam-Webster)
    Webster's New World Dictionary of the American Language (Simon & Schuster)

    Other professional dictionaries include:
    The Dictionary of Business, Finance, and Investment
    The Dictionary of Computers

    There are also foreign-language dictionaries that are particularly helpful to the executive assistant or secretary who must translate correspondence and reports or look up foreign words and phrases. Such dictionaries list words or phrases in two ways, for example, French to English in one section and English to French in another section.

7. *Encyclopedias:* As a general rule, encyclopedias are designed as general reference books on a wide variety of topics. Some encyclopedias are designed to provide very detailed information, while others may be directed toward children's use or people within a particular profession. Many encyclopedias have annual supplements available that describe key highlights and events of the past year. Here is a sample list of some encyclopedias available today:

    The Encyclopedia Americana (Grolier)
    Encyclopedia of Associations (Gale Research Company, Detroit)
    Encyclopaedia Brittanica (Encyclopaedia Brittanica, Brittanica Centre, Chicago)
    Encyclopedia of Information Systems and Services
    Funk & Wagnalls New Encyclopedia (Funk & Wagnalls)
    International Encyclopedia of the Social Sciences
    Random House Encyclopedia (Random House)

The World Book Encyclopedia (World Book)

8. *Etiquette References:* Current references on etiquette focus on conventional requirements of social behavior and conduct as established within any class or community or for any occasion. Two of the more well-known references are:

Baldridge, Letitia, *Amy Vanderbilt's Complete Book of Etiquette,* Doubleday & Company, Inc., New York (latest edition)

Post, Elizabeth L., *The New Emily Post's Etiquette,* Funk & Wagnalls, New York (latest edition)

9. *Financial Services:* Subscription services are available to the financial community that will give the latest information on stock prices, industry developments, legislative changes affecting organizations, and other pertinent business and financial information.

Babson's Reports, Inc.: *Investment and Barometer Letter, Washington Forecast Letter*

The Conference Board, Inc.: *Business Scoreboard, Road Maps of Industry Focus, Conference Board Record*

Moody's Investors Service, New York:

Moody's Bank and Finance Manual: Biweekly news reports for banking institutions, insurance, investment, mortgage, real estate, and finance companies.

Moody's Bond Record: Monthly publication that covers over 15,000 bond issues and gives the user information on market position and statistical background.

Moody's Bond Survey: Weekly publication that reports on the bond market and comments on individual issues.

Moody's Dividend Record: A biweekly publication that covers 9,500 issues; each January the *Annual Dividend Record* is also published.

Moody's Handbook of Widely Held Common Stocks: Quarterly publication of summary reports on selected common stocks, including dividends and earnings.

Moody's Industrial Manual: A biweekly report that provides background and financial information on industrial firms in the United States and abroad which are listed on the New York and American Stock Exchanges.

Other manuals or surveys published by Moody's include:

Moody's Municipal and Government Manual

Moody's Public Utility Manual

Moody's OTC Industrial Manual

Moody's Stock Survey

Moody's Transportation Manual

Standard & Poor's Corporation, New York:

Standard and Poor's Fixed Income Investor: This quarterly publication presents a basic analysis of 69 major domestic companies.

Standard and Poor's Industry Surveys: This quarterly publication presents a basic analysis of 69 major domestic companies.

Standard and Poor's Stock Reports, American Stock Exchange: This publication is a quarterly service that reports on over 1,200 companies listed on the American Stock Exchange. Income statements and balance sheets are included with an analysis of earnings reports.

Standard and Poor's Stock Reports, New York Stock Exchange: This is a quarterly publication that reports on over 1,400 companies listed on the New York Stock Exchange. Information on sales, earnings, and potential dividends is included, as well as projections on the overall long-term outlook.

Standard and Poor's Stock Reports, Over the Counter: This quarterly service reports on companies' OTC transactions and those listed on regional stock exchanges. The report includes income statement, balance sheet items, earnings reports and information on dividends, price ranges, and capitalization.

10. *Newsletters and Reports:* Some organizations publish weekly or monthly newsletters or reports that present relevant, up-to-date information on new developments in particular business-related areas. Professional organizations often publish newsletters for members.

    Kiplinger Washington Letter, Kiplinger Washington Editors, Inc., Washington, D.C. (published weekly): A letter service that covers developments and trends in business and government.

    John Naisbitt's Trend Letter, John Naisbitt's Trend Letter, Inc., Washington, D.C. (published twice monthly): An authoritative report on forces transforming the economy, business, technology, society, and the world from 1982 to present.

    Seybold Outlook on Professional Computing, Seybold Group, Inc., Santa Clara, California (published monthly): Newsletter for and about the computer industry, with emphasis on desktop and portable equipment and software used in business.

11. *Newspaper Indexes:* To make it easier for people to research particular topics or subjects that appear in the daily newspapers, some of the larger newspapers in the country have established a printed index to the newspaper issues.

    The New York Times Index, New York Times, New York (published semimonthly): This index provides a subject index valuable to researchers in many fields of study. Included in the index are brief abstracts of articles found in the *New York Times* newspaper, along with date, column number, and page where the entire article may be found.

    Wall Street Journal Index, Dow Jones & Company, Inc., New York: This published index includes reference to every news item published in *The Wall Street Journal.*

12. *Office Administration Reference Books:* The professional secretary

will find a wide variety of reference books dealing with office administration extremely helpful. Here is a representative list of some of the reference books available:

Clark, James L., and Lyn Clark, *How 6: A Handbook for Office Workers,* Sixth Edition, Wadsworth/Kent Publishing Company, Boston, 1991.

House, Clifford R., and Kathie Sigler, *Reference Manual for Office Personnel,* South-Western Publishing Company, Cincinnati, latest edition.

Kutie, Rita, and Virginia Huffman, *The Wiley Office Manual,* John Wiley & Sons, Inc., New York, latest edition.

Sabin, William A., *The Gregg Reference Manual,* McGraw-Hill Book Company, Inc., New York, latest edition.

13. *Parliamentary Procedures:* The appropriate conduct of business meetings will depend upon the application of parliamentary procedures by the people involved. Here are two references that serve as excellent guides:

    Jones, O. Garfield, *Parliamentary Procedure at a Glance,* Hawthorn Books, Inc., New York (latest edition).

    Robert's Rules of Order Newly Revised, Scott, Foresman and Company, Chicago (latest edition).

14. *Mailing and Shipping Publications:* Changes in postage rates, directions for using ZIP codes, and shipping information will be applied more easily if some of the following references are used:

    Address Abbreviations, U.S. Postal Service Publication No. 59 (or more recent edition), U.S. Government Printing Office, Washington, D.C.

    Bullinger's Postal and Shippers Guide for the United States and Canada, Bullinger's Guides, Inc., Westwood, New Jersey (published annually).

    Directory of International Mail, U.S. Government Printing Office, Washington, D.C. (latest edition).

    Dun & Bradstreet Exporters' Encyclopedia, Dun & Bradstreet, Inc., New York (latest edition).

    National ZIP Code and Post Office Directory, U.S. Government Printing Office, Washington, D.C. (current edition)

    Postal Service Manual, U.S. Government Printing Office, Washington, D.C. (current edition).

15. *Quotations:* The professional secretary who assists the executive in preparing speeches or other presentations may find these books of quotations helpful:

    Bartlett, John, *Bartlett's Familiar Quotations,* Little-Brown.

    The Oxford Dictionary of Quotations, Third Edition (or more recent), Oxford Press.

    Stevenson, Burton, *Home Book of Quotations,* Tenth Edition (or more recent), Dodd, Mead & Company, Inc., New York, 1967.

16. *Thesauri:* A *thesaurus* is a lexicon (dictionary) or similar book of words or information that focuses on synonyms and antonyms. Here are two thesauri that are used frequently:

    Roget's International Thesaurus (Thomas Y. Crowell Co., New York)

    Roget's Thesaurus in Dictionary Form (Berkley Publishing Company)

    Roget's II: The New Thesaurus (Houghton-Mifflin)

    Webster's Collegiate Thesaurus (Merriam-Webster)

    Webster's New World Thesaurus (Simon & Schuster)

17. *Travel and Transportation Guides:* Current editions of travel and transportation guides, atlases, and road maps are available through bookstores, automobile associations or motor clubs, and oil companies. Here are some of the most commonly used travel and transportation guides:

    Business Traveler's Road Atlas and Guide to Major Cities (Rand McNally, Chicago), 1990

    Commercial Atlas & Marketing Guide (Rand McNally & Company, Chicago)

    Hotel & Motel Red Book, published annually (American Hotel and Motel Association, New York)

    The New York Times Atlas of the World (The New York Times Company, Inc., New York)

    The Official Airline Guide Electronic Edition Travel Service (Official Airline Guides, Oak Brook, Illinois)

    The Official Airline Guide, North American, Worldwide, and International Edition (Official Airline Guides, Oak Brook, Illinois)

    The Official Airline Guide Travel Planner Hotel & Motel Red Books, North America, Europe, Pacific Asia, published quarterly (Official Airline Guides, Oak Brook, Illinois)

    The Official Airline Guide Worldwide Cruise and Shipline Guide, published six times per year (Official Airline Guides, Oak Brook, Illinois)

    ... plus road maps obtained from various automobile associations, motor clubs, and oil companies.

18. *Word Books:* The availability of at least one word book is very important to the secretary who operates a typewriter, a computer with word processing software, or dictation-transcription equipment. A word book presents an alphabetical list of the most frequently used words and indicates the spelling, syllabication, and recommended hyphenation.

    Kaethe, Ellis, ed., *The Word Book,* Second Edition, Houghton-Mifflin Company, Boston, Massachusetts, 1983.

    Zoubek, Charles E., and G. A. Condon, *20,000 Words,* Eighth Edition, McGraw-Hill Book Company, New York, 1985.

Chapter 5: Review Questions

Part A: Multiple-Choice Questions

DIRECTIONS: Select the best answer from the four alternatives. Write your answer in the blank to the left of the number.

_____ 1. In conducting any meaningful research, you must first know

    a. all possible sources of information.
    b. the purpose of the research.
    c. the names of individuals you want to contact for interviews.
    d. the types of records you should access.

_____ 2. All except one of the following represent types of information that need to be included on a bibliography card. Which one is not necessary?

    a. Title of magazine article
    b. Name of publisher of the article
    c. Date of publication of the article
    d. An additional reference that might be helpful

_____ 3. When copying an article that is stored on microfiche, you must

    a. observe copyright laws carefully.
    b. return the microfiche to its jacket as soon as possible.
    c. use a microfiche reader to produce any printed copies you need.
    d. never make a photocopy of any of the material stored on it without permission.

_____ 4. The library classification system that is based on the premise that all knowledge can be classified into ten primary groups is known as

    a. the Library of Congress classification system.
    b. the Dewey Decimal System.
    c. interlibrary loan system.
    d. in-house research service.

_____ 5. Businesses, government agencies, and universities have organized business documents that have historical value into

    a. in-house research services.

b. computer information banks.
c. active records storage.
d. business archives.

_____ 6. If you were looking for a new book entitled *Business Trends for the Year 2000* and you knew the publisher but not the author, which of the following sources would help you locate the name of the author?

    a. Ayer's Directory of Publications
    b. Webster's Biographical Dictionary
    c. Books in Print
    d. Reader's Guide to Periodical Literature

_____ 7. If you were researching companies involved in specific types of manufacturing, you would find the following reference the most helpful:

    a. The Thomas' Register
    b. Ayer's Directory of Publications
    c. Moody's Handbook of Widely Held Common Stocks
    d. Forbes

_____ 8. Which of the following would serve as a guide to weekly developments and trends in business and government?

    a. Reader's Guide to Periodical Literature
    b. Roget's International Thesaurus
    c. The New York Times
    d. Kiplinger Washington Letter

_____ 9. If you were looking for updates on some of the forces (economic, social, business) that are currently affecting global business situations, you could subscribe to

    a. the Kiplinger Washington Letter.
    b. the New York Times Index.
    c. John Naisbitt's Trend Letter.
    d. Standard & Poor's Stock Reports.

_____ 10. One of the following references is essential to have on hand so the use of parliamentary procedure for conducting a meeting can be checked if there are points of order during a meeting:

    a. The United States Government Manual
    b. Robert's Rules of Order
    c. Barron's
    d. The Congressional Record

Reference Materials 155

Part B: Matching Sets

Matching Set 1

Match the appropriate type of directory (A-E) with the types of information sought (11-15). Write the letter of your answer in the blank to the left of each number.

Types of Directories

A. Periodical Directory
B. Biographical Directory
C. Book Directory
D. Professional Association Directory
E. Business Directory

TYPES OF INFORMATION SOUGHT

_____ **11.** The name of the author(s) of a 1973 edition of an office management book.

_____ **12.** The name of the publisher of *Business Week*.

_____ **13.** Information about the famous doctor and researcher, Jonas Salk.

_____ **14.** A listing of dentists currently practicing in Des Moines, Iowa.

_____ **15.** The names of women who are currently corporate presidents or vice-presidents.

Part C: Problem Situations

DIRECTIONS: For each of the following problem situations, select the best answer from the four alternatives. Write your answer in the blank to the left of the number.

Problem 1

Your manager, Sylvia Silverstone, has asked you to research the ways in which the computer is being used by executives in preparing business graphics for speeches and other presentations. You have set up an appointment with John Symonds, president of your company, to obtain specific information about his use of graphics in preparing sales presentations.

16. Which of the following is the most important for you to do prior to your appointment with Mr. Symonds?

   a. Confirm the appointment with Mr. Symonds' secretary as soon as possible.
   b. Develop a short synopsis of your research results thus far to share with Mr. Symonds.
   c. Send Mr. Symonds a copy of the questions you wish to ask during the interview.
   d. Check with Sylvia Silverstone again to be sure that Mr. Symonds is one of the people she wants you to contact.

Problem 2

The responsibilities of Paula Allen as a paralegal for Bailey & Swift, a Chicago law firm, is to research past court cases in order to obtain information relative to present cases for the preparation of briefs and other legal documents.

17. A subscription service that is available for this purpose is referred to as

   a. an in-house research service.
   b. a computer information service.
   c. a business archive.
   d. a records center.

Chapter 5: Solutions

Part A: Multiple-Choice Questions

	Answer	Refer to Chapter Section
1.	(b)	[A-1] It is essential that you understand the purpose of the research as you begin your task.
2.	(d)	[A-5-a] The other choices refer to items that should appear on a bibliography card.
3.	(a)	[A-5-c] Legally you can always make one copy of stored materials for your own use. Copyright laws prohibit the making of additional copies for distribution to other people.
4.	(b)	[B-1-a(1)] The Dewey Decimal System is the classification system referred to here.
5.	(d)	[B-2-c] Historical records need to be preserved in archives.
6.	(c)	[C-3] The only source identified in the choices that lists books that have been published and are still in print is *Books in Print* (R. R. Bowker Company, New York), which is published annually. The name of author(s) and publisher are readily available in this source.
7.	(a)	[C-4-c] The Thomas' Register is the only publication indicated in the choices which provides a directory of manufacturing companies.
8.	(d)	[C-10] This newsletter is the only publication indicated in the choices that is a weekly publication and would present current trends about business and government events.
9.	(c)	[C-10] This newsletter is published twice monthly and contains futuristic views on the national and international business situation.
10.	(b)	[C-13] *Robert's Rules of Order* is the primary and oldest authority on parliamentary procedure.

Part B: Matching Sets

Matching Set 1

11.	(C)	[C-3]
12.	(A)	[C-3]
13.	(B)	[C-2]
14.	(D)	[C-4-a]
15.	(E)	[C-4-c]

Part C: Problem Situations

16.	(c)	[A-5-d(1)] If Mr. Symonds sees a copy of your interview questions prior to your meeting, he would most likely have a

better opportunity to be prepared with responses for you. This procedure tends to save time in the research process.

17. (b) [B-1-e] Several computer information services are available to the legal profession. Most law firms find it a necessity these days to subscribe to at least one.

CHAPTER 6

Conferences and Meetings

OVERVIEW

Many executives are involved in planning, organizing, and/or attending company-sponsored conferences or association-sponsored conventions. Often executives will be invited to serve as speakers at such conferences. The secretary becomes involved in making sure that appropriate procedures are followed to assure the executive's participation at such conferences or perhaps the executive's leadership activities at conferences or conventions.

Managers tend to spend approximately one-third of their time in meetings each week, according to some estimates, and in many organizations as much as 15 percent of personnel budgets are spent directly on meetings. Meetings are important in order to act upon items of business affecting the entire organization. This chapter reviews the methods used to organize business meetings: informal (committee and office) meetings and formal (in-house, teleconferencing, and out-of-town) meetings.

Knowing the correct procedures for setting up meetings is especially important for the administrative assistant or executive secretary. There are many arrangements for meeting rooms, materials, and notifying participants that must be taken care of efficiently in order for the meeting to be a success. This chapter ends with a brief discussion of parliamentary procedure and its importance in conducting meetings.

DEFINITION OF TERMS

AD HOC COMMITTEE. A small group formed to investigate a particular event or problem that has occurred within the organization; this committee has a temporary appointment and will serve until a report is presented to the executive board or committee.

AGENDA. A list of items of business to be discussed or presented during the meeting.

AUDIOCONFERENCE. A type of teleconference; only voice or sound communication takes place.

COMPUTER CONFERENCE. A meeting with communication between participants taking place using computer terminals to transmit information; all records produced, documents transmitted, and written comments are stored in the computer; a form of electronic mail.

CONFERENCE. A formal meeting of a group of people with a common purpose; may be company-sponsored or association-sponsored meetings.

ELECTRONIC BLACKBOARD. A device used with teleconferences to display business graphics on a pressure-sensitive blackboard and transmit these visuals to other meeting locations.

FORMAL MEETING. A meeting that is planned in advance, usually held in a conference room or special meeting room, with a prepared agenda.

INCIDENTAL MOTION. Motion that arises from pending question; may be introduced at any time and must be decided before the question to which it is incidental is decided.

INFORMAL MEETING. A meeting with a small number of people (two to four) to discuss a particular business matter; a specific business matter has brought these people together for a meeting.

IN-HOUSE MEETING. A formal meeting that is held on company premises.

MAIN MOTION. A motion that states an item of business; has the lowest precedence in rank among all types of motions; must be seconded and is subject to discussion, debate, and amendment.

MINUTES. The official record of the meeting which summarizes the business that has been transacted, reports that have been presented, and any other significant events occurring at the meeting.

MOTION. The presentation of an item of business to the group.

PARLIAMENTARY PROCEDURE. The set of rules that govern the conduct of a formal meeting (*Robert's Rules of Order* is an example of such a set of rules).

PETITION. A formal statement, signed by individuals who are eligible to sign the statement, asking that some specific action be taken.

PRIVILEGED MOTION. A motion with the highest order of precedence which affects the comfort of the members of the group that is meeting.

QUORUM. The required number of voting members who must be present in order to transact business.

RESOLUTION. A formal statement of an organization's appreciation, congratulations, or sympathy.

STANDING COMMITTEE. A small group of members who are appointed for a definite term with specific objectives assigned for which the group is responsible during the term.

STORYBOARD. A frame-by-frame plan for the preparation of an audiovisual presentation; shows the description of the picture or illustration plus any narrative that will accompany the picture.

SUBSIDIARY MOTION. A motion that assists, modifies, or disposes of the main motion.

TELECONFERENCE. A meeting of several people, who may be in different geographical locations, that is held through telephone communications so that the individuals can speak with each other about matters of business.

TRANSPARENCY. An acetate sheet that contains an image burned or drawn on it that can be projected on a screen or wall.

UNCLASSIFIED MOTION. A motion that is appropriate but cannot be classified as a main motion, a subsidiary motion, an incidental motion, or a privileged motion.

VIDEOCONFERENCE. A formal meeting that is a type of teleconferencing; a meeting where participants who are located in different geographical locations are able to view one another on closed-circuit television (slow scan, freeze frames, or full motion) and talk in turns during the same time period.

A. Conferences

A *conference* is defined as a formal meeting of a group of people with a common purpose. Types of conferences include company-sponsored conferences and association-sponsored conventions. The two terms *conference* and *convention* are treated as synonymous terms in this context.

1. *Types of Conferences:* Conferences or conventions are sponsored by individual companies or by business or professional associations.

    a. *Company-sponsored conferences:* Conferences are sometimes sponsored by companies for the purpose of discussing timely topics or business events. Such a conference might be sponsored only for company personnel to bring them up to date on new products, services, or research developments within the industry.

    (1) *Location:* The conference may be held on the company premises or at a nearby hotel. Usually the company prefers to have the conference at or near the corporate headquarters so that it is easier to show displays of new products, work with company personnel, or conduct training sessions.

    (2) *Personnel to chair conference:* Depending upon what the basic purpose of the conference is, an executive within the company with responsibilities related to the conference may be appointed chairperson of the conference. A committee of company personnel would be appointed to assist in planning the event. Secretarial support is extremely important since there are many arrangements

that are necessary before, during, and after the conference.
- (3) *Travel to and from conference:* Since some of the participants may be coming from other parts of the country or world, travel arrangements will need to be coordinated carefully. If the conference is only for company personnel, the plan may be to obtain all travel reservations through the corporate travel department. If others from outside the company are invited to participate, it will still be important to know what their travel arrangements are in order that appropriate ground transportation can be provided. If travel expenses are to be paid, procedures for reimbursement should be included.
- (4) *Supportive services:* Consultation will be necessary with the reprographics or in-house printing department to be sure that program booklets, handout materials, and other materials to be printed will be able to be produced in house. In addition, an inquiry service might be established so that callers inquiring about the conference will receive all pertinent information from a secretary assigned this responsibility.

b. *Association-sponsored conventions:* Numerous annual conventions are sponsored by professional business associations primarily for the benefit of the members of the association.

EXAMPLE: Joe Hixson is the administrative manager for AJAX Company, and he is a member of the Administrative Management Society. In addition to participating in local chapter events, Joe attends the national convention each year, which is held in different locations throughout the country.

EXAMPLE: Barbara Canfield, an executive secretary, is an active member of Professional Secretaries International. This year she is serving as secretary of the local chapter, and in July she will be attending the PSI International Convention as a delegate.

- (1) *Location:* Conventions are usually held in hotels and civic centers where there will be adequate meeting room space, hotel rooms available, and accessibility to public transportation. Trade shows and exhibits are another feature of conventions that help participants become more up to date in their field.
- (2) *Personnel in charge of convention:* Such a convention is planned by a committee from the professional association sponsoring the convention. Normally a vice-president is in charge of programs and serves as the chair of the program planning committee. Many times there is a

Conferences and Meetings 163

local committee (from the city area where the convention will be held) assisting with local arrangements.

(a) If you are the secretary for an executive who is in charge of a professional convention, you will no doubt be involved in assisting with the arrangements for the convention.
(b) Correspondence about the convention and arrangements for attending will also be handled by you if your executive plans to attend a convention.

(3) *Travel to and from convention:* Executive travel to and from the convention will need to be handled through the travel department or the travel agency handling company business. The secretary who coordinates the travel arrangements with the agency will need to be sure that dates, times, flights, or other travel information are verified with business travelers to be sure they are correct.
(4) *Supportive services:* A file folder should be established for any materials relating to the convention. If the executive is in charge of the convention, then a series of folders will need to be prepared to house all of the correspondence and related materials that will accumulate in the planning stages.

2. *Planning a Convention:* Attending a convention as a participant is relatively easy, but planning a convention for others to attend is very difficult and requires long hours of detailed preparation. There are procedures before, during, and after the convention that are vital to the success of the convention.

a. *Before the convention:* Typical activities that need to be accomplished in the preconvention time period include the following:

(1) Selecting the site for the convention, if that has not already been done by the association.
(2) Establishing the convention budget.
(3) Reserving adequate meeting-room space in hotel or convention center, and making sure that appropriate audiovisual equipment will be available.
(4) Meeting with the Convention Services Manager of the hotel or convention center to review arrangements for the convention.
(5) Making preliminary meal arrangements with hotel or convention center.
(6) Preparing preregistration materials to mail out to participants, including sample program, registration information, and fee schedule.

(7) Contacting convention speakers by telephone and letter confirming speaking arrangements.
(8) Contacting exhibitors for the trade show, if there is one scheduled.
(9) Preparing a printed convention program and handbook.
(10) Preparing publicity for local newspapers, radio, and television coverage.
(11) Arranging special tours for spouses and convention participants.
(12) Reserving a block of hotel rooms for convention participants.
(13) Arranging hospitality rooms and other courtesies for the participants.
(14) Arranging for audiovisual or video equipment and technicians for recording or taping any of the convention sessions.
(15) Contacting the agents for any special entertainment that will be scheduled during the convention and arranging for performances.
(16) Arranging ground transportation (buses, limousines) to transport participants from airport to hotel or convention site.

b. *During the convention:*

(1) Setting up and supervising the convention registration desk.
(2) Checking in all exhibitors and issuing exhibit spaces assigned.
(3) Handing out special packets of materials to guest speakers as they arrive.
(4) Making arrangements for speakers to be met at the airport and transported to the convention site.
(5) Setting up information desk for distributing information about tours, community, restaurants, etc.
(6) Checking to see that audio-visual equipment is in place prior to each convention session.
(7) Presenting special folders to hosts, hostesses, recorders for the various convention sessions.
(8) Finalizing number of people attending each meal function.

c. *After the convention:*

(1) Preparing checks for honorariums and expenses for guest speakers.
(2) Preparing a financial statement for the entire convention.
(3) Sending thank-you letters to all of the speakers, hotel

Conferences and Meetings 165

  and/or convention personnel, and participants (if the number of participants is rather small).

(4) Sending thank-you letters/memos to all who assisted with the convention: registration workers, hosts, hostesses, chairs for sessions, recorders, etc.

(5) Monitoring the publication of the proceedings of the convention if this is the usual procedure for this particular association.

(6) Creating a reference file of all procedures used and suggestions for the next convention.

The items listed under A-2-a, A-2-b, and A-2-c are not listed in any particular order of priority. Within each category, priorities would need to be established and deadlines set for the activities required when actually planning and carrying through a convention program.

B. Meetings

It is estimated that managers spend approximately one-third of their time in meetings each week and that many organizations spend up to 15 percent of their personnel budgets directly on meetings. With technology and change enveloping the office, it has become even more important in recent years that people communicate with each other in small and large groups in order to meet the objectives of the organization. A large number of businesses or other organizations could not survive without meetings.

1. *Planning and Organizing Meetings:* Meetings tend to be organized either as *informal meetings* or as *formal meetings*.

   a. *Informal meetings:* Usually an informal meeting involves an informal discussion by a small number of people (two to four) to discuss a particular business matter. Normally, a specific business matter has brought these people together for the meeting. The meeting is scheduled in one person's office or in a small conference room.

   (1) *Committee meeting:* The individuals who are meeting may be members of a committee and must meet to further the work of the committee.

   EXAMPLE: The Computer Advisory Committee will meet on Thursday from 9 to 11 A.M. to discuss the utilization of the computer in the Office Services Department.

   (a) *Standing committee*: Members of a standing committee are appointed for a definite term, for example, one year, two years. The standing committee has definite objectives assigned for which it is responsible during the term.

EXAMPLE: Betty serves on the Program Committee for the Maywood Business Women's Association. As a member of this committee, she is working with the other three members to establish a schedule of programs for the monthly meetings for this year.

(b) *Ad hoc committee:* An ad hoc committee is formed to investigate a particular event or problem that has occurred within the organization. The committee has a temporary appointment and will serve until a report is presented back to the standing committee or management.

EXAMPLE: The ABC Company has a standing committee, the Computer Selection Committee, whose primary goal is to select a new computer system for the company. An ad hoc committee has been formed that will investigate how each of four departments plans to use computers and various software programs in their operations. The ad hoc committee will then report back to the Computer Selections Committee.

(2) *Office meeting:* Sometimes problems arise in the day-to-day operation of an office that require two or three people to meet to discuss the problems. A department manager may find it necessary or helpful to ask two or three employees to come into his/her office to discuss some business matter.

b. *Formal meetings:* A more formal meeting would definitely have to be planned in advance so that the participants in the meeting would be aware of the meeting and know the agenda items that would be covered at the meeting. Formal meetings are usually held in conference rooms or special meeting rooms. All types of conferencing—teleconference, videoconference, or computer conference—can be arranged through a national or an international communications network, depending upon the needs of the organization. This makes it possible for people who are separated by great distances to participate in business matters.

(1) *In-house meeting:* A formal meeting might be held in-house on company premises. A meeting or conference room would be reserved, and all people who need to attend would be notified well in advance. The purpose of the meeting would be of a more formal nature, too.

Conferences and Meetings

EXAMPLE: *The Board of Directors is planning to hold its next meeting on Wednesday, May 15, at 3 P.M. in the Board Room.*

EXAMPLE: *The XYZ Corporation is inviting all of the regional marketing representatives to attend a one-day sales meeting at the corporate headquarters on April 4.*

The in-house meeting may be for company personnel only, or it may be for outside professionals, depending upon the purpose of the meeting.

EXAMPLE: *The XYZ Corporation is planning to have a one-day Office Automation seminar for administrative office managers from the northern Ohio region. The purpose is to demonstrate the office automation systems that XYZ Corporation is presently marketing.*

(2) *Teleconference:* A formal teleconference might be set up so that several business executives from different geographical locations can "meet" through telephone communications. Instead of having to travel to a particular site for the meeting, the conferees can "meet" by speaking with the others directly from their own offices. *Audioconference* is another term for teleconference.

EXAMPLE: *Jan Stevens made an appointment with George Richards (New York office), Nancy Whitley (Atlanta office), and Bernard Clifton (San Francisco office) for a teleconference on Monday morning at 10 A.M. She wants to share with them some marketing strategies that the company is trying to promote. She will be able to communicate with the telephone network and an electronic blackboard so that the statistics and graphics she presents from her own location will be transmitted to each of the other three locations. In this way the other participants will find it easier to follow the discussion.*

(3) *Videoconference:* Another type of formal conference is the videoconference, which is really an extension of teleconferencing. Again, an appointment must be set up for the scheduled date and time. Participants are able to view each other on closed-circuit television. Slow scan (freeze frames) as well as full-motion video is possible. The videoconference closely approximates a face-to-face conference. Hard copies of visuals and data are transmitted via intelligent copiers or facsimile equipment.

(4) *Computer conference:* Participants in a computer conference use computer terminals to transmit information to

other members of the group. The response may be simultaneous or on a delayed basis, so participants do not have to participate with each other at the same time. Information or messages may be stored for later responses. All records produced, documents transmitted, and written comments are stored in the computer. This type of conference, as a form of electronic mail, may be accomplished on a national or international network.

(5) *Out-of-town meeting:* Business travel to out-of-town meetings is very common for business executives. If the corporation has numerous branch offices, this is one way for the executive to monitor business operations at the different branches. If the scheduling for the meeting has to come from the executive's office, the secretary will need to be sure that all reservations for the travel and the meeting are arranged.

EXAMPLE: George White, Vice President for Marketing, just told Brenda, his executive secretary, that he will be traveling to Montreal on June 3 and 4 to meet with the marketing people in the Canadian region. Brenda will need to make whatever travel, hotel, and meeting room reservations that will be necessary.

2. *Arranging Meetings:* Informal and formal meetings will run smoothly only if all of the necessary arrangements for the meetings are completed ahead of time. The busy executive has no time to worry at the last moment about what room is reserved, where the handouts are, or whether people were notified.

   a. *Selecting convenient date and time:* The first thing to do is to select a date and time that is convenient for those people who must attend. This may mean that you will need to check with each person to find out alternative times so that, when each person has responded, the best possible time can be chosen. It will no doubt be quicker to select a time if you are able to consult each person's calendar through an electronic calendaring system, find out the best possible time, and immediately schedule the meeting.

   b. *Notifying participants of meeting date/time:* Of course, no meeting can take place without participants being present so each one needs to be notified of the meeting date, time, and location.

   (1) *Telephone call:* The secretary should telephone each participant to let him or her know as soon as possible the meeting date, time, and place and to ask them to put this on their calendars immediately. Through the voice mail network, if one is available, the secretary will be able to leave a complete message for each participant.

(2) *Electronic mail:* If a computer network is available, a memorandum can be transmitted to each participant to let him or her know the meeting date, time, and place and to ask them to put this meeting on their calendars immediately.

(3) *Follow-up letter:* A written reminder of the meeting and a confirmation of the date, time, and location should follow. It is helpful to the participants if they also know what the agenda is ahead of time.

(4) *Telephone follow-up:* If no response is received from the participant, the secretary should follow up by telephone to see if the individual plans to attend the meeting.

c. *Notifying executive of those attending:* Once you have responses from all who should attend the meeting, let your executive know exactly who will be attending. This is a double check to be sure that you have not forgotten to invite someone.

d. *Preparing materials for meeting:* Copies of materials to be distributed during the meeting should be prepared ahead of time.

e. *Preparing an agenda:* An *agenda* is a list of items of business to be discussed or presented during the meeting. Copies of the agenda should be prepared so that they are available at the beginning of the meeting. Sometimes copies of the agenda will be sent out in advance. The usual order of business is as follows:

- Call to order by presiding officer
- Attendance
- Announcement of quorum
- Reading of minutes of previous meeting
- Approval of minutes
- Reports of officers
- Reports of standing committees
- Reports of special committees
- Old (or unfinished) business
- New business
- Appointment of committees
- Nominations and elections
- Date of next meeting
- Adjournment

See Figure 6-1 for a sample agenda.

f. *Taking notes at meeting:* If requested, the secretary should take notes during the meeting so that a complete set of minutes may be prepared. (If the executive is the secretary for the meeting, the executive's secretary may be called upon to take complete notes during the meeting.)

THE CHICAGO INFORMATION PROCESSING ASSOCIATION

Parker Hotel--Chicago Room
Wednesday, August 21, 199-

AGENDA

```
1.   Call to Order:  Denise Thomas, President
2.   Secretary's Report:  Minutes of July Meeting
3.   President's Report
4.   Treasurer's Report:  Thomas F. Whitney
5.   Standing Committee Reports:
     a.   Program Committee:  Eleanor Watson, Vice-President
     b.   Fundraising Committee:  Suzanne Weir, Chair
6.   Old Business
7.   New Business:
     a.   Theme for Next Year's Information Processing
          Conference
     b.   Representation at the International Convention
8.   Adjournment
```

Figure 6-1
Sample Agenda

    g. *Noting important dates on executive's calendar:* After the meeting is over, the secretary should scan through the notes from the meeting to see if important dates for future meetings were mentioned. These dates should be recorded on the appropriate office calendars.

    h. *Getting room ready for next meeting:* After the meeting is over, the meeting room should be left in proper order for any other meetings which follow. All extra handout materials should be collected.

    i. *Transcribing notes:* It is best to transcribe meeting notes immediately so that no important details resulting from the meeting will be forgotten or ignored.

    j. *Sending minutes or meeting report:* After the minutes or meeting report have been prepared, the secretary should send one copy to each of the participants for approval. *Minutes* are a record of the proceedings of a meeting. (See Section B-2-f in this chapter.)

3. *Conducting Meetings:* Executives spend at least one-third of their working time in meetings, either as participants or as the chairpersons of the meetings. In addition to planning and organizing meetings, it is vital that the meetings be conducted in an expeditious manner. The meeting time should be used effectively so that each participant feels that the order of business is handled efficiently. The use of parliamentary procedure establishes a definite routine for conducting a meeting in an efficient and orderly manner.

    a. *Using meeting time effectively:* There are many techniques that can be used to permit meeting time to be used as effectively as possible. Here are only a few of the more important ones:

(1) *Time frame for meeting:* A definite time frame should be established for the meeting when it is scheduled so that participants know the amount of time to plan for. This time frame can be announced to the participants ahead of time so they know how much time must be devoted to the meeting.

EXAMPLE: The monthly staff meeting is always scheduled for Wednesday afternoon from 1:00 to 2:30 P.M. Having this time already scheduled on calendars means that those who participate will not allow any other conflicts during this time frame.

(2) *Distribution of agenda and handout material:* If possible, the agenda and supportive handout material should be distributed at least one day prior to the meeting to give people sufficient time to read these materials. Too often people arrive at a meeting and are given a "stack" of materials that take time to look through, and there is not sufficient time at the meeting to do this expeditiously.

(3) *Promptness in starting meeting:* People appreciate starting meetings on time. If the meeting is scheduled for 9:00 A.M., then it should start at 9:00 A.M. As a general rule, people do not expect a meeting to start on time; but if starting on time becomes the general rule, people will be more prompt in getting to the meeting.

(4) *Agenda items:* An agenda helps to organize the order of business for the meeting and to keep the participants on target. If an item is not on the agenda, it should not be discussed at this meeting.

   (a) Routine items on the agenda, for example, reading of secretary's minutes and treasurer's report, should be handled quickly since there will usually be minor revisions in wording and few questions asked.

   (b) Taking care of routine items quickly will leave more time to present and discuss other agenda items which are the primary reason for the meeting.

(5) *Summary of important points:* During the meeting the chairperson should act as a facilitator, taking the time to summarize key points that are made so that everyone understands the importance or meaning of particular action taken.

(6) *Closing the meeting:* When the business itemized on the agenda has been acted upon, the meeting should be adjourned promptly. The meeting might be scheduled for two hours, but if the business can be taken care of in less time, people will appreciate having those extra few minutes to return to other work that needs to be handled.

b. *Using proper parliamentary procedures:* Parliamentary procedure is a necessary part of conducting a formal meeting because its use enables the meeting to be conducted in an efficient and orderly manner. Some have defined parliamentary law as "common sense used in a gracious manner." *Robert's Rules of Order* (first published in 1876) has been revised numerous times over the past 100 years and still is the basis for acceptable parliamentary procedure followed in formal meetings. It is the responsibility of the parliamentarian (someone appointed to be present at the meeting) to be sure that the meeting is conducted according to these rules. A copy should be on hand for reference.

   (1) *Basic principles of parliamentary procedure:* In order for a group of people to arrive at group decisions in an efficient and orderly manner, the basic principles of parliamentary procedure must be followed:

   (a) Courtesy and justice must be accorded to all who are participating in the meeting.
   (b) Only one topic is considered at one time. (This is the reason that an agenda is so important at a meeting.)
   (c) The minority must be heard; every person has an equal opportunity to be heard.
   (d) The majority will prevail; a majority vote will result in a motion passed.

   (2) *Conducting the meeting with parliamentary procedure:* Each matter of business to be presented during the meeting for action by the group must be introduced to the group in the form of a *motion* made by one group member who has secured the floor by being recognized by the chairperson for the meeting. The motion must receive a *second* by another person.

   (a) *Types of motions:* Items of business are presented, one by one, to the group in the form of *motions*. Once a motion has been made and seconded, the item can be discussed thoroughly. There are five different types of motions: main motions, subsidiary motions, incidental motions, privileged motions, and unclassified motions.

   - *Main motions:* A main motion is a motion that states an item of business. The main motion has the lowest precedence in rank among all types of motions. The main motion must be seconded and is subject to discussion, debate, and amendment. The motion may be reconsidered or have a subsidiary motion attached to it, and the motion needs a majority vote to pass.

EXAMPLE:
George: "I move that we accept the report of the Special Committee on Human Resource Development."
Rita: "I second the motion."

- *Subsidiary motions:* A subsidiary motion may assist, modify, or dispose of the main motion. A subsidiary motion supersedes the main motion and must be acted upon before the group returns to the main motion. The following subsidiary motions may be applied:

  To table motion (to lay aside until later).
  To call for the vote.
  To refer the motion to committee for further consideration.
  To amend a main motion.
  To postpone indefinitely action on a motion.

- *Incidental motions:* Incidental motions are motions that arise from pending questions. They may be introduced at any time and must be decided before the question to which they are incidental is decided. Here are the incidental motions that may be used:

  To suspend a rule temporarily.
  To close nominations.
  To reopen nominations.
  To withdraw or modify a motion.
  To rise to a point of order.
  To appeal from decision of the chair.

- *Privileged motions:* Privileged motions are called convenience motions since they affect the comfort of the members of the group that is meeting. These motions have the highest order of precedence. The most typical privileged motions include:

  To call for orders of the day.
  Questions of privilege: to bring up an urgent matter such as noise, discomfort, etc.
  To take a recess.
  To adjourn.
  To set next meeting time.

- *Unclassified motions:* Other motions that are appropriate but cannot be classified in the other four categories include the following:

To take motion from table.
To reconsider.
To rescind decision on a motion.

(b) *Quorum:* The bylaws of the organization usually specify the number of voting members who must be present in order to transact business at a meeting of the organization. The required number of voting members who must be present in order to transact business is called a *quorum.*

4. *Preparing and Using Visual Aids:* Presentations of factual information at meetings are greatly enhanced by the use of visuals to complement the verbal or written presentation. Some typical kinds of visuals representing other types of media than paper are transparencies and slides.

   a. *Overhead transparencies:* A *transparency* is an acetate sheet that contains an image burned or drawn on it that can be projected on a screen or wall. Preparing typed or drawn copy for use in making an overhead transparency requires you to use carbon-based materials. There are many different kinds of transparencies you can make: colored background with white or black letters/images; clear background with black/colored images; shaded transparencies; or multiple-part transparencies.

      (1) *Preparing typewritten or drawn copy:* Transparencies are prepared by using a thermographic copier (see *Module VI*, Chapter 6, Reprographics Technology). This means that the original copy will be run through a copier with a special sheet of transparency acetate on top so that the original image can be burned through the transparency.

         (a) If you are typing the copy, be sure to use a Selectric typewriter with the lift-off feature so that you can correct errors as you go along. Errors must be removed entirely from the page, not covered up, because of the burning process.
         (b) If a typing error is made, it must be corrected either by lifting off, if the typewriter has that feature, or by erasing with a typewriting eraser. The error cannot be covered up with correction fluid or cover-up correction paper. The image would look like a strikeover on the transparency.
         (c) The best element to use in the typing process is an Orator or Orator Presenter element. This is a 10-pitch element that appears very large on the page and is much easier to read from a distance during

the presentation. It is very important to have a *readable copy* on the screen in a meeting.

(d) All copy should be prepared on white bond paper in the format desired.

(e) All typed or drawn copy should be proofread very carefully so that any errors will be found *before* the transparency is prepared. The cost of transparency material is high (as much as 40 cents per sheet), and a misspelled word can result in a transparency being discarded.

(f) To include a tracing or drawing as a part of the copy, use a pencil or special transparency marker to do the actual drawing. Remember that everything you want reproduced must be prepared *only* with carbon-based material (film ribbon, pencil, special pen).

(g) If it is necessary to paste up a page with both illustrated material and text, prepare a photocopy of the material (this photocopy is carbon based) and make the transparency from the photocopy.

(h) Copy may also have been prepared on the computer with graphics software and printed on a laser printer. Type styles and typefaces can be varied on the same illustration by inserting appropriate commands into the document prior to printing.

(2) *Preparing the overhead transparency:* The way the material is burned on the transparency acetate will depend on the type of acetate that is being used. Transparencies may be purchased that have colored background and either white or black letters and images will be burned into the transparencies.

(a) Shaded transparencies may be prepared by either shading in the areas with a felt-tip marker (permanent or water based, depending on the permanency desired) or with acetate shading material that can be cut to size and attached to the transparency.

(b) Multiple-part transparencies are often called progressive transparencies. This means that one transparency will be used to illustrate several steps in a process. Each time the speaker moves to the next step another portion of the transparency can be flipped over as an "overlay" for the parts already presented.

(c) Always turn the dial on the thermographic copier to the right location for the making of the transparencies. Usually there is a special mark for this location. Once the original copy (with the transparency acetate sheet) has been run through the copier, the transparency is ready for projection.

(d) Cardboard frames are available to use in framing each transparency. These frames make it easier for a speaker to handle the transparencies, and it is possible to mark on each frame an appropriate label describing what is displayed.

Transparencies may be prepared on a number of different types of copiers. Acetate sheets are placed in the paper carrier, just as bond paper is, and run through the copier in the same way. The image is burned into the acetate, creating the reproduction of the text or drawing.

b. *35mm slides:* Many speakers prefer to use photographic slides for presentations. Some companies have photographers whose job it is to prepare slides and other photographs for company personnel. The user's responsibility becomes one of planning the content, ordering the preparation of the slides, and arranging the slides in sequence when they are ready.

(1) *Preparing copy for slides:* A *storyboard* is a frame-by-frame plan for the preparation of an audio-visual presentation on specially designed sheets that show the description of the picture or illustration plus any narrative that will accompany the slide. The storyboard is prepared to show exactly what slides are needed before any photography or art work is undertaken. In this way the correct sequence of the presentation can be entirely planned out so that the slides can be photographed in the correct sequence.

(a) The storyboard gives a brief description of each slide desired—exactly what features/events should be photographed.

(b) The storyboard contains the written script that will accompany each slide in the presentation. This script is especially helpful when a cassette tape or a "canned" presentation will be prepared to accompany the slide series.

(2) *Previewing slides:* Once the slides are processed, the user should preview the slides, comparing them with the prepared script, to see if there are any discrepancies.

EXAMPLE: A particularly useful device in previewing slides is the multiple-slide lighted tray in which a large number of slides can be placed. They can be moved around, and the sequence changed, until the final order of presentation is agreed upon.

c. *Electronic blackboards:* A relatively new way of displaying business graphics is the electronic blackboard, a device used with teleconferences to transmit visuals to other locations. The electronic blackboard consists of a pressure-sensitive blackboard, microphone, and speaker at one location and a television monitor, microphone, and speaker at a second location (there may be additional locations as well). As someone writes on the blackboard, the coordinates are picked up electronically and transmitted to the monitor at the other location(s) where an image of the blackboard is displayed.

5. *Preparing Resolutions and Petitions:* Formal statements of an organization's appreciation, congratulations, or sympathy may be expressed as a *resolution*. The resolution is a formal expression from an entire group. A *petition* is a formal statement of reasons for introducing and asking for a specific action to be granted. The petition is a formal expression from the individuals who sign the petition.

   a. *Resolution:* As stated above, the resolution is a formal statement from an entire group. Preparation of the resolution will require the following steps:

   (1) *Advance preparation:* The resolution must be prepared in advance by a resolutions committee appointed for that purpose. Then the resolution must be reviewed by the presiding officer of the group (chairperson or president) or by the executive board or committee.
   (2) *Presentation of resolution:* The resolution may be presented orally or in writing at the meeting. The most effective way of presenting such an expression is in writing, however.
   (3) *Final form:* After the meeting, the secretary must prepare the resolution in final form and have it signed and included as a part of the official proceedings of the meeting. Since the language used in the resolution is formal, the rationale for the resolution is introduced with the word WHEREAS preceding each reason given. The final paragraphs that state the official action to be taken are introduced by the word RESOLVED or, if there is more than one action taken, RESOLVED FURTHER (typed in all capitals and followed by a comma and a capital letter). See Figure 6-2 for an example of a typewritten resolution.

   b. *Petition:* A petition is a formal statement, signed by individuals who are eligible to sign the petition, asking that some specific action be taken. The petition is a formal expression only from the individuals who sign the petition.

RESOLUTION

Adopted November 28, 199-

WHEREAS, Georgia L. Stratton has been a member of Kishwaukee Chapter, Professional Secretaries International, for fifteen years, and

WHEREAS, Ms. Stratton has contributed significantly to the professional activities of the Chapter, having served as Secretary, First Vice-President, and President, and

WHEREAS, Ms. Stratton is retiring from her position as Executive Secretary for Dr. Gerald R. Kuhlson, Vice-President for Field Operations, Rockville Manufacturing Company, where she has been employed for twenty-five years, therefore be it

RESOLVED, That the members of Kishwaukee Chapter, Professional Secretaries International, go on record as expressing their sincere appreciation of Georgia L. Stratton's many services to the Chapter; and be it

RESOLVED FURTHER, That the members of Kishwaukee Chapter sincerely congratulate Georgia L. Stratton on her retirement from the secretarial profession and wish her happiness in her retirement years.

_____   _____
Secretary   President

Figure 6-2
Sample Resolution

(1) *Advance preparation:* The petition must be prepared in advance with an adequate number of signature lines. Next, the petition needs to be circulated so that the required number of signatures may be obtained.

(2) *Presentation:* Once the required number of signatures has been obtained, the petition may be presented orally and in writing at the meeting. The written petition, with signatures affixed, is the official document. Further action by the group will be discussed at the meeting.

6. *Preparing Minutes of Meetings:* The minutes of a meeting are the official report of the meeting. The purpose of *minutes* is to summarize the business that has been transacted, reports that have been given, and any other significant events occurring at the meeting.

   a. *Preliminary writing:* The secretary should transcribe the notes from the meeting in the format desired by the organization. (See Chapter 11, Preparing Communications in Final Format, Section F-1, for discussion of format to be used for preparing minutes.) Using the agenda as a guide is an excellent idea, because the agenda serves as an outline of the items discussed at the meeting. Complete information, including motions, committee reports, and announcements, must be included in the minutes.

      b. *Approval by presiding officer:* The preliminary draft of the minutes should be approved by the presiding officer before it is finalized and duplicated for distribution to the other members of the executive board or committee.

      c. *Distribution of minutes:* The minutes need to be distributed at the next meeting for approval. The agenda includes the approval of the secretary's minutes as one of the first items of business.

Minutes are the official record of the meeting. Therefore, the secretary must exhibit a very professional attitude toward the accurate preparation of the minutes so that the official proceedings are correctly filed.

Chapter 6: Review Questions

Part A: Multiple-Choice Questions

DIRECTIONS: Select the best answer from the four alternatives. Write your answer in the blank to the left of the number.

_____ 1. With technology resulting in organizational change within the office, there will be

    a. less emphasis on small- or large-group communication in the firm and more emphasis on individual participation.
    b. more emphasis on small- or large-group communication in the firm and less emphasis on individual participation.
    c. more formal meetings rather than informal meetings within the organization.
    d. more informal meetings rather than formal meetings within the organization.

_____ 2. Which of the following committees established by the board of directors of a professional association would be categorized as a standing committee?

    a. Next year's program committee
    b. Computer selection committee
    c. Membership committee chair
    d. Committee liaison for state curriculum committee

_____ 3. A committee formed to investigate a specific problem or event that has occurred within the organization is known as

    a. a standing committee.
    b. a status committee.
    c. an ad hoc committee.
    d. an advisory committee.

_____ 4. A meeting of ABC Company's Board of Directors would be categorized as

    a. an informal meeting.
    b. a formal meeting.
    c. an advisory meeting.
    d. a stockholders' meeting.

5. A formal meeting set up so that people located in different parts of the country can use telephone communications to meet is called

   a. a teleconference.
   b. a professional conference.
   c. a computer conference.
   d. a video conference.

6. A list of items of business to be discussed during a meeting is called

   a. a quorum.
   b. minutes of the meeting.
   c. a motion.
   d. an agenda.

7. One of the basic principles of parliamentary procedure is that

   a. only one topic can be considered at one time.
   b. the majority must be heard.
   c. the minority will prevail.
   d. all topics must be covered at the meeting.

8. Once a motion has been made and seconded

   a. a vote may immediately be requested by the chair of the meeting.
   b. the motion is now ready for discussion, debate, or amendment.
   c. a recess may be called.
   d. only the voting members will be allowed to vote.

9. Which of the following motions is a main motion?

   a. "I move to amend the motion that we hold the conference at the Sea Pines Resort to include the dates, July 18 and 19."
   b. "I move that we close nominations for the office of president."
   c. "I move that we postpone action on this motion until our next meeting."
   d. "I move that we approve the minutes as presented."

10. To table a motion means to

    a. put it aside until a later meeting.
    b. refer the item to a committee for further examination.
    c. postpone action on the motion indefinitely.
    d. discuss the motion.

Conferences and Meetings

_____ **11.** A motion to take a recess is called

   a. an incidental motion.
   b. a subsidiary motion.
   c. a privileged motion.
   d. a main motion.

_____ **12.** The required number of voting members who must be present in order to transact business at a meeting is called

   a. a majority.
   b. an agenda.
   c. ex-officio members.
   d. a quorum.

_____ **13.** Many executives are involved in making presentations before professional groups. Which of the following represents the most economical way of preparing visuals of typewritten material to show to a group?

   a. Photographic slides
   b. Transparencies
   c. Electronic blackboard
   d. Computer graphics

_____ **14.** The first step in planning a slide presentation is to

   a. record a script onto a cassette tape.
   b. preview the slides and compare them to the script.
   c. prepare a description of each slide needed for the program.
   d. sequence the slides according to the script.

_____ **15.** A record of the proceedings of a meeting usually duplicated for the members is called

   a. a quorum.
   b. an agenda.
   c. minutes of the meeting.
   d. a motion.

Part B: Matching Sets

Matching Set 1

Match each of the planning functions (A-C) with the appropriate convention activities (16-22). Write the letter of your answer in the blank to the left of each number.

Planning Functions

    A. Before the Convention
    B. During the Convention
    C. Following the Convention

ACTIVITIES

_____ 16. Supervise the convention registration desk.

_____ 17. Prepare honorariums for speakers.

_____ 18. Establish convention budget.

_____ 19. Monitor publication of convention proceedings.

_____ 20. Place audiovisual equipment in rooms where needed for sessions.

_____ 21. Prepare preregistration materials.

_____ 22. Create a reference file for the next convention.

Part C: Problem Situations

DIRECTIONS: For each of the questions relating to the following problem situations, select the best answer from the four alternatives. Write the letter of your answer in the blank to the left of the number.

Problem 1

Marian Smythe, your office manager, tells you that she will be attending the convention of the American Business Communications Association to be held at the Hilton Hotel in Phoenix next month.

_____ 23. Which of the following should you proceed to do right now?

    a. Complete travel authorization forms for Marian to sign.
    b. Arrange for hotel and air reservations.
    c. Complete and send in the convention preregistration forms.
    d. All of the above.

Conferences and Meetings

Problem 2

You are the executive secretary for Tom Sullivan, who is the program chair for this year's Administrative Management Society Seminar on Office Automation.

_____   24. Before the conference, you should

   a. set up the conference registration desk.
   b. prepare checks for honorariums and expenses for guest speakers.
   c. reserve adequate meeting-room space with audiovisual equipment needed.
   d. check in all exhibitors and issue exhibit spaces previously assigned.

Problem 3

Your executive has just told you that a special meeting of the Executive Committee must be scheduled for next Monday afternoon at 2 P.M.

_____   25. Which of the following items is the *first* thing you should do?

   a. Send a memo to each member of the committee notifying each one of the meeting.
   b. Telephone each member of the committee telling each one of the meeting.
   c. Review materials needed for the meeting with your executive.
   d. Schedule the conference room for the meeting.

Chapter 6: Solutions

Part A: Multiple-Choice Questions

	Answer	Refer to Chapter Section
1.	(b)	[B] There will be more emphasis on group communications in business decisions affected by technology.
2.	(a)	[B-1-a(1)(a)] A standing committee is appointed to achieve definite objectives for which it is responsible. A standing committee also serves a definite term of office.
3.	(c)	[B-1-a(1)(b)] An ad hoc committee is formed as a result of some special event or happening within the organization. Its work will terminate when the problem is solved.
4.	(b)	[B-1-b(1)] A formal meeting is one that is planned in advance and has a prepared agenda. A board of directors meeting would be such a meeting.
5.	(a)	[B-1-b(2)] A teleconference makes use of networked telephone systems so that three or more people can talk with each other at the scheduled time. Teleconferencing is just like scheduling a business appointment except the participants are located in different geographic areas and talk together by telephone.
6.	(d)	[B-2-e] An agenda is prepared so that there is a definite order of business followed at the meeting.
7.	(a)	[B-3-b(1)] In parliamentary procedure the minority as well as the majority has a right to be heard. Only one topic is considered at a time as the group moves through the agenda items.
8.	(b)	[B-3-b(2)(a)] No discussion, debate, or amending can take place until a motion has been made and seconded.
9.	(d)	[B-3-b(2)(a)] A main motion is a motion that states an item of business. Answer (a) is a subsidiary motion, answer (b) is an incidental motion, and answer (c) is a privileged motion.
10.	(a)	[B-3-b(2)(a)] A motion to table is a subsidiary motion.
11.	(c)	[B-3-b(2)(a)] A privileged motion is also called a motion of convenience, affecting the comfort of the participants.
12.	(d)	[B-3-b(2)(b)] The number of people constituting a quorum has been previously determined by the group and can be found in the organization's bylaws.
13.	(b)	[B-4-a] Transparencies are especially helpful in creating meaningful visuals of material for presentation to a group.
14.	(c)	[B-4-b(1)] The initial step is to plan the slides that will be needed for the program.
15.	(c)	[B-6] Minutes provide a summary of the matters of business transacted at the meeting.

Part B: Matching Sets

Matching Set 1

16.	(B)	[A-2-b(1)]
17.	(C)	[A-2-c(1)]
18.	(A)	[A-2-a(2)]
19.	(C)	[A-2-c(5)]
20.	(B)	[A-2-b(6)]
21.	(A)	[A-2-a(6)]
22.	(C)	[A-2-c(6)]

Part C: Problem Situations

23. (d) [A] All of the procedures mentioned need to be taken care of now.

24. (c) [A-2-a(3)] Adequate meeting-room space must be reserved prior to the conference.

25. (b) [B-2-b(1)] You should notify the committee members before making any other arrangements for the meeting. It may be that some of the committee members could not come at that particular time and want the meeting time changed. Once the meeting time and date are established, meeting-room arrangements should be made.

CHAPTER 7

Reprographics Management

OVERVIEW

Reprographics is the office system with primary responsibility for preparing copies of documents needed during the operation of the organization. Some reprographics processes, such as copying, enable the operator to make only one copy as needed, while others are more complex, permitting the rapid reproduction of hundreds or thousands of recorded images.

Reprographics processes may be divided into copying, duplicating, phototypesetting and composition, desktop publishing, imaging, and finishing processes (see *Module VI, Office Technology*). The management of these reprographics processes requires that the reprographics needs of the organization be studied in order to see the feasibility of specific procedures within the organization. Many reprographics processes are centralized within firms because of the high cost involved—personnel costs as well as equipment costs. Although many production jobs are handled through in-house reprographics services, some custom work may be handled by commercial printing firms.

Above all, analyzing the costs involved in reprographics processes is very important and crucial to increasing the effectiveness of the services offered. Attention needs to be given to the selection of appropriate equipment, matching the production needs with the process, and establishing operations procedures and control.

DEFINITION OF TERMS

AUDITRON. A device that controls use of a convenience copier through the use of a plastic card, key, or other insert device to activate the copier.

AUTHORIZATION. The procedure implemented that permits only certain personnel to use the reprographics equipment.

CENTRALIZED CONTROL. The organizational pattern used to locate reprographics operations in one physical location in the organization under the direction of one manager.

COMMERCIAL PRINTING FIRM. An outside business organization that provides services such as artwork, graphic design, or special printing requirements through contracts with the organization.

COPY QUALITY. An examination of the appearance of the copy produced to be sure that it has been prepared accurately and according to instructions.

COPYRIGHT LAWS. Legislation that has been enacted to prohibit making copies of copyrighted material without the written permission of the publisher.

DECENTRALIZED CONTROL. The organizational pattern used to locate reprographics operations within the various departments where they are utilized; usually under the direction and supervision of the department manager.

IN-HOUSE REPROGRAPHICS SERVICES. Those duplicating and printing services that are provided within the organization by specialized personnel trained to perform these functions.

PROCEDURES. Steps used to complete a given office task and governed by operations controls.

REPROGRAPHICS. The office system with primary responsibility for making copies of documents needed during the operation of the business.

A. Determining Reprographic Needs

Before decisions are made as to the type of reprographics service needed for the in-house operation, the copying and duplicating requirements of the organization must be examined carefully. The nature and quantity of the materials to be copied and duplicated will be the basis of this needs assessment. The following factors must be considered in determining reprographic needs.

1. *Original Documents:* The types of business forms, reports, correspondence, or other documents that will need to be copied or reproduced are a primary concern. Specific characteristics of these documents that require special attention include text, drawings, photographs, halftones, and boxes.
2. *Production Requirements:* Special production requirements will also influence decisions relating to reprographics services. Such requirements as the use of color, reduction, enlargement, and paper stock available are important considerations when reprographics services are examined.
3. *Copies Needed:* The number of copies of each document used within the business must be determined as well as to whom the copies will be distributed; how copies will be prepared, stored, and retrieved; and the length of time a copy is retained.

4. *Quality Required for Copies:* Image sharpness, uniformity of duplicating, resistance to smudging, and frequency of duplicating specific documents help to determine the quality needed during particular processes.
5. *Turnaround Time:* The users need to provide estimates of the turnaround times that affect them on their jobs, while people performing reprographic functions need to estimate the time required for them to handle routine and custom jobs assigned to them.

B. **Organizing Reprographic Systems**

Reprographics systems are managed differently in small and large firms, depending on the organization of centralized or decentralized office support services within the organization. The size of the firm and its specific reprographic needs have a strong effect on the personnel needed to operate and manage reprographics systems. Monitoring controls are needed to move toward a cost-effective and efficient operation. A basic concern is whether the actual production can be handled efficiently in the in-house reprographics center as opposed to the commercial print shop.

1. *Decentralized vs. Centralized Control:* Decentralized operations take place in various locations throughout the organization, wherever the work needs to be done. Each department within the organization would have its own reprographics equipment and services. With centralization, an individual is usually assigned the overall responsibility for managing the reprographics operations which are typically located in a center with all departments having easy physical access to the services offered.

   a. *Advantages of decentralized control:* Organizing reprographics services with decentralized control means that each department would supervise and manage its own copying and duplicating functions. Some of the advantages of decentralized control include the following:

   (1) *Self-service:* Workers within the department are able to perform copying and duplicating functions as needed. Basic equipment would be available within the department.
   (2) *Flexibility:* Each department could establish its own policies and procedures in regard to what is copied or duplicated, when the equipment is to be used (during work hours), and how many copies may be produced.
   (3) *Quick access:* The amount of travel time to and from the copier, for example, would be reduced. Access to the equipment would be quick and easy since it is located within the department.

(4) *Turnaround time:* Individual office employees performing reprographics functions will be able to control turnaround time as needed since fewer people will be involved in the operation. Priorities can more easily be set within the department.

Of course, there may be disadvantages of decentralized control as well. Once certain types of office support services are departmentalized, it becomes more difficult to maintain organization-wide control over the use and maintenance of equipment. More supervision is no doubt necessary to be sure that *all* individuals using reprographics equipment know and understand basic operation.

b. *Advantages of centralized control:* If the reprographics operation is centralized, an administrative manager will typically be assigned to oversee the system. In addition, there may be at least one reprographics supervisor who manages the specific functions within the reprographics center itself. Here are some of the advantages of centralized control:

(1) *Specialized personnel:* High-quality copying and duplicating work will be accomplished through the use of specialized personnel for typesetting, composition, desktop publishing, layout and design, equipment operation, and photographic work required.
(2) *Equipment variety:* Because the work is centralized, duplicate equipment will not be necessary and a greater variety of reprographics equipment is possible because of the nonduplication. Perhaps the only reprographics equipment needed within the departments will be small copiers.
(3) *Flexibility:* With a centralized operation, there can be more flexibility in the kinds of production jobs accepted. With specialized personnel available to assist, a large variety of reprographics work can be done in-house.
(4) *Work scheduling:* Production jobs can be scheduled more easily in a centralized operation so that quality work will result. Lead time is required in order to be sure that the work gets done on time.
(5) *Productivity:* The objective for centralizing reprographics operations is to increase the productivity. A variety of equipment is available, with specialized personnel available to help, which should lead to increased productivity on the part of other office personnel.

Perhaps the most significant disadvantage is the fact that, once more people are involved in the production process, the work may take longer than anticipated. Some people do not allow enough lead time to permit a quality job to be done.

2. *In-House Reprographics Services vs. Commercial Printing:* Many organizations have initiated in-house reprographics services because of the need to control the copying, duplicating, and printing needs of the organization. For specialized custom work, commercial printing firms may be the best answer because of the expertise involved in designing and printing these types of jobs.

   a. *In-house services:* The types of duplicating needs vary from small organizations to large organizations. In small firms one copier and one duplicator may meet the particular needs of the firm. In large firms, however, it may be necessary to organize a centralized reprographics department to service all departments within the organization. Some of the specific applications for in-house services include:

      (1) *Forms:* All the forms used within the business may be printed in quantity to maintain a sufficient inventory.

      EXAMPLES: Letterhead stationery, envelopes, memorandum forms, order forms, estimates, sales slips, insurance policies, contracts, agreements, and other legal forms.

      (2) *Public relations materials:* Posters, company newsletters, and annual reports are typical kinds of public relations materials that the organization may need to have printed.

      (3) *Desktop publishing services:* With the relatively new capabilities of desktop publishing, the reprographic center can offer services that will convert word processing files created by secretaries and other administrative assistants into published materials. Such items as newsletters, brochures, and statistical information may be redesigned from word processing formats into desktop publishing formats, which can include illustrations, drawings, and columnar text.

      (3) *Miscellaneous items:* Other items that may be duplicated or printed in an in-house facility include business cards, internal recordkeeping forms (log forms, job request forms, production sheets), and special packaging needed for products.

   b. *Use of commercial services:* Some documents demand special attention because of artwork, graphic design, or printing requirements. It is sometimes to the company's advantage to contract the work to be designed and/or printed by an outside commercial printing service.

      EXAMPLES: Such production work might include brochures that advertise the company's products, photographic posters highlighting new products, annual fiscal reports of the company (produced in booklet format primarily for stockholders), magazines, and newsletters for which the in-house reprographics equipment is not well suited.

Some factors to consider in deciding whether to use a commercial service include the following items:

- The costs for producing certain quantities, for example, a single copy, 100 copies, 10,000 copies.
- The quality of the prepared copy.
- The additional cost for finishing processes such as collating, binding, and folding.
- The total time required for completion of a specific production job.

C. Controlling Reprographic Systems

Of all the office support services available within a firm, the reprographic processes tend to be among the most expensive. The cost of specialized labor, equipment, paper inventories, composition, and other miscellaneous costs must be analyzed in terms of the services being provided by reprographics personnel. Adequate attention must be given to the selection of appropriate equipment, matching the production job to the appropriate reprographics process, and establishing operating controls for handling routine as well as custom production work.

1. *Selecting Reprographics Equipment:* Initial investment in reprographics equipment will be relatively high. In a small- to medium-sized firm, the investment may be as much as $50,000 to $100,000, while in a large firm the investment can be anywhere from $100,000 to $300,000 or more. Selection of appropriate equipment to handle the copying and duplicating needs of the organization requires attention to the following factors:

    a. *Specific applications:* Determining the specific applications for which the equipment is intended is essential. Consideration should be given to those special features of the equipment that make it possible to perform certain functions.

    EXAMPLE: A high-speed copier is needed to handle the large copy volume of the ABC Company. In addition to its copying capability, the copier's collating and stapling features will enable these operations to be performed quickly with only minimal manual labor.

    b. *Basic equipment operation:* The ease of operating the new equipment will make it easier to implement new procedures into the operations of the reprographics center. In addition, the speed of operation is also an important consideration.

    c. *Training needed by operators:* The training ease of the new system is important in determining the amount or kind of training needed by operators of the system. Most estimates indicate that it takes anywhere from three to six months for an operator to become productive with a new equipment system. Therefore, the initial cost of training to the organization is high—from the time "lost" through retraining to time spent in special seminars sponsored by various professional associations and vendors.

d. *Equipment cost:* Of course, the initial cost of the equipment is an especially important consideration. This includes the cost of maintenance and service contracts for the particular equipment selected.

e. *Estimated delivery time:* Most orders for reprographics equipment will take a few weeks to a few months for delivery, outside of copiers. Most vendors of copy equipment have models ready for immediate purchase and delivery. An important factor in selecting equipment will be the estimated delivery time from manufacturer to vendor to purchaser.

EXAMPLE: The X & Z Company anticipates that in three months it will start printing a special report for one of its clients. A new equipment system is on order and is scheduled to be delivered within the next three weeks. That should leave adequate time for the operator to be trained on the new system. A delay in receiving the new equipment as scheduled will mean a delay in being able to serve the client.

2. *Matching Production with the Process:* With more than one reprographics process available for producing copies, the production job must be matched with the reprographics process that will give the desired appearance and quality. Factors that may be used in determining which process would be the most appropriate for the specific production job include the following items:

a. *Copy quality desired:* When the various copying and duplicating processes are compared, there are considerable differences among these processes. The quality of the paper used for the run as well as the care taken in preparing the original copy or the master also affect the appearance of the copies that are copied or duplicated. Here are some specific questions that need to be answered.

- How important is the appearance of the copy?
- How will the copy be used within the office?
- How will the copy be transmitted externally to other organizations?
- Who will see the copy? someone within the organization? or someone outside the organization?

b. *Number of copies needed:* Depending on the process used, the number of usable copies will vary. Refer to Figure 7-1 to note

Process	Equipment Base Cost	Average Cost Per Copy	Copy Quality	Economical Quantity
Offset Duplicator	Expensive ($3,500-$16,000)	Low to Medium (.005-.015)	Excellent	10-10,000
Convenience Copier	Medium to Expensive ($800-$30,000)	Medium to Expensive (.03-.06)	Good to Excellent	1-20
High-speed Copier	Expensive ($25,000+)	Medium (.035)	Excellent	Over 20

Figure 7-1
Comparison of Reprographics Processes

the economical quantity that can be produced in each kind of copying and duplicating process referred to in this chapter.

c. *Copy costs:* You will want to choose the reprographic process that produces the quality you need at the lowest possible cost. Refer again to Figure 7-1, and note the average cost per copy for each process.

d. *Preparation time:* When selecting a reprographics process, it is important to consider the amount of time needed to make copies. Time required for keyboarding into the computer, word processing, equipment setup, and turnaround equal the total preparation time needed to ready the document and prepare the required number of copies.

3. *Establishing Operations Procedures and Controls:* Often policies and procedures are established for operations and controls within a specific department area. This is important especially when the department or service area is performing work orders for the entire organization. *Procedures* are steps used to complete a given office task. Naturally, these procedures need to be governed by some controls so that those people performing the various operations will know better what is expected of them.

a. *Operations procedures:* Rather than trying to remember all of the specialized procedures involved in certain types of production work or with certain types of reprographics equipment, personnel have been involved in developing procedures manuals that explain what is actually being done in given office situations. These sets of procedures tend to *standardize* the methods used in performing certain work functions.

(1) *Personnel procedures:* Specific procedures must be established for personnel to follow in the operations involved in reprographics.

(a) *Training:* One or more individuals need to be trained in machine operation, depending on their expertise. In addition, equipment maintenance and service are of vital importance to reprographics operations. The training should include a basic understanding of ways to keep costs down in reprographics operations.

(b) *Authorization:* Only authorized personnel should be permitted to use the reprographics equipment. This is due primarily to the specialized nature of the equipment itself. The technical nature of the work plus computerized applications require reprographics personnel to handle very sensitive operations.

(c) *Equipment misuse:* Delays in the completion of production work can be caused by employee misuse of equipment. Once the equipment is "down," valuable time is lost and, of course, productivity suffers. Deadlines for copying and printing may not be met as well.

(2) *Records procedures:* In any business procedure, there are certain records that are needed, either to monitor the work being done or to monitor the equipment usage.

(a) *Request forms:* Whenever a user wishes to request work to be done by the reprographics center, a job request form (similar to the one used in word processing or document preparation) should be completed which describes the copying or duplicating required.

(b) *Equipment usage forms:* In reprographics it is important to keep track of the amount of equipment usage per job. A chargeback procedure may be used to charge individual departments for costs associated with specific jobs, and these costs may include equipment costs or depreciation.

(c) *Equipment repair records:* Detailed records of equipment repair per machine are extremely important in monitoring the effectiveness of the equipment in specific procedures.

EXAMPLE: An offset duplicator that requires continuous repair, almost on a daily basis, will not be very effective in preparing needed copies of documents.

b. *Operations controls:* The administrative manager (or whoever is in charge of the reprographics operations) must impose certain operations controls so that the reprographics service will function effectively. Here are some of the possible controls that might be used.

(1) *Copy monitoring:* An *auditron* is one way of controlling use of a convenience copier. This is a plastic card, key, or other insert device that activates the copier for use and keeps a record of the number of copies produced.

(2) *Copyright controls:* Any organization today must be concerned about the handling of copyrighted materials and appropriate procedures to use for making copies, with or without the written permission of the publisher.

EXAMPLE: Copyright laws do permit materials to be copied in certain circumstances. A single copy is usually permitted so that an individual can use it for his/her own research. However, multiple copies are permitted only in very special circumstances.

(3) *Time controls:* Some copiers are in use only during the business day, from 8 A.M. to 5 P.M.

(4) *Trained operator:* Sometimes it is more efficient to have an operator available either to run the copies needed or to be available in case there is a problem with the equipment or the supplies.

(5) *Restricting the number of copies prepared:* Since large numbers of copies can be reproduced more economically using other methods, the use of the copier may be restricted to ten or less copies.

4. *Controlling Reprographics Costs:* The primary cost factors in reprographics operations include personnel, equipment, space, and supply costs. Each of these cost factors (and other types of "hidden" costs) must be considered in the per copy costs for reprographics services. "Hidden costs" include costs for ordering reprographics supplies and equipment, costs for storage of supplies (especially large quantities of paper), costs involved in keeping accurate stock inventories, and mailing costs, among others. Procedures need to be implemented to reduce excess costs, and these need to be enforced, too. Here are some specific ways utilized by some organizations to reduce and control reprographic costs:

a. *Selecting most appropriate reprographics process:* This has been mentioned earlier in this chapter in relation to the cost analysis involved. Sometimes the fastest method of obtaining copies may be the most expensive.

EXAMPLE: Ellen has to reproduce 30 copies of a one-page report. If she decides to copy the page on a convenience copier, the cost will be approximately 5 cents per copy or a total of $1.50. If she uses an offset process to produce the 30 copies, she will probably be able to produce them at approximately 1 cent per copy after the master has been produced. Time may be an important factor for her in deciding which process to use.

Reprographics Management

b. *Standardizing equipment and supply usage:* If compatible equipment is used in various locations around the company, supplies can be ordered for all compatible equipment at the same time, thus taking advantage of quantity ordering. From a maintenance point of view, too, obtaining service on the same equipment brands will reduce the costs since more than one piece of equipment could be serviced during a single visit from a repair technician.

EXAMPLE: Some companies have established satellite centers in various areas of the company, each with the same type of equipment system. Therefore, the same supplies can be used in each location. The only drawback occurs if the particular brand seems to require a great deal of constant repair. In this case, the administrative manager should examine the quantity of usage and whether this particular brand can withstand the amount of usage required.

c. *Conducting departmental surveys:* Departments should be made aware of usage and cost figures for reprographics services incurred at least on a monthly basis. Cumulative figures for annual operations would be helpful in planning annual budgets. Sometimes individuals are never shown the figures that would substantiate exactly how much the equipment is actually used. These figures can be helpful in determining future equipment needs or in establishing guidelines for the usage of the different duplicating methods available within the firm.

One of the primary responsibilities of the administrative manager is to reduce office costs in order to make the office a more productive function within the firm. Controlling the reprographics costs incurred is one way of reducing possible waste of valuable resources within the firm.

D. Innovations and Trends in Reprographic Systems

The move toward "the paperless office" has certainly not materialized in recent years. If anything, more records and more paper have been created as a result of using computers and office automation technology to speed up various processes. The importance of the production of quality paper documents cannot be underestimated. Technology is permitting the creation of higher-quality paper documents, produced in much less time, for use in promoting new products and new services.

1. *Integration of Reprographics with Other Systems:* The interface of reprographics with computer systems and computer software has produced some miraculous results. Text created through word processing, spreadsheet, and graphics software, recorded on disk, can be converted easily to publishing systems. Much time is saved when

the secretary can key in the original text with a word processing software, convert it to an appropriate systems file, which can then be converted to publishing software by reprographics personnel.

2. *Increased Use of In-House Facilities:* More copying and duplicating can be handled more easily in-house rather than sending work outside the firm. The computer is enabling very sophisticated composition and desktop publishing work to be handled with much more ease and speed by office support personnel.

3. *Laser Printing:* One of the most profound innovations in reprographics is the laser used for high-speed printing. Copies may be reproduced in different colors, or business forms may be produced with very intricate designs. Small laser printers are used with microcomputer systems and enable the use of a wide variety of typefaces and type styles in printing original copy.

4. *Facsimile Transmission (FAX):* During the latter 1980s and early 1990s there has been a revolution in the use of FAX. Although facsimile transmission has been available for years, it has always been considered an expensive process. Now the costs are low enough that for $1 to $2 per page, you can FAX information anywhere by telephone in just a matter of minutes.

5. *Voice Processing:* Research is still being conducted with communication devices that permit reproduction in print from the human voice. Voice messages are being used in all types of new systems—voice mail as well as computer networks. Direct lines are available to the computer for storage of information, which integrates voice processing with records management.

6. *Visual Information Display:* Information is retrieved from computer storage through the use of a visual display or terminal. By keying in the right codes into the keyboard, copies of information may be ordered. Choices are available for hard copy as well as soft copy.

7. *Optical Character Recognition (OCR):* With OCR equipment, it is not necessary to key information into the system. Hard copy, either typewritten or handwritten, can be read by the system. The information can be transferred to a magnetic storage medium for later viewing or conversion to printed copies. OCR will continue to play an important role in office systems of the future.

Keeping up to date with the latest reprographics technology will require specialized personnel to participate in professional seminars and trade shows to become familiar with the latest equipment and techniques being used within the industry.

Chapter 7: Review Questions

Part A: Multiple-Choice Questions

DIRECTIONS: Select the best answer from the four alternatives. Write your answer in the blank to the left of the number.

_____ 1. A business organization needs to conduct a needs assessment in order to determine the reprographic needs of the organization. The basis for such a needs assessment is primarily which of the following?

   a. To determine the types of business documents that need to be reproduced in a given period of time.
   b. To identify specialized personnel who will perform specific reprographics functions.
   c. To select the equipment that will be used for the process.
   d. To provide quick access to the reprographics center.

_____ 2. If reprographics functions are decentralized, which one of the following is an advantage?

   a. Specialized personnel are available for the layout and design work that needs to be done.
   b. Workers within a given department are able to perform all copying and duplicating functions as needed.
   c. Production jobs are more easily scheduled so that enough lead time is allowed to get the job done.
   d. There will not be duplication of reprographics equipment, even copiers, within the firm.

_____ 3. Which of the following is a disadvantage of a decentralized reprographics operation?

   a. The setting of priorities within the department.
   b. Departmental policies and procedures affecting reprographics operations.
   c. The control of turnaround time to get a document produced.
   d. The control over the use and maintenance of equipment.

_____ 4. Sometimes centralized reprographics centers are established within the organization to provide

   a. specialized service in handling a limited number of production jobs.
   b. production work completed within the shortest possible time.

c. specialized personnel for desktop publishing.
d. self-service opportunities to increase production time.

_____ 5. Which of the following is a disadvantage of centralized control over reprographics operations?

   a. Production may take longer because of the specialized personnel and equipment involved.
   b. A large variety of reprographics work can be done in-house.
   c. Office productivity is decreased because of the time involved to complete production jobs.
   d. It is more difficult to schedule production jobs that need to be completed.

_____ 6. Which of the following items would best be produced in an in-house reprographics service?

   a. An advertising brochure for a new product.
   b. Annual fiscal report of company.
   c. Company newsletter.
   d. Periodical published by the company.

_____ 7. Which of the following items would best be produced with the help of a commercial printing firm?

   a. Business forms for the company.
   b. Photographic posters illustrating a new product.
   c. Company newsletter.
   d. Special packaging needed for a product.

_____ 8. Of all the office support services available, the reprographic processes tend to be

   a. more expensive in terms of equipment investment.
   b. the least expensive office support services provided.
   c. approximately the same cost as word processing services.
   d. more expensive because of the use of commercial services.

_____ 9. When more than one reprographics process is available for producing copies of documents, the selection of the appropriate process depends upon

   a. the procedures that will be used to complete the process.
   b. the basic equipment operation.

Reprographics Management

        c. the training needed by operators.
        d. the amount of time that will be needed to prepare the copies.

_____ **10.** The term *copy quality* refers to

        a. the costs involved in producing the document.
        b. the appearance of the document copies.
        c. the preparation time involved in producing the document.
        d. the number of copies required.

_____ **11.** One of the devices used to monitor the number of copies that are produced on a copier is to

        a. limit the number of supplies available for use with the copier.
        b. reduce the number of people who have access to the equipment.
        c. require that an auditron be used to activate the copier.
        d. conduct a departmental survey to see how much the copier needs to be used.

_____ **12.** One of the ways to control the reprographics costs involved in producing documents is to

        a. purchase compatible equipment to be used in various locations around the company.
        b. pay close attention to copyright laws.
        c. provide access to facsimile transmission for more efficient message communication.
        d. establish specific procedures for users who wish to submit production work.

_____ **13.** Reprographics management within an organization will be affected <u>most</u> by which one of the following developments?

        a. The use of word processing to create document text.
        b. Laser technology in high-speed printing.
        c. The per-copy cost of producing documents.
        d. General management of reprographics services provided by an administrative manager.

Part B: Matching Sets

Matching Set 1

Match the operations functions (A-B) with each of the descriptive statements (14-18). Write the letter of your answer in the blank to the left of each number.

Operations Functions
    A. Operations Procedures
    B. Operations Controls

DESCRIPTIVE STATEMENTS

_____ 14. Only authorized personnel should have access to reprographics systems.

_____ 15. A record is kept of the number of copies produced.

_____ 16. Individuals need to be trained depending on their skill and expertise.

_____ 17. Individual departments are charged for costs related to specific work orders.

_____ 18. Written permission is required to make copies of copyrighted material.

Matching Set 2

Match the types of organizational structure (A-B) to each of the features (19-25). Write the letter of your answer in the blank to the left of each number.

Types of Organizational Structure
    A. Decentralized Control
    B. Centralized Control

FEATURES

_____ 19. Each department establishes its own regulations for equipment usage and copies to be produced.

_____ 20. Each department manages its own copying services.

_____ 21. Specialized personnel are available to assist with custom work requiring layout and design as well as desktop publishing.

_____ 22. More lead time may be needed to get the work completed.

Reprographics Management

_____ 23. It is more difficult to maintain company control over equipment use and maintenance.

_____ 24. Copying and printing priorities are set within the department.

_____ 25. A large variety of production jobs can be scheduled during the same period of time.

Part C: Problem Situations

DIRECTIONS: For each of the following problem situations, select the best answer from the four alternatives. Write the letter of your answer in the blank to the left of each number.

Problem 1

Jack Martin is the manager of the Reprographics Center for Smith-Tyson Toys, Inc., a manufacturer of specialty toys including train sets, electronic vehicles, and small mechanical toys. There are three other people working in the center: Ruth is a desktop publishing and composition specialist, Jane is in charge of layout and design, and George is the copying and printing equipment technician/operator.

_____ 26. Fran Miller, the marketing manager, has brought in a work order for a sales brochure for a new toy robot. In considering the requirements of the task, Jack would most likely

   a. recommend that Fran seek the assistance of a commercial printing firm in the production of the sales brochure.
   b. accept the work order and then talk with Ruth and Jane later about the feasibility of designing the brochure.
   c. ask Fran to discuss the plans for the brochure with Ruth and Jane to see if it is a task that can be done in-house.
   d. accept the work order and tell Fran that there should be no difficulty in meeting the deadline.

_____ 27. Jack finds that keeping up with the changing technology is one of the most difficult concerns he has at present. Which of the following procedures would demonstrate that he is making a strong effort to keep his co-workers involved in change?

   a. He recommends to his superiors that each summer, during a somewhat slack period, he and the other three employees in his department be granted permission to attend the annual seminar of the American

Graphics and Printing Association. For the past two years, they have agreed to sponsor attendance.
b. He has subscribed to a number of technical magazines and has them on display within the department.
c. He is a member of the state professional association in graphics and printing and attends all of the state conferences held each year.
d. He is active in several community organizations where he is in contact with managers from other nearby companies.

28. Ruth saw a particularly interesting article on a newsletter design in the latest issue of one of the word processing magazines that the department receives and decides to make a copy of the article for her sample file. She keeps samples so that when people throughout the organization want to see an example she will have some to show. Which of the following statements about copying is true?

a. All articles in a magazine are copyrighted; therefore, no copies whatsoever can legally be made of the article.
b. Ruth must contact the publisher to ask permission to make a copy of the article.
c. Anyone can make one copy of a copyrighted article for personal use only.
d. Ruth may make as many copies of the article as she wishes.

Chapter 7: Solutions

Part A: Multiple-Choice Questions

	Answer	Refer to Chapter Section
1.	(a)	[A] Knowing the types of documents to be reproduced through copying or duplicating processes is the basis for defining the need for reprographics services within an organization.
2.	(b)	[B-1-a(1)] All of the other choices are characteristics of centralization, not decentralization.
3.	(d)	[B-1-a] All of the other choices are advantages of decentralization, not disadvantages.
4.	(c)	[B-1-b(1)] Specialized service would be available to handle a variety of production jobs, including desktop publishing.
5.	(a)	[B-1-b] Production may take longer because work orders are being handled for all departments, and the priority set for one job must mesh with the priorities set for all other jobs.
6.	(c)	[B-2-a(3)] Answers (a), (b), and (d) are all items that might best be produced through a commercial printing firm because of special artwork, graphic design, or printing requirements.
7.	(b)	[B-2-b] Answers (a), (c), and (d) are all items that might best be produced in an in-house reprographics center because of the routine nature and formats used in documents like these.
8.	(a)	[C] The equipment investment in copying, composition, desktop publishing, and printing equipment is high, but the need for increased office productivity requires the utilization of high-speed equipment.
9.	(d)	[C-2-d] Of the four choices, only *time* is a factor which would determine choice of process.
10.	(b)	[C-2-a] Copy quality refers to the appearance of the copies—how these copies appear on the page, type styles and typefaces used, size of type, error-free copy.
11.	(c)	[C-3-b(1)] An auditron helps with two aspects of copy management: providing access to the copier for an authorized person and keeping a record of the number of copies produced by an individual or department.
12.	(a)	[C-4-b] The use of compatible equipment in various locations/departments throughout the organization may help to keep the maintenance costs down. Maintenance of a number of like systems can typically be handled through one contract or one technician.
13.	(b)	[D-3] Technology and automated systems have drastically affected all reprographics operations. With laser technology not only has the image quality improved but the production speed as well.

Part B: Matching Sets

Matching Set 1

14.	(A)	[C-3-a(1)(b)]
15.	(B)	[C-3-b(1)]
16.	(A)	[C-3-a(1)(a)]
17.	(A)	[C-3-a(2)(b)]
18.	(B)	[C-3-b(2)]

Matching Set 2

19.	(A)	[B-1-a(2)]
20.	(A)	[B-1-a]
21.	(B)	[B-1-b(1)]
22.	(B)	[B-1-b]
23.	(A)	[B-1-a]
24.	(A)	[B-1-a(4)]
25.	(B)	[B-1-b(3)]

Part C: Problem Situtations

26. (c) [B-2] Because of the specialized nature of a sales brochure for a new product, Jack should include Ruth and Jane in the discussion and planning of the new brochure. They would be in a better position to tell the marketing manager what the capabilities of the equipment are, how long the job would take to complete, and other information relating to the work order itself. In addition, they could respond to questions.

27. (a) [D] Participation in professional seminars is one of the best ways of keeping up to date with the latest technology. Trade shows and seminars enable specialized personnel in the area of reprographics to learn some of the latest techniques being used within the industry.

28. (c) [C-3-b(2)] Usually an individual can make one copy of any copyrighted article for personal use without violating any laws. Making multiple copies is questionable.

PART II   Communication

CHAPTER 8

Composing Communications

OVERVIEW

Business communication, both oral and written, is the lifeblood of any organization. In your position as a professional secretary, your communication skills will have a tremendous effect on your relationship with executives, co-workers, organization leaders, and customers. Although oral communication is an hourly activity, the skills involved in composing and recording communication in written form for later reference and review is the main purpose of this chapter. Many of these guidelines, however, are applicable to oral communications. The chapter concludes with a section on listening and oral communication skills.

As a professional secretary, you have the responsibility of developing clearly written communication. Many executives rely on the secretary to handle the majority of the office correspondence as well as to critique the executive's writing. Realizing this, the secretary must understand that communication is more than stating those facts which an executive feels are important.

Saying or writing what you have to communicate is called *encoding* the message. However, that message may be delivered to the receiver through a variety of channels: verbal, telephone, formal report, messenger, electronic mail, or computer, to mention only a few. The choice of channel is important in persuading the receiver to listen to the message and interpret it correctly. Message interpretation requires the receiver to *decode* the message. As a writer, your responsibility is to strive to have the decoded message be the same as the encoded message. A means for assessing whether this has been accomplished is to seek feedback.

Communicating is much more than just stating what is important to you. Full consideration must be given to all aspects of the communication process, or the communication will be weak and ineffective.

DEFINITION OF TERMS

ABSTRACT LANGUAGE. The quality of words and thoughts where meanings can be interpreted differently by different people, even in the same situation.

ACTIVE WORDS. Words that denote action on the part of the individual.

APPENDIX. Supplementary research material included in a supplementary part of the report.

BIBLIOGRAPHY. An alphabetical list of all information sources used for a report included at the end of the report.

CLARITY. A criterion of effective sentence and paragraph construction that requires that any message be written in an accurate and nonconfusing manner.

COHERENCE. A quality shown by writing that is consistent in style, word choice, and word usage, resulting in sentence and paragraph unity and unity of the work.

COMBINATION LETTER. A message in which there is both a positive and a negative response.

CONCISENESS. Writing in a brief but comprehensive manner.

CONCRETE LANGUAGE. The use of words and terms that are precise in meaning; the opposite of abstract language.

CONSTANT INFORMATION. Wording that will stay exactly the same on every message produced.

DATA BASE. A complete record of variable information.

DEDUCTIVE STYLE. The direct approach to writing in which the main idea is stated first, followed by supporting details.

DESCRIPTORS. Adjectives and adverbs that are used as key words to denote certain aspects or characteristics found in business writing.

EMPATHY. An understanding of the feelings or emotions of another person.

EMPHASIS. The attachment of greater importance to particular aspects of a message; placing special stress on a particular thought, word, or syllable.

EXPERIMENTAL RESEARCH. The conduct of a study to determine whether a change in one factor or variable causes a change in another factor or variable.

EXTERNAL REPORT. Business writing which will be disseminated outside the organization.

FORM LETTER. Correspondence with some identical parts that may be sent to more than one person or company for a specific purpose.

GLOSSARY. An alphabetical list of terms defined for the reader.

GOODWILL. A positive feeling between organizations or between people working within organizations that results in positive, clear, and courteous communication.

HORIZONTAL REPORT. Business writing that is distributed from department to department or division to division within the organization; communication at the same administrative level.

INDEX. A list of names and subjects, with page references in order to find specific information contained in the report quickly; appears at end of report.

INDUCTIVE STYLE. An organizational approach that implies that the writing will lead the reader to the main idea; the details and supporting information are presented first, with the main idea following.

INFORMAL REPORT. Business writing used to transmit meaningful information to other people within the organization or outside the organization; usually no more than five pages at the most.

INTEROFFICE COMMUNICATION. Message transmission from one office to another within an organization.

JARGON. Words used in business writing which are generally understood only by others in the profession; often referred to as "slang" language in business writing.

MEAN. The arithmetic average of a group of responses obtained by computing the sum of all the responses and dividing by the number of responses; a measure of central tendency.

MEDIAN. The midpoint in a distribution of responses; a measure of central tendency.

MEMORANDUM. The most common medium for corresponding within the firm; used for communication whenever the writer and the receiver of the message work for the same organization.

MODE. The response that occurs the most frequently in a distribution of responses; a measure of central tendency.

NARRATIVE REPORT. A report that includes primarily text material (words).

NEGATIVE LETTER. Correspondence that conveys a "no" response or some other form of "bad news"; an indirect approach is used to write this type of correspondence.

NONTECHNICAL REPORT. A report that conveys information to people who do not have backgrounds in the subject area; an effort is made to refrain from using technical language.

OBSERVATIONAL RESEARCH. The conduct of a study that permits the researcher to actually see the actions or results of individual or group activity.

PARALLELISM. The statement of ideas that are equal in thought in identical grammatical form.

PASSIVE WORDS. Words that denote inaction or waiting for something to happen.

SCHEDULED REPORT. A report that is issued at regularly stated intervals.

PERSUASIVE LETTER. Correspondence that tends to be positive but complex in nature, requesting the receiver to take some action after justification for such action is presented in the letter.

POSITIVE LETTER. Favorable correspondence that says "yes" or otherwise presents "good news" to the receiver.

PRIMARY RESEARCH. An investigation to gather original information to use as current data in a report.

PROGRESS REPORT. A report that identifies work in process and gives the present status of a project.

RANGE. The difference between the value of the highest response and the value of the lowest response in a distribution.

RELIABLE DATA. Data that are measured consistently and accurately.

REPETITIVE LETTER. Form correspondence that is prepared and sent to a list of different people, each with personal name and address inserted; some small amounts of information may vary.

REPORT. The result of a process whose purpose is to transmit meaningful data to an individual(s) for either information or decision-making purposes.

ROUTINE LETTER. Correspondence with the primary purpose of exchanging day-to-day information; sometimes called a neutral letter.

SECONDARY RESEARCH. An investigation to gather information others have prepared to use as a supportive basis for a report.

STANDARD DEVIATION. A measure of the degree of scattering of a frequency distribution about its arithmetic mean.

STATISTICAL REPORT. A report that includes primarily numerical data.

SURVEY RESEARCH. A study to determine opinions, beliefs, or reactions to specific phenomena; may be administered in written (a questionnaire) or oral form (an interview).

TECHNICAL REPORT. Business writing that conveys information to professionals within the field who will understand the specialized vocabulary and terminology included in the report.

TONE. The manner in which a certain attitude is expressed in writing.

UNBIASED LANGUAGE. The expression of thoughts and ideas so that equal treatment is given to everyone (men and women, minority groups, and job holders).

UNITY. A coherent flow of ideas throughout a written work—within sentences, within paragraphs, and between paragraphs.

VALID DATA. Data that measure what they are intended to measure.

VARIABLE INFORMATION. Any text material that must be inserted to complete the message; this information will change on each letter produced.

VERTICAL REPORT. Business writing prepared for someone at a higher level or a lower level within the organizational structure of the company.

A. **Fundamentals of Writing**

Written messages must be coherent and logical so the reader can understand the messages. The reader has no opportunity to ask questions in case any of the ideas presented are not clear. Improper selection of words will prevent the reader from understanding the ideas being presented. Word choice, sentence and paragraph construction, and parallelism affect the presentation of clear, understandable messages. Language must be used that will evoke clear mental images as the message is being read.

1. *Effective Word Selection:* Words selected for use in the message must be appropriate for the situation. Words with the right denotative meaning (literal meaning) and connotative meaning (feeling or impression conveyed) must be selected. The key to effective word selection is to use specific nouns, action verbs, and descriptive adjectives and adverbs.

   a. *Positive language:* Writing needs to be positive in nature. People react to positivism by wanting to do, to act, and to listen.

      (1) Messages should be written from the reader's viewpoint. Direct the message to the reader. Focus on the use of pronouns such as *you, your* rather than *I, me*.

         (a) What has already been accomplished should be the focus rather than what should have been done or what cannot be done. Express what has been done in a positive manner.
         (b) The reader's interest in the subject of the message should be emphasized.
         (c) If appropriate for the situation, the receiver of the message should be complimented.

      (2) Messages should limit the use of negative expressions. A letter or memo should not be written in a moment of anger.

         (a) Avoid using the word *not* or contractions containing *not* too often in a message.

            EXAMPLES:
            Yes: Remember to call us the next time you need help with your office decor.
            No: Don't forget to call us for help with your office decor.

         (b) Avoid using negative expressions that tend to express doubt or sorrow or accuse the reader unnecessarily. Words like *regret, unfortunately, apologize, neglected,* and *failed* have negative connotations.

            EXAMPLE: You failed to enclose a check to pay for the order.

   b. *Tone:* Tone is defined as the manner in which a certain attitude is expressed. What you choose to say and how you say it determine the tone of the writing. The business writing tone that is more effective is friendly, conversational, businesslike, objective, and personalized. Tone, along with style, forms the overall impression for the reader.

   c. *Familiar words:* In conversation and writing during a typical business day, most people use only 1,000 to 1,500 words out of more than 700,000 words in our language. Most words in the English language are unfamiliar to many of us.

     (1) Use commonly known synonyms for unfamiliar words.

     (2) Avoid confusing unfamiliar words with technical words. Technical words may be used without an explanation when writing to a member of the same profession. However, these same terms may need to be explained when writing to an individual not in the profession.

     (3) Use the English equivalent for foreign expressions. It is undesirable to use foreign expressions in business writing.

     (4) Refrain from using jargon in business writing. *Jargon* is defined as "slang" language. Jargon used in business writing is generally understood only by others in the profession.

     (5) Spell out acronyms when first used in a document followed by the acronym in parentheses. An *acronym* is a word formed by the initials of words in a set phrase. Thereafter, the acronym can be used.

EXAMPLE: The American Management Association (AMA) is a professional organization for business people. The AMA also offers membership to college and university professors of business.

   d. *Concrete language:* Being precise and specific in your writing is very important. The use of words and terms with meanings that people generally agree upon helps to make language more concrete. Some words are too general to convey a message effectively. *Concrete* language refers to the use of words and terms that are precise in meaning. *Abstract* language refers to the quality of language where meanings can be interpreted differently by different people, even in the same situation.

     (1) A word or phrase may be added to an abstract word to define it more precisely.

EXAMPLE: building
The Sears Tower, the tallest building in the world...

     (2) The abstract term may be explained within the sentence.

EXAMPLE: application
You may use this software package to prepare a mailable letter.

("Prepare a mailable letter" refers to the specific application.)

(3) The most specific, concrete word possible should be used when it is important to the meaning of the message.

EXAMPLE: building
bank, restaurant, library

(4) Short, simple words convey the meaning much more directly and more clearly than long, complex words. Of course, choose the word most appropriate to the reader.

EXAMPLES:

Short, simple words	Long, complex words
later	subsequent
people	personnel
car, truck, bus	vehicle
use	application

e. *Active words:* Active words denote *action* whereas passive words denote *inaction* or *waiting for something to happen.* The use of active verbs, descriptive adjectives, and descriptive adverbs will create more action in your writing.

(1) *Active verbs:* Verbs denote the action that is taking place. An *action* verb conveys a precise meaning, which is what is needed in business writing. Such verbs convey the degree of precision in the action being expressed.

EXAMPLES:

Active	Passive
speaks	is conversing
writes	is composing
participates	will be meeting

(2) *Descriptive adjectives:* Adjectives are used to describe nouns or subjects and to support active verbs. Descriptive adjectives are sometimes called key words or *descriptors*. As descriptors, adjectives may be precise or imprecise in the way they describe a noun.

EXAMPLES OF IMPRECISE DESCRIPTORS:
good better best
fine
real

EXAMPLES OF PRECISE DESCRIPTORS:
This electronic, self-correcting typewriter is a sophisticated system because such routines as centering and underlining are automatic functions.

(3) *Descriptive adverbs:* Adverbs modify verbs, adjectives, or other adverbs. Adverbs, too, need to be descriptive so that a precise meaning is conveyed to the reader.

EXAMPLES OF IMPRECISE DESCRIPTORS:
nearly   well   fairly   barely   likely

EXAMPLES OF PRECISE DESCRIPTORS:
neatly   courteously   concisely   frequently

Martha politely asked for the accurately written report.

The use of active words will make your communication more meaningful to the receiver. Here are two examples of how exact information can be more helpful:

EXAMPLES:
Imprecise: *Come in early tomorrow morning, and Mr. Smith will see you.*
Precise: *Come in at 9:15 tomorrow morning, and Mr. Smith will see you.*

f. *Contemporary words and expressions:* The selection of contemporary words and expressions makes the writing more relevant through up-to-date expressions.

EXAMPLES:
word processing   modular work station
hard copy   soft copy
disk operating system (DOS)

g. *Unbiased language:* If due caution is not used, bias can creep into business writing very easily. Equal treatment must be given to everyone (men and women, minority groups, and job holders). Sometimes people become stereotyped into particular jobs or positions, even though both men and women can be effective job holders. Here are some basic guidelines that may be followed so that unbiased language will be used in all business writing.

(1) *Sex-fair language:* Language in business writing must be free of sexual bias.

(a) Whenever people are referred to in general, asexual words and phrases should be used instead of masculine or feminine words.

EXAMPLES:
manpower   peoplepower
manhours   working hours

Here are some ways in which these changes in word usage can be achieved:

- Sentences may be reworded to remove unneeded pronouns.
- The number can be changed from singular to plural.
- Masculine pronouns can be replaced with *s/he*, *her or his*, *one*, or *you* to decrease the use of sexist language.

A variety of these techniques may be used to avoid monotonous, repetitious writing or difficulty in reading the material.

EXAMPLE:
Each secretary needs a complete report on file by the end of the week.
Instead of:
Each secretary needs to complete her report by the end of the week.

(b) Men and women should be referred to as equals, and references to them should be consistently phrased. You should use the person's full name in the first reference to that person; then you may use either the first name, last name, or proper pronoun in later reference.

EXAMPLE:
Sylvia Gerald was recently appointed the chairperson of the Awards Committee. Ms. Gerald has been with the company since 1975.

(c) Unnecessary labels and stereotypes should not be used in business writing.

EXAMPLES:
female executive	*executive*
just like a man	*(this phrase should not be used)*

(d) The words *man* or *woman* should not be used as a prefix or suffix in job titles.

EXAMPLES:
chairman	*chairperson*
	chair
	presiding officer
foreman	*supervisor*

(e) When referring to people by sex, parallel language should be used.

EXAMPLES:
the ladies and the men
should be:
the women and the men
or
the ladies and the gentlemen

man and wife
should be:
husband and wife

(f) When referring to people by name, parallel language must be used in expressing their names.

EXAMPLES:
Please telephone one of our marketing representatives, either Bill Gray or Mrs. Brown, with the description of the cabinet.

Instead, say:
Please telephone one of our marketing representatives, either Bill Gray or Muriel Brown, with the description of the cabinet.

(g) General expressions used should refer to both men and women. Use generic titles or descriptions for both women and men.

EXAMPLES:

male secretary	*secretary*
female executive	*executive*
male programmer	*programmer*

(2) *Racially or ethnically unbiased language:* Equal treatment of people within certain racial or ethnic groups is a necessity in business writing so that the audience will not be offended by the writing.

(a) Qualifiers may be used to reinforce racial or ethnic stereotypes. Do not add information that suggests that a person is an exception to a racial or ethnic norm.

EXAMPLE:
George Kim, an exchange employee from Korea, has very good spelling skills.
(Does this sentence imply that Koreans, as a general rule, have difficulty with spelling?)

(b) The identification of racial or ethnic origin should not appear in the writing unless it is pertinent to the message being conveyed. In proofreading and editing, watch for bias that is sometimes implied in context.

(3) *Job-related language:* In business writing, the types of jobs held by people should not be stereotyped. In other words, examples should be used of both men and women in positions which might easily be stereotyped.

EXAMPLES:
Shirley, a secretary in the Financial Department, is responsible for the drafting of all research reports. (Are all secretaries female?)

Glenn, a secretary in the Loan Department, supervises the five part-time employees.

2. *Effective Sentence and Paragraph Construction:* Sentences and paragraphs need to be constructed carefully to be effective in meaning. The following points should help to improve the quality of the sentences and paragraphs produced.

a. *Constructing effective sentences:* A sentence is a complete thought expressed in words that are understandable. A sentence must have a subject and a predicate.

(1) *Types of sentences written:* The types of sentences written should be varied. A variety of sentence types adds interest to a message or sometimes changes the emphasis or tone.

(a) A combination of simple, compound, and complex sentences adds variety to the sentence structure.

(b) Simple sentences must have a subject and a verb and may have modifiers—adjectives, adverbs, or complements. *Complements* are additional words for complete meaning.

EXAMPLE:
Frugal   Mary   worked   for   33   years.
(Adjective)
        (Subject)
                    (Verb)
                                    (Complement)

(c) Compound sentences consist of two independent clauses joined by a comma and a conjunction (and, but, or, nor . . .), a semicolon, or a conjunctive adverb (also, however, therefore . . .). An independent clause conveys a complete thought and can stand alone as a sentence.

EXAMPLE:
<u>Sales increased in June</u> *(independent clause),* but *(conjunction)* <u>the vice president of Marketing expected a greater sales increase</u> *(independent clause).*

(d) Complex sentences consist of an independent clause and one or more dependent clauses. A dependent clause is incomplete; it cannot stand alone as a sentence. Dependent clauses begin with a connecting word showing its subordinate relationship. The connecting word is either a relative pronoun (who, which, that) or a subordinate conjunction (if, because, when, since . . .).

EXAMPLE:
<u>As far as Henry determined</u> *(dependent clause),* <u>there was no problem with the local area network in the Accounting Department</u> *(independent clause).*

(e) A compound-complex sentence consists of two or more independent clauses and one or more dependent clauses. Compound-complex sentences should be used sparingly.

(2) *Length of sentences:* Sentences should normally average from 15 to 20 words. There needs to be a combination of short, medium, and long sentences to keep reading interesting. A sentence that exceeds 40 words, however, should be rewritten into two or more sentences.

(3) *Connectives:* Sentences should be joined when the thought continues. The expression of related ideas needs to be clearly constructed.

EXAMPLE: The word processing supervisor reviews each document before it leaves the center; this is an important responsibility.

(4) *Sentence formats:* Some ideas are better stated as questions rather than as statements. A clause or a phrase may begin a sentence, which adds variety to the format. Certain words may be underlined, italicized, or set in boldface.

b. *Developing organized paragraphs:* Groups of related sentences are formed into paragraphs, with each paragraph having at least one central idea or theme. When the idea changes, a new paragraph results. A paragraph has one main idea presented, with detailed information to support that idea.

(1) *Deductive style:* This organization is direct. The main idea is stated followed by supporting details.

(2) *Inductive style:* This organization is indirect. Supporting details are presented first; then the main idea is presented.

There must be parallel construction in order to develop organized paragraphs so there is equal treatment of ideas that are comparable.

c. *Criteria for effective sentence and paragraph construction:* As effective communicators, sentences and paragraphs need to be constructed with several qualities in mind: coherence, emphasis, unity, conciseness, variety, clarity, and accuracy.

(1) *Coherence:* Thoughts are developed with coherence if the writing shows consistency in style, word choice, and word usage. Coherence means that the sentences and paragraphs are constructed so each word contributes to the sentence, each sentence contributes to the meaning of the paragraph, and each paragraph contributes to the entire message. The following techniques can help the writer maintain cohesion.

(a) *Emphasis:* Coherence is shown by emphasizing certain aspects of the message, that is, placing special stress on a particular thought, word, or syllable. Repeating a word from the preceding sentence emphasizes that thought. Sometimes specific items need to be emphasized equally. Comparing or contrasting to show similarities or differences is another way to emphasize a point. Sometimes information must be presented in rank order, depending on its importance. Another way to emphasize is with the use of different sizes of type, underlining, or format change.

(b) *Word choice and usage:* Sentences are directly linked when a pronoun is used to represent a noun from the preceding sentence.

- Begin sentences with connecting words: however, therefore, also. Connecting words imply continuation of the same topic.
- Use words that are commonly found together:

state/federal
employer/employee
graduate/undergraduate
winter/spring/summer/fall

(c) *Parallelism:* Ideas that are equal in thought should be stated in identical grammatical form. Violations of parallel construction lead to misinterpretation and awkward sentence formats.

EXAMPLE: The purpose of the meeting is to organize *our plan for a new data processing system and* implementing *procedures for writing the proposal. (The words that are underlined are not parallel.)*

The purpose of the meeting is to organize *our plan for a new data processing system and* to implement *procedures for writing the proposal. (The underlined words are parallel.)*

(2) *Emphasis:* Emphasis is a very important part of developing coherence in writing; the two criteria are closely related. Emphasis means that greater importance is attached to a particular fact.

(a) *Word choice and order:* Key information should be placed at the beginning of sentences or messages so that the reader will be sure to see it. Selecting words that relate precisely to the idea being conveyed permits you to emphasize the idea correctly.

(b) *Balance:* Items of equal value should be emphasized equally in the writing.

(c) *Restatement:* Sometimes a fact or detail needs to be restated, in different words, so that the reader will be more likely to pay attention to that fact.

EXAMPLE: The importance of setting up appropriate procedures for accepting work will save personnel time. In other words, the procedure for logging in work will enable you to organize the work in less time.

(d) *Format:* Sometimes the format is changed within a document to add emphasis to specific details. Within the body of a letter, a statistical table might be included to emphasize facts that would otherwise be obscured in the body of the message. Type sizes and styles help to vary the format as well.

(3) *Unity:* The term *unity* suggests that there is a coherent flow of ideas throughout a written work—within sentences, within paragraphs and between paragraphs.

    (a) *Detailed information:* Factual information to support the main ideas is included within the paragraphs.
    (b) *Connectives:* Conjunctions and other connecting words are used to form relationships between and among words and sentences.
    (c) *Repetition:* Sometimes key ideas are summarized at the end of the message in order to emphasize their importance and also as reminders to the reader.

(4) *Conciseness:* Business writing needs to be concise because a busy executive will usually look briefly at the first page of a document to see if it is worthwhile to read further. *Conciseness* is defined as writing in a brief but comprehensive manner. In preparing communication that is concise, you must first identify the main purpose of the correspondence and plan your approach.

    (a) *Planning:* Planning what you are going to write will result in more concise writing. Determine what is really necessary to say, keeping in mind that the communication must be clear. What is not required is stating the obvious.
    (b) *Revision:* In the revision stage, when reviewing the communication from the reader's viewpoint, look for short, simple sentences and the use of active voice. Using a conversational style will also lead to more concise writing.

(5) *Variety:* In order to maintain a reader's interest in what you are attempting to say, use a variety of techniques to enhance the message you are conveying. The use of synonyms helps to vary the word usage and the choice of words. Individual sentences may be constructed in different ways. Entire messages may need to be varied in cases where the same letter is being sent to a number of different people—remember to keep the reader's perspective in mind.

    (a) *Word usage:* A thesaurus is a reference that is helpful in determining other words that have the same meaning as the one being conveyed in the message. Look for synonyms to add variety to the writing.

        EXAMPLES:
        action: *performance, movement, working, operation*

record: account, minutes, diary, journal, proceedings

(b) *Sentences:* The use of a combination of simple, compound, complex, and occasionally a compound-complex sentence will help to vary the sentence construction. There should also be a combination of short, medium, and long sentences to keep the reader interested in the writing. Sentences should normally average about 15 to 20 words.

(c) *Messages:* To make the writing more interesting to the writer as well as the reader, messages need to be varied so that they are appropriate for the person receiving them and the purpose for which they are intended. Variable information needs to be inserted so that each message is personalized.

EXAMPLE: In word processing, form letters and form paragraphs are used to express the same messages to a number of different people. Even though the basic message can stay the same, paragraphs or other variable information pertinent only to one individual can be inserted to personalize the message. The receiver of the message feels that the message was written personally, even though the basic message is standard to all recipients.

(6) *Clarity:* Any message needs to be written in a clear, accurate manner. Knowing the purpose of the message first will help you accomplish clarity in your writing. Combining clarity with the use of the "you" approach will help to direct the message to the reader.

(a) *Purposes:* It is helpful for writers to outline what they wish to accomplish before they begin writing. By identifying the reasons for writing the message, the writer should be able to focus on those points first rather than "going off on tangents."

(b) *Review:* Once the message has been written, it is a good idea to set the material aside for a short time. Rereading it later may help to achieve clarity. Another technique used is to have a co-worker read the material to see if the message is clear.

Secretaries and executives need to work together to read and react to one another's writing. Such a critique can be a very helpful strategy in improving the writing that is transmitted from the office, especially in cases where the writing concerns sensitive issues.

Composing Communications

225

(7) *Accuracy:* Any type of business writing should be accurate—accurate in terms of message, format, and language.

   (a) *Message:* The message should contain accurate data and other detailed information. Specific references to data sources are extremely important, especially if the reader needs to know the credibility of the data. The message should present the information in a logical, sequential manner so that the reader can follow the accuracy of the message.

   (b) *Format:* The message should be produced in a document format that is accurate; the margins should "frame" the writing so the appearance is pleasing to the eye. Also, material can be placed in columns within the document to enhance the presentation of key material. The secretary plays a very important role in being sure that the document format is determined *before* the message is prepared in written form.

   (c) *Language:* A message must be produced in document format in grammatically correct language. What impression will the reader have of the message or the firm if poor English and inaccurate punctuation exist within the sentence construction? The typical reaction to a poor communication is that the firm probably produces an inferior product too.

d. *Development of goodwill:* Each message conveyed from one organization to another has the capacity of creating goodwill between the organizations. Goodwill develops when people work together, within the organization or with others outside the organization, and communicate positively, clearly, and courteously.

(1) *Considerateness:* Communication that will create goodwill needs to express consideration for the other person. In other words, the writer must think of the receiver of the message and the effect that message will have upon that individual. A genuine interest in the reader must be emphasized in the communication.

EXAMPLE: A message of welcome to the new secretary in the office may be a warm, considerate step for others in the office to take. When an employee has been out of the office due to illness, a "welcome back" message may help bridge the gap for that person—that first day back to work may be difficult.

(2) *Empathy:* The "you" approach in business writing helps to create empathy in writing. The writer must be able to see the difficulty or problem from the reader's point of view. *Empathy* refers to an understanding of the feelings or emotions of another person. (It is important to know the difference between sympathy (feeling sorry for) and empathy (understanding feelings).

EXAMPLE: Moving to a new location has not been an easy task for you and your family, and I want to be as helpful as I can with the transition.

(3) *Courtesy:* Concern for the reader will help you deliver a courteous message. The "pleases" and "thank yous" come naturally when you consider the best interests of others. The best tone your letter can produce is a natural one. A technique that often shows courtesy is the inclusion of the reader's name throughout the correspondence; it gives the reader the feeling of importance.

EXAMPLE: Please send us your report as soon as it is convenient for you, Bob. Your writing is always of the highest quality so I know that only minor revisions may be necessary. Thank you for your willingness to help us with this report.

(4) *Sincerity:* Sincerity is a genuine expression of confidence and trust shown in other people. In some business writing it is important to keep confidential certain facts and data. Sincere writing eliminates excessive humility, flattery, or overstatement of information.

EXAMPLE: We know that you will be able to give us the information we need because of your expertise in this area. We want to reassure you, however, that your responses to our questions will be held in strict confidence and analyzed as part of the total response from the sample.

(5) *Respect:* Effective business communication requires that respect be shown for the company represented, for products or services being provided, and for the reader of the message. The use of tact, consideration, and courtesy is very important in business writing *if* you want the reader to respond in a given way. Respect needs to be shown not only for the individual but for the individual's position within the firm as well.

EXAMPLE: We are very eager to have you try our latest product—the Correcto ribbon—because we think you will find it more adaptable to your needs than other ribbons on the market. Sometimes ribbons break or tear while being used. Ours will not! Your experience as a secretary will enable you to give us an honest evaluation of this new product.

Goodwill developed among people is very important in today's business world, and secretaries can do much to further the development of goodwill through attention to considerateness, empathy, courtesy, sincerity, and respect created through effective business communication.

B. Business Letters

The business letter is associated with *external* communication. It is the type of written communication used most often for corresponding with others outside the organization. The sender uses the letter as a means to inform the receiver of various kinds of business news and events. Business letters need to be written from the reader's viewpoint by using the "you" approach.

1. *Positive Letters:* Of course, the most pleasant type of letter to write or receive is the *positive* or *favorable* letter—the letter that says "yes" or otherwise presents good news to the reader. The main purpose of the positive letter is to transmit needed information that will please the receiver.

    a. *Types of positive letters:* There are numerous reasons for writing positive or favorable letters. Here are some of the more typical types of positive correspondence.

        (1) *Order for goods or services:* Especially in small companies or in situations where a purchase order is not used in ordering goods or services, a letter will initiate such an order. Complete information needs to be included identifying the exact purchase:

- Name of item(s) or service(s).
- Descriptions: sizes, order numbers, or type of service requested.
- Prices, if known.
- Shipping information.

        (2) *Letter granting refund or adjustment:* It is most important to describe the claim briefly and to explain the exact refund or adjustment made. Such information as purchase order or invoice numbers must be included.

        (3) *Response to inquiry for information:* Frequently letters are received that request certain types of information. The direct approach enables the writer to provide answers to those questions asked.

EXAMPLES: Inquiries might include requests for subscription information for a new computer magazine, information needed to obtain a credit account, and information on a new training program available for prospective word processing specialists.

(4) *Goodwill message:* The primary purpose of some correspondence is to generate goodwill (a favorable attitude and feeling) toward you and your organization from others with whom you conduct business. A goodwill message can express sympathy, congratulations, or thanks.

EXAMPLES:
THANKS: A letter thanking Paula Robinson, a business consultant, for presenting a seminar on "Communication Techniques for the Professional Secretary" at the November meeting of the local chapter of Professional Secretaries International.

SYMPATHY: A letter to Betty Jacobson, one of the company's clients, expressing condolence on the death of her father.

CONGRATULATIONS: A letter congratulating Alice Moore-Young on being promoted to administrative manager of the Kendall Corporation.

b. *Writing approach:* The direct or deductive approach is used in writing positive letters. When your correspondence carries good news, get to the point immediately. Why bother with the details when the reader is most interested in hearing the good news first? Then, you can follow up with the facts and close the message with a positive, forward-looking comment.

(1) *Direct or deductive approach:* Since goodwill is created in the first paragraph, begin with a general statement of the main point of the message. With the direct approach, you immediately provide the reader with the information he/she wishes to receive.

EXAMPLE: Mr. Randy Daily, our computer operator, will be glad to speak to your trainee group on Tuesday, December 4. (This first paragraph says "yes" immediately, indicating a favorable response.)

(2) *Detailed follow-up:* In the next paragraph, the necessary details should be explained. It is important that the recipient understand any conditions or other details relating to the message.

Composing Communications 229

EXAMPLE: Mr. Daily will meet with the group in Conference Room B from 1:30 to 3:00 P.M. From your suggestions, he plans to discuss job submission, preparing the system, watching for down signals, and system demands. (This paragraph covers the details of the presentation.)

(3) *Closing statement:* The message should close with a general positive statement or a request for action (a courteous request). If you need action by a given date, this deadline should be included as well as any special reasons for needing this information by then.

EXAMPLE: Please review these areas with the trainees prior to December 4. There should be some good discussion following his presentation. It is always exciting to exchange information with interested, young people entering the field. (This paragraph includes a positive note about a stimulating discussion with the trainee group.)

Figure 8-1 illustrates the complete example of the positive or favorable letter.

```
Dear Ms. Stanley

Mr. Randy Daily, our computer operator,
will be glad to speak to your trainee
group on Tuesday, December 4.

Mr. Daily will meet with the group in
Conference Room B from 1:30 to 3:00 P.M
From your suggestions, he plans to
discuss job submission, preparing
the system, watching for down signals, and
system demands.

Please review these areas with  the
trainees prior to December 4.  There
should be some good discussion followin
his presentation.  It is always excitin
to exchange information with interested
young people entering the field.

Sincerely
```

Figure 8-1
Example of Positive or Favorable Letter

2. *Routine or Neutral Letter:* The primary purpose of the routine letter is to exchange day-to-day information. Routine or neutral letters are written more often than any other type of letter. The routine nature of the letters results in a favorable reception to these letters.

   a. *Types of routine letters:* Primarily, routine correspondence includes either requests for information or responses to information requests received. Here are some typical types of routine or neutral letters:

(1) *Request for information:* A simple request for information can be stated precisely and sometimes briefly.

EXAMPLE: A letter requests a vendor to send pricing information for a new computer just being marketed.

(2) *Response to information request:* Sometimes inquiries are received which need to be answered within a short period of time.

EXAMPLE: An inquiry is made about appropriate procedures to use in securing an automobile loan from the credit union.

b. *Writing approach:* Again, the direct or deductive approach is used in writing routine or neutral correspondence.

(1) *Direct or deductive writing:* The main point of the message is presented in the first paragraph.

EXAMPLE: Would you please give me your opinion on a storage problem? (This opening sentence is a direct request for advice.)

(2) *Detailed follow-up:* Factual information should follow so the reader understands the need for information.

EXAMPLE: Recently we purchased a two-year supply of steel moldings. When these moldings were purchased, we had access to our factory warehouse. With a decision to expand operations, the warehouse is needed for manufacturing materials. Our production manager suggested that the steel moldings be stockpiled outdoors. (This paragraph follows up with factual information.)

My concern with stockpiling outdoors is the effect of rust and pitting. I understand your company has used this method of storage for a number of years with much success. In your opinion, is there any serious risk in exposing steel moldings to weather conditions for as long as two years? (This paragraph identifies major concerns and makes the actual inquiry.)

(3) *Closing statement:* A summarizing statement in the closing paragraph reemphasizes the main point of the message or requests some type of action, sometimes according to a specific deadline.

EXAMPLE: I would appreciate any advice you can offer about outdoor storage. We plan to have our next meeting on June 15. Could I hear from you before that time? (This closing paragraph asks for action and sets a time line for a reply.)

Figure 8-2 shows the complete example of the routine or neutral letter.

```
Dear Mr. Boyce

Would you please give me your opinion on
a storage problem?

Recently we purchased a two-year supply
of steel moldings.  When these moldings
were purchased, we had access to our
factory warehouse.  With a decision to
expand operations, the warehouse is
needed for manufacturing materials.  Our
production manager suggested that the
steel moldings be stockpiled outdoors.

My concern with stockpiling outdoors is
the effect of rust and pitting.  I
understand your company has used this
method of storage for a number of years
with much success.  In your opinion, is
there any serious risk in exposing steel
moldings to weather conditions for as
long as two years?

I would appreciate any advice you can
offer about outdoor storage.  We plan to
have our next meeting on June 15.  Could
I hear from you before that time?

Sincerely
```

Figure 8-2
Example of Routine Letter

3. *Negative Letter:* When correspondence conveys a "no" response or some other form of bad news, you should use the *indirect* approach. This approach may also be referred to as the *inductive* approach. Many times the reader is more likely to do what you hope s/he will do and is more willing to accept the bad news if the details are presented first. Otherwise, the facts may not be read. Some feel that the bad news should be placed within a paragraph in the middle of the letter. If this approach is used, you must be very careful that the news you are relaying to the reader is clear. And, of course, you will want to close the message with a forward-looking comment which can be positive for both you and the reader. The negative letter is also referred to as an *unfavorable* letter.

    a. *Types of negative letters:* The letter that says "no" or includes a refusal is necessary in many different types of business situations. Here are a few types of negative letters that may be written:

        (1) *Refusal to send information:* You may receive an inquiry for some information that is not readily available or

cannot be released. In this case, a refusal letter must be written in a polite, courteous manner, so the reader will not be offended.

(2) *Refusal to give assistance:* A request for assistance might be received, asking for help with a particular problem. You may feel that you are not the right person to ask or do not have the time to adequately carry out the request.

(3) *Problem with order for goods/services:* An order that has been received may not be able to be filled at this time. Perhaps the inventory is low, and the order will not be filled until that inventory is replenished. A letter will need to be sent explaining the delay in shipment.

(4) *Refusal to grant particular action:* Perhaps you are unable to grant the particular action requested by the writer. In cases where you will be unable to grant a claim or extension of time, a refusal letter must be written.

b. *Writing approach:* The indirect, or inductive, approach is recommended for writing negative letters.

(1) *Buffer paragraph:* Since the facts need to be read and understood *before* the bad news is communicated, a beginning paragraph setting the stage may be necessary. Such a paragraph is called a *buffer paragraph.* One must be careful not to be too wordy, or the reader will begin to read between the lines, assume the news, and not read the important part of the letter—the facts.

EXAMPLE: You can count on a large, interested readership for the article you are writing about the importance of sales letters in business.
(This paragraph demonstrates a buffer beginning, yet is not too lengthy.)

(2) *Rationale for refusal:* Next, reasons must be stated for the refusal, followed by a clearly stated refusal. The facts must be put into perspective from two viewpoints:

(a) The philosophy of the business, realizing the goals of the organization.
(b) The reader's viewpoint, realizing the wants and concerns of the reader.

This is where the balancing act will come into play. By carefully outlining these two viewpoints, the message can be developed in an honest approach, never losing sight of the reader's wants and concerns. The message needs to be delivered in as tactful and understanding manner as possible.

EXAMPLE: Our company depends on effective sales letters to interest new clients. Through the years, we have tested our letters extensively to find the most effective sales techniques for the written message. Our writers are continually revising, conducting test mailings, and comparing returns. The best letters used by Appleton Enterprises represent a considerable investment in both time and money.

(This paragraph presents reasons. Even though the reasons are based on company policy, company policy is an internal matter and cannot be used as a reason in an external communication. Also, reasons given are logical enough that there is no need for an apology.)

(3) *The bad news:* Once the rationale has been given, the refusal or other "bad news" should be presented.

EXAMPLE: Because of the time and research put into our sales letters, several other companies have expressed an interest in using our material. Therefore, it was necessary to copyright all our sales letters and confine them to company use. Should we release them for publication, we would incur the same expense once again because their effectiveness for us would be decreased.

(This paragraph implies "no." Yet, this explanation is written clearly enough so the reader understands that the letters cannot be used in the article.)

(4) *Closing statement:* The ending of the letter will either ask for action on the part of the reader or present a forward look if the news was unfavorable. Since you are hoping to continue correspondence with the reader, you will want a pleasant closing for your message. Avoid being apologetic. If the facts are well thought out, they will be logical and no apology will be necessary.

EXAMPLE: I am enclosing two bulletins and a bibliography we have found helpful in developing our letters. You may also find the material helpful with your article. I look forward to reading your article in the Writer's Guide when it is published.

(This letter closes with a positive note stating interest in reading the article when it is published. In addition, reference materials were sent to the reader in an effort to help.)

In writing a negative or unfavorable letter, you must take the time to write a tactful, courteous letter with the reader's feelings in mind. If the letter discusses a particularly sensitive issue, set it aside for a short time. Then reread it and revise it so the message is clear and will be interpreted correctly by the reader. Or, have a co-worker read the letter for clarity, empathy, sincerity, and goodwill. Figure 8-3 shows the complete example of the negative letter.

4. *Combination Letter:* There are times when you can say "yes" to the reader for only part of what is requested. In this case, the message should begin with the positive response, followed by facts that support both the positive and the negative responses. The "no" response needs to be clearly stated, with the letter closing on a positive note.

   a. *Types of combination letters:* Letters that contain both a positive and a negative response may be written for a variety of reasons. Here are a few examples of how the combination letter might be used:

```
Dear Ms. Brothers

You can count on a large, interested
readership for the article you are writing
about the importance of sales letters in
business.

Our company depends on effective sales
letters to interest new clients.  Through the
years, we have tested our letters extensively
to find the most effective sales techniques
for the written message.  Our writers are
continually revising, conducting test
mailings, and comparing returns.  The best
letters used by Appleton Enterprises
represent a considerable investment in both
time and money.

Because of the time and research put into our
sales letters, several other companies have
expressed an interest in using our material.
Therefore, it was necessary to copyright all
our sales letters and confine them to company
use.  Should we release them for publication,
we would incur the same expense once again
because their effectiveness for us would be
decreased.

I am enclosing two bulletins and a
bibliography we have found helpful in
developing our letters.  You may also find
the material helpful with your article.  I
look forward to reading your article in the
Writer's Guide when it is published.

Sincerely
```

Figure 8-3
Example of Negative Letter

(1) *Partial order being filled:* Perhaps only part of a sales order can be filled at this time. The combination letter must identify the part of the order that can be filled, followed by reference to the part of the order that cannot be filled.

(2) *Partial response to information request:* A request for information may include some questions that can be answered as well as some questions that need replies from other departments or individuals.

b. *Writing approach:* In writing a combination letter, it is best to start with the positive aspect of the message.

(1) *Opening paragraph:* Begin the first paragraph with the positive or "yes" response to the original message, being careful not to lead the reader into thinking the "yes" is for everything.

EXAMPLE: Your four rose bushes should arrive by May 20, just in time for spring planting. They were shipped via AR Express, one of our most reliable shipping companies.
   (The opening paragraph says "yes," making it clear which part of the request is positive.)

(2) *Detailed follow-up:* Follow the "yes" statement with facts supporting both the positive and the negative aspects of the message.

  (a) The presentation of these facts needs to be logical.
  (b) It should be clear to the reader which facts relate to the positive part of the message and which ones relate to the negative part of the message.

EXAMPLE: You will be more than happy with the blossoms these rose bushes yield. These bushes should be planted in a sunny area, keeping the ground moist with evening waterings. For your climate, it is best to use rose mounds or cones for winter protection.
   (Facts relating to the good news are presented in this paragraph and will be separated from the facts in the following paragraph which carries the bad news.)
   The peach trees you ordered ordinarily bloom in April, a time when the Illinois climate varies between 35 and 50 degrees. These peach trees would almost certainly bloom before the last freeze of the winter season. For trees that bloom after the danger of freezes in your area, we recommend the Ambrosia. This peach tree produces peaches similar to those of the trees you ordered. The Ambrosia blooms in

late May; details are presented in the enclosed brochure.

(This paragraph advises that the item ordered is not the best choice, and facts about the tree ordered are compared with facts of an alternative choice so that the reader can decide what action to take. A brochure with more detailed information is enclosed for more detailed information.)

(3) *Closing statement:* The letter should close with a positive, forward-looking request for action on the part of the reader. The "no" response to the reader must be clearly stated.

EXAMPLE: Just indicate your instructions on the enclosed post card. If we hear from you prior to May 1, we can change your order to the Ambrosia for the same price. Also, you would still be able to plant your trees to take advantage of this season's growth and have them in bloom next year.

Figure 8-4 is the complete example of the combination letter.

```
Dear Ms. Wieland

Your four rose bushes should arrive by May
20, just in time for spring planting.  They
were shipped via AR Express, one of our most
reliable shipping companies.

You will be more than happy with the blossoms
these rose bushes yield.  These bushes should
be planted in a sunny area, keeping the
ground moist with evening waterings.  For
your climate, it is best to use rose mounds
or cones for winter protection.

The peach trees you ordered ordinarily bloom
in April, a time when the Illinois climate
varies between 35 and 50 degrees.  The peach
trees would almost certainly bloom before the
last freeze of the winter season.  For trees
that bloom after the danger of freezes in
your area, we recommend the Ambrosia.  This
peach tree produces peaches similar to those
of the trees you ordered.  The Ambrosia
blooms in late May; details are presented in
the enclosed brochure.

Just indicate your instructions on the
enclosed post card.  If we hear from you
prior to May 1, we can change your order to
the Ambrosia for the same price.  Also, you
would still be able to plant your trees to
take advantage of this season's growth and
have them in bloom next year.

Sincerely yours
```

Figure 8-4
Example of Combination Letter

Composing Communications

5. *Persuasive Letter:* A persuasive letter presents positive information to the reader, but the nature of the information is more complex. The writer requests that the receiver take some action. However, the writer has the task of providing enough justification for the action that the receiver will be motivated to act.

   a. *Types of persuasive letters:* Letters that are persuasive in nature may be used for many different reasons. Here are some typical types of persuasive communication that might be used:

      (1) *Special requests for assistance:* Community agencies or nonprofit organizations may engage in fund-raising activities to help economically disadvantaged or handicapped groups. Requests for assistance may be sent out to mailing lists to encourage contributions to be made.

      (2) *Special requests for information:* People who are engaged in research find it necessary to make special requests to individuals who are known in a field to help with certain types of information. Such a request must persuade the receiver to cooperate and assist with the study.

      (3) *Marketing goods, services, or ideas:* A frequently used persuasive letter is the sales letter, which attempts to interest the receiver in a new service, product, or idea. Such a letter must be written with the receiver in mind so that the new goods or service would appeal to that age group, a person in that particular position, or a person with specific types of needs.

   b. *Writing approach:* The approach used most often in writing the persuasive letter is the Attention-Interest-Desire-Action approach (also known as the A-I-D-A approach).

      (1) *Opening paragraph:* The opening paragraph must get the reader's attention. This may be accomplished by appealing to the reader's interests, problems, or responsibilities. Sometimes it is helpful to begin with a question for the reader.

      EXAMPLE: May we have your help again this year? Thanks to your very generous donation in the past, we have been able to keep our Animal Shelter open. This Christmas we need your thoughtfulness and kindness again.

      (This paragraph introduces the reader to the problem and, hopefully, gets the reader's attention.)

      (2) *Detailed follow-up:* Next, you need to emphasize the

reasons why the reader should respond positively to the request. Describe the details of your request by using words that help the reader identify with the positive benefits of responding favorably to your request. You want the reader to react positively to your message.

EXAMPLE: The animals we house at the Animal Shelter must be kept warm, clean, and fed through the winter months. Here are some of the ways in which we use your donations:
1. *Homes are provided for many stray dogs and cats until they are adopted.*
2. *Veterinarian care is provided for hurt, sick, or abused animals.*
3. *Programs on responsible pet care are made available to the general public.*
4. *Visits with the animals to the senior citizens retirement centers are very therapeutic and bring much happiness to the residents.*

(3) *Closing statement:* Explain to the reader courteously what action should be taken. In the closing statement, appeal to the reader's interest in helping solve the problem.

EXAMPLE: Please use the enclosed reply envelope to send your contribution today. Your Christmas donation will show your continued love and concern for animals and those who benefit from the shelter's service.

Figure 8-5 is the complete example of the persuasive letter.

6. *Form Letters:* Correspondence with some identical parts may be sent to more than one person or company for a specific purpose. Perhaps an individual has not paid a bill, and a form letter (always sent to a person who does not pay a bill within the first 30 days) is prepared and sent. Word processing has made it possible for form documents to be created so the secretary has the timesaving capability of only providing the variable information that must be inserted. Form letters may be of three types: personalized repetitive letters, letters with variable information, and letters created from standard form paragraphs.

   a. *Personalized repetitive letters:* Repetitive letters are form letters that are being prepared and sent to a list of different people. One of the purposes of word processing is to help personalize these repetitive letters. Each letter should appear as if it had been individually prepared and typed for the

Composing Communications

```
Dear Mrs. Donaldson

May we have your help again this year?
Thanks to your very generous donation in the
past, we have been able to keep our Animal
Shelter open.  This Christmas we need your
thoughtfulness and kindness again.

The animals we house at the Animal Shelter
must be kept warm, clean, and fed through the
winter months.  Here are some of the ways in
which we use your donations:

1.   Homes are provided for many stray dogs
     and cats until they are adopted.

2.   Veterinarian care is provided for hurt,
     sick, or abused animals.

3.   Programs on responsible pet care are
     made available to the general public.

4.   Visits with the animals to the senior
     citizens retirement centers are very
     therapeutic and bring much happiness to
     the residents.

Please use the enclosed reply envelope to
send your contribution today.  Your Christmas
donation will show your continued love and
concern for animals and those who benefit
from the shelter's service.

Sincerely yours
```

Figure 8-5
Example of Persuasive Letter

receiver. In addition, the letter may contain personalized messages for the recipients—a postscript on some messages, the use of the individual's name in the body of the message. Here is a typical message that is intended for a large group of people.

EXAMPLE: Every year the Royal Travel Service serves hundreds of Milwaukee area residents who wish to escape from the winter snows and bask in the sunny climate of Florida for the winter.

We have groups leaving Milwaukee during the first week of every month from December through March so they can spend from two to four weeks at their favorite vacation spot. Our service allows you to "leave the flying to us"; let us arrange your flight, ground transportation, and hotel accommodations if needed.

Our next vacation group leaves from Milwaukee on January 4 for sunny Florida. Won't you let us help you plan your winter vacation in Florida?

(1) *Use of personal names:* Personal names are used mostly in the inside address, the salutation, and perhaps one reference within the body of the message. With repetitive letters, it is important to keep the letter as standard as possible, with very little change from letter to letter.

EXAMPLE:
Mr. and Mrs. Robert Stevens
433 West Wisconsin Avenue
Milwaukee, WI 53215

Dear Mr. and Mrs. Stevens:
Every year the Royal Travel Service serves hundreds of Milwaukee area residents like Robert and Mary Stevens who wish to escape from the winter snows and bask in the sunny climate of Florida for the winter.
   [Note: The rest of the message would stay the same.]

(2) *Use of postscripts:* When a number of repetitive letters are being prepared, it may be necessary to add a postscript to some of them in order to personalize the message. Here is an example of a postscript that might be added to the foregoing example:

EXAMPLE:
P.S. Bob and Mary, we are looking forward to the possibility of having you with us again this year. Didn't we have fun last year? By the way, be sure to ask for the 10 percent discount available to those who have traveled with us before.

b. *Letters with variable information:* A repetitive letter may have variable information as well as constant information. *Constant information* is the wording that will stay exactly the same on every letter produced. *Variable information* is any text that must be inserted to complete the message; this information will change on each letter produced. The letter used in the preceding example may be changed to include variable information.

EXAMPLE: Every year the Royal Travel Service serves hundreds of   (1)   area residents who wish to escape from the winter snows and bask in the sunny climate of   (2)   for the winter.
   We have groups leaving   (1)   during the first week of every month from December through March so they can spend from two to four weeks at their favorite vacation spot. Our service allows you to "leave the flying to us"; let us arrange your flight, ground transportation, and hotel accommodations if needed.

Our next vacation group leaves from ___(1)___ on ___(3)___ for sunny ___(2)___. Won't you let us help you plan your winter vacation in ___(2)___ ?

Variables:
*Letter to Mr. and Mrs. Robert Stevens
  433 West Wisconsin Avenue
  Milwaukee, WI 53214*

  *(1) Milwaukee
  (2) Florida
  (3) January 4*

*Letter to Mr. George P. Hendricks
  5554 North Michigan Avenue
  Chicago, IL 60656*

  *(1) Chicago
  (2) Arizona
  (3) January 10*

Two methods that are used in word processing for the preparation of letters with variable information include the use of merge codes for keying in variable information or the use of data bases to create records of variable information to merge with form letters and other types of forms.

(1) *Use of merge codes:* The form letter is recorded on some form of word processing media, for example, disks, with appropriate input codes inserted at the "spots" where the variables should be keyed. The insertion of each variable is a manual operation. Once a variable has been keyed and inserted into the document, the secretary can continue the automatic operation until the next point where variable information needs to be inserted.

(2) *Data bases of information:* A complete record of variable information may be available in the form of a data base. In word processing this is usually referred to as a mail-merge function that requires the preparation of a primary document (the form letter) and a secondary document (the variables). This data base of information can include the following types of data:

- Name, address, and telephone number of each person
- Account number
- Employment
- Employer address
- Any other variable information that might be pertinent

When the form letter is prepared, merge commands are inserted at the points where variable information will be inserted into the final letter. These merge commands are prompts that ask for specific information from the data base. In the final preparation of the letter, the form letter is merged with appropriate information from the data base. Additional variable information, only appearing once, can be inserted manually into the final document.

c. *Letters from form paragraphs:* Business organizations use many kinds of form paragraphs to create form letters. Some form paragraphs say "yes," others say "no" or persuade. A series of form paragraphs pertaining to particular situations can be stored so the secretary can recall only those paragraphs that are appropriate for a given situation. The result is a personalized letter for each recipient.

EXAMPLES OF FORM PARAGRAPHS:
(1) Every year the Royal Travel Service serves hundreds of (1) area residents who wish to escape from the winter snows and bask in the sunny climate of (2) for the winter.
(2) Every year the Royal Travel Service serves hundreds of (1) businesses who wish to schedule conferences in other parts of the country. Getting away from the winter snows and spending time in a sunny climate may appeal to you and your business associates.
(3) We have groups leaving (1) during the first week of every month from December through March so they can spend from two to four weeks at their favorite vacation spot. Our service allows you to "leave the flying to us"; let us arrange your flight, ground transportation, and hotel accommodations if needed.
(4) We can schedule a group tour, if you wish, at any time during the month and at any time of the year. Special rates are available, depending upon the length of your conference. Our service allows you to "leave the flying to us"; let us arrange any flight, ground transportation, hotel, or meeting accommodations your organization may require.
(5) Our next vacation group leaves from (1) on (3) for sunny (2). Won't you let us help you plan your winter vacation in (2)?
(6) Please contact our local representative, (4), at (5) to obtain more details on our conference service to business organizations in the area. Try us—you'll like us!

EXAMPLE OF MERGED LETTER:
This example combines form paragraphs (2), (4), and (6).

Robert Jensen & Associates
5430 North Michigan Avenue
Chicago, IL 60656

Dear Mr. Jensen:

Every year the Royal Travel Service serves hundreds of Chicago *businesses who wish to schedule conferences in other parts of the country. Getting away from the winter snows and spending time in a sunny climate may appeal to you and your business associates.*

We can schedule a group tour, if you wish, at any time during the month and at any time of the year. Special rates are available, depending upon the length of your conference. Our service allows you to "leave the flying to us"; let us arrange any flight, ground transportation, hotel, or meeting accommodations your organization may require.

Please contact our local representative, C.S. Moore, *at* (312) 555-2300 *to obtain more details on our conference service to business organizations in the area. Try us—you'll like us!*

Sincerely,

Paulette S. Bronson
General Manager

[Note: The underlined information represents the variable information that would be entered from the data base or manually.]

The more routine, repetitive letters are designed as form letters and prepared using word processing software, the more time the secretary will have for customized work. Anytime a letter must be prepared more than once with identical information, this type of procedure should be considered.

C. Interoffice Communication

The most common form of communication *within* an organization is through interoffice communication. *Interoffice* means from one office to another within an organization. *Intraoffice* communication would be communication from one organization to another (external form of communication). Interoffice communication takes the form of memoranda or short, informal reports.

1. *Memorandums:* The most common medium for corresponding within the firm is the interoffice memorandum. The memo (as it is often called) can always be used for communication whenever the writer and the receiver of the message work for the same organiza-

tion. Just as with business letters, memorandums can be prepared that are favorable, unfavorable, or persuasive in nature.

- **a.** *Favorable memorandums:* When writing a memorandum that is favorable in nature, the same principles that are used for writing favorable business letters can be applied.

    (1) *Types of favorable memorandums:* Here are some of the more common reasons why favorable memorandums may be written:

    (a) *Request for information:* The memo is written to present an explanatory summary of information.
    (b) *Response to information request:* The memo may be an answer to a previous memo which requested certain information.
    (c) *Request for assistance:* The memo may be a request for help in locating specific information from the files or records.
    (d) *Directives:* The memo may issue a directive from a superior with complete instructions for performance of a particular assignment.

    (2) *Writing approach:* The direct or deductive approach is used in writing favorable memorandums. The style of writing may vary somewhat depending on the purpose of the memo.

    (a) *Direct or deductive approach:* Begin the memo with a statement of the general objective.

    EXAMPLE: The attached list of clients who have utilized our services at least once in the last six months will give you the information you requested for your semiannual report.

    (b) *Presentation of details:* Follow the general opening statement with the information supporting the ideas presented in the memo. It is usually a good idea to present information to only one objective in each memo. Otherwise, there is the problem of determining under what name or title the memo will be filed for later reference.
    (c) *Closing statement:* A closing comment or statement is required if it is necessary to summarize or give an opinion or recommendation. In addition, an offer to help further provides a courteous closing to the message.

- **b.** *Unfavorable memorandums:* Memorandums that are unfavorable in nature and carry a "no" response should be written using the *indirect*, or *inductive*, approach. The position and status of the writer and the receiver of the message should also be considered very carefully so that lines of authority are observed in the tone and style of the memorandum. Similar techniques to those used in writing negative letters should be used.

(1) *Types of unfavorable memorandums:* Here are some of the more common purposes of unfavorable memorandums:

   (a) *Refusal of information request:* You may receive a request for information that is confidential in nature and cannot be released or information that is not available to you. Reasons should be given in the memorandum demonstrating why it is impossible for you to supply the information.

   (b) *Refusal to give assistance:* You may be asked for your help, but it may be necessary for you to consult with your superior to see if it would be all right for you to help. When you find it necessary to refuse, you should do it in a courteous way, perhaps suggesting an alternative.

   (c) *Performance evaluation:* A memorandum that explains an unfavorable performance evaluation should be handled with care. The contents of the memorandum should be explained in person as well as in written form so that the individual being evaluated has an opportunity to question or discuss aspects of the evaluation with the supervisor.

(2) *Writing approach:* The indirect, or inductive, approach is recommended for unfavorable memorandums. The writing style used will depend upon the position of the individual who is receiving the memo as well as the nature of the message being presented.

   (a) *Buffer paragraph:* A beginning paragraph should set the stage for the explanation to follow. A brief introduction to the nature of the memo should be stated clearly.

   (b) *Rationale for refusal:* The basic reasons for having to refuse to assist or give information should be explained briefly and clearly. The details must be presented so that the views of the organization as well as the reader are considered important.

   (c) *The bad news:* The refusal or other bad news should be stated definitely so that there will be no misunderstanding on the part of the recipient.

   (d) *Options:* Following the refusal, you may present available options: make a referral, offer a substitute,

or suggest an alternative procedure. Offering an option is called refusing *with* recourse.

(e) *Closing statement:* The ending of the memo may ask for some further action on the part of the receiver or present an alternative that might be considered.

c. *Persuasive memorandums:* A similar approach to that used for persuasive letters should be used in writing memorandums that are persuasive in nature. The *Attention-Interest-Desire-Action* approach should be used to develop a message that results in some positive action taken by the recipient.

(1) *Types of persuasive memorandums:* Usually a persuasive memorandum is designed to get someone else to act or to do something for you. Here are some typical reasons for using persuasive memorandums:

(a) *Special request for information:* You may find that you need some information for research you are doing. A special request to someone in charge of records for the company may provide you with needed information to complete your research.

(b) *Special request for assistance:* In office work there arise times when assistance is needed in handling a particularly difficult problem. A special request in the form of a memorandum would be needed in situations where a brief explanation of the problem would help the individual decide whether or not to help.

(c) *Selling a service or idea:* An offer to help another person within the organization, through a service or an idea, should be put into writing so that the recipient will have time to consider the importance of the offer to particular work being done. A serious offer such as this requires time so the recipient of the message can consider alternatives.

(2) *Writing approach:* The writing approach used for persuasive letters will also be used for writing persuasive memorandums. The primary objective of the memorandum is to encourage someone to act positively toward a request that is being made.

(a) *Opening paragraph:* The opening paragraph of the memorandum must get the reader's attention. Sometimes an opening question will appeal to the reader's interest.

(b) *Details:* The rationale for a positive reaction to the

request needs to be presented next. You need to emphasize the reasons why the reader should respond favorably to your request, and you need to provide details so that the reader understands your request completely.

(c) *Closing statement:* End the memo with a courteous request that a certain action be taken. In this paragraph, you need to appeal to the reader's interest in helping to solve the problem or act in a specific way.

[See Chapter 11, Preparing Communications in Final Format, for an explanation of the document format to use in preparing interoffice memorandums.]

2. *Informal or Short Reports:* Another form of interoffice communication is the informal or short report. This type of report is used to transmit meaningful information to other people within the organization or outside the organization. Perhaps the most important aspect of the report, besides its content, is the fact that it is *informal* and *short*. Typically, an informal report is no more than five pages at the most. In fact, the fewer the pages the better; the busy executive will look at the first page of such a report and will need to be persuaded through the message to read further.

a. *Types of informal or short reports:* There are numerous ways in which the informal or short report can present business information. Some of the more common types of short reports include:

(1) *Proposals:* The development of new office procedures or new equipment may necessitate the development of a proposal. The proposal includes information such as *what* the new development is, *why* it is important to the continued efficient operation of the office, *how* it will be used, and *how much* it will cost to implement. A short report should give enough information to management so that the decision can be made whether to continue with the plan.

(2) *Feasibility study:* An analysis of business systems and procedures obtained through a feasibility study may be reported to management in the format of an informal or short report. An explanation of the procedures used as well as the results will provide management with a summary of the highlights of the research.

(3) *Progress report:* Sometimes it is necessary to make a progress report that outlines steps already completed in a project and others that still need to be handled. The format for an informal or short report is very appropriate

for this type of progress report. (Sometimes this is referred to as a *work-in-process report*.)

Any business report can be written as an informal, short report. In fact, most reports are written in this form.

    b. *Acceptable formats:* Basically, three formats are used for informal or short reports: memorandum report (in the form of a memorandum), letter report (in the form of a business letter), and short report in manuscript form. (See Chapter 11, Preparing Communications in Final Format, for further explanation of memorandum, letter, and report formats.)

    c. *Writing approach:* The direct, or deductive, approach is often used in writing an informal or short report. Some managers prefer to find out results or solutions first and then the detailed information relating to those results. The inductive approach is popular, too, especially for persuasive reports.

        (1) *Personal style:* The writing style may be personal and conversational, with limited self-reference. Writing in the first or second person is acceptable if not overused.

        (2) *Presentation of information and analysis:* Depending on the problem pursued, both basic information and detailed analysis may be included in the report. Attention should be focused on brevity, however, since this is a short report of no more than five pages. The data analysis, if any, need not be as detailed as in a more formal report. A limited number of visual aids may be used to support findings.

        (3) *Supplementary information:* The report itself, without supplementary parts like appendices and bibliographies, may be the most important to the reader. Sometimes the informal or short report includes only the highlights or outline of events that were studied, with a final notation that if the reader wishes access to more detailed information, bibliography, or appendices, a request should be made.

D. Business Reports

The purpose of the business report is to transmit meaningful data to an individual(s) for either information or decision-making purposes. A business report may be an oral report or a written report. (The concentration in this chapter is on the written report.)

    1. *Types of Reports:* Reports are classified according to type of text or data material, time interval, informational flow, context, function, and message style.

        a. *Material:* Reports that include primarily text material (words) are referred to as *narrative* reports. Reports that include primarily numerical data are referred to as *statistical* reports.

b. *Time interval:* Reports known as *scheduled* reports are issued at regular, stated intervals—weekly, monthly, quarterly. *Progress* reports may be prepared in the middle of projects to report on the status of the project. *Special* reports may be prepared to handle unusual or nonroutine requests for information; these reports are prepared on demand.

c. *Informational flow:* A *vertical* report may be prepared for someone at a higher level within the organizational structure of the company or for someone at a lower level. A *horizontal* report is communication at the same administrative level and may be distributed from department to department or division to division within the organization. An *external* report is one which will be disseminated outside the organization. Sometimes these reports are called *radial* reports, reports that cut across levels of authority or move both inside and outside an organization.

d. *Context: Nontechnical* reports convey information to people who do not have backgrounds in a subject area; an effort is made in writing such a report to refrain from using technical language. *Technical* reports are designed for conveying information to professionals within the field who will understand the specialized vocabulary and terminology included in the report.

e. *Function:* Reports may be informational or analytical in nature.

   (1) *Informational report:* Facts are presented in an organized, structured manner within an information report. Sometimes the report is prepared using a standardized format, such as in the case of an inspection report or an accident report.

   (2) *Analytical report:* In addition to presenting basic information and facts, the analytical report analyzes these facts and provides an interpretation of them. A thorough analysis of the findings will lead to the development of conclusions and recommendations based upon the report.

f. *Message style:* The style used in preparing the report may be *chronological* (according to the sequence in which events occurred), *logical* (according to patterns of reasoning), or *psychological* (according to the receiver's needs).

2. *Planning, Designing, and Conducting Research:* Prior to doing the actual research for a report, it is necessary to plan in detail exactly what the research will entail. The report is the *result* of the research. Therefore, if care is exercised in planning the research study, the information required in the final report will be collected in a systematic manner.

a. *Definition of problem:* First of all, you need to know what problem needs to be solved. It is important that you distinguish the problem from the symptoms of the problem. A clear definition of the problem, as well as any limitations, is necessary.

   (1) *Research questions:* The problem may be defined in terms of specific research questions that need to be answered through the study being conducted.
   (2) *Subproblems:* The problem might be further defined into subproblem areas that will be undertaken in the study.
   (3) *Preliminary research:* In order to become familiar with the problem, find out how the organization has been involved in this type of problem solving. Research other types of background information that will help you plan the report. Included in this phase is the review of related periodical literature that may give current, practical information from business. (See Secondary research data, Section D-2-b(1) in this chapter.)
   (4) *Limitation of the problem:* Defining the problem requires that the problem be limited. Usually the general topic of the report must be narrowed so a particular problem can be pursued. Some typical questions to ask in narrowing the problem include:

   - *What* do you want to do?
   - *Why* is this important?
   - *When* will the study take place?
   - *Where* will the study take place?
   - *Who* or *What* are being studied (the sample or population)? (This is relevant if people are involved.)

   (5) *Scope of the problem:* Another consideration in defining the problem is to determine the breadth of the problem—exactly what will be studied and what will *not* be studied.
   (6) *Identification of factors or variables:* Key elements of the research are independent variables, dependent variables, and other factors affecting the design of the study and report. The identification of these elements tends to give structure to the study (and the future report). Such factors as employee attitudes, work flow, and equipment help to frame the focus of the study to precise aspects of the problem being studied.

   The problem must be defined before the subsequent steps in the process may be pursued effectively. The rest of the report format depends upon the data that need to be collected.

b. *Collecting data:* Once the problem has been defined and approved by superiors, the collection of research data may begin. Data collection is the accumulation of data or facts from secondary and primary sources in order to analyze the problem thoroughly and evaluate possible solutions to the problem.

(1) *Secondary research data:* An examination of secondary research data (research done previously) enables you to gain much background information relating to the subject of your study. Secondary research is an investigation to gather information others have prepared to use as the basis for your primary research.

   (a) *Prior research:* A review of prior research will show what research has been done already. This information is valuable to you in determining what direction your research should go—especially in terms of new directions.
   (b) *Related areas:* You may find related areas that also need to be considered in your research, some not previously considered.
   (c) *Justification for need:* A review of prior research and literature pertaining to the problem should lead to the supportive information needed to justify this particular research study or report. The comment is often made that if the research has already been done, why not use the result of that research rather than taking the time and spending the money to conduct our own?
   (d) *Supporting evidence:* Sometimes you need supportive information for procedures you choose to use or actions you hope to take to solve a problem. If someone has already used a particular procedure, this could support your use of the same procedure in a different research setting.

   Secondary research data may be obtained from company publications, general reference books, government documents, periodicals, information banks, and other types of research studies.

(2) *Primary research data:* When you conduct primary research, you are conducting an investigation to gather original information to use as current data in a report. There are three types of primary research that are conducted: experimental, observational, and survey research.

   (a) *Experimental research:* The purpose of experimental research is to determine whether a change in one factor or variable causes a change in another factor or variable. The research design must insure that any change that results is due to the factor in question.

(b) *Observational research:* The purpose of observational research is to actually see or observe the actions or results of individual or group activity. Such research may be conducted in person, actually spending time in the research location observing the behavior of people, or through an intermediary process such as videotaping or filming a work process for later review and analysis.

(c) *Survey research:* In survey research, the primary purpose is to determine opinions, beliefs, or reactions to specific work situations. The types of questions asked could range from questions about the actual work process to questions concerning the environment, technology used, or opinions about the future. A survey can be administered either in written form (a questionnaire) or oral form (an interview).

(3) *Data collection procedures:* Procedures used in collecting valid and reliable data must be planned and monitored carefully. *Valid* research procedures measure what they are intended to measure. *Reliable* data are data that are measured consistently and accurately. Care in using sampling techniques and developing questionnaires will help to increase the validity and reliability of data that are collected.

(a) *Questionnaire:* Factual data, attitudes, and opinions may be obtained through the use of a questionnaire. A questionnaire is a written form that includes all questions to be answered, space for providing the answers on the form or on an additional answer form. The use of optical character recognition (OCR) response forms will improve the speed and accuracy of data input for analysis. Specific techniques should be used in developing items for a questionnaire. Here is a sampling of some of these techniques.

- The items must be worded in a parallel manner so that they will be interpreted accurately.
- Only one response should be obtained per item; ask only one question per item.
- Responses to the questions should not be influenced by how the question is written. The statement or question should be stated as objectively and nonjudgmentally as possible.

- Only items that pertain to the research problem should be included.
- Write items that will lead to bias-free answers.
- Include items that can be answered quickly and easily. The format of the question will help in making it relatively easy for someone to respond.
- The items should be sequenced in a logical, coherent order. Sometimes it is a good idea to group all items pertaining to a particular subproblem together.

The overall format used for the questionnaire should be designed in such a way that the data will be collected in the order in which you plan to present the results in the report. The tabulation and evaluation of the data will always appear in the same sequence.

(b) *Mail questionnaire:* Many questionnaires are designed to be administered through the mail. A questionnaire will be mailed, with a letter of explanation, to each individual in the sample. Directions will be given for completing the questionnaire, and the deadline for return of the completed questionnaire will be indicated. Sometimes a self-addressed envelope is included for ease in responding.

(c) *Personal interview:* Another technique that is used to obtain responses to a questionnaire is the personal interview. An interview allows you to obtain responses to questions in person. It is important to make an appointment ahead of time for such an interview to be sure that the respondent has set aside adequate time to respond to the questions. If numerous interviews are being conducted, each one should be conducted in exactly the same way, with the questions being asked in the same sequence. The personal interview has the advantage of providing the opportunity for a more in-depth response than the mail questionnaire.

(d) *Telephone interview:* The telephone can be an important research tool as well. An interview can be conducted over the telephone, asking the respondents the same questions that would be asked in a mail questionnaire. The telephone interview must be designed to take very little time in administering. Sometimes the data are keyed directly into a computer as the respondent answers the questions. In questions with subquestions (or branches), the computer can be programmed to skip to the next appropriate question.

EXAMPLE:
If the question is this:

Do you believe that the open plan has contributed to better communication in the office?
Yes ____ No ____

If you answer "yes," skip to Questions 15-18.

The interviewer would ask the respondent the question. If the respondent answers "yes," then the computer will immediately branch to Question 15 when the interviewer enters the "yes" answer on the keyboard.

The telephone interview is still not as effective as the personal interview. A relatively small number of questions can be included in the telephone interview as compared with the personal interview, but, of course, the personal interview is more expensive.

(4) *Question format:* The format of the question plays an important role in data analysis. Select a format that makes data analysis easy. Question formats can be closed, open, or scaled.

 (a) *Closed question:* The closed question provides the respondent with a choice of answers. Choices can be as simple as *Yes, No, Don't Know* or *Agree, Disagree, No Opinion*. Sometimes the closed question requires a selection from a list.

 EXAMPLES:
 Current Occupation *(please check)*

 ___ *Student*
 ___ *Blue-collar worker*
 ___ *White-collar worker*
 ___ *Professional*
 ___ *Unemployed*
 ___ *Retired*
 ___ *Other:* _____

 Household Income *(please check)*
 (Husband/Wife Combined)

 ___ *Below $10,000*
 ___ *$10,000 - 24,999*
 ___ *$25,000 - 39,999*
 ___ *$40,000 - 59,999*
 ___ *$60,000 - 74,999*
 ___ *$75,000 and Over*

The respondents are to circle or check their responses. Sometimes it is important to clarify the choice so the respondent understands what you mean by the category. For current occupation, it may be helpful to provide a definition of blue-collar worker, white-collar worker, and professional. Notice, in all cases, a choice for alternative answers (Other, $75,000 and Over) is provided.

(b) *Open question:* The open question requires the respondent to provide an answer. No choices are provided. The possible difficulty of the open question is data analysis because of the variety of responses. Two respondents may use different terminology but may in fact mean the same answer. Many open questions can be made into closed questions. If open questions are used, provide enough space for the respondent's answer.

EXAMPLE:
What advice would you give a recent high school graduate about entering the secretarial profession?

_____

(c) *Scaled question:* Rating scales allow the respondent to rank a list of items or to respond according to a continuum. This question format also makes data analysis easy.

EXAMPLES:
Please rank the job characteristics in order of importance to you. Use 1 for most important, 2 for second most important, and so forth, until you have ranked all the items. Two blank lines have been provided for you to write in other important job characteristics.

__ *Challenge*
__ *Interaction with people*
__ *Job responsibility*
__ *Salary*
__ *Task variety*
__ _____
__ _____

For each job characteristic, please circle the degree to which the characteristic is important to you.

CHALLENGE

1	2	3	4	5
Unimportant		*Moderately Important*		*Very Important*

INTERACTION WITH PEOPLE

	1	2	3	4	5
	Unimportant		*Moderately Important*		*Very Important*

    c. *Analyzing data:* The next step is to analyze, evaluate, and interpret the data that have been collected. Data are really nothing until this phase of the research; this is the step that gives meaning to the data.

        (1) *Data organization:* Once the data are collected, they need to be organized for further evaluation and interpretation. Some of the data organization should have occurred during the development of the questionnaire, at least in the grouping of categories of questions on the questionnaire.

            (a) *Data classification:* Data need to be classified into appropriate groups. These groups should be meaningful so that results of the data analysis will have meaning.

            (b) *Data editing:* Data must be examined carefully to see if there are missing or inaccurate data. It is likely that a respondent did not follow the directions carefully enough in completing the questionnaire. If there are missing data, there are procedures you can use in handling the response, depending on the computer program you are using to assist in the analysis of the data. There may be cases where you will want to eliminate the respondents' answers to the entire questionnaire if there is too much inconsistency in responding.

            (c) *Data coding:* If data are to be entered and analyzed by a computer program, the data coding procedure is very important. Coding means that a number is assigned to each response classification.

            (d) *Data tabulation:* The number of responses in each classification for each statement or question will need to be counted. Frequency distributions are created from the data. The counting can be done manually or by the computer.

            (e) *Statistical analysis:* Statistics can be generated that will result in percentages, measures of central tendency, and measures of dispersion.

                • *Percentages:* Ratios that show relationship between one or more response classifications; a base of 100.

                • *Measures of central tendency:* Statistics that mea-

sure the center value of a distribution of data. The *mean* is the arithmetic average of a group of responses obtained by computing the sum of all the responses and dividing by the number of responses. The *median* is the midpoint in a distribution of responses. The *mode* is the response that occurs the most frequently in a distribution of responses.
- *Measures of dispersion:* Values that show the variation of the data in a distribution. The *range* is the difference between the value of the highest response and the value of the lowest response in a distribution. The *standard deviation* is a measure of the degree of scattering of a frequency distribution about its arithmetic mean.

(2) *Evaluation and interpretation of data:* The summary statistics that have been computed can be used to make specific inferences from the data about the problem that was defined earlier. Any inferences are made about the population (even though you might have only used a sample) and are based upon the accuracy, significance, and relationships shown in the same data. It is during this stage that meaning is derived from the data, and you must use logical reasoning in order to develop any conclusions based upon the data. The result of the evaluation and interpretation of the data is the development of a set of *findings* (or facts) derived from the study.

d. *Reporting findings and drawing conclusions:* The findings are usually reported immediately following the presentation of the data supporting the findings. In other words, in the data analysis section of the report, the narrative sequence would include the presentation of the data within the paragraphs, followed by the statistical table representing the supportive evidence. Presentation of the complete set of findings and conclusions derived from these findings are presented in a summary chapter or section of the report.

(1) *Findings:* The bulk of a report discusses data in order to derive findings. A summary of the findings is presented immediately following the presentation of the data. This summary provides a capstone to the data analysis section of the report. The findings (or key findings) may also be summarized in the final chapter (or section) of the report if there is a section for such a summary.

(2) *Conclusions:* An informational report merely presents facts to the reader that may be useful in further study or review. However, if your research involved the collection

of data that were subsequently analyzed, conclusions should be drawn that are based upon the data analysis. The conclusions *must* be based only upon the data that were analyzed and nothing else because there would be no proof present for any other inferences. If you found significant differences between two sets of data, reporting the significance is a finding. A conclusion can be drawn from the finding that can present an explanation of what this finding means to the entire population.

(3) *Recommendations:* The conclusions drawn as a result of the findings form the basis for any recommendations that are indicated. There might be recommendations for further research and study, new materials to be developed, or training programs to be initiated. Sometimes there are implications for organizations that should be considered as well, even though the exact consequences might not be known. There may be implications for organizations in terms of additional personnel needed, changes in business systems utilized, or developmental plans that should be considered.

e. *Organizing the report:* Developing the final written report will depend most upon how well the plan for the report is organized. The sequence of the report must be decided, whether the report will be written inductively or deductively. In addition, the outline for each of the sections of the report needs to be determined.

(1) *Inductive organization:* Inductive writing leads from the specific to the general. This is the most prominent plan used for formal reports. The report begins with an introduction, statement of the problem, definition of terms, eventually leading to the findings, conclusions, and any recommendations that are included.

(2) *Deductive organization:* Deductive writing begins with a presentation of general information, followed by the more specific information involved in the research. The conclusions and recommendations are presented first, then the statement of the problem, definition of terms, and identification of procedures used. The data analysis and findings follow, and a summary is included as the final section of the report.

(3) *Other types of organization:* Sometimes a report will be presented chronologically because of the importance of the time frame for the report. Such a report might be divided into phases or sections based upon certain periods of time. Reports might also be presented that highlight activities or functions affecting different aspects of the company, for example, sales according to geographic regions.

The report should be planned in such a way that an outline can be developed of the major headings that will be used throughout the report. This outline serves as a guideline for the writer and eventually will become the table of contents (with the addition of subheadings inserted as the writing goes along). The writer needs to be consistent in outlining, using appropriate outline symbols and sequences. (See Chapter 11, Preparing Communications in Final Format, for information on how an outline should be developed.)

f. *Writing the report:* The final step in the research process is the writing of the report itself. Whether formal or informal style is used to write the report depends upon the situation and the needs of individuals for whom the report is being prepared. A formal, impersonal style may be used for longer reports written primarily for people outside your organization or on the executive level. A more personal, less formal style may be used when memorandum reports or letter reports are prepared. In this section we have emphasized the long, formal report. A formal report may be subdivided into three primary sections: preliminary parts, body of the report, and supplementary parts. The features of each of these three divisions are defined briefly here:

(1) *Preliminary parts:* These parts are included prior to the main body of the report and help to provide the kind of organization needed in the report.

   (a) *Letter or memorandum of transmittal:* Sometimes a letter or memorandum must accompany a report as a brief introduction to the report. The transmittal correspondence begins with a general introduction to the report and may present a brief summary of findings and conclusions. Its purpose is to lead the reader to read the enclosed report.

   (b) *Title page:* The information to be included on the title page includes the title of the report; the name, title, and address of the writer; and the date.

   (c) *Authorization form:* A signed authorization from the individual authorizing the research must be included. This is a form that was completed and signed prior to the start of the research.

   (d) *Table of contents:* Every report should have a table of contents which indicates the major subdivisions of the report along with page references.

   (e) *Table of illustrations:* All figures and illustrations included in the body of the report should be itemized in a table of illustrations along with the specific page references.

(f) *Abstract:* Sometimes an abstract is requested to precede the report itself. This abstract is usually 300 to 500 words in length and provides a brief summary of the conduct of the study and the reporting of the data, findings, and conclusions of the study.

(2) *Body of the report:* The body of the report is usually subdivided into the introduction, data analysis and findings, and summary of conclusions and recommendations.

   (a) *Introduction:* The main purpose of the introductory section is to present the reader with the problem of the study, research questions, hypotheses, limitations of the problem, the rationale for the study or report (with supporting information), definitions of terms used, and procedures used in the study.
   (b) *Data analysis and findings:* In this section the complete data analysis must be presented. Each finding must be explained in terms of the statistical analysis that was conducted. These statistical analyses are normally presented in tables accompanied by appropriate narrative.
   (c) *Conclusions and recommendations:* The summary provides an overview of the study and a look at the complete set of findings, or selected findings if appropriate. In addition, conclusions derived from the findings are included in this section as are recommendations that can be drawn directly from the conclusions.

(3) *Supplementary parts:* The last section of the report includes the bibliography, glossary, appendix (or appendices), and index.

   (a) *Bibliography:* An alphabetical list of all information sources used for the report.
   (b) *Glossary:* An alphabetical list of terms defined for the reader.
   (c) *Appendix (or appendices):* Supplementary research material, such as sample questionnaire, sample letters written to respondents, and detailed data analysis not included in the report.
   (d) *Index:* A list of names and subjects, with page references in order to quickly find specific information contained in the report.

The business report is a very important business document and must be prepared with care so that it will be functional in assisting in the decision-making process. (For more information on business report formats, see Chapter 11, Preparing Communications in Final Format.)

E. **Dictation Skills**

Dictating messages in the automated office is very important. As a secretary or administrative assistant, you may be required to interpret the dictated message or you may have to dictate the message. Dictated messages are typically recorded in three ways—on a dictating machine, voice mail, or answering machine.

1. *Interpreting Dictation:* When interpreting the dictated message, you assume the responsibility of making sure the information is accurate. It becomes your responsibility to verify the accuracy of all data.

    a. *Numeric data:* Addresses, dollar amounts, percentages, and any important fact or figure must be accurate. Many times you will be given a hard copy containing the correct information, perhaps some previous correspondence. Otherwise, the data are usually in the company files. If you cannot verify the information and you are suspicious of inaccuracy, bring the matter to the attention of the individual who originated the message.

    b. *Grammar and punctuation:* The use of dictionaries, office manuals, and automated word processing tools should minimize spelling, grammar, and punctuation errors. Careful proofreading of the document should eliminate any other errors. All documents should be free of spelling, grammar, or punctuation errors.

2. *Dictating Messages:* In an automated office, dictating messages on a machine is very common. The feedback from face-to-face dictation is missing in the automated environment. The dictator needs to provide complete instructions and speak clearly when using the dictation machine, voice mail, or answering machine.

    a. *Dictation machine:* To effectively use a dictation machine, you must be proficient in using the English language and in organizing ideas for letters, memos, or reports.

        (1) *Predictation:* It is important that you plan what needs to be covered in the communication. Gather all information necessary to prepare your reply. Number any items you will be referring to so the person doing the transcription can easily reference these materials.

        (2) *Beginning the dictation:* Indicate who you are, the type of correspondence, and special format instructions. It is important for the transcriber to know from the beginning the general instructions for the correspondence and the

name of the person who is dictating. Identifying yourself is particularly important when the transcription is being handled in word/information processing centers. General instructions should include:

(a) The type of correspondence which follows, for example, memo, letter, short report, rough draft.
(b) Letter format (blocked letter style is recognized as the most efficient format).
(c) Punctuation style (open punctuation, with no punctuation after salutation or complimentary closing, is recognized as the most efficient style).

(3) *Dictating:* Dictate at a moderate pace in thought groups and enunciate clearly. Phrases and clauses help to dictate long sentences in thought groups; pause at those points. Also, pause before and after instructions provided within the dictation.

Adhering to the following dictation guidelines makes the transcription easier:

(a) Do not dictate the inside address and ZIP code when they are available to the transcriber from a document provided. At the time the address and ZIP code are dictated, say "The address and ZIP code are on the letter (or appropriate document reference) in the folder." All materials provided to the transcriber should be enclosed in a folder or similar carrier to be returned to the dictator with the finished transcribed document. By following this practice, all materials are kept together for efficient followthrough on the next phase.
(b) Spell out unusual names.

EXAMPLE:
"Mrs. Smyth (that's spelled S - m - y - t - h) will be able to..."

(c) Overemphasize the dictation of initials. Many times it is helpful to follow the initial with a word reference.

EXAMPLE: "B as in boy."

(d) When a word typically spelled in lower case should be capitalized, indicate that it should be capitalized. The same is true when a word should be entirely capitalized.

EXAMPLE: The statement "The new Marble top on the credenza..." would be dictated as follows:

"The new (PAUSE) (typist, capital M) Marble (PAUSE) top on the credenza..."
or
"The new (PAUSE) (typist, all capital letters) MARBLE (PAUSE) top on the credenza..."

(e) To indicate the beginning and ending of quoted material, say "quote" and "unquote." For material to be in bold print, say, "boldface," and, "unbold."

EXAMPLE: *"In an ex post facto design, (PAUSE) (boldface)* **(PAUSE) inferences about relations among variables (PAUSE)** *(unbold) (PAUSE) are made without direct intervention..."*

(f) When a word is to be underlined, pause, then say "underline" followed by the word, then pause. If a phrase is underlined, pause, and say, "underline the phrase," before the phrase.

(g) When you prefer that a character be keyed a particular way, indicate your preference just prior to the character.

EXAMPLE:
For instructions on making a dash, say: "Secretary, make the dash by typing one hyphen preceded and followed by a blank space."

See Chapter 9, Section B-2-d for other dash formats.

Once you have indicated your preference, the typist should be consistent throughout that document. When the dictation is transcribed in a word/information processing center, do not assume that the same typist will key succeeding documents even though they were dictated at the same time on the same diskette. Repeat a special instruction the first time it is needed in a document.

b. *Voice mail:* Voice mail should be used for short messages. When sending voice mail, you know in advance that you will be recording a message. Plan what is important to put in the message before activating the system. Identify yourself, the date and time, and the purpose of the mail at the beginning of the message. Speak clearly using short, complete sentences. When finished, indicate that the mail is complete. Many voice mail systems incorporate a closing command which indicates the end of the message.

c. *Answering machine:* Today most office telephones include an answering system. When placing a phone call, be prepared to leave a short message. Important facts to include in the message are: your name, date and time, number where you can be reached (if this varies, provide appropriate information), purpose of the message. If you are calling to obtain an answer to a question, ask your question. When the call is returned, your answer should be provided.

Office personnel must not abuse the automated environment and avoid face-to-face conversations. Communication is important to all organizations. Many times the most effective delivery system is through face-to-face meetings.

F. Listening and Oral Communication Skills

Research studies indicate that most office personnel spend approximately 40 percent of their workday listening. Poor listening habits result in communication problems which can be costly to the organization—missed meetings, errors in shipments, inaccurate correspondence.

Listening is *hearing* what someone else said followed by *interpreting* what was said. Interpreting is determining what the speaker meant. Listening is an energetic process. A good listener recognizes this and works at developing good listening skills.

1. *Suggestions for Better Listening:* Listening is a skill which can be learned. The following suggestions can improve your listening habits:

   a. *Avoid distractions:* Do not create distractions by doing other things, noting annoying habits of the speaker, or allowing others to distract you from the conversation.
   b. *Identify a purpose:* Is the purpose of the conversation to inform, persuade, or entertain? Informative and persuasive conversations usually include important facts and information. Adapt to the purpose and concentrate on what is being said.
   c. *Understand the main ideas:* Relate facts and ideas to comprehend the real message.
   d. *Control emotions:* Do not get upset. Many important remarks are missed this way. Concentrate on the message, hear the speaker through, discuss any necessary points, and then make judgments.
   e. *Stay alert:* The normal speaking rate is 100 to 125 words per minute. People think four times faster. Use this "thinking time" to evaluate what the speaker is saying and to anticipate the speaker's direction. Make mental summaries for further discussion.

2. *Listening Techniques:* Repeating the information, asking questions, and making affirmative comments are three listening techniques.

These techniques are best used in various combinations when taking directions, giving instructions or orders, and sharing ideas.

a. *Taking directions: Repeat the directions* (information) to make sure you have accurately heard and interpreted what was said.
b. *Taking instructions:* When taking instructions, it is important that you understand the speaker. Be sure to *ask questions* to clarify any vagueness. Also, it is wise to *repeat the instructions* once the speaker has finished.
c. *Taking orders:* When a customer is placing an order, it is helpful to let them know you are giving them your full attention. *Making affirmative comments* can accomplish this. When this order is complete, *repeat the information* to assure accuracy.
d. *Sharing ideas:* When sharing ideas with colleagues, they need to know you are giving them your full attention. *Making affirmative comments* accomplishes this. When you feel you do not understand what is being said, *ask questions*. Finally, by *repeating information* others have said, you are indicating your understanding of the conversation and allowing for corrective feedback when there has been a misunderstanding.

Chapter 8: Review Questions

PART A: Multiple-Choice Questions

DIRECTIONS: Select the best answer from the four alternatives. Write your answer in the blank to the left of the number.

_____ 1. Which statement best reflects a positive message?

   a. I apologize for not contacting you sooner.
   b. I have mailed the material by air express.
   c. If further information is needed, do not hesitate to FAX your request.
   d. Please contact us if you decide to pursue this alternative.

_____ 2. Which of the following techniques would demonstrate that concrete language is being used?

   a. Acronyms are used to eliminate unnecessary wording.
   b. Commonly known antonyms are substituted for unfamiliar words.
   c. Industry-specific jargon is frequently used in the writing.
   d. Specific words with precise meanings tend to dominate the writing.

_____ 3. Which of the following uses unbiased language in expressing an idea?

   a. As a result of legislation, Mary Kennedy, a black, was able to return to school.
   b. Both women and the men in the audience gave the speaker a standing ovation.
   c. C. R. Adams, our top salesman, reported that sales for May had increased 7 percent.
   d. The young woman lawyer prepared a brief that was highly regarded by her peers.

_____ 4. To be effective, a sentence included in business writing should

   a. average about 25 words.
   b. be joined to another when the thought continues.
   c. be a simple sentence.
   d. have a main clause and a dependent clause.

_____ 5. Which one of the following is parallel?

   a. graduate / junior
   b. plan / organize / staffing / direct / control

267

c. president / vice-president / secretary
d. state / United States

_____ 6. Placing key information at the beginning of a sentence so the reader will be sure to see it is an example of

   a. balance.
   b. clarity.
   c. emphasis.
   d. variety.

_____ 7. A reference book for identifying synonyms is

   a. a dictionary
   b. an office reference manual.
   c. a thesaurus.
   d. a word-division manual.

_____ 8. Understanding a situation from the reader's point of view shows _____ toward the reader.

   a. empathy
   b. respect
   c. sincerity
   d. sympathy

_____ 9. As a type of formal written communication, the business letter is used most often for

   a. external communication.
   b. horizontal communication.
   c. internal communication.
   d. vertical communication.

_____ 10. Which of the following examples would be considered a favorable letter?

   a. A response to an information inquiry.
   b. A request for information.
   c. A letter explaining why information cannot be released.
   d. A letter marketing a new product.

_____ 11. When the direct writing approach is used for a business letter

   a. the first paragraph is a buffer paragraph that sets the stage for what follows.
   b. the first paragraph is written to get the reader's attention.

Composing Communications 269

   c. the first paragraph begins with a general statement of the main point of the message.
   d. the constant and variable information needs to be identified in the first paragraph.

_____ 12. When a negative letter needs to be written

   a. company policy should be used as rationale for the refusal.
   b. reasons for the refusal should be clearly presented in the first paragraph followed by a goodwill paragraph.
   c. the first paragraph should set the stage so the rationale for the refusal (presented in the second paragraph) is read.
   d. the refusal should be clearly stated and immediately followed by a rationale.

_____ 13. If you are involved in marketing a new product and wish prospective customers to know about the product, you would send

   a. a combination letter.
   b. a persuasive letter.
   c. a positive letter.
   d. a routine letter.

_____ 14. The primary purpose of a form letter is to

   a. compose a letter with little or no variable data.
   b. personalize a letter by including the addressee's name and address.
   c. send letters with some identical parts to more than one person or organization.
   d. take advantage of word processing capabilities.

_____ 15. Text that stays the same on every form letter produced is called

   a. constant information.
   b. merged information.
   c. personal information.
   d. variable information.

_____ 16. In word processing, a mail-merge function requires the preparation of

   a. a primary document and a form letter.
   b. a primary document and a secondary document.
   c. a secondary document and a database.
   d. a secondary document and a variable document.

17. A mail-merge database includes the

    a. constant data.
    b. form letter.
    c. merged data.
    d. variable data.

18. The most common form of correspondence within the firm is the

    a. business letter.
    b. business report.
    c. informal report.
    d. interoffice memorandum.

19. Which of the following approaches would be most effective in writing a company directive with complete instructions for completing an assignment?

    a. Detailed approach
    b. Direct approach
    c. Indirect approach
    d. Inductive approach

20. Which type of communication is best for a performance evaluation which requires skill improvement?

    a. Favorable memorandum
    b. Unfavorable memorandum
    c. Formal report
    d. Informal/short report

21. A three-page informal report presenting some information on a new office system planned for purchase needs to be communicated to several other people within the organization. This specific type of informal report is called a

    a. feasibility study.
    b. progress report.
    c. proposal.
    d. technical report.

22. A report on the work-measurement study just conducted in the word processing center by Suzanne Weir, the word processing manager, is

being communicated to Jan Dailey, administrative vice-president. This is considered

a. an external report.
b. a nontechnical report.
c. a periodic report.
d. a vertical report.

_____ 23. In planning a report that will require both primary and secondary research, the first thing you need to do is

a. conduct primary research to become familiar with the problem.
b. define the problem that needs to be solved.
c. develop a questionnaire to gather factual data.
d. identify the variables of the study.

_____ 24. If you were interested in studying the behavior of secretaries on the job, with the purpose of recommending to the office manager how individual assignments could be changed, which of the following research methods would be the *best* to use?

a. Experimental research
b. Observational research
c. Secondary research
d. Survey research

_____ 25. The statement, "The parts were sent to Karl Johnson via air express," should be dictated as follows:

a. The parts were sent to Karl Johnson via air express.
b. The parts (PAUSE) were sent (PAUSE) to Karl Johnson (PAUSE) via air express.
c. The parts were sent to Karl (that's spelled K - a - r - l) Johnson via air express.
d. The parts were sent to Karl (with a K as in keep) Johnson via air express.

_____ 26. Since listening is a skill that can be learned, which of the following should be practiced to improve listening skills?

a. Allow emotions to guide your response.
b. Make sure you understand the purpose of the message.
c. Notice any unusual speaking patterns of the speaker so you can inform the speaker of these distractions.
d. Pay close attention as people speak faster than you can listen.

PART B: Matching Sets

Matching Set 1

Match each definition (27-31) with the appropriate term (A-J). Write the letter of your answer in the blank to the left of the number.

Terms

A. Deductive Style
B. Horizontal Report
C. Inductive Style
D. Mean
E. Median
F. Mode
G. Parallelism
H. Primary Research
I. Progress Report
J. Secondary Research

DEFINITIONS

_____ 27. Business writing distributed at the same administrative level.

_____ 28. Gathering information prepared by others.

_____ 29. Direct approach to writing; main idea followed by supporting details.

_____ 30. Ideas equal in thought should be stated in identical grammatical form.

_____ 31. Midpoint in a distribution of responses; measure of central tendency.

Matching Set 2

Match each definition (32-36) with the appropriate term (A-J). Write the letter of your answer in the blank to the left of the number.

Terms

A. Analytical Report
B. Bibliography
C. Closed Question
D. Glossary
E. Goodwill
F. Listening
G. Open Question

Composing Communications 273

      H. Scaled Question
      I. Scheduled Report
      J. Voice Mail

           DEFINITIONS

_____ **32.** An alphabetical list of terms defined for the reader.

_____ **33.** Hearing and interpreting what was stated.

_____ **34.** Questionnaire format which allows the respondent to react to a continuum.

_____ **35.** A report issued at the end of every month.

_____ **36.** Dictated communication used for short messages.

Part C: Problem Situations

      DIRECTIONS: Follow the directions given with each problem situation. Write the letter of your answer in the blank to the left of the number.

Problem 1

      Identify the following sentences as one of the following:

      A. Simple
      B. Compound
      C. Complex
      D. Compound-Complex

_____ **37.** This evening I will demonstrate how to use Harvard Graphics with WordPerfect to create clear, effective, and attractive graphics within your reports.

_____ **38.** Harvard Graphics will be used to produce the charts for the report, and WordPerfect will be used to produce the body of the report.

_____ **39.** You need to save the graph in the normal Harvard Graphics format as well as export the picture in a WordPerfect readable format.

_____ 40. After completing the chart, it is important to save the graph so it can be imported into the WordPerfect document.

_____ 41. With a little practice, the process is simple, and there are significant benefits when you integrate the two business software programs.

_____ 42. A hands-on session is helpful if you encounter questions.

Problem 2

Below are outlines of letters. Identify the letter outlines as

A. Positive
B. Routine (Neutral)
C. Negative
D. Combination
E. Persuasive

_____ 43. (1) Refund $40
(2) Inspection: defective valve
(3) See you at Open House

_____ 44. (1) Need price of laser printer
(2) Importance of quality printing
(3) Other suggestions?
   Need by _____

_____ 45. (1) Explain new office policy
(2) How policy is to be administered
(3) Policy should clarify future situations.

_____ 46. (1) Importance of topic
(2) Constraints in participating
(3) Identify another possible participant

_____ 47. (1) YES—can speak on "Database Management"
(2) Discuss background in topic
(3) Do not have expertise in "Normalization"
(4) If Database Management is sufficient, need to know by May 12—preparation time

_____ 48. (1) Attention getter
(2) Create interest/desire
(3) Make action easy

Chapter 8: Solutions

Part A: Multiple-Choice Questions

	Answer	**Refer to Chapter Section**
1.	(d)	[A-1-a]
2.	(d)	[A-1-d]
3.	(b)	[A-1-g(1)(b)]
4.	(b)	[A-2-a]
5.	(c)	[A-2-c(1)(c)]
6.	(c)	[A-2-c(2)]
7.	(c)	[A-2-c(5)(a)]
8.	(a)	[A-2-d(2)]
9.	(a)	[B]
10.	(a)	[B-1-a(3)]
11.	(c)	[B-1-b(1)]
12.	(c)	[B-3]
13.	(b)	[B-5-a(3)]
14.	(c)	[B-6]
15.	(a)	[B-6-b]
16.	(b)	[B-6-b(2)]
17.	(d)	[B-6-b(2)]
18.	(d)	[C]
19.	(b)	[C-1-a(2)]
20.	(b)	[C-1-b]
21.	(c)	[C-2-a(1)]
22.	(d)	[D-1-c]
23.	(b)	[D-2-a]
24.	(b)	[D-2-b(2)(b)]
25.	(c)	[E-2-a(3)(b)]
26.	(b)	[F-1]

Part B: Matching Sets

Matching Set 1

27.	(B)	[D-1-c]
28.	(J)	[D-2-b-1]
29.	(A)	[A-2-b(1)]
30.	(G)	[A-2-c(1)(c)]
31.	(E)	[D-2-c(1)(e)]

Matching Set 2

32.	(D)	[D-2-f(3)(b)]
33.	(F)	[F]
34.	(H)	[D-2-b(4)(c)]

35.	(I)	[D-1-b]
36.	(J)	[E-2-b]

Part C: Problem Situations

37.	(A)	[A-2-a]
38.	(B)	[A-2-a]
39.	(A)	[A-2-a]
40.	(C)	[A-2-a]
41.	(D)	[A-2-a]
42.	(C)	[A-2-a]
43.	(A)	[B-1]
44.	(B)	[B-2]
45.	(B)	[B-2]
46.	(C)	[B-3]
47.	(D)	[B-4]
48.	(E)	[B-5]

CHAPTER 9
Editing Communications

OVERVIEW

One important responsibility for most secretaries is providing the final approval to a written document prior to sending it to the receiver. This talent requires English skills: both grammatical construction and punctuation, spelling, format knowledge, and an ability to produce a document that has visual appeal. The evaluation of these characteristics requires proofreading and editing skills.

Tying these skills together results in a document which has a clear, concise, and courteous tone. The purpose of this finishing touch is to produce a document that will appeal to the receiver. Possessing the ability to communicate in as few words as possible, be understood, and communicate with a "smile" is an asset for both secretaries and executives.

DEFINITION OF TERMS

COPY EDITING. Revising a draft of a document for consistency, conciseness, and grammatical accuracy by making revisions within the body of the document. The edited copy is returned to the author for verification.

HARD COPY. Typewritten or printed pages of a document.

PROOFREADING. Checking the final copy for spelling, punctuation, and adherence to formatting guidelines.

PROOFREADING MARKS. Symbols written within the margins of a typed document so the error can be viewed and corrected.

SOFT COPY. The pages of a document stored on disk and viewed on a computer screen.

A. Proofreading

Proofreading is the process of checking final copy for spelling, punctuation, and formatting. When the final copy is not on a word processor, proofreading marks are made with light pencil markings within the margins of the document. The error can then be corrected and the light pencil marks erased without the entire page being retyped.

The procedure for proofreading soft copy depends upon the proofreader's responsibility and authority. If the proofreader is to only flag necessary corrections, then the proofreader will make proofreader marks within the hard copy document.

If the proofreader also has the authority and responsibility of making the changes, then the proofreader can read the copy on the cathode ray tube (CRT) (computer screen). All necessary corrections are made within the soft copy document at the time of proofreading. This eliminates the need for proofreader marks.

1. *Proofreading Methods:* Whether proofreading is done alone or with someone else, the material must be proofread both for typographical errors and for content.

    a. *Proofreading for typographical errors:* Proofreading for typographical errors should be done by reading backward. This allows the proofreader to concentrate on each word separately and to check spelling. This method cannot be used for content. For example, if the word *to* was typed as *so*, the error would go undetected.

    b. *Proofreading for content:* All material should be read slowly, concentrating on the grammatical accuracy of the message. Many proofreaders find that reading aloud helps them to concentrate on the content of the message.

    c. *Proofreading by other personnel:* Because proofreading is so important, many firms have proofreading departments. Before a document is released, it is sent to the proofreading department where it is read by someone other than the originator, copy editor, or typist. In many instances, the proofreading is done by two individuals, one reading the material aloud from the writer's copy and another checking the final document. This technique can also be adopted by secretaries working together within a firm. The original document should be proofread by someone who was not involved in preparing the document. The one who reads from the writer's copy could be someone who was involved in preparing the document.

2. *Proofreading Techniques:* Whether proofreading is done alone or others are assigned to do the proofreading, the following techniques should be used.

a. *Reading the copy:* When proofreading, read the copy slowly and concentrate on the material.
b. *Aligning copy:* Use a ruler to follow the line of print on hard copy. This is particularly helpful with statistical copy. The ruler is also helpful in making sure a line is not skipped in reading. Scrolling one line at a time when proofreading soft copy assures that a line is not skipped.
c. *Proofreading vertically:* If the material is similar to a table and was typed horizontally, proofread the copy vertically. This is particularly helpful when proofreading alone.
d. *Counting entries:* If there are lines of entries that can be counted, count the number of entries in the original and compare that with the number of entries typed in the final document.
e. *Delaying final proofreading:* If time permits, do not do the final proofreading immediately after typing or keying in the material. If you wait for an hour or more, errors are more likely to be found. The longer the wait, the better—the proofreader will be more objective in making judgments about the composition of the document (see Chapter 8, Section A, Fundamentals of Writing.

3. *Proofreading Symbols:* When proofreading hard copy text, the proofreading symbols illustrated in Figure 9-1 should be used. Also, the marks on a final document should be made lightly with pencil within the margins of the document to possibly avoid the need of retyping the entire page.
4. *Proofreading Software:* Most word processing software includes a spell-check feature. The purpose of the spelling feature is to check the document for *spelling* errors.

a. *Activating the spell-check feature:* When the spell check is activated, the spell-check software scans the soft copy document for words it does not recognize—words that are *not* in the spell-check dictionary.

(1) The unrecognized word is highlighted on the CRT for the proofreader to verify the spelling of the word.
(2) If the word is correct, the proofreader activates the continue command.
(3) If the word is incorrect, the proofreader can usually correct the word immediately before continuing the spell-check function. A spell check may also give the proofreader some possible spellings to choose from. Variations on spell-check features are explained in the word processing operations manual.

b. *Adding unrecognized words to dictionary:* Some spell-check programs allow the proofreader the option of adding a new word to the spell-check dictionary before continuing.

Meaning	Symbol	Example	Final Edited Copy
TRANSPOSE	∽	cha(ng)e the letters around	change the letters around
DELETE	ℓ	to take ~~something~~ out	to take out
CLOSE UP	⌒	to bring to⌒gether	to bring together
INSERT	∧	the insert symbol∧a caret (is)	the insert symbol is a caret
SPACE	#	insert a#space	insert a space
PARAGRAPH	¶	Using the symbol means to begin a new paragraph. ¶ A new thought means a new paragraph.	Using the symbol means to begin a new paragraph. A new thought means a new paragraph.
MOVE LEFT	[	[Align the material to the left.	Align the material to the left.
MOVE RIGHT	]	Align the material to]the right.	Align the material to the right.
SPELLING or SPELL OUT	(sp) or ◯	When a word is spelled incorrectly, write *sp* in a circle above the misspelled word. When an (abbrev) is to be spelled out, circle the word.	When a word is spelled incorrectly, write *sp* in a circle above the misspelled word. When an abbreviation is to be spelled out, circle the word.
CAPITAL LETTERS	≡ or CAPS	underline all letters that are to be capital letters or write the letters CAPS in the margin.	Underline ALL letters that are to be capital letters OR write the letters CAPS in the margin.
LOWER CASE	/ or lc	Draw a line through letters that should be /ower /case /etters OR write the letters *lc* in the margin.	Draw a line through letters that should be lower case letters OR write the letters *lc* in the margin.
LET STAND	..... or *stet*	Keep it the ~~original~~ way. Writing *stet* in the margin also means "let it stand."	Keep it the original way. Writing *stet* in the margin also means "let it stand."
INSERTION OF PUNCTUATION	∧ ∨ ⌄	When a comma needs to be inserted∧use the caret symbol but don't use it for an apostrophe or quotation marks. Use the inverse caret.	When a comma needs to be inserted, use the caret symbol but don't use it for an apostrophe or quotation marks. Use the inverse caret.

Figure 9-1
Proofreading and Copy Editing Symbols

    c. *Checking grammar:* Proofreaders who use the spell check feature should be aware that spell checks are not grammar conscious. A spell check only verifies that a word is spelled correctly.

        EXAMPLE: **There** *is a correct spelling of a word. However, if the word in the document should be* **their**, *the spell-check feature will not highlight the word for the proofreader to verify grammatical accuracy. (See Use of Editing Software, Chapter 9, B-9.)*

Therefore, it is still very important—and necessary—for the proofreader to copy edit for grammatical accuracy.

B. Editing for Technical Correctness

Command of the English language develops in two ways. First, it develops from everyday usage—speaking, reading, and writing the language. Second, it develops through English reviews which reinforce and expand upon rules learned in primary and secondary education. Like any skill, English needs to be reviewed and practiced in order to maintain accuracy and proficiency.

Command of the English language entails using correct grammar, punctuation, capitalization, spelling, and numbering. The language is further enhanced by appropriate formatting and consistent language style.

1. *Grammar and Word Usage:* The English language is easy as well as difficult to study. It is easy to study because the language has been used since early childhood and developed over the years. It is difficult because many adults feel they already know and understand the language and are not interested in restudying what they already know. However, the English language is varied and changing. Most adults use what would be classified as informal English—language characterized by short sentences, "chatty" construction, and use of local jargon. Many call this conversational English.

In business writing, many of the documents are expected to have a "conversational" tone and yet be formal. Formal English is characterized by strict adherence to language rules and specialized vocabulary. The purpose of the language guide which follows is to review the structure of the English language, the rules which govern the English language, and the format and language style which packages the business document.

a. *Elements of a sentence:* For a sentence to be complete it must contain a subject and a verb (predicate). Most sentences also contain an object or a complement. The four components of a sentence are subject, verb, object, and complement.

Secondary sentence elements encompass the use of modifiers, phrases, and clauses.

(1) *Subject:* Each sentence requires one or more subjects. The subject of a sentence is a noun or noun equivalent which is the topic of the sentence. A simple subject consists of a single word, such as *secretary*. A complete subject consists of the simple subject as well as any other words which modify that subject, such as *knowledgeable secretary*.

EXAMPLES:
A knowledgeable <u>secretary</u> *aspires to become a CPS. (noun)*

He *aspires to become a CPS. (noun equivalent—pronoun)*

What you study *is important to passing the CPS exam. (noun equivalent—noun clause)*

Studying *is important to passing the CPS exam. (noun equivalent—gerund)*

To study *requires self-discipline. (noun equivalent—infinitive)*

(2) *Verb:* The verb of a sentence tells what the subject has done, is doing, or will be doing, or the verb can express a condition about the subject. When the verb expresses a condition, it is a linking verb; otherwise, it is an action verb.

The verb must agree with the subject. If the subject is singular, the verb must be singular. If the subject is plural, the verb must be plural. Agreement between subject and verb is important, and sometimes writers do have problems. Questions about agreement usually arise when verbs have compound subjects or when the subject is separated from the verb by many other words. Typically, the verb follows the subject.

EXAMPLES:

I always ask *questions to ensure complete understanding. (Present tense, singular, action)*

We ask *questions of each other while studying. (Present tense, plural, action)*

I asked *for a raise.*
(Past tense, singular, action)

We asked *for a new photocopier.*
(Past tense, plural, action)

I will ask *for a word processor for this office.*
I am going to ask *for a word processor.*
(Future tense, singular, action)

We will ask *for help during the tax season.*
We are going to ask *for help during the tax season.*
(Future tense, plural, action)

I am *happy with the word processor.*
(Present tense, singular, linking verb)

We are *happy with the word processor.*
(Present tense, plural, linking verb)

I was *happy when the word processor arrived.*
(Past tense, singular, linking verb)

We were *happy when the word processor arrived.*
(Past tense, plural, linking verb)

I will be *happy when the word processor arrives.*
(Future tense, singular, linking verb)

We <u>will be</u> *happy when the word processor arrives.*
(Future tense, plural, linking verb)

(3) *Object:* Action verbs are usually followed by a *direct object*. The direct object of the verb completes the sentence by answering the question "what" or "whom" after the verb. The direct object is either a noun or noun equivalent.

Verbs such as buying, giving, asking, telling, and the like are followed by an *indirect object*. The indirect object names the receiver of the direct object and precedes the direct object and answers the questions "to whom," "to what," "for whom," or "for what."

EXAMPLES OF A DIRECT OBJECT:
Secretaries who are rushed usually make mistakes.
Make "what"? mistakes (noun)
Martha likes him *for a manager.*
Likes "whom"? him (noun equivalent—pronoun)
Clarice knows what skills are required.
Knows "what"? what skills are required (noun equivalent—noun clause)
Richard enjoys hunting *every fall.*
Enjoys "what"? hunting (noun equivalent—gerund)
The committee voted to adjourn.
Voted "what"? to adjourn (noun equivalent—infinitive)

EXAMPLES OF AN INDIRECT OBJECT:
Many people gave United Way *a fair share contribution.*
Gave "what"? contribution
"to whom"? United Way

Dr. Jones should give the tree *a pruning.*
Should give "what"? pruning
"to what"? tree

David bought Mother *50 stock certificates yesterday.*
Bought "what"? certificates
"for whom"? Mother

(4) *Complement:* When the verb expresses a condition about the subject (linking verb), it usually is *followed* by a complement. A complement is a noun that refers to the subject or an adjective that describes the subject. Because the linking verb expresses a condition rather than action, *a complement is related to the subject* by that linking verb.

A noun or noun equivalent is called a predicate noun; an adjective is called a predicate adjective.

The most common linking verbs are the various forms of *be*: is, am, are, was, were, has been, might be.

EXAMPLES:
Mr. Johanson is a dynamic speaker.
Is "what"? speaker (predicate noun)
My manager might be unhappy *with the committee's decision.*
Might be "what"? unhappy (predicate adjective)

b. *Secondary elements of a sentence:* Most sentences have modifiers, clauses, or phrases. These are considered secondary elements of a sentence.

(1) *Modifiers:* Single words used as modifiers usually relate to the element of the sentence they modify. The most common modifiers are adjectives and adverbs. Adjectives relate to nouns, whereas adverbs can relate to the sentence as a whole or modify a particular word (verb, adjective, or adverb).

Adjectives and adverbs assist the writer in being more specific. These modifiers usually add descriptive details or specific definition to key words. The adjective or adverb is usually near the word it modifies, and most adverbs are made by adding *ly* to an adjective.

EXAMPLES:
Our home *office is located in Memphis.*
   Subject: *office*
Adjective: *home (describes which office)*
Jean speaks quite clearly *over the telephone.*
    Verb: *speaks*
  Adverb: *clearly (describes how Jean speaks)*
  Adverb: *quite (describes how clearly)*
Mack's extremely *small frame makes it difficult to find a comfortable working desk.*
   Noun: *frame*
Adjective: *small (describes frame)*
  Adverb: *extremely (describes small)*

(2) *Clauses:* Clauses can be either independent or dependent. An independent clause contains a subject and verb (predicate) and can stand by itself as a sentence. Usually a comma separates two independent clauses when the sentences are connected with a conjunction (*and, but, or*) or a conjunctive adverb (*however, consequently, then*). If there is no conjunction or conjunctive adverb between two independent clauses, then the sentences are separated by a semicolon.

A dependent clause also contains a subject and verb (predicate); however, it is part of the sentence and cannot stand by itself as a complete sentence. It is connected to the main sentence by a connecting word that shows its subordinate relationship: either a conjunction (*since*, *when*, *because*, *if*, *after*) or a relative pronoun (*who*, *which*, *that*). When a dependent clause begins a sentence, a comma follows. When a dependent clause appears within a sentence, commas are included before and after the clause.

EXAMPLES:
The new word processor arrived this morning, *and Micro-Systems will be out tomorrow to review the operations.*
(Two independent clauses connected by the conjunction and*)*

Margaret is at the board meeting; she should be back at 4 P.M.
(Two independent clauses, no conjunction)

If you are serious about taking the CPS exam, *you should register for the review course which begins next month.*
(Dependent clause beginning the sentence)

Let me know when the coffee is ready.
(Dependent clause ending the sentence)

Mrs. Johnson, who is our new director, *will meet with the board of directors tomorrow.*
(Dependent clause within the sentence)

(3) *Phrases:* A phrase is a group of related words connected to a sentence by a preposition or a verb. Such a phrase cannot stand by itself because it has no subject or verb (predicate). Such phrases are modifiers and may or may not require punctuation marks.

A prepositional phrase functions like an adjective or adverb depending on what it modifies. The phrase begins with a preposition (*from*, *at*, *by*, *of*) and is followed by a noun or noun equivalent.

A verbal phrase does not function as a verb. A participle phrase functions as an adjective; a gerund phrase functions as a noun; and an infinitive phrase functions as either a noun, an adjective, or an adverb. The phrase consists of the verbal element plus the object or complement and modifiers of the phrase.

EXAMPLES:
The cabinet by his desk *contains our department manuals.*
(Prepositional phrase—adjective)

Mr. Klein spoke in a loud voice.
(Prepositional phrase—adverb)

Ashley, having passed the CPS exam on the first try, *feels very good about herself.*
(Verbal phrase—participle phrase)

<u>Passing the CPS exam</u> *opened new directions for Mark.*
(Verbal phrase—gerund phrase as the subject)

Sara gave me plenty of work to do *before she left.*
(Verbal phrase—infinitive phrase as an adjective modifying the noun work*)*

The students in the CPS course want to review *their grammar.*
(Verbal phrase—infinitive phrase as an adverb modifying the verb want*)*

2. *Punctuation:* The use of correct punctuation is extremely important for the secretary. What is said or written can easily be changed by the misuse of a punctuation mark. This section of the language guide provides a quick summary of the ways in which major forms of punctuation are used correctly in transcripts.

   a. *Apostrophe:*

   (1) *To show possession:* The apostrophe may be used to show possession.

   (a) *Singular nouns:* Add the apostrophe and an *s* to all singular nouns (unless the singular noun ends in *s*). For singular nouns that end in *s*, only the apostrophe is necessary. However, it is also correct to add an apostrophe and an *s*, particularly if the extra syllable is pronounced.

   EXAMPLES:
   author's manuscript
      (singular noun)
   boss' standards*
      (singular noun ending in <u>s</u> *)*
      (boss's is also correct)
   James' invention*
      (one-syllable proper name ending in <u>s</u> *)*
      (James's is also correct)
   Marlys' family*
      (two-syllable proper name ending in <u>s</u> *)*
      (Marlys's is also correct)
   *Once you decide how you prefer to show possession, do be consistent throughout the document.

   (b) *Plural nouns:* Add the apostrophe and an *s* to plural nouns that do not end in an *s*. For plural nouns that end in an *s*, add only the apostrophe.

   EXAMPLES:
   women's organization
      (plural noun not ending in <u>s</u> *)*
   accountants' pins
      (plural noun ending in <u>s</u> *)*

Editing Communications

(2) *For plurals:* For the sake of clarity with small letters, the plural is formed by adding *'s*. An apostrophe is generally used to form the plurals of capital letters and numbers; however, just the capital letter and an *s* is sufficient. The only capital letters which should always have an apostrophe before the *s* are *A*, *I*, and *U*, primarily for clarity. Again, once you choose a style, be consistent throughout the document.

EXAMPLES:
a's   A's   Bs or B's   1s or 1's
b's   I's   Cs or C's   2s or 2's
c's   U's   Ds or D's   3s or 3's

(3) *With symbols:* The apostrophe is used as the symbol for *feet* on business forms and in tables. As part of a sentence within a paragraph of a letter or a report, the word *feet* is spelled out in full.

EXAMPLE:
2' x 4' (meaning 2 feet by 4 feet)
A sentence within a letter would read:
The board must be 2 feet by 4 feet.

(4) *Contractions:* The apostrophe is used to indicate the omission of a letter or letters.

EXAMPLES:
it's   (it is)
wouldn't   (would not)
can't   (cannot)

b. *Colon:* When the colon is used in typewritten material, it is always followed by two spaces. The only exception is when the colon is used in indicating time [see Section B-2-b(2) in this chapter].

(1) *After an introduction:* A colon is used after a statement that introduces a long direct quotation, enumerated items, or a series which is introduced with the expressions *these*, *as follows*, or *the following*.

EXAMPLES: The motion was: "The regular meetings will be held on the second Wednesday of each month at 7 P.M. at the Winchester Library Meeting Room."

My presentation is divided into three areas:
1. The CPS Examination
2. Preparation for the Examination
3. Taking the Examination

[For enumeration format, see Period, B-2-i(5) and Parentheses, B-2-h(1) in this chapter.]

The ten o'clock workshop sessions are as follows: word processing, communication, or integration of data processing and word processing.

(2) *Time:* The colon is used to separate the hours from the minutes when time is expressed in figures. There is no space after the colon. The time is always followed by a correct form of *A.M.* or *P.M.* When the time is an even hour, only the hour is used. However, if both even hours and hours with minutes are used within the same sentence, all time is expressed with hours and minutes for consistency.

Variations for typing *A.M.* and *P.M.* are: *a.m.*, *A.M.*, *am*, and *AM*; *p.m.*, *P.M.*, *pm*, and *PM*. For clarity, the more frequent use is with periods. Otherwise, *am* and *AM* could be mistaken for the word *am*. Be consistent with your format and type *A.M.* and *P.M.* notations in the same way. (See Guidelines for Proper Use of Numbers, Section B-7 in this chapter.)

EXAMPLES:
The meeting begins at 2 P.M.
Since the meeting begins at 2:00 pm, meet me at 1:30 pm to review the agenda.

c. *Comma:*

(1) *After an introduction to a sentence:* An introduction can be a word (*However, Therefore*), a phrase (*By hurrying, In case you didn't know*), or an adverbial clause (*As soon as the package arrives, When this meeting is called to order*). A comma is used to separate this introduction from the main sentence.

EXAMPLES:
Finally, the meeting began at 3 PM.
(Word)
Because of the weather, it looks like the company picnic will have to be postponed.
(Phrase)
As soon as the package arrives, alert the Accounting Department.
(Adverbial clause)

(2) *Series:* When there are more than two items in a series of words or phrases, a comma is used to separate the items. If a conjunction (*and, or, nor*) precedes the last word in a

series, a comma is not necessary before the conjunction. The comma itself represents the conjunction. However, many times the comma is used before the conjunction for clarity. Sometimes the items within the series contain conjunctions. Again, for clarity, a comma should precede the conjunction before the last item in the series. If *et cetera* (*etc.*) is part of the series, use a comma before and after *et cetera*. If the series contains a series, semicolons are used to separate the main series while commas are used for the inner series [see Semicolon, Section B-2-l(2) in this chapter].

EXAMPLES:
Mary ordered the paper, folders and gummed labels.
The shipment contained regular paper and legal paper, pencils and pens, and rulers.
The order for spring slacks, skirts, blouses, etc., from the Marks Department Store was shipped yesterday.
The Harris shipment on Friday included two pink, green, and gold chairs; one green sofa; and one glass end table.

(3) *Compound sentences:* When two complete sentences are connected with a conjunction (and, but, or) or a conjunctive adverb (also, however), a comma precedes the conjunction or conjunctive adverb. Sometimes the conjunction is used because of a compound verb; then the comma is not used.

EXAMPLES:
One week our secretary was out sick, but we obtained an excellent replacement from Temporaries, Inc.
You should reconsider your decision to cancel the order and instruct us to reinstate it.
(Compound verb: should reconsider *and* instruct*)*

(4) *Direct quotes:* A comma is used to set off a direct quotation (the exact words of the speaker) and quotation marks ("") are placed around the exact words. [See Colon, Section B-2-b(1) in this chapter for the exception and example.] Periods and commas go inside the quotation marks. [For rules pertaining to punctuation marks used with quotations, see the Note following Quotation Mark, Section B-2-k(3) in this chapter.]

EXAMPLES:
Mr. Jackson said, "Pay the bill immediately."
"Pay the bill immediately," were Mr. Jackson's exact words.
Mr. Jackson said, "Pay the bill immediately," in a very emphatic tone.

(5) *Parenthetical:* When a word, phrase, or clause is used that is not necessary to the grammatical completeness of the sentence, it is considered a *parenthetical expression*. A parenthetical expression is set off by commas; but if it comes at the end of the sentence, only one comma is needed.

EXAMPLES:
Martha, however, is not applying for the position.
(Word)
Mr. Smith, I am sure, will be able to handle the matter.
(Phrase)
I have prepared a cover letter, a copy of which should be inserted in each booklet.
(Clause)

(6) *Apposition:* An appositive is a word, phrase, or clause that identifies or explains a noun, pronoun, or other term. An appositive is set off by commas unless it is at the end of the sentence where only one comma is necessary.

EXAMPLES:
The meeting will be on Wednesday, April 15, in the main conference room.
(April 15 is the appositive. It is easy to recognize by saying, "Which Wednesday?")
Mrs. Sally Francis, our PSI President, will attend the International Conference.
(Our PSI President is the appositive. You can identify the appositive by saying, "Which Mrs. Francis?")

(7) *Nonrestrictive clauses:* Nonrestrictive clauses begin with *which*, *who*, or *whose*. These clauses may be omitted without changing the meaning of the sentence. A clause beginning with *that* usually is restrictive (essential to the sentence). Only nonrestrictive clauses are set off with commas.

EXAMPLES:
The formula, which was tested at the Medical Laboratories Institute, has really been an advancement for the medical profession.
Sara Emmory, who can type 98 words per minute with 97 percent accuracy, is being considered for the new position.

(8) *And omitted:* When two adjectives modify the same noun and the *and* is missing, a comma is used to replace the

missing *and*. However, if the first adjective modifies the combination of the second adjective plus the noun, the comma is not used.

EXAMPLES:
The train is a quiet, smooth way to travel. (The words quiet *and* smooth *modify* way.*)*

This is just a short, friendly reminder that your payment is now due. (The words short *and* friendly *modify* reminder.*)*

The beautiful spring bouquet was a nice touch to the head banquet table. (The word beautiful *modifies the combination* spring bouquet.*)*

d. *Dash:* Typically, a dash is used for greater emphasis. For the dash to have any impact, however, you must be selective in using the dash as a substitute for other punctuation marks. The forcefulness of the dash is greatly diminished if overused.

EXAMPLES:
Mrs. O'Miria—an excellent physician—has been honored by her colleagues.
(The dash is used here instead of parentheses or commas. This is also the preferred style for typing the dash.)
Our favorite place to vacation — Alaska. (The dash is used here instead of a colon.)
I like the new typewriter—the new control keys make typing so much easier.
(The dash is used here instead of a semicolon.)

Note: The dash is typed with two hyphens and no spaces (preferred typing style), with two hyphens together and one space before and after the hyphens, or with one hyphen and one space before and after the hyphen. Once a style is selected, use the same format throughout a document; consistency is important. Never type a dash as one hyphen with no space before and after the hyphen. A single hyphen with no spaces is used within a compound word (see Hyphen, Section B-2-g in this chapter).

e. *Exclamation point:* After a word, phrase, or sentence, an exclamation point is used for emphasis. The exclamation point is followed by two spaces.

EXAMPLES:
The exam is in two days!

Yes! I am impressed with that community project.

f. *Ellipsis:* Ellipsis marks are used to show the omission of words within a sentence. An ellipsis is typed with three periods, with a space before and after each period. If the ellipsis comes at the end of the sentence, the end-of-sentence punctuation is typed as normal (next to the word); then leave a space before typing the ellipsis. If the end-of-sentence punctuation is never typed, only the ellipsis is used.

EXAMPLE:
The president said, "With the rising cost of energy . . . we will keep our thermostat at 72 degrees year round. . . ." She was very emphatic with this statement.
The president said, "With the rising cost of energy . . . we will keep our thermostat at 72 degrees . . ."

g. *Hyphen:* The hyphen is typically used for word division or as a part of a compound word.

(1) *Compound adjective:* If two adjectives (descriptive words) precede a noun, a hyphen is used to make these two adjectives into a compound word.
   Note: Do not confuse this rule with the *and omitted* rule [see Comma, Section B-2-c(8) in this chapter].

   EXAMPLE:
   The first-class mail is delivered to all departments by 10 A.M.

(2) *Replace "to" or "through":* In statistical writing, tables, or charts, the hyphen can be used to replace the words *to* or *through.*

   EXAMPLE:
   The report covers Tables 19-35.

(3) *Prefixes:* When a prefix is added to a word, the word may be written as a single word or as a hyphenated word. Preferred usage calls for words with prefixes to be spelled as single words without hyphens whenever possible. Typically if a prefix is a word, for example, *self,* a word with the prefix *self* will be hyphenated.

   EXAMPLES:
   preemployment   self-imposed

(4) *Word division:* The hyphen is used to indicate the division of a word at the end of a typed line. Correct hyphenation rules must be followed [see Guidelines for Word Division and Hyphenation, Sections B-8-a and B-8-b in this chapter].

   EXAMPLE:
   When you are typing a lengthy manu-

script, correct hyphenation rules must be followed.

(5) *Suspended hyphen:* In a series of hyphenated words having the same ending, the hyphen is retained with all the hyphenated words. One space follows each suspended hyphen.

EXAMPLE:
Either the blue- or black-colored chairs will match the decor of the new office.

Note: A hyphen is typed with no spaces before or after it except in word division [see B-2-g(4)] or suspended hyphen [see B-2-g(5)].

h. *Parentheses:*

(1) *Enumerated items:* Enclose numbers or letter in parentheses when the enumerations are continued on the same line.

EXAMPLE: The CPS Exam has six parts: (1) behavioral science in business, (2) business law, (3) economics and management, (4) accounting, (5) office administration and communication, (6) office technology.

(2) *Instead of comma or dash:* If you wish to deemphasize an expression that is not necessary to the meaning or completeness of a sentence, you may use parentheses instead of a comma or dash to set it off from the rest of the sentence.

EXAMPLE:
The office picnic (scheduled for August 15) will be held at Tinley Park.

(3) *References:* When references to tables, pages, diagrams, or other similar references are made for further clarification, these references are placed in parentheses.

EXAMPLE:
The section on buying stocks (pages 35-42) is very helpful.

(4) *Around a complete sentence:* If a complete sentence is placed in parentheses, the sentence would begin with a capital letter and the ending punctuation mark would fall inside the parentheses.

EXAMPLE:
Dr. Carmichael's data processing presentation lasted over an hour. (However, the time was well spent!) After the

presentation, there was a question-and-answer period (requested by the audience).

Note: Punctuation following a parenthesis within a sentence goes outside the parenthesis, and the first word within the parenthesis is not capitalized. See B-2-h(4) for punctuation rule when a complete sentence is placed within the parentheses.

i. *Period:*

(1) *After sentences:* Use a period to mark the end of a complete declarative sentence. The period is followed by two spaces.

EXAMPLE:
I plan to attend the PSI seminar on the office of the future. Reservations are needed by October 15.

(2) *After a polite request:* Use a period to mark the end of a question that is a polite request.

EXAMPLE:
Will you attend the meeting for me next week.

(3) *With abbreviations:* Periods are to be used with personal and professional abbreviations, academic abbreviations, and seniority abbreviations. The ending period is followed by one space unless it ends a sentence; then there are two spaces. There is no space after a period within an abbreviation.

EXAMPLES:
Ms.   Dr.   Ph.D.   B.A.   Jr.   Sr.

(4) *With numbers:* Use a period to denote the decimal point for money accounts and fractions. Omit decimal and two ciphers after even-money amounts unless the figure is included in a sentence with dollars-and-cents amounts. (See Guidelines for Proper Use of Numbers, Section B-7-d in this chapter.) In a decimal fraction, the figures are considered as one number. Therefore, no space follows the period.

EXAMPLES:
We still owe $1,537.75 on our microcomputer, which amounts to 3.5 percent of the total bill.
You gave a $50 donation last year.

(5) *Following an enumeration:* A period follows each number or letter of an enumeration which is listed. The periods are to be aligned, and two spaces follow the period.

EXAMPLE:
Please include the following administrators on the invitation list:
1. Mr. George White, Board of Directors
2. Miss Martha Phiffel, Second Vice President
3. Mrs. Kathy McDoughel, Director of Personnel

(6) *Within an outline:* A period follows each letter or number used to introduce each item in an outline. The periods are to be aligned, and two spaces follow the period.

```
EXAMPLE:

     I.  Business Letters
         A.  Styles
             1.  Block
             2.  Modified Block
         B.  Format

    II.  Tables
```

(7) *With paragraph headings:* When you use a paragraph heading, it is followed by a period and a dash or two spaces. The heading is always underlined. [See Chapter 11, Section D-2.]

EXAMPLE:
<u>February usage</u>. *The Executive Dining Room was used eight times during the month of February for luncheon meetings.*
<u>February usage</u>.—*The Executive Dining Room was used eight times during the month of February for luncheon meetings.*

j. *Question mark:* Use a question mark after a sentence that asks a direct question. The question mark is followed by two spaces.

EXAMPLE:
Will Julie be sitting for the CPS exam in May? If so, which testing site does she prefer?

k. *Quotation mark:*

(1) *With direct quotes:* Quotation marks are placed around the exact words that were spoken or written. [See Comma, B-2-c(4), and Colon, B-2-b(1) in this chapter.]

EXAMPLES:
Did Mary really say, "Since I did not get the promotion, I am going to resign."
Your advertisement must include the following: "Warn-

ing! Use of this product may be hazardous to your health."

(2) *With titles:* Quotation marks are used to enclose chapters of books and titles of articles, lectures, or reports.

EXAMPLE:
My lecture, "Office Automation," is going to be published in <u>Today's Secretary</u> *as "The Office of the Future is Here Today."*

(3) *Single letters:* When reference is made to a single letter within the alphabet, that letter may be placed in quotation marks for ease of reading. [For alternate format, see Underscore, B-2-m(4).]

EXAMPLE:
You only need to add an "s" to form the plural of all numbers.

Note: Periods and commas are the only punctuation marks that always go inside the closing quotation mark. The question mark, exclamation point, and closing parenthesis go inside the closing quotation mark only when they are part of the quotation. Semicolons and colons always go outside the closing quotation mark. If quoted material comes at the end of a sentence, the punctuation mark that ends the quotation is used to also end the sentence. This is true even when the punctuation mark for the end-of-quotation sentence and the end of the sentence are not the same.

l. *Semicolon:*

(1) *Compound sentences:* When a sentence consists of two complete sentences with no conjunction, a semicolon is used to separate the sentences. See Comma, B-2-c(3) in this chapter, for use of a comma with a conjunction or a conjunctive adverb.

EXAMPLE:
Our secretary also had the flu; however, she was out for only two days.

Note: When punctuation is required within either of the sentences, follow correct punctuation rules. "However" is an introduction to the second sentence; therefore, it is followed by a comma [see Comma, B-2-c(1) in this chapter].

(2) *Series:* When a series contains a series, semicolons are used to separate the main series while commas are used for the inner series.

EXAMPLE:
The fall order includes women's slacks, skirts, blouses, and sweaters; men's slacks, shirts, and sweaters; and children's pants, t-shirts, and sweaters.

m. *Underscore:*

(1) *Titles:* All titles (books, magazines, newspapers, movies, plans, etc.) are underscored.

EXAMPLE:
The president is an avid reader of the <u>Wall Street Journal</u>, <u>Money</u>, and the two local newspapers.

(2) *For emphasis:* An underscore may be used to emphasize a word, phrase, clause, or sentence. However, for the underscore to have any effect, be selective with its use.

EXAMPLE:
The <u>main</u> reason for wanting word processing in our office is because we edit many of our materials before making final copies.

(3) *Paragraph headings:* All paragraph headings are to be underscored so they stand out from the balance of the material in the paragraph. Other headings (centered and side) may or may not be underscored. [See Chapter 11, Section D-2.]

(4) *Single letters:* When reference is made to a single letter within the alphabet, that letter may be underscored for ease in reading. [For alternate format, see Quotation Mark, Section B-2-k(3) in this chapter.]

EXAMPLE:
You only need to add an <u>s</u> to form the plural of all numbers.

Note: If you have italic type on your typewriter or printer, italics can be used in place of the underscore.

3. *Capitalization:* Proper capitalization is like having good manners. Improper capitalization makes a written document appear sloppy and difficult to read.
Note: An explanation of all capitalization possibilities is impossible in a review manual such as this. Therefore, only the most frequent use of capital letters will be covered in this section.

a. *Beginning a sentence:* Capitalize the beginning of every sentence or expression which ends with a punctuation mark (period, question mark, or exclamation mark).

EXAMPLE:
When is the meeting? It is scheduled for 9 A.M. tomorrow.

b. *A sentence within parentheses:* When a complete sentence within parentheses stands by itself, it is capitalized. If, however, a sentence within parentheses is part of another sentence, it does not begin with a capital letter.

EXAMPLE:
A good synonym and antonym reference book is important to writers. (The Roget's International Thesaurus is a popular reference book.)
The teacher requires several reference books (we need them for the next session).

c. *Beginning a quotation:* The first word of a complete sentence from a direct quotation is to be capitalized.

EXAMPLE:
In the letter Dr. Johanson wrote, "The stock will double within the year."

d. *Pronoun I:* The pronoun *I* is always capitalized to distinguish it as a word by itself.

EXAMPLE:
Judge Rand and I will take care of the banquet arrangements.

e. *Titles of people:* When a title is used as part of a person's name, it should be capitalized. This is also true for names of family relationships unless preceded by a possessive or used as a common noun. When any title is a descriptive word, it is not capitalized.

EXAMPLES:

Part of the Name	Descriptive Word
Judge Fia Mathews	She is the new judge.
Dr. Andrews	Your doctor called.
The President vetoed the bill. (U.S. President)	The president resigned. (a company president)
I called Mother.	She is a grandmother.

f. *Books and articles:* The first word, nouns, pronouns, verbs, adjectives, adverbs, and prepositions of more than five letters are capitalized in titles of books and magazine or newspaper articles.

EXAMPLES:
Molloy's Live for Success
The World Is Made of Glass
"Communication—An Important Link Between Secretary and Executive"

g. *Academic courses:* Specific high-school or college course titles are capitalized; general subjects are not capitalized unless they are languages.

EXAMPLES:
Business Letter Writing	*English*
Administrative Office Management	*management*
Human Relations 101	*psychology*
Conversational Spanish	*language*

h. *Geographic locations:* Specific geographic locations and directions used to identify geographic areas are capitalized. When used to indicate direction, the word is not capitalized.

EXAMPLES:
Minnesota	*the Midwest*	*west of the Mississippi*
Savannah	*a Southerner*	*a southern custom*
Indonesia	*the Far East*	*east Asia*

i. *Organizations:* Names (and abbreviations) of social organizations, business organizations, and clubs are capitalized. When the words *senior, junior, sophomore,* and *freshman* refer to organized groups or functions, they are capitalized.

EXAMPLES:
Professional Secretaries International (PSI)
League of Women Voters
American Management Association (AMA)
Junior Prom
Sophomore Bleacher Bums

j. *Institutions:* Specific public and private institutions are capitalized. When the name applies to a whole class of institutions, it is not capitalized.

EXAMPLES:
Guilford High School	*our high school*
Green Public Library	*the public library*
Daily Medical Clinic	*the medical clinic*

k. *Groups:* Names of national, political, religious, or racial groups are capitalized. Names of social and economic groups are not capitalized.

EXAMPLES:
English	*Finnish*
Democrat	*Republican*
Lutheran	*Jew*
Negroid	*Caucasian*
upper class	*senior citizens*

l. *Objects:* Specific objects (brand-name products, structures, documents, artifacts) are capitalized.

EXAMPLES:
Kodak film   *Jefferson Memorial*
Declaration of Independence

m. *Elements of time:* Capitalize words designating specific months, days, holidays, events, and periods. Names of seasons are not capitalized.

EXAMPLES:
June	*Monday*
Memorial Day	*World War II*
the Renaissance	*summer*

4. *Format and Appearance:* When a written document is seen for the first time, the reader will be more eager to read the document if the format and appearance are familiar and attractively displayed. People are comfortable with what is familiar and has a neat, attractive appearance.

    a. *Format:* Because the visual impact of a document has an impact on the reader before the material is even read, it is important to be familiar with formatting guidelines.

        (1) *Format of an envelope:* The two major envelope styles are the conventional style and the OCR style. The position of the address in relation to bar codes on the envelope is another important consideration.

        (2) *Format of a letter:* The three most common letter styles are blocked letter style, modified blocked letter style, and simplified letter style. The style used depends on individual preference. When the reader encounters a style that is familiar and is used properly, the reader develops confidence in a writer. Also, one must decide on either open or mixed punctuation style.

        (3) *Other business documents:* All business documents have guidelines to follow. This is true of preprinted forms as

well as original material such as interoffice memorandums. Even rough-draft copy has guidelines to be followed which make it easy for the writer to edit the material.

b. *Appearance:* A neat, attractive appearance means proper spacing of the document; few and neat corrections; clear, dark print; and a nonglossy paper that is easy to read.

Besides the picture-frame appearance, neat corrections are extremely important. With modern technology, many office personnel have the advantage of word processing systems, correcting typewriters, or electronic typewriters. However, there are times when possessing skillful correction techniques is advantageous. A secretary who can produce a mailable copy that is neat, clean, and "looks perfect" is much appreciated. That perfect look can be accomplished by making use of the following correction tips:

(1) *Preparing the original document:* The first step toward that perfect look is preparing the original document. The ink from the ribbon is absorbed into the typing paper; therefore, the sooner a correction is made, the better. However, there is always a certain amount of surface ink. When the original sheet is rubbed and there is some smudging, this indicates a high degree of surface ink. This is caused from either the type of ribbon used or the amount of absorbancy of the paper. A neater correction will be obtained if some of the surface ink is lifted from the original paper before making a correction. This surface ink can be lifted by using a soft drafting eraser or gummed typewriter cleaner. The drafting eraser is rolled or gently stroked over the error. The typewriter cleaner is like Silly Putty and picks up the excess ink when pressed over the error.

(2) *Choosing the proper correction device:* Once the document is prepared by lifting off the surface ink, the proper correction device must be selected: correction fluid, correction paper, or an eraser.

(a) *Correction fluid:* On the original copy, correction fluid may be used in areas where correct words will be typed over the correction and if the correction is small.

- Check to make sure the correction fluid is thin. Shake the bottle to mix the ingredients. If the liquid does not "slosh" in the bottle, add some thinner and mix thoroughly.
- With a small amount of fluid on the brush, paint over the error like an artist drawing that letter.

Applying the correction fluid in this manner allows the small amount of liquid to drop into the crevice made by the letter. In this way, only the error is covered and a neat correction is made. Sometimes the correction is almost invisible depending on the letter being typed over the error.
- Permit the corrected area to dry thoroughly before typing over the correction. Drying time can be from 10 to 30 seconds depending on the brand of correction fluid used and how thin the fluid is (age of the fluid).
- With extensive use of photocopiers, many office employees use the original as a file copy and send a photocopy to the recipient. In such a situation, larger corrections are made with correction fluid, and fluid is even used in areas where nothing is typed over the correction. It is important to realize, however, that if a file copy is kept for many years, the correction fluid may become dry and brittle and flake off the paper, exposing the error.

(b) *Correction paper:* On the original copy, correction paper may be used for areas where correct words will be typed over the correction and if the correction is small.

- Position the typed document so you can strike over the error.
- Slip a fresh piece of correction paper on top of the paper with the chalky side toward the typing paper.
- Type out the incorrect letter(s).
- Make sure you always use a clean section of the correction paper while typing the incorrect letter(s).

(c) *Eraser:* Making a correction with an eraser is the most permanent form of correction as well as being the best choice when nothing is to be typed in the area where the incorrect letter(s) is being removed. However, patience is necessary when correcting an error with an eraser. The grit from the eraser acts like sandpaper. If the eraser is pressed firmly against the paper and moved with rapid motion, a hole is likely to appear in the paper. The key to a neat correction with an eraser is

- Use the white typing eraser (coarse) for original copies and the pink carbon eraser (soft) for carbon copies.

- Press lightly against the paper.
- Move in a circular motion for oval letters (o, c, e, O) as well as for circular portions of letters (p, b, d, q).
- Move in an up-and-down motion for straight letters (t, i, l, w) as well as for straight portions of letters (p, b, d, q).
- As the grit accumulates, brush or blow it away from the paper and the typewriter.
- Before erasing, be sure the eraser is clean. If an eraser is dirty, it will leave smudge marks on the copy. An eraser can easily be cleaned by rubbing it on an emery board. An emery board in the desk drawer specifically for that purpose is helpful.
- When using a typewriter with a movable platen, it is a good idea to move the platen so it extends to the left or to the right of the typewriter before beginning to erase. Move the platen so it extends to the left when the correction is on the left half of the typing paper; vice versa if the error is on the right half of the typing paper. It is also advisable to move the typing font or daisy wheel away from the error when using a typewriter that does not have a movable platen.

(d) *Other correction techniques:* You may want to consider two other correction techniques—a strikeover and camouflaging with chalk.

- *Strikeovers:* On a few typewriters one letter can be typed over another and the strikeover is invisible. Some possibilities are an *o* or an *e* over a *c*; a *p, q, d, g,* and *b* over an *o*; or an *f* over an *i*. Test your typewriter with various letter combinations but be cautioned to use this technique *only* if there is no visible sign of the incorrect letter underneath. One must be very careful with this technique because what will cover up on one typewriter may not work on another typewriter. This technique must always be checked with different typewriters, and the typist must be very particular that the strikeover is absolutely invisible.

You may combine the strikeover with correction fluid or chalk to camouflage that portion of the letter not covered properly by the strikeover.

- *Camouflaging with white chalk:* After erasing with an eraser, the paper sometimes has worn thin and white paper looks grayish in color. By using white chalk and rubbing over the back of the area, much of the original color will come back to the paper. (Use yellow chalk for buff paper.)

(3) *Reinserting paper for correction:* Even though all highly conscientious secretaries proofread the material before removing the paper from the typewriter, there are times when an error is detected later. Reinserting the paper and aligning the print takes practice and familiarity with the typewriter. Using the typewriter scale as a special realignment tool or utilizing the tissue paper technique are two easy methods for paper alignment.

   (a) *Realignment with the typewriter scale:* The scale on the typewriter is designed to assist in realignment of the paper. Scales vary from machine to machine; therefore, time must be spent becoming familiar with the typewriter.

   - Insert a piece of practice paper.
   - Type some material.
   - Examine the position of the typewriter scale to the letters typed. (Make sure to examine the left scale over the print as well as the right scale. Many times the scales on a typewriter are just slightly different from one another.)
   - Remove the typing paper.
   - Reinsert the paper using the typewriter scale to visually "judge" exact position.
   - Use the ratchet release to freely move your typing paper to the left or right (horizontally) if it is out of alignment in that direction.
   - Use the variable line-space regulator to move the paper up or down (vertically) if it is out of alignment in that direction.

   (b) *Tissue-paper technique for originals:* The tissue-paper technique can be used to reposition originals as well as carbon copies.

   - First, eliminate the incorrect letter with correction fluid or an eraser. (The only time you may try to erase an error once the paper has been reinserted is if correction paper or self-correcting ribbon is being used. However, it is very difficult to align the paper exactly so the incorrect letter is covered adequately by the correction paper or lifted off by the self-correcting ribbon.)

- Reinsert the paper using the typewriter scale, ratchet release, and variable line-space regulator to visually "judge" exact position.
- Insert a piece of tissue paper over a letter next to the incorrect letter which was eliminated when the paper was out of the typewriter.
- Type the aligned letter on the tissue paper. If it is aligned exactly over the original, only one letter will be visible. If not, adjust the original using the typewriter scale, ratchet release, and variable line-space regulator. Test it again to see if only one letter is visible.
- Once the original is aligned properly, remove the tissue paper and type the correct letter on the original.

(c) *Tissue-paper technique for carbon copies:* The tissue-paper technique can also be used with carbon copies.
- First, erase the error with a pink carbon-copy eraser (soft) before realigning the paper in the typewriter.
- Use the typewriter scale, ratchet release, variable line-space regulator, and tissue paper to realign the carbon copy. Follow the steps explained with originals.
- Once the carbon copy is aligned, insert a piece of carbon paper on top of the copy being corrected, insert a piece of scrap paper on the top of the carbon paper, and then type the correct letter. This gives the corrected letter the same appearance as when first typed.

5. *Consistent Style:* The word *consistent* means compatible or uniform. Style in business writing is the manner in which we express ourselves. Each person has a unique writing style, like no one else's. However, business writing requires that the style should not draw attention from the reader, who should be concentrating on the content of the writing. Therefore, the writing style needs to be examined in the editing phase to be sure that there is a consistent, uniform pattern to the writing—but not one that will detract from the attention the reader will pay to the content of the message.

a. *Format patterns:* The format used in business writing will help to create a consistent style. Rules of setting margins and tabs according to acceptable formats should be followed so that within a given document the *same* margins and tabs will be used. Here are some of the format features that need to be consistent throughout the report:

(1) Top, bottom, and side margins for first page of document.
(2) Top, bottom, and side margins for succeeding pages of document.
(3) Indentions of paragraphed material.
(4) Placement of footnotes or endnotes.
(5) Placement of headings and subheadings throughout the document.

b. *Word usage:* Any word that can be written in more than one way should be written only one way throughout a document. When the word is combined with a number, be sure to check the number rules to see how the term should be typed.

c. *Tone:* In editing a document that has already been prepared, evaluate the tone. Tone, as defined in the previous chapter, is the manner in which a certain attitude is expressed. Again, the tone needs to be consistently informal or consistently formal, depending on the purpose of the document.

d. *Punctuation:* Some rules for punctuating sentences are more flexible than others and provide the writer with choices. The comma is a good example.

EXAMPLE: The comma is used in a series of three or more items. If a conjunction precedes the last word in a series, a comma is optional before that conjunction. However, many times it is still used before the conjunction for clarity. If you decide in your writing to include the comma before the conjunction in a series, then be consistent in the entire document so that a comma always appears before the conjunction in the series. (Tom, Sue, and Bob attended the management seminar.)

The editing process is the final opportunity to make any changes in business writing before it is distributed to the receiver. It is crucial that editing be considered an absolutely necessary step to the final approval of the document before it is put to use outside the organization. Every document that leaves the firm creates an image, either favorable or unfavorable.

6. *Spelling and Keyboarding Accuracy:* There has been a cry raised in public education for a return to the basics of education. Much of this is due to entry-level office employees who cannot read, write, or spell.

There is a similar concern in the administrative secretarial field. While seeking better office systems and taking advantage of improved office technologies, many are neglecting the basics. Executives still expect quality basic skills. The question here is, "Are you an expert speller?"

English spelling would be easier if each sound were represented by a single letter or a combination of letters. Absolute correctness in spelling is not easy to achieve. Most errors can be avoided, however, if time and effort are spent in

- Memorizing the spelling of difficult words
- Using the dictionary when in doubt
- Proofreading what has been written
- Reviewing the following spelling rules

a. *ie and ei:* The grammar-school rhyme is most helpful with this rule: "*I* before *e* except after *c*, or when sounded like *a* as in neighbor and weigh."

   EXAMPLES:
   freight   receive   achieve   lien

   EXCEPTIONS TO BE MEMORIZED:
   counterfeit   either   foreign   leisure
   neither   weird

b. *ie ending:* When a word ends in *ie*, it is changed to *y* before the suffix *ing*.

   EXAMPLES:
   die   dying   lie   lying

c. *Silent e ending:* Words ending in silent *e* drop the *e* before a suffix beginning with a vowel. The *e* is retained before a suffix beginning with a consonant except when the *e* is immediately preceded by another vowel other than an *e*.

   EXAMPLES:
   conceive   conceivable   achieve   achievement
   true   truly   imagine   imaginary
   definite   definitely   nine   ninth

   EXCEPTIONS (RETENTION OF E BEFORE A VOWEL BECAUSE OF PRONUNCIATION):
   changeable   noticeable   outrageous   vengeance

d. *Silent e with compounds:* Silent *e* is retained with compounds whether the second word begins with a vowel or a consonant.

   EXAMPLES:
   hereafter   household

e. *ee ending:* When a word ends in *ee*, both *e's* are retained with adding a suffix except when the suffix begins with an *e*. To form the plural of the word, add only an *s*.

   EXAMPLES:
   agree   agreeable   free   freed
   lessee   lessees

f. *cle and cal:* Words ending in *cle* are nouns; words ending in *cal* are adjectives derived from other words ending in *ic*.

EXAMPLES:
article   icicle   logical   comical

EXCEPTIONS/WORDS BOTH NOUNS AND ADJECTIVES:
chemical   periodical   radical

g. *ph, gh, ch, i:* In many words, the *gh* and *ph* sound like *f*; the *ch* sounds like *k*; the *i* sounds like *y*.

EXAMPLES:
enough   physician   architect   companion
laugh   multigraph   scheme   familiar

h. *cede, ceed, sede:* No rule for verbs with any of these endings; the words just need to be memorized.

EXAMPLES:
accede   precede   exceed   supersede
concede   recede   proceed
intercede   secede   succeed

i. *y ending preceded by a vowel:* When a word ends in *y* and is preceded by a vowel, the *y* is generally retained when adding a suffix. To form the plural of the word, add only an *s*.

EXAMPLES:
convey   conveyance
display   displayed
turkeys   pulleys

j. *y ending preceded by a consonant:* When a word ends in *y* and is preceded by a consonant, the *y* is generally changed to *i* when adding a suffix except when the suffix begins with *i*. To form the plural of the word, change the *y* to *i* and add *es*.

EXAMPLES:
rely   relied   relying
liquefy   liquefied   liquefying
remedies   dictionaries

k. *ful:* The suffix *ful* is spelled with only one *l*. The *l* does not double when adding another suffix except for the suffix *ly*. To form the plural of the word, add only an *s*.

EXAMPLES:
powerful   helpfulness   cheerfully
handfuls

l. *Doubling the ending consonant:* The ending consonant is doubled before adding a suffix when

(1) the suffix begins with a vowel.
(2) the final consonant is preceded by a single vowel.
(3) the word is accented on the last syllable.

EXAMPLES:
gripping   pinned   controllable
occurrence

m. *Compounds:* A compound word consists of two or more words which are written as one word, written as separate words, or hyphenated. There is no rule for the use of the hyphen; the decision is based on common usage. However, typically phrases used as adjectives are hyphenated before a noun.

EXAMPLES:
<u>Closed (one word)</u>
toastmaster   workbench

<u>Open (separate words)</u>
attorney general

<u>Hyphenated</u>
public-spirited   one-half   hard-hat

7. *Guidelines for Proper Use of Numbers:* Typing of numbers within documents requires your concentration in order to maintain consistency throughout the document. The following guidelines for typing numbers should be helpful in deciding exactly how numbers should appear.

a. *Numbers from one through ten:* The numbers from one through ten are usually spelled out; numbers above ten should be in figures.

EXAMPLES:
We ordered ten cases of yarn; however, they shipped only four.
Please send us 35 copies of your latest bulletin.

b. *Specific numbers ten or under:* Even though the number is ten or under, the following specific types of numbers should be written in figures: measurements, temperature readings, dimensions, election returns, market quotations, chemical terms, and scores.

EXAMPLES:
The temperature today is only 5 degrees.
The Rebels won the soccer game with a score of 5 to 2.
The room was 8 feet by 12 feet.

c. *Sets of numbers within sentence:* Be consistent when several sets of numbers are within the same sentence. Use figures for all numbers.

EXAMPLE:
In our firm there are 9 exempt employees and 18 nonexempt employees.

d. *Money:* Sums of money are expressed as figures.

EXAMPLES:

Correct	Incorrect
$5.41	$5.41¢
92 cents	92¢ (unless used in material which contains many price quotations)
	$0.92 (unless in a table with other dollar-and-cents figures)
$25	25$
	$25.00 (unless other amounts within sentence have dollars and cents)

e. *Percentages:* Express percentages in figures followed by the word *percent*. The word is correctly spelled as *percent* or *per cent*. Once you choose a spelling, be consistent throughout the document. If the percentage is used in technical material, the percent symbol (%) can be used.

EXAMPLE:
There will be a 35 percent markup on this group of merchandise.

EXAMPLE OF TECHNICAL MATERIAL:
The Federal Government requires this food product to contain 95% natural ingredients; our product is 96.3% natural.

f. *Mixed numbers:* Express mixed numbers (whole numbers and fractions) in figures with a space between the whole number and the fraction. Type the fraction with a number, a slash, and another number (no spaces). If the only fractions within the document are fractions on your keyboard, these keys may be used. In other words, be consistent with the format.

EXAMPLES:
The board should be 28 1/4 inches by 35 5/8 inches by 1 1/2 inches.
The frame measures 5½ by 3¼ inches. (This sentence is not in the same document as the first sentence; therefore, the fraction key on the keyboard could be used.)

g. *Beginning sentence with number:* When a sentence begins with a number, write it as a word or rearrange the sentence.

EXAMPLES:
Seventy of our secretaries are going to the convention.
The convention will be attended by 70 of our secretaries.

h. *Hyphens in numbers:* Use hyphens in numbers between 21 and 99 when the numbers are written as words.

EXAMPLES:
twenty-one
three hundred seventy-eight

i. *Two numbers for one item:* If two numbers compose one item, express the smaller number as a word. Where this is impractical, separate the two numbers with a comma.

EXAMPLES:
There are 30 fifteen-cent stamps.
In 1990, 5,654,098 packages were delivered by our company.

j. *Dates:* Dates are expressed as figures unless used in rigidly formal writing such as an invitation or announcement. The day is written without the suffix (*st*, *nd*, *th*, . . .) unless the day is typed before the month.

EXAMPLES:
The open house is Wednesday, June 19.
The 19th of June would be a good date for the open house.

k. *Time:* Time is written in figures unless used with the word *o'clock*. Variations for typing A.M. and P.M. are: a.m., A.M., am, and AM; p.m., P.M., pm, and PM. For clarity, the more frequent use is with periods. Otherwise, am and AM could be mistaken for the word "am." Be consistent with your format, and type A.M. and P.M. in the same way. Do not use the two ciphers with the even hour unless it appears with another figure containing minutes.

EXAMPLES:
The meeting will begin at two o'clock.
The meeting will begin at 2 P.M.
The time set aside for the meeting is 2:00 to 2:30 P.M.

l. *Grouping of numbers:* No commas should be used in large serial numbers, policy numbers, page numbers, or telephone numbers. It is permissible, and often desirable for clear reading, to insert spaces within large serial numbers or policy numbers. The number is usually clustered in groups of three or four digits. However, when copying a number, type the number exactly as the originator has typed it. Area codes for telephone numbers are placed within parentheses and the phone number is typed with a hyphen.

EXAMPLES:
Our insurance policy is No. 378 9605 789.
Our telephone number is (815) 399-5678.
Assign the new job number 38976.

m. *Expressing large numbers:* A number in the millions or billions is typed as a combination of the word and figure. If a number in the thousands must be written, write it in hundreds rather than thousands (a shorter form).

EXAMPLES:
Our goal is 10 million orders for this fiscal year.
Sixteen hundred orders have already been placed.

n. *Spelling out other forms of numbers:* Spell out numbers when they appear as *first*, *second*, *third*, etc.

EXAMPLE:
This is our third notice. Please call if there is a problem.

o. *Numbers in legal copy:* In legal copy, money is expressed in both figures and words.

EXAMPLE:
The defendant agrees to pay the sum of four hundred fifty dollars ($450) for services rendered.

p. *Descriptive numbers:* Express numbers that follow such words as *chapter*, *volume*, *page*, *floor*, or *apartment* in figures. The word *number* is not used.

EXAMPLES:
Chapter 2 begins on page 56.
I moved to apartment 8.

q. *Age:* Age is expressed as a word unless days and months are given.

EXAMPLES:
He is two years old.
He is 2 years, 3 months, and 15 days old.
She will be eighty-five on her next birthday.

r. *Street names:* A street name should be typed in the same form as it is typed by the city or on company letterheads.

EXAMPLES:

Harrison Interiors in Rockford, Illinois, is located on Sixth Street.

Ada International is located on 5th Avenue in Des Moines, Iowa.

  s. *Plurals:* Express the plural of figures by adding an apostrophe and an *s* or just adding an *s* is sufficient. Generally, the apostrophe is used. Once you choose a style, be consistent throughout the document.

EXAMPLES:
7's or 7s 35's or 35s

8. *Guidelines for Word Division and Hyphenation:* In some instances, it is necessary that words be divided in order for the right margin to be somewhat even. The most desirable point for dividing a word is really a matter of opinion. By basing word division on the principles of pronunciation and spelling, much time and effort are saved.

You can develop a "feeling" for correct syllabication through careful observation and study of word pronunciation and spelling and through reference to the dictionary. The following general suggestions developed from document format and business protocol.

  a. *General suggestions for word division:*

    (1) Divide a word only when it is absolutely necessary.
    (2) When a word division must be made, it is best to have enough of the word on the first line to be able to conceptualize the entire word and to carry enough of the word to the next line to balance the division somewhat equally.
    (3) Avoid dividing a word at the end of the first line of a paragraph. The last word in the paragraph should *never* be divided.
    (4) The last word on a page should *never* be divided. Type the complete word on the page where you achieve the best balance between the two lines of print.
    (5) Avoid dividing words at the end of more than two consecutive lines.
    (6) If you can possibly avoid it, do not divide a proper name. The pronunciation of a proper name is not always revealed by the spelling; there may be some doubt as to the correct syllable division. [See Section B-8-b(15) in this chapter.]

  b. *Rules for word division:* Specific rules for word division are helpful in making appropriate decisions in hyphenating words. In the following examples, the period (.) identifies syllables where it is not advised to divide a word and the hyphen (-)

identifies syllables where it is acceptable to have a word division.

(1) Only divide words between syllables. Therefore, one-syllable words cannot be divided.

EXAMPLES:
One-syllable words: *cream*   *sound*
Correct word division: *for-ward*   *mo.ti-va-tion*

(2) Words of four or five letters should never be divided, and the division of six-letter words should be avoided. A divided syllable should have three or more characters in the division.

EXAMPLES:
a.lone   *a.part-ment*   *co.her-ence*
vouch.er   *caf.e-te.ri.a*

(3) Hyphenated words are to be divided only at the hyphen.

EXAMPLE:
self-ad.dressed

(4) Compound words should be divided between the elements of the compound.

EXAMPLES:
busi.ness-men   *grand-fa.ther*

(5) The addition of the past tense to a word does not necessarily add an extra syllable.

EXAMPLES:
guessed   *missed*   *laughed*

(6) When a word containing three or more syllables is to be divided next to a one-letter syllable, the division should come after the one-letter syllable.

EXAMPLES:
crit.i-cism   *sep.a-rate*   *af.fil.i-ate*

(7) When there is a double consonant within a word, the word *may* be divided between the consonants. The pronunciation of the word will help you determine if it is proper to divide the word at this point; that is, you *could* divide a word with a double consonant sound. [Also, see Examples (8) and (9).]

EXAMPLES:
bel.lig-er-ent   strug-gling
vac-ci-nate

(8) When a final consonant is doubled before a suffix, the additional consonant goes with the suffix. [Also, see Examples (7) and (9).]

EXAMPLES:
be.gin-ning   de.fer-ring

(9) When the double consonant is the ending of a root word, separate the suffix from the root word. [Also, see Examples (7) and (8).]

EXAMPLES:
ad.dress-ing   a.gree-ing

(10) Words ending in *able, ible, ical, cian, cion, sion, gion,* and *tion* should be divided between the stem of the word and the terminating syllable.

EXAMPLES:
a.gree-able   con-ta-gion   sus-pi-cion
cler-i.cal   mu.si-cian   am.bi-tion
de.duct-i.ble   ap.pre-hen-sion

(11) Some word endings are *ble* and *cal* instead of *able*, *ible*, or *ical*. In these cases, the "a" or "i" is part of the preceding syllable.

EXAMPLES:
char.i-ta-ble   au.di-ble
fan-tas-ti-cal

(12) When a word is to be divided at a point where two one-letter syllables (vowels) occur together, the division should be made between the vowels.

EXAMPLES:
e.vac.u-a.tion   grad.u-a.tion

(13) A syllable that does not contain a vowel must not be separated from the remainder of the word.

EXAMPLES:
did.n't   would.n't

(14) A date can be divided only between the day and the year and not between the month and the day. In this case, no

hyphen is needed; the date (year) is just continued on the next line.

EXAMPLE:
September 18,   NOT: *September*
199-   *18, 199-*

(15) Do not divide a proper name if you can possibly avoid it. [See Section B-8-a(6) in this chapter.] If, however, a complete name cannot be typed on one line, separation of the parts of the name must be made at a logical reading point. A title should not be by itself on a line. A middle name should be typed with the first name. When a name is separated between two lines, no hyphen is used.

EXAMPLES:
Ms. Carla M.
Johanson
NOT

Ms.   or   *Ms. Carla*
Carla M. Johanson   *M. Johanson*

(16) If it is not possible to type a street address on one line, the address should be separated at a logical reading point. There are many variations of a logical reading point; you must use your best judgment. The city, state, and ZIP Code can be separated between the city and the state, but not between the state and the ZIP Code. No hyphen is needed for this type of separation.

EXAMPLE:
Harrisonburg,   or   *Harrisonburg,*
Virginia 22801   *VA 22801*

(17) Do not divide figures, amounts of money, figures from an identifying term, or abbreviations.

EXAMPLES:

Correct	Incorrect	
34576539	3456-6539	
$50,000	$50,-000	$-50,000
page 45	page 45	
11 inches	11 inches	
A.T.&T.	A.T.-&T.	

c. *Hyphenation with word processing:* Word processing software uses word wrap to move an entire word to the next line whenever a word would extend beyond the right margin. If the hyphenation feature in the word processing software is used, words can be divided between two lines. The hyphenation feature commands are explained in the word processing operations manual. Most hyphenation features, however, are programmed with an automatic or manual function.

   (1) *Automatic hyphenation feature:* The automatic hyphenation feature hyphenates the word according to the rules established within the word processing software. The word processing hyphenations may or may not be consistent with the rules for word division as accepted by most businesses.
   (2) *Manual hyphenation feature:* The manual hyphenation feature prompts the user (secretary) to decide whether the word should be hyphenated and, if so, where the hyphen should be inserted. The manual function provides the operator with the flexibility to follow the rules for word division as accepted by most businesses.

   Familiarity with the hyphenation function within the word processing package will guide the user to select the automatic hyphenation feature or the manual feature.

9. *Use of Editing Software:* Word processing software can be enhanced by the addition of software that checks grammatical construction. The purpose of grammar software is to check the document for correct word usage and complete sentences. Checking for correct grammatical usage is a sophisticated process. Most software in this category checks for basic grammatical construction.

C. Copy Editing for Application of Writing Fundamentals

Editing has been in existence for many years, but the term traditionally has been associated with the publishing industry. Secretaries in all types of offices have been performing copy editing, but many times the task has been incorrectly referred to as *proofreading*, another important secretarial skill which has previously been covered. It is important to recognize the difference between these two skills.

A daily phenomenon is the busy executive hurriedly writing down ideas or dictating thoughts to the secretary. After the draft has been written or dictated, the next step—copy editing—is often the primary responsibility of the administrative secretary. *Copy editing* is the revision of a draft or a document for consistency, conciseness, and grammatical accuracy. Revisions are marked within the body of the document using proofreading and copy editing symbols (Figure 9-1). The edited copy is returned to the author for verification. After all revisions have been made and the document is typed in final form, the secretary will *proofread* the document for typing accuracy.

1. *Guidelines for Preparing Copy for Editing:* Copy to be edited can be prepared in rough-draft format. Four guidelines for typing rough-draft copy should be followed.

   a. *Side margins:* Side margins should be wide. Side margins should be 1 inch at a minimum.
   b. *Spacing:* Triple spacing should be used so corrections can easily be inserted. Never single-space rough-draft copy.
   c. *Paragraphs:* Indent paragraphs so a new paragraph can easily be identified. An alternative is to quadruple-space between paragraphs if triple spacing is used for the document and triple-space between paragraphs if double spacing is used for the document.
   d. *Readability of copy:* Even though this is a rough-draft copy, typing neatness should be maintained. When using a word processor, format codes (hyphenation, page advance) are *not* included. These codes are included before printing the final copy. When using a correcting typewriter or a standard typewriter, corrections do not need to be as neat and camouflaged as with the final copy. In rare cases, putting an *x* over incorrect word(s) is acceptable, and strikeovers (even though noticeable) are also used when it is a clear coverup, for example, *l* over an *i*, *t* over an *l*.

      Readability is the key factor. Rough-draft copy will be read for revisions, and reading is easier if the copy is neat.

2. *Basic Skills for Editing:* A superior secretary will develop a strong background in English skills, especially grammatical construction and punctuation. Copy editing requires grammar, punctuation, spelling, and composition skills as well as the ability to maintain consistency in both format and language usage throughout the document. These skills are the underpinnings of the editing process when reading a document for completeness and accuracy.

   a. *Grammar skills:* Because of the complexity of the English language as well as changes made to update grammar rules, a current English handbook should be available and used by every secretary. An executive secretary maintains and updates office skills through review and practice.
   b. *Punctuation skills:* A periodic brushup on punctuation skills is also vitally important.
   c. *Spelling skills:* Spelling can be improved by using the dictionary or a word book and concentrating on vocabulary building. There is always the *jargon* of the field to learn. When entering a new field, learn new terminology by adding one word to a vocabulary list every day. This technique can also be used for regular vocabulary expansion. The words should be

Editing Communications

used in daily communication, and periodically a spelling test should be taken on the words.

d. *Composition skills:* Composition is the ability to accurately tie grammar, punctuation, and spelling together into a written communique. A well-written document is one that is understood (clear), is stated in as few words as necessary (concise), and appeals to the reader (empathy). To develop effective communication skills, much practice is required and a "receiver" needs to evaluate the writing.

(1) *Reading for content:* When reading the copy for content, put yourself in the receiver's position. The aim of all communication is to produce a document that will appeal and communicate to the receiver. Sometimes reading for content can best be accomplished by reading aloud. Also, when someone else (coworker) reads the document for content, that person should evaluate the document from the receiver's perspective.

(2) *Checking accuracy of content:* Someone other than the author of the document should be reading for accuracy. Usually an author reads what he/she wants to say, not what has been written.

3. *Effective Word Selection:* When copy editing, it is very important to edit for content; in other words, examine the copy to determine what was intended by the author is the same as what is written. Content editing is accomplished by reading and concentrating on word selection, sentence structure, sentence completeness, train of thought, and tone.

Effective word selection comes with practice. There are a few English words which are used incorrectly, and their proper usage should be reviewed.

a. *Accept and except: Accept* means to receive or approve of; *except* means not to include.

EXAMPLES:
I accept your apology.
I have everyone's timecard except yours.

b. *Advise and advice: Advise* is a verb meaning to make a recommendation; *advice* is a noun meaning counsel.

EXAMPLES:
My manager advised me to sit for the CPS exam.
I think that is good advice.

c. *All ready and already: All ready* is an adjective phrase meaning everyone or everything is prepared; *already* is an adverb meaning before.

EXAMPLES:
The executives are all ready for the communications workshop.
Dr. Pascal already responded.

d. *Among and between: Among* refers to more than two; *between* refers to only two. The word *and* should always be used between the choices.

EXAMPLES:
Poor communication causes dissatisfaction among employees.
Between you and me, I think I received my raise.
I cannot choose between green and yellow and red and yellow.
(green and yellow is one item; red and yellow is a second item)

e. *Awhile and a while: Awhile* is an adverb meaning a period of time; *a while* is a noun with an article.

EXAMPLES:
Can you stay awhile?
(adverb modifying stay*)*
Can you stay for a while?
(noun—object of the preposition for*)*

f. *Bad and badly: Bad* is the adjective; *badly* is the adverb. *Badly* is used after linking verbs when emphasis is on the verb. However, *bad* is the *preferred* adjective form after linking verbs.

EXAMPLES:
The stock maneuver looks bad.
(adjective modifying the subject maneuver*)*

Since the accident, Sally limps badly.
(adverb describing limps*)*

Tom feels badly about the sale.
Tom feels bad about the sale.
(Many people object to use of badly *as the adjective after a linking verb; therefore, it is best to use* bad.*)*

g. *Complement and compliment:* Both can be used as a noun or a verb. *Complement* means finished or fitting together. *Compliment* is used when referring to praise.

EXAMPLES:
The new wall hangings complement the furniture.
(meaning fit together)
I must compliment Dan for his choice in wall hangings.

h. *Effect and affect: Effect* is a noun meaning result; *affect* is a verb meaning influence.

Editing Communications

EXAMPLES:
The effects of datacommunications have had a great impact.
(Effects = subject of the sentence)
The weather affected our plans.

i. *Good and well: Good* is an adjective; *well* is either an adjective or an adverb. The most common error is using the adjective *good* in place of the adverb *well*. *Good* and *well* are both used as predicate adjectives with the verb *feel*; however, the connotation is different.

EXAMPLES:
Everyone had a good time at the department party.
(adjective modifying the noun time*)*
All is well with the new couple.
(adjective modifying the subject all*)*
After the hurricane, the cleanup went well.
(adverb modifying the verb went*)*
Jon doesn't feel well.
(referring to Jon's health)
Eric felt good about building the addition.
(referring to Eric's mental feeling—happiness)

j. *Lay and lie: Lay* is a verb meaning to put or place; it takes an object. *Lie* is a verb meaning to recline; it does not take an object.
The principal parts of lay are lay, laid, laid.
The principal parts of lie are lie, lay, lain.

EXAMPLES:
I do not know where I laid my folder.
(folder is the object of the verb laid*)*
Grandpa should lie down for a rest.

k. *Lose and loose: Lose* is a verb meaning misplace; *loose* is an adjective meaning not tight or a verb meaning let go.

EXAMPLES:
Don't lose my place.
The dress is too loose.
Mark loosened the dog's collar.

l. *Most and almost: Most* is an adjective meaning large in number; *almost* is an adverb meaning nearly.

EXAMPLES:
Most secretaries sitting for the CPS exam take a review course.
(adjective modifying the subject secretaries*—meaning the majority; referring to large in number)*
Her writing almost meets specifications.
(adverb modifying meets*)*

m. *Proceed and precede: Proceed* means to continue; *precede* means to go before.

EXAMPLES:
We must proceed with our plans.
Learning the concepts precedes lab application.

n. *Principal and principle: Principal* is a noun or adjective meaning first in importance; *principle* is a noun meaning rule or basis for conduct.

EXAMPLES:
The new principal is planning major revisions.
To adhere to one's principles is important.

o. *Real and really: Real* is an adjective; *really* is an adverb.

EXAMPLES:
The real way to make progress is to work hard.
Everyone is really working hard at the office.

p. *Set and sit:* Both *set* and *sit* are verbs. *Set* takes an object; *sit* does not take an object.

EXAMPLES:
Please set my papers in the red in-basket.
(Set "what"? my papers
 "where"? in the red in-basket)
Please sit down on the couch.

q. *Site, cite, and sight: Site* is a noun meaning location. *Cite* is a verb meaning quote or recognize. *Sight* is a noun meaning vision.

EXAMPLES:
The new office site has a beautiful view.
Joel cited many abuses of the policy.
Joanne's sight was impaired because of the injury.

r. *Their, there, and they're: Their* is the possessive form of they. *There* is either an adverb or subject. *They're* is a contraction for they are.

EXAMPLES:
Their car was totaled.
Put the plant over there. (adverb)
There is a message on the spindle for you. (subject)
They're going to the theater for the performance. (contraction for they are)

Editing Communications

    s. *Then and than:* **Then** is an adverb; *than* is a conjunction usually used in comparisons.

        EXAMPLES:
        Call me this afternoon. We can then set a time.
        I like the Model 8032 better than the new one.

    t. *To, too, and two:* **To** is a preposition. *Too* is an adverb meaning also or very. *Two* is the number.

        EXAMPLES:
        Please bring the car to the garage for repair.
        The steak was too rare.
        We have two disk drives with our computer.

    u. *Who, which, and that:* **Who** is used when referring to a person and *which* when referring to things. *That* can be used to refer to either a person or a thing; it is usually used with restrictive clauses. A restrictive clause is one that is necessary to the completeness of the sentence.

        EXAMPLES:
        Secretaries who have word processors encounter less frustration with editing.
        (*who have word processors refers to secretaries*)

        This manual, which was written by the data processing manager, is very easy to follow. (*which was written by the data processing manager refers to "manual"—it is a clause that is not required, or nonrestrictive*)

        This is a word processor that can be learned quickly. (*that can be learned quickly is a restrictive clause referring to the word processor*)

4. *Effective Sentence and Paragraph Construction:* Common sentence errors are incomplete sentences, run-on sentences, and improper division for train of thought.

    a. *Incomplete sentence:* An incomplete sentence is one that is missing a subject or a verb (predicate). Incomplete sentences occur frequently in speech; therefore, often these sentences appear in written documents. An incomplete sentence can be corrected in one of these ways:

        (1) *Supplying the missing subject or verb (predicate):* Many times incomplete sentences follow complete sentences to which the sentence thoughts are connected. It is important to watch for incomplete sentences and supply the missing subject or verb.

EXAMPLE:
The new chair for the word processing unit was delivered today. Believe it's adjustable.
(The subject in the second sentence is missing. Corrected: I believe it's adjustable.*)*

(2) *Connecting it to another sentence:* Sometimes it is more convenient to connect the incomplete sentence to another sentence which has related thoughts.

EXAMPLE:
The report was sent to the Finance Department yesterday. The report on building expansion.
(The verb in the second sentence is missing. Corrected: The report on building expansion was sent to the Finance Department yesterday.*)*

(3) *Dropping the sentence:* Many times incomplete sentences are explanatory phrases or clauses which can be dropped from the written material.

b. *Run-on sentences:* Just the opposite of an incomplete sentence is running two or more complete sentences together. These sentences can be either made into two separate sentences or connected with correct punctuation.

(1) *Two separate sentences:* Because of the length of a run-on sentence, sometimes it is best to separate it into two separate sentences. Also, it is important that a written document have some variety in the length of sentences.

EXAMPLE:
A four-year degree in Office Administration is required for the new position because it is a supervisory position in the Administrative Services Department that is the department responsible for information processing.
(Corrected: ... in the Administrative Services Department. That is the department responsible for information processing.*)*

(2) *Correct punctuation for run-on sentences:* When two complete sentences are connected with punctuation it is called a *compound* sentence. If the run-on sentence does not have a conjunction, a semicolon is to be used between the two sentences. [See Section B-2-l(1) in this chapter.] If the run-on sentence has a conjunction, a comma is used between the two sentences. [See Section B-2-c(3) in this chapter.]

c. *Paragraph construction:* A paragraph represents the writer's thoughts on a portion of the whole subject. The entire document represents the writer's thoughts on the whole subject. Therefore, all skilled writers will organize their separate thoughts pertaining to the whole subject in a logical manner before they attempt to write. Writing manuals always advise an outline prior to writing. When writing skills are being developed or improved upon, the outline is usually written out on paper. As writers become more skillful with their writing, some choose to organize their thoughts mentally. However, many writers consistently produce a paper sketch of the topic before writing. It is important to recognize when this step is required in order to produce logical and clearly written material.

Even though paragraphs will vary in length and purpose, most paragraphs are composed of three types of statements.

(1) *Overview statement:* Many paragraphs contain a statement at the beginning which is general in nature and provides an overview of what is to follow. Such a statement can be a restatement of previous material when the paragraph is an expansion on a previous point. Sometimes an overview statement comes at the end of a paragraph summarizing what was presented in the paragraph.

(2) *Supporting statement:* Supporting statements are sentences within the paragraph presenting the ideas the writer has on this particular point of the topic.

(3) *Detail statement:* Good writing consists mainly of detail statements, statements which present facts about the topic. Generalizations and opinions are best supported by accurate facts.

5. *Tone, Goodwill, Considerateness, and Writing Style:* Tone is determined by what needs to be said and the point that needs to be made. Tone is the manner in which the attitude is expressed. Even with negative newsletters, goodwill is desired. Therefore, the majority of writing has the tone of goodwill, considerateness, friendliness, and being objective and personal.

6. *Editing for Organization:* Before checking to see whether a written document is organized, the copy editor must be organized. The topic should be well understood, the purpose of the document should be well understood, the approach used should be identified, and an outline should be followed while reading the material. All written documents should be clearly written and logical.

    a. *Communication between writer and copy editor:* Open communication between the writer and copy editor is very important. The communication needs to be clearly explained. This requires that either the writer or the copy editor must be a listener while the other one is speaking. This dialogue will help in making sure the topic and purpose of the document is well understood.

    b. *Approach used:* The copy editor needs to know whether the document was written in the direct approach (sometimes referred to as deductive approach) or the indirect approach (sometimes referred to as inductive approach). Letters, interoffice memorandums, and short reports can use either approach depending on the content of the document and the anticipated reaction by the reader.

        (1) *Direct approach:* This approach explains the main point immediately and then presents the facts to support the main point.

            (a) *Good news:* The direct approach is used when the material conveys good news.

            (b) *Analytical reports:* Analytical reports follow the direct approach. With an analytical report, it is important to establish goals. These goals include a statement of the problem and the purpose of the report. These two goals are included at the beginning of the report under the subheading(s), *Statement of the Problem* and *Purpose*.

        (2) *Indirect approach:* This approach gives the facts before the whole picture is presented. This approach is followed when it is believed the reader needs supporting evidence so the main point will be viewed with an open mind.

            (a) *Negative news:* Material that conveys negative news should follow the indirect approach.

            (b) *Persuasive writing:* When the material in the document needs to overcome feelings by the reader, the indirect approach should be used.

    c. *Outline:* The outline used by the writer for organizing his or her thoughts can also be used by the copy editor. However, some writers prefer that the communication between the writer and the copy editor be used by the copy editor to develop an outline to follow for editing. This method allows for a possible different approach to the subject. Utilization of this method will require time. If the copy editor approaches the topic differently, the writer and editor will need time to work out these differences.

7. *Editing for Completeness and Content Accuracy:* There are four basic rules of copy editing that an administrative secretary must keep in mind when editing for completeness and content accuracy: look it up, check and double-check, be consistent, and maintain the author's writing style.

a. *Looking it up:* When in doubt, look up the punctuation rule, the correct spelling, or the grammar rule. Reference manuals are the secretary's "right hand" and should be used without hesitation while copy editing.

b. *Checking and double-checking:* Checking and double-checking means being inquisitive as well as discriminating. The secretary editing the material can never assume that the facts and/or structure are correct. The copy editor's job is to check everything for accuracy. An executive secretary will not remain in that position for long if the excuse, "Well, that's exactly what you wrote," is ever used.

EXAMPLES:
When a document indicates facts and figures, check that these figures are correct.
If a word seems to be incorrectly used, question its use.
When a specific reference does not seem accurate, check the original source.

c. *Being consistent:* It is obvious that excellent grammar and punctuation skills will be important for copy editing. However, these skills must be matched with the skill of being observant. A copy editor must be observant of inconsistencies such as

(1) Transposition of letters and/or words.
(2) Information that is left out of the copy.
(3) Incomplete sentences in the document.
(4) Repetitive use of information.

EXAMPLE:
When reference is made to a conference in Dallas on the first page of a report, and later Houston is mentioned as the conference site, this discrepancy must be detected by the copy editor.

d. *Maintaining the author's writing style:* The document is the writer's, and the writing style of the writer must be maintained. This skill develops as the writer and copy editor work together over a period of time. However, it can be developed more quickly if an effort is made to identify the writing characteristics peculiar to the writer. Of course, this does not mean that a copy editor should allow incorrect writing habits to continue. A tactful conference between the writer and copy editor can help identify those writing characteristics which the writer will want unhesitatingly changed. There may be certain characteristics which the author may not allow to be changed; these writing characteristics are to remain in the material as the author's style.

8. *Copy Editing Style Sheet:* The saying, "practice makes perfect," is apropos to the development of copy editing skills. When a long document must be edited, a style sheet is a very helpful tool. The function of the style sheet is to assist the copy editor in remembering all the formatting points the author expects to be followed as well as all the editing decisions made while reading the material. The style sheet helps the copy editor maintain consistency throughout the document. The headings of a style sheet will vary to meet the individual needs. The style sheet illustrated in Figure 9-2 was developed by an executive secretary to meet the needs of the personnel department within a manufacturing organization. Figure 9-3 illustrates how the style sheet is used.
9. *Copy Editing Symbols:* To make copy editing easier, the symbols illustrated in Figure 9-1 are used. When copy editing, these symbols are made within the body of the document. It is helpful when these editing symbols are written with a colored pencil so they stand out from the black type. Also, the symbol must be clearly written. This aids the author when the material is reread for verification as well as the executive secretary when the material is being typed in final form.
10. *Word Processing and Copy Editing:* With current advancement in office technology, the word processor has become a timesaving editing tool. When the executive makes revisions on the first draft, neither the executive nor the secretary need hesitate in making revisions. With the text stored on magnetic media, it is a simple matter to change the order of the material, reword sentences, insert new text, or delete text not needed.

   a. *Using word processing:* Many documents dictated by the executive will be typed in final form the first time. If word

SPELLING	PUNCTUATION	REFERENCES	FORMAT NOTATIONS		OTHER NOTATIONS
NUMBERS	CAPITALIZATION	FACTS			

Figure 9-2
Editing Style Sheet

SPELLING	PUNCTUATION	REFERENCES	FORMAT NOTATIONS ¶ ~~Head~~	OTHER NOTATIONS
per cent a.m. p.m.	① No comma before and in series — unless for clarity. ② boss' for possession.	① Popular Computing Jan. 199- p. 75-78 "Tools for Writing"	① Use style w/ dash. EX. HEADING.-- Begin	
NUMBERS	CAPITALIZATION	FACTS ① Surveyed 80 local businesses. ② 87% return.		

Figure 9-3
Editing Style Sheet Used by an Executive Secretary

processing is used, the secretary can proceed with the keying and editing of the document directly on the computer screen, storing the document on disk, and then printing the document. Later revisions will be an easy matter because the text is stored on diskettes. Format codes should be inserted after all editing is complete and the final document is ready for printing.

b. *Using a typewriter:* If a standard typewriter (with or without correction devices) is used, the secretary should read the dictated notes completely prior to typing to be sure that all necessary changes will be made while typing. Reading through the author's input (whether in handwriting, in shorthand from oral dictation, or recorded on a dictation unit) should guarantee a more accurate copy, thus saving much time in the long run.

Chapter 9: Review Questions

Part A: Multiple-Choice Questions

DIRECTIONS: Select the best answer from the four alternatives. Write your answer in the blank to the left of the number.

_____ 1. Proofreading marks should be

   a. made with colored pencil so they are easily distinguishable.
   b. made with light pencil marks within the body of the document.
   c. made with light pencil marks within the margins of the document.
   d. recorded on a separate sheet of paper.

_____ 2. When proofreading

   a. check tables by reading vertically if the material was typed horizontally, or vice versa.
   b. count the number of lines in the original and compare this with the final copy.
   c. page a screen at a time on soft copy to make sure material is not skipped.
   d. read slowly for content while checking for typographical errors.

_____ 3. Proofreading software for computer systems

   a. is in the early stages of development and therefore not reliable.
   b. corrects all misspelled words relieving the proofreader of this responsibility.
   c. highlights all words that do not match the spell-check dictionary; the user (proofreader) verifies and correct spelling.
   d. prompts the user (proofreader) when the word is spelled here and it should have been hear; the user makes necessary corrections.

_____ 4. In the sentence—The survey, *conducted in the spring of 1991*, revealed that electronic mail is used by over 80 percent of the firms.—the italicized phrase, *conducted in the spring of 1991*, is

   a. an adjective.
   b. an independent clause.
   c. a participle phrase (verbal phrase functioning as an adjective).
   d. a prepositional phrase (functioning as an adjective).

5. Which sentence is punctuated correctly?

   a. Dr. Jones is pleased with the conference. (She called from Boston.)
   b. Mr. Paris article, *Management for the 1990s*, covers the importance of the administrative secretary.
   c. We need to finish these projects today; minutes of yesterdays board meeting, monthly stock report, the presentation for Mark's retirement dinner, and the Jagger Yancy report.
   d. The next conference is in California. I need plane reservations because its a fast convenient way for me to travel.

6. The correct sentence is

   a. Charlotte is taking a course in management information systems from a University in West Texas.
   b. The League of Women Voters is holding an open forum at the Newburg Public Library to discuss the state mandates with Senator Lewis.
   c. The Mayor has an editorial about last week's article "City services will be cut."
   d. 150 senior citizens attended the first meeting on Wednesday, 6-10.

7. The appearance of a document

   a. deals with selecting one of the more common letter styles: block, modified block, or simplified.
   b. deals with proper spacing and formatting; having few and neat corrections; having clear, dark print; and using nonglossy paper.
   c. is important for all documents except rough-draft copies.
   d. is important for external documents; however, requires minimum attention for internal documents.

8. When making corrections, a drafting eraser or gummed typewriter cleaner is used for

   a. camouflaging the letter to be corrected.
   b. cleaning typing erasers.
   c. correcting carbon copies.
   d. lifting the surface ink from the original before making a correction.

9. Which correction technique is *not* acceptable?

   a. Apple, Inc.'s letterhead is on buff paper. In proofreading the letter, Pat used yellow chalk to camouflage a correction.
   b. In using the electronic typewriter, Meg realized that an *f* covers an *i*.

Editing Communications

Meg corrected the word *iig* (correct spelling *fig*) with a strikeover - *f* over the first *i*.
c. Mark had to use the electric typewriter and needed to erase the word *by*. He gently used horizontal and vertical strokes with the eraser.
d. Sally is preparing a document for photocopying. She deleted a statement with correction fluid.

_____ 10. When preparing documents, consistency is important to

a. format.
b. punctuation.
c. word usage.
d. all of the above.

_____ 11. When typing numbers

a. always spell out numbers under 10.
b. be consistent when several sets of numbers are within the same sentence.
c. express percentages as 23%.
d. spell out fractions.

_____ 12. The correct sentence is

a. The meeting is scheduled for June 5th at 2:00 a.m.
b. The 1st letter referred to policy number 378,469,201.
c. Their new address is Suite 3, East Sixth Avenue, EauClaire, Wisconsin.
d. There should be 30 5-pound boxes of candy.

_____ 13. When dividing a word

a. it is best to have enough of the word on the first line to be able to conceptualize the entire word.
b. make sure the pronunciation of a proper name is followed.
c. the last word on a page should contain most of the letters so the word is easily conceptualized without having to turn the page.
d. the previous line cannot also end with a divided word.

_____ 14. The correctly divided word is:

a. Mr. John   R. David
b. page 105
c. should-   n't
d. $132,   000

_____ 15. Which statement is correct with regard to hyphenation with word processing?

   a. The automatic hyphenation feature prompts the user to determine whether the word should be hyphenated.
   b. The automatic hyphenation feature hyphenates the word according to hyphenation rules established within the word processing software.
   c. The manual hyphenation feature provides the least amount of flexibility in following hyphenation rules as accepted by most businesses.
   d. With word wrap, hyphenation should seldom be necessary.

_____ 16. Editing is

   a. checking the final copy for spelling and punctuation accuracy.
   b. checking the document for typing accuracy.
   c. correcting the format of the document.
   d. revising a draft for consistency, conciseness, and grammatical accuracy.

_____ 17. When editing, the purpose is a well-written document which

   a. adheres to correct document format.
   b. adjusts the writing style to the editor's perspective.
   c. is clear, concise, and appeals to the reader.
   d. reflects the author's personality.

_____ 18. A copy editing style sheet

   a. is helpful in maintaining the author's writing style.
   b. is seldom used because such a sheet usually does not meet the needs of diverse departments.
   c. is a useful tool for maintaining consistency when editing long documents.
   d. should have only three areas of concentration for comments.

Part B: Matching Sets

Matching Set 1: Hyphenation Test

DIRECTIONS: For each word, match the word with the correct hyphenation. Write the letter of your answer in the blank to the left of the number.

Editing Communications

_____   **19.** DETAILED

       a. de-tailed
       b. detail-ed
       c. detailed

_____   **20.** CROSS-COUNTRY

       a. cross-country
       b. cross-coun-try
       c. cross-co-untry

_____   **21.** GRANDPARENTS

       a. grand-parents
       b. grandpar-ents
       c. grandparents

_____   **22.** IMPERATIVE

       a. im-perative
       b. imper-ative
       c. impera-tive

_____   **23.** RESTOPPING

       a. re-stopping
       b. restop-ping
       c. restopp-ing

Matching Set 2: Spelling Test

DIRECTIONS: Select the word in each pair which is spelled correctly. Write the letter of your answer in the blank to the left of the number.

_____   **24.** a. alloted
          b. allotted

25. a. bicycal
     b. bicycle

_____

26. a. commitment
     b. committment

_____

27. a. committes
     b. committees

_____

28. a. concede
     b. conceed

_____

29. a. cut-and-dried pattern
     b. cut and dried pattern

_____

30. a. geologist
     b. geologyst

_____

31. a. historical
     b. historicle

_____

32. a. achieveing
     b. achieving

_____

33. a. kameleon
     b. chameleon

_____

34. a. landlady
     b. land-lady

_____

35. a. lotterys
     b. lotteries

Editing Communications 337

_____ 36. a. mouthfull
 b. mouthful

_____ 37. a. neice
 b. niece

_____ 38. a. occuring
 b. occurring

_____ 39. a. outrageous
 b. outragous

_____ 40. a. periodical
 b. periodicle

_____ 41. a. phosphorus
 b. phosforus

_____ 42. a. procede
 b. proceed

_____ 43. a. relaying
 b. relaing

_____ 44. a. sincerly
 b. sincerely

_____ 45. a. square root
 b. squarroot

_____ 46. a. tieing
 b. tying

_____   47. a. whole-sale
                   b. wholesale

_____   48. a. weird
                   b. wierd

Part C: Problem Situations

DIRECTIONS: The following problem situations will give you practice with punctuation, capitalization, and the use of numbers in copy. Follow the directions given with each problem.

Problem 1

Punctuate and capitalize the following sentences. Insert the corrections into the copy that follows, or retype the sentences and insert the punctuation and capitalization as you go along.

49. The meeting is scheduled to begin at ten with lunch starting at 12:30.

50. David received his order for sunflight rosefire and angleglow lilies gardenwonder and white perfection dahlias and oriental poppies all in the same day!

51. Carol should reconsider her decision to move to California and apply for the assistants position at Montclare state college.

52. The contract stated The lease will run for two years... Monthly payments of $750.00 ... on the First of the Month.

53. The guests included pastor Olsen and three members of the board.

Problem 2

Correct the following sentences for accuracy in keying (typing) numbers. Insert corrections into the sentences that follow, or type the sentences and make corrections as you go along.

54. We were surprised when the part cost only 75c.

55. The formula calls for 51/4 caps of red dye and 2 5/8 caps of neutralizer.

56. 25 members attended the 4 of July picnic.

57. 1500 patients received the vaccination today!

58. When Grandpa was 69, he started chapter one of his book.

Chapter 9: Solutions

Part A: Multiple-Choice Questions

	Answer	Refer to Chapter Section
1.	(c)	[A]
2.	(a)	[A-2-c]
3.	(c)	[A-4-a]
4.	(c)	[B-1-b(3)]
5.	(a)	[B-2-h(4)]
6.	(b)	[B-3, B-3-e, B-3-i, and B-3-j}
7.	(b)	[B-4-b]
8.	(d)	[B-4-b(1)]
9.	(c)	[B-4-b(2)(c)]
10.	(d)	[B-5]
11.	(b)	[B-7-c]
12.	(c)	[B-7-p and B-7-r]
13.	(a)	[B-8-a(2)]
14.	(b)	[B-8-b(17)]
15.	(b)	[B-8-c]
16.	(d)	[C]
17.	(c)	[C-2-d]
18.	(c)	[C-8]

Part B: Matching Sets

Matching Set 1: Hyphenation Test

19.	(c)	[B-8-b(2) and (5)]
20.	(a)	[B-8-b(3)]
21.	(a)	[B-8-b(4)]
22.	(c)	[B-8-b(2) and (6)]
23.	(b)	[B-8-b(2) and (8)]

Matching Set 2: Spelling Test

24. (b) [B-6-l(3)] Double the ending consonant before adding a suffix when the word is accented on the last syllable.

25. (b) [B-6-f] Words ending in *cle* are nouns.

26. (a) [B-6-l] The suffix does not begin with a vowel, the final consonant is preceded by a single vowel, and the word is accented on the second syllable. Therefore, the ending consonant is not doubled before adding the suffix.

27. (b) [B-6-e] To form the plural of a word ending in ee, add only an s.

28. (a) [B-6-h] There is no rule for the *cede* ending. The word just needs to be memorized.
29. (a) [B-6-m] The phrase *cut and dried* is used as an adjective, modifying the noun *pattern*. Therefore, it is hyphenated.
30. (a) [B-6-j] When a word ends in *y* and is preceded by a consonant, the *y* is generally changed to *i* when adding a suffix which begins with a consonant.
31. (a) [B-6-f] Words ending in *cal* are adjectives derived from other words ending in *ic*.
32. (b) [B-6-c] Words ending in silent *e* preceded by a consonant drop the *e* when adding a suffix beginning with a vowel.
33. (b) [B-6-g] The *ch* has the *k* sound.
34. (a) [B-6-m] A compound word consists of two or more words which are written as one word, as separate words, or hyphenated. The word *landlady* has typically been written as one word.
35. (b) [B-6-j] To form the plural of a word which ends in *y* and is preceded by a consonant, change the *y* to *i* and add *es*.
36. (b) [B-6-k] The suffix *ful* is spelled with only one *l*.
37. (b) [B-6-a] "*I* before *e* except after *c*, or when sounded like *a* as in neighbor and weigh."
38. (b) [B-6-l(1)] Double the ending consonant when the suffix begins with a vowel.
39. (a) [B-6-c] This is an exception to the rule. The silent *e* is retained before a suffix beginning with a vowel because of pronunciation.
40. (a) [B-6-f] Words ending in *cal* are adjectives derived from other words ending in *ic*. The word *periodical* is an exception to this rule and can be either a noun or an adjective, however.
41. (a) [B-6-g] The *ph* has the *f* sound.
42. (b) [B-6-h] There is no rule for the *cede*, *sede*, or *ceed* endings. The words must be memorized.
43. (a) [B-6-i] When a word ends in *y* and is preceded by a vowel, the *y* is generally retained when adding a suffix.
44. (b) [B-6-c] Words ending in a silent *e* preceded by a consonant retain the *e* when adding a suffix beginning with a consonant.
45. (a) [B-6-d] When two words are consolidated, making a compound word, a silent *e* on the first word is retained with the compound word.
46. (b) [B-6-b] When a word ends in *ie*, it is changed to *y* before the suffix *ing*.
47. (b) [B-6-m] A compound word consists of two or more words which are written as a single word, as separate words, or hyphenated. Typically, the word *wholesale* has been written as one word.
48. (a) [B-6-a] This is an exception to the "*i* before *e*" rhyme. This word needs to be memorized.

Editing Communications

Part C: Problem Situations

49. The meeting is scheduled to begin at 10:00 A.M. with lunch starting at 12:30 P.M.
    [B-2-b(2)] Note: AM, a.m., am, PM, p.m., and pm are also correct; just be consistent.
50. David received his order for sunflight, rosefire, and angleglow lilies; gardenwonder and white perfection dahlias; and oriental poppies all in the same day!
    [B-2-c(2)] Note: Comma before the *and* is optional. [B-2-l(2)] [B-3-l] Note: These are not brand-name objects.
51. Carol should reconsider her decision to move to California and apply for the assistant's position at Montclare State College.
    [B-2-a(1), B-2-c(3), B-3-j]
52. The contract stated, "The lease will run for two years. . . . Monthly payments of $750 . . . on the first of the month."
    [B-2-c(4), B-2-i(4), B-3-c, and B-3-m]
53. The guests included Pastor Olsen and three members of the board.
    [B-2-c(2), B-3-e and B-3-j]
54. We were surprised when the part cost only 75 cents.
    [B-7-d]
55. The formula calls for 5 1/4 caps of red dye and 2 5/8 caps of neutralizer.
    [B-7-f]
56. Twenty-five members attended the 4th of July picnic.
    [B-7-g, B-7-h, and B-7-j]
57. Fifteen hundred patients received the vaccination today!
    [B-7-g and B-7-m]
58. When Grandpa was sixty-nine, he started Chapter 1 of his book.
    [B-7-p and B-7-q]

CHAPTER 10
Abstracting Communications

OVERVIEW

The ability to accurately and concisely summarize articles, reports, books, or letters is an invaluable skill. Most executives receive volumes of material that must be read. As an executive and secretary team move up within an organization, more and more material must be absorbed. Yet, there are still only 24 hours in a day. Therefore, an executive secretary who is able to summarize material for executives and managers is a secretary who possesses a special skill. Like all skills, summarizing material requires practice. In this chapter, a distinction is made between preparing an abstract or précis and annotating.

DEFINITION OF TERMS

ABSTRACT. A summary of a document using key words from the document.
ANNOTATING. Marginal notations on a document answering questions or presenting facts related to material in the document.
PRECIS. A paraphrased summary of a document.

A. Techniques

There are several ways in which material can be summarized. Many times all that is necessary is photocopying sections of material or highlighting key points. However, an executive secretary must also be able to prepare an abstract or précis of key points or be able to use computerized services.

1. *Photocopying:* With the sophisticated photocopying equipment in offices, sections of material can easily be copied for reference and later use. Many times it will be the secretary's responsibility to identify material important for the executive and to take the initiative for photocopying the material. Also, the executive will identify material that needs to be photocopied.

   a. *Efficient use of the photocopier:* The photocopy machine can be housed in the reprographics department where it is operated by the reprographics staff, or it can be located where it is available for all office staff to use. Some instances may require the use of photocopying services from external organizations.

   (1) *Use by all staff:* Many times a photocopying machine is made available for all office personnel, even though there is an in-house reprographics department. When a photocopying machine is available to be used at one's discretion, it is important to schedule the time. Scheduling eliminates unnecessary trips to the photocopier and saves time. Efficient use of a decentralized photocopier involves:

   (a) *Organizing material:* Accumulate the material that needs to be copied in one place.
   (b) *Scheduling photocopying:* Schedule one or two times during the day to use the photocopy machine. The amount of times scheduled will depend on your photocopying work load. One situation a secretary will want to avoid is scheduling only one or two times during the day and spending 15 minutes or more at the machine because of the volume that needs to be copied. With massive volumes, two times in the morning and two times in the afternoon may be necessary. A typical schedule would include one time in the morning and one time in the afternoon.

   (2) *Departmentalized or external use:* If material to be copied must be sent to a centralized department or out of house, turnaround time must be taken into consideration. Usually a photocopy request form must be completed which will allow you to state, "when needed." Also, it is the secretary's responsibility to make sure all material sent is returned and to make sure when the material is returned that the copy request was completed accurately.

Abstracting Communications 347

(a) *Logging requests:* In order to make sure that all materials sent to be copied are returned, requests should be logged. When the material is returned, a notation should be made on the log. Illustrated in Figure 10-1 is a photocopying request log.

(b) *Completing the request form:* It is important that all information required to do the photocopying is stated on the request form.

- Date of request
- Page numbers to be copied
- Collating and stapling requirements
- Date needed

(c) *Turnaround time:* Because the material needs to be sent to a department or out of the organization, this needs to be taken into consideration along with the volume of photocopying normally done by the reprographics service. A secretary must plan ahead to make sure the material is returned by the time it is needed. If it is a rush item, many departments can handle these requests if they are infrequent. Sometimes a rush item may have to be delivered to the photocopying service area in order for it to be completed on time.

b. *Legal use of the copier:* The author of any document has spent time researching, composing, and editing the written word. For this reason, copyright laws have been established for the protection of authors and publishers. *Fair uses* of copyrighted

DESCRIPTION OF ITEM	NUMBER OF COPIES	DATE SENT	EXPECTED RETURN	RETURNED

Figure 10-1
A Photocopying Request Log

work provide exceptions to the copyright holder's exclusive right to the work. Fair uses include:

(1) Making one copy for the purpose of studying and highlighting the material.
(2) Using the copyright material for limited purposes in a classroom training situation. This is permissible if the work is short, and it would be impractical to obtain the consent of the author or publisher.

Module 2, Business Law contains more complete coverage of copyrights in Chapter 6, Section B.

2. *Highlighting Key Points:* Highlighting key points is an effective and efficient means of emphasizing important information within a document. Sometimes the secretary can do this on the original, but usually highlighting is done on a copy so the original is unaltered. Highlighting should be done by underlining or overmarking with a bright-colored marker, pen, or pencil.

    a. *Underlining:* Some executives prefer a thin line underneath the key information. This can easily be accomplished with a fine-pointed marker, a pen, or a pencil. Whichever is used should be in a color other than blue or black. A ruler should be used so the underline is straight.

    EXAMPLE: The most <u>common source</u> *of information for business reports is information obtained from* <u>observations</u>.

    b. *Overmarking:* Some executives prefer a wide mark drawn over the key points. A wide-end, light-colored marker and a ruler are the best tools for this method.

    EXAMPLE: The **first source** *for help in library research is the card catalog.*

    c. *Colored marker, pen, or pencil:* With highlighting, it is important to use a colored writing instrument other than the typical colors of blue and black.

        (1) *Underlining:* When underlining, a bright, dark color should be used. Good underlining colors are red or green.
        (2) *Overmarking:* When overmarking, a bright, pale color should be used. Good overmarking colors are light blue, pink, yellow, or orange.
        (3) *Colorcoding:* Through the use of several colors, the material highlighted can also be organized by color code.

3. *Summarizing Key Points:* The task of summarizing is referred to as an abstract or a précis. An abstract or a précis is a concise summary

of all key points. Some executives will only require that abstracts be prepared, others will require only précis, and others will require both.

- **a.** *Abstract:* Many summaries are condensations of the original material so the executive does not have so much to read. Such a summary is referred to as an abstract. An abstract contains key points of the original, usually in the exact wording of the original.

    (1) *Length:* Depending upon the depth of the information contained in the original, an abstract can be from one-fourth to one-half the length of the original.
    (2) *Format:* There are two formats for presenting an abstract. It can be in paragraph format or in outline format.

- **b.** *Précis:* Many times the summary is used to develop lectures or reports. In this case, it is important that the material paraphrase the original. A précis is a summary of material in your own words.

    (1) *Length:* A précis is usually one-third the length of the original.
    (2) *Format:* A précis is typed in paragraph format.

4. *Computerized Services:* Computerized services provide information on many topics. Some services are totally dedicated to one topic—law, medicine, political data. These commercial database services are collections of articles, abstracts, and bibliographic citations from books, periodicals, reports, and theses. Several popular commercial database services are Bibliographic Retrieval System (BRS), NewsNet, and Dialog.

    - **a.** *Subscription:* In order to electronically search the database information, one must subscribe to the computerized service. Subscribers are then provided with database access codes. Database search commands (words or phrases) are used for the information retrieval process. The subscriber is charged for database search time as well as the electronic transmission of the information. Charges are usually higher for daytime access than evening or weekend access.
    - **b.** *Database search:* A good way to begin a search is with general terms or topics. Using the search commands, the topic is narrowed to more specific, pertinent information. Moving from the general to the specific provides a broader search of the database. Usually topics are previewed and narrowed to eliminate those not needed before sending the information.

B. Effective Abstracts and Précis

An abstract or a précis is a concise summary of all key points. Whether an abstract or a précis is needed, all relevant information must be included, major conclusions must be mentioned, the original must be documented, the language must be consistent with the original, and the format must be easy to read.

1. *Concise Summary of Key Points:* The length of the summary will depend on the depth of the material in the original. It must be kept in mind, however, that the purpose of an abstract or précis is to summarize the key points of the original so time is saved for the executive when reading the material.

    a. *Abstract:* An abstract can be from one-fourth to one-half the length of the original material.
    b. *Précis:* A précis is usually one-third the length of the original. In writing a précis, the original material is recomposed, omitting illustrations, amplifications, or flowery language.

2. *Relevant Information:* Since the purpose of the abstract is to condense the original so more material can be read in the same amount of time, it is not necessary for the secretary to spend time rewording the material. With a précis, time will be spent on recomposing the original while maintaining the author's point of view, writing style, and tone without using the author's exact words or phrases.

    Both an abstract and a précis must include the key points of the original. There are four writing characteristics which can be used as flags to identify key points:

    a. *Facts:* The easiest to identify are facts. Facts are usually represented in figure format. This information clearly stands out from the written word. The secretary must make sure that only relevant facts are contained in the abstract or précis and that the summary includes other key points from the original.
    b. *Listings:* Many authors list important points as 1, 2, 3, and so forth. Another listing technique is to make a point without any listing notation and follow up with the word *second* when the author is making a succeeding point. The word *second* would be a flag that a point has previously been made and that there may be more to follow. The word *last* is many times used to indicate a concluding point.
    c. *Headings:* Headings throughout the material should be followed for the summary. Headings are usually flags for key points to be discussed. At the end of the material within the heading, there usually will be summary statements.
    d. *Topic sentences:* Sometimes a new paragraph is a continuation of the previous paragraph including new thoughts. When a completely new idea or concept is introduced, the paragraph normally begins with a topic sentence. This sentence can be

used to identify a key point. Many paragraphs end with a summary statement or the paragraph itself is a summary of a section.

3. *Reporting Major Conclusions:* Many authors conclude their writing with a summary statement, paragraph, or section. To understand the gist of the material, read the concluding summary material first. For a book, the preface should be read first.

   Understanding the concluding remarks will help the secretary locate key points within the document. Also, these concluding points should be part of the abstract or précis.

4. *Complete Documentation:* Credit must be given to the original author; therefore, it is important to include all bibliographical information on the photocopy, abstract, or précis.

   a. *Bibliographical information:* The bibliographical information includes:

   (1) Title of the report, book, or magazine
   (2) Name(s) of author(s)
   (3) Page number when material is written verbatim
   (4) Title of article in the magazine
   (5) Date of publication
   (6) Name of publisher and location

   b. *Placement of bibliographical information:* Exactly where to include the bibliographical information can vary. The executive and secretary should identify the format preferred and follow that format for all documentation.

   (1) *Photocopies:* On photocopies, the information can be included on either the front of the first page or back of the last page. Sometimes the information is included on the back of the first page or bottom (at the end) of the last page.
   (2) *Abstract and précis:* The abstract and précis will contain source title, author, and title of the article in the main heading of the summary. Page numbers will be included within the abstract as needed. Other bibliographical information may be included in the main heading or at the end of the summary in footnote format.

5. *Level of Language Consistent with Original:* When summarizing the material, it is important to maintain the tone and thought of the author. Even when preparing an abstract, the thought can be completely altered by leaving out a word, punctuation mark, or key point. Also, even though a précis is recomposing the original material, it is important to maintain the author's point of view.

   Following guidelines for writing an abstract or précis will help maintain consistent language with the original.

a. *Summaries within original:* Read any summary sections or paragraphs first. This helps establish the general idea of the document.
b. *First reading:* Quickly read the entire material; do not take notes. If the material is lengthy, quickly read the first major division. This also helps to establish the general idea.
c. *Second reading:* With the second reading, look up unfamiliar words or references to unfamiliar material. With the unfamiliar clarified, you are better able to understand the material and will more accurately note only the important ideas. Following this procedure will help distinguish amplifications from key points.
d. *Taking notes:* With the third reading, you are ready to take notes. Record only the important ideas and facts using the guidelines presented in Section B-2 of this chapter. If you are writing a précis, use your notes to summarize the material in your own words.
e. *Rough copy:* Type the summarized notes in rough-draft format. Remember, the purpose of an abstract or précis is to be concise yet clear!
f. *Edit:* Compare the abstract or précis with the original for accuracy. Edit the summary, eliminating unnecessary words and making sure the wording is clear.
g. *Final copy:* Type the abstract or précis in an easy-to-read format.

6. *Easy-to-read Format:*

   a. *Abstract format:* An abstract can be typed in outline form or in paragraph form. The decision as to whether the format should be in paragraph or outline form will depend on the executive's preference. If there is no preference, then the format is left to the secretary's discretion. Choose the format which you consider easiest to follow and most appropriate for the material.
   b. *Précis format:* A précis is always typed in paragraph form.

   An example of an abstract in outline form is illustrated in Figure 10-2. Figure 10-3 illustrates an abstract of the same article in paragraph form.

7. *Distinguishing Abstracts from Précis:* For the secretary who needs to prepare both abstracts and précis, it will be important to indicate when the summary is an abstract and when it is a précis. This is necessary for the executive in order to determine how the information might be used in a letter, a speech, or a report. Also, it is important when the secretary retrieves the summary from the file several months later; the code will help both the secretary and the executive remember whether the material is a direct quote or a paraphrase.

TITLE: "Build Your Future As a Small Investor"
SOURCE: THE SECRETARY, November/December 1991, pp. 10-14
****
I. Small Investor: Sets aside $1,000 or less to invest
II. Initial Steps
   A. Determine short- and long-term goals (include retirement)
   B. Evaluate current financial situation
      1. Monitor expenses: 2-3 months
      2. Categories
         a. Household
         b. Food
         c. Insurance
         d. Clothing
         e. Medical/dental
         f. Taxes
         g. Charitable contributions
         h. Entertainment
         i. Education
         j. Transportation
         k. Investment/savings
         l. Other: Carefully evaluate
      3. Enemy: credit-card debt/finance charges
   C. Assess risk-tolerance; all investments have risks
      1. Low risk-tolerance / conservative investments
      2. Sources: <u>Money</u> and <u>Consumer Reports</u>
III. Evaluate Possibilities
   A. Go it alone
      1. Requires research
      2. Cautions
         a. Personal biases
         b. Limited or inaccurate knowledge
   B. Obtain services of reputable financial services firm
      1. Good for first time investors
      2. Discuss current financial wellness and retirement needs
IV. Investment Options
   A. Certificates of deposit
   B. Treasury notes, bonds, and bills
   C. Individual stocks
   D. Annuities
   E. Municipal bonds
   F. Mutual funds
      1. Advantages for small investors
         a. Diversification
         b. Professional management
            (1) Load funds: Up to 8.5% per purchase
            (2) No-load funds: Sold by fund management companies
         c. Liquidity
      2. Bond mutual funds
         a. Ratings
            (1) AAA (tops) to D (default)
            (2) BBB or higher recommended
         b. Municipal bonds: Some protect income from taxes
V. Other Factors
   A. Inflation erodes value of money
   B. Delay taxation through tax-deferred investments
      1. 401(k) plans through companies
         a. Up-front tax savings
         b. High maximum contribution; up to 13% of gross
      2. Individual Retirement Account (IRA): Annual maximum
         a. Individual $2,000
         b. Married with 1 nonworking spouse $2,250

Figure 10-2
Abstract in Outline Form

```
VI.     Other Needs
        A.      Children's education
                1.      Zero coupons
                2.      Mutual fund
        B.      Liquid reserves for emergencies
                1.      Includes: cash, money market accounts,
                        general securities
                2.      Rule of thumb: 3-6 months of normal net
                        income
VII.    Action
        A.      Pick No. 1 investment choice:  Invest
        B.      Choose dollar-cost averaging
        C.      Periodically review plan
```

Figure 10-2 *(con't)*

```
                BUILD YOUR FUTURE AS A SMALL INVESTOR[1]

Initial steps for small investors include: determine short- and
long-term goals, evaluate current financial situation, and
understand personal risk-tolerance.

Two possible directions: do own investment research or utilize
services of reputable finance firm.

Good investment option for small investor is mutual funds because
of diversification, liquidity, and fund managed.

Load funds can add an additional 8.5% for management.

Bond mutual fund ratings range from AAA (top) to D (default); BBB
or higher is recommended.

Tax-deferred investments include 401(k) through companies or
Individual Retirement Account (IRA).

Zero coupons and mutual funds are good for children's education.

When investing, make sure to retain liquid reserves for
emergencies.

When starting an investment plan, consider dollar-cost averaging.

Periodically review investments made.
```

---

[1] Georgia Adamson, CPS, "Build Your Future As a Small Investor," <u>The Secretary</u>, November/December 1991, pp. 10-14.

Figure 10-3
Abstract in Paragraph Form

Usually a capital *P* in parenthesis or circled identifies the material as a précis; a capital *A* is used for an abstract. This code can be recorded on the front of the first page, top, right corner or on the back of the last page, top, right corner. Or possibly the executive and secretary will identify a different location or code. Whatever is decided upon, however, should be consistently followed for all abstracts and précis.

8. *Using the Abstract or Précis:* In using the material for speeches, training sessions, or other writing, the executive would be plagiarizing if credit was not given to the original author. Bibliographical information can be provided in a footnote, or reference to the author and source can be incorporated in the body of the material.

When the material is quoted verbatim (abstract), quotation marks are required around the material. When the material is paraphrased (précis), quotation marks are not required around the material. In both instances, the original author must receive credit for the material.

Chapter 10: Review Questions

Part A: Multiple-Choice Questions

DIRECTIONS: Select the best answer from the four alternatives. Write your answer in the blank to the left of the number.

_____ 1. When material needs to be sent to a photocopy department or out of house to be photocopied, it is important to keep a photocopy request log so

   a. photocopy requests not returned can be tracked down.
   b. sufficient turnaround time is scheduled.
   c. the material sent for photocopying will be returned quickly.
   d. the photocopy department will know what to copy and how many copies.

_____ 2. Fair use of copyrighted work

   a. allows a single copy to be made for the purpose of studying and highlighting material.
   b. allows continued (unlimited) photocopying as long as it is for classroom training situations.
   c. means material should seldom be photocopied.
   d. protects the author's exclusive right to the work.

_____ 3. Using a wide-point marker to shade with a light color is

   a. annotating.
   b. highlighting.
   c. overmarking.
   d. underlining.

_____ 4. Underlining should be done with a

   a. bright, dark red or green thin marker.
   b. bright, pale pink or yellow wide marker.
   c. dark blue or black thin marker.
   d. dark red or purple wide marker.

_____ 5. A paraphrased summary is

   a. an abstract.
   b. an annotation.

  c. a photocopy.
  d. a précis.

_____ 6. In conducting a computer search for summaries on a legal issue, begin the search

  a. from a broad legal perspective, narrow it down to the issue, and finally screen out information not needed.
  b. using one term which references the issue.
  c. with general terms pertaining to the issue; then narrow it down to specific information.
  d. with a specific case pertaining to the legal issue in order to cross-reference related cases.

_____ 7. Key points in the original document can be identified by

  a. lists.
  b. statements written in the form of a question.
  c. subheadings.
  d. all of the above.

_____ 8. Bibliographical information for a précis should include

  a. title of the material, author, and publisher.
  b. title of the material, author, publication date, and publisher.
  c. title of the material, author, publication date, publisher, and page numbers.
  d. title of the material, author, publication date, publisher, page numbers, and editor.

_____ 9. The level of the language of the summary

  a. can vary from the original when writing an abstract.
  b. must vary from the original when writing a précis because a précis is a paraphrased summary.
  c. needs to be consistent with the original on verbatim material only.
  d. should be consistent with the original.

_____ 10. When using material from a précis for other writing

  a. a bibliography is sufficient for credit to the original author.
  b. the executive should reword the précis material to avoid plagiarism.
  c. the original author does not have to be referenced since a précis is a paraphrase.
  d. quotation marks should enclose the précis wording.

Abstracting Communications

Part B: Matching Sets

Matching Set 1

Match each statement (11-15) with the appropriate term or symbol (A-L). Write the letter of your answer in the blank to the left of the number.

TERMS/SYMBOLS

    A. (A)
    B. (ABS)
    C. Abstract
    D. Bibliographical Information
    E. Colorcoding
    F. Copyright
    G. Fair Use of Copyright
    H. Overmarking
    I. Paraphrase
    J. Précis
    K. Underlining
    L. **

STATEMENTS

_____ 11. Code to distinguish the summary as an abstract.

_____ 12. Exceptions to an author's exclusive right to the material.

_____ 13. Outline summary of key points using the exact wording of the original work.

_____ 14. Providing credit to the original author.

_____ 15. Using a fine-point marker to highlight key information in a bright, dark color.

Part C: Problem Situation

DIRECTIONS: Read the following problem situation carefully. Record the appropriate transactions on the Photocopy Log shown on the next page.

16. The following items were handled by Barbara Jamison on June 14 and June 15.

Monday, June 14

AM Harris Report to Reprographics Department, 10 copies, 1-day turnaround.
Mortgage Contract for Jon Misic to Reprographics Department, 2 copies, same-day turnaround.

PM Fox Center Development Contract to Reprographics Department, 30 copies, 2-day turnaround.
Mortgage Contract for Mr. and Mrs. Dan Coughlin to Reprographics Department, 2 copies, next-day turnaround.
Mortgage Contract for Jon Misic, 2 copies received.
Burpee Plans, 6 copies received, 1 copy unusable, next-day rush.

Tuesday, June 15

AM FAX letter to Jon Misic, need reply by end of week.
Burpee Plans, 1 copy received.
Harris Report, 9 copies received, same-day rush.

PM Mortgage Contract for Mr. and Mrs. Dan Coughlin, 2 copies received.

DESCRIPTION OF ITEM	NUMBER OF COPIES	DATE SENT	EXPECTED RETURN	RETURNED
Robin Estate	25	6/11	6/15	
Burpee Plans	6	6/11	6/14	

Chapter 10: Solutions

Part A: Multiple-Choice Questions

	Answer	Refer to Chapter Section
1.	(a)	[A-1-a(2)(a)]
2.	(a)	[A-1-b]
3.	(c)	[A-2-b]
4.	(a)	[A-2-c(1)]
5.	(d)	[A-3-b]
6.	(c)	[A-4-b]
7.	(a)	[B-2-b]
8.	(b)	[B-4-a]
9.	(d)	[B-5]
10.	(a)	[B-8]

Part B: Matching Set

11.	(A)	[B-7]
12.	(G)	[A-1-b]
13.	(C)	[A-3-a]
14.	(D)	[B-8]
15.	(K)	[A-2-a and A-2-c(1)]

Part C: Problem Situation

16.

DESCRIPTION OF ITEM	NUMBER OF COPIES	DATE SENT	EXPECTED RETURN	RETURNED[c]
Robin Estate	25	6/11	6/15	
Burpee Plans	6	6/11	6/14	14 (5 good)
Harris Report	10	6/14[b]	6/15	15 (9 copies)
Misic MC	2	6/14	6/14	14
Fox Contract	30	6/14	6/16	
Coughlin MC	2	6/14	6/15	15
Burpee Plans	1	6/14	6/15 AM	15 AM
Harris Report	1	6/15	6/15 PM	

Note: FAX letter to Jon Misic (Tuesday, June 15, AM) does not belong on Photocopy Log.

[a] Can also spell out mortgage contract, but must identify whose mortgage contract (Misic, Coughlin).
[b] May also indicate AM or PM; seems to be two pickup times. Where time is recorded in answer, it is a special situation—RUSH.
[c] Notes of resubmits are helpful for later review or service. Also, it is best to record a new entry for resubmit; easier to monitor. All blank areas in RETURNED column mean not returned.

CHAPTER 11
Preparing Communications in Final Format

OVERVIEW

Document format is the key to the creation of an attractive, accurately typed business paper. Such factors as vertical and horizontal placement; use of acceptable style; correct punctuation, capitalization, word usage, and word division; and acceptable correction techniques determine the usability of a particular document. Without proper application of all these factors, a typed document is unmailable or unusable. Therefore, attention to document formatting must be given high priority in preparing all typed business papers.

The first impression any document makes on the reader depends on the visual quality of the document. In the discussion of various document formats, appropriate horizontal and vertical placement for each format will be emphasized and examples shown to demonstrate how each format is used.

Office personnel must make many judgments with regard to document format in the course of the workday. The more the fundamental knowledges and skills of document format are applied, the more effective the document.

DEFINITION OF TERMS

ANNOTATED BIBLIOGRAPHY. A listing of all references used in the report, in alphabetical order, with a brief paragraph following each entry commenting on the content and value of the reference.

BAR GRAPH OR CHART. An illustration that shows a comparison from one time period to another; uses bars of equal width to show quantities (values) on one axis and the factor to be measured on the other axis.

BIBLIOGRAPHY. An alphabetical list of all references consulted by the author that contributed to the content of the report; usually placed at the end of the report on a separate page.

BLOCKED LETTER STYLE. A standard letter style which begins all lines of the letter, including the opening and closing lines at the left margin.

COPY NOTATION. Special notation used only when a copy of the letter is being sent to another person or persons and is typed a double space after the reference initials.

DOCUMENTATION. The creating, collecting, organizing, storing, citing, and disseminating of descriptive information in writing; in report writing, refers to reference notes (footnotes or endnotes) and bibliographic information.

ENDNOTE. A reference note that appears on a separate page at the end of the report.

FOOTNOTE. A reference note that appears on the bottom of the page where the reference is made.

GRAPHIC AID. An illustration that is used to clarify data presented within a report.

GRAPHICS. Visual representations of successive changes in the value (quantity) of one or more variables.

IBID. Term used when reference is made to the immediately preceding footnote or endnote.

INSIDE ADDRESS. The address to which the letter will be mailed.

INTEROFFICE MEMORANDUM. Correspondence between individuals, departments, and branch offices of the same company; interoffice memorandum forms may be used.

ITINERARY. An executive's travel plan that specifies all details concerning the business travel.

LINE GRAPH OR CHART. An illustration consisting of a series of connected lines showing a particular trend in business data for a period of time.

LOC. CIT. Term which refers to the same page reference as the previous footnote.

MINUTES. A summary of the events of a meeting; serves as the official report of the meeting.

MIXED PUNCTUATION. In business letters, there is a colon after the salutation and a comma after the complimentary closing.

MODIFIED BLOCKED LETTER STYLE. A standard letter style in which the date line begins at the centerpoint or ends at the right margin, the complimentary closing and signature line begin at the centerpoint, and paragraphs may be blocked or indented.

NEWS RELEASE. A message to be disseminated to newspapers or magazines with business news about the organization.

OP. CIT. Term used when reference is made to a previous source, but there are intervening reference notes.

OPEN PUNCTUATION. No punctuation is typed after the salutation or the complimentary closing in a business letter.

OPTICAL CHARACTER RECOGNITION (OCR). The process used to scan characters for machine identification using light-sensitive devices; used by the U.S. Postal Service to scan addresses.

OUTLINE. Key words coded in descending order, using Roman numerals, numbers, and letters of the alphabet to show the basic topics of a report or speech.

PAGINATION. The number of document pages from the first page through the last page.

PIE GRAPH OR CHART. An illustration that represents the parts that make up a whole; the circle equals 100 percent, and the sections are divided off parts of the whole, or smaller percentages of the whole.

PRIMARY MEMORY. Internal computer memory used for processing.

READING POSITION. Placement of a table three lines above exact vertical placement.

REFERENCE INITIALS. The initials of the typist of the letter; may also include the writer's initials.

REFERENCE NOTES. Notations used to acknowledge various sources of information; also called reference citations, footnotes, or endnotes.

SALUTATION. The greeting to the person to whom the letter is being sent.

SELECTED BIBLIOGRAPHY. An alphabetical listing of those references pertaining to the topic that have been cited previously in the reference notes.

SIMPLIFIED LETTER STYLE. A standard letter style in which all lines begin at the left margin, there is no salutation or complimentary closing, and a subject line is typed in all capital letters a triple space after the inside address and a triple space before the body of the letter; first introduced by the National Office Management Association, now the Administrative Management Society.

TABLE. Text material presented in a columnar format.

WIDOW LINE. One line from a paragraph by itself on a page.

A. Business Letter Format

One important business paper created in the office today is the business letter. The format used for preparing the letter will help to create attractive, well-placed copy.

1. *Format of Business Letter:* Proper placement of a letter on an 8½ by 11-inch sheet of letterhead or bond paper can be determined by using the Letter Placement Table (Figure 11-1). Once the total number of words in the body of the letter has been determined, the table can be used to decide the length of line, the line on which the date will be typed, and the blank lines between the date and the inside address.

   a. *Date:* The current date, with the month spelled in full followed by the day and the year, should be used.

Number of Words in Body of Letter	Length of Line	Date on Line	Blank Lines Between the Date and Inside Address[a]	Date on Line[b]	Blank Lines Between the Date and Inside Address[c]
Up to 100 Words (Short)	50-space line	2 lines below letterhead (usually around line 12)	6-10	15-18	3
100-200 Words (Medium)	60-space line		4-7	14-16	3
Over 200 Words (Long)	70-space line		3-5	13	3
Over 300 Words (2-page)	70-space line		3-5	13	3

[a]Blank lines mean you would need one more return to begin your typing. The space varies because of pica (10-pitch) or elite (12-pitch) type and word length in the body of the letter. Pica would have fewer blank lines between the date and inside address than elite type. Special notations would be placed within the blank space. There should be a minimum of 3 blank lines between a special notation and the inside address.

[b]The position of the date line depends on the type used (pica or elite) and word length in body of letter. Pica type requires fewer blank lines. More words in the letter require fewer blank lines. A special notation after the date line requires fewer blank lines.

[c]Blank lines mean you would need one more return to begin your typing. When a special notation is typed after the date, use 3 blank lines between the special notation and the inside address.

Figure 11-1
Letter Placement Table (Using Letterhead)

EXAMPLE: September 19, 199-

   b. *Inside address:* The address to whom the letter will be mailed is called the *inside address*. Use the Letter Placement Table (Figure 11-1) for correct spacing between the date line and inside address.

      (1) *Titles:* A title should precede all individual names. Titles include *Mr., Ms., Honorable, Dr.,* etc.

      (2) *State:* In the inside address, the state can be abbreviated with the two-letter state abbreviation, or it can be spelled in full. On the envelope, it should be the two-letter state abbreviation in order to be read by the optical character reader (OCR) at the post office.

All addresses should be addressed to an individual or an organization; should have a mailing address (a post office box or a street); and should have a city, state, and ZIP code as the last line. The post office *prefers* that envelope addresses be no longer than four lines.

EXAMPLES:

MR TERRY ADDAMS
567 WILLS DRIVE
ROCKFORD IL 61108-1917

MRS MARTHA BOES
PERSONNEL DEPARTMENT
COLONIAL BROTHERS INC
1111 RAILWAY BLVD
CLIFTON NJ 00186-0500

HARRINGTON BANK
PO BOX 345
BUTTERNUT WI 54514-9504

HONORABLE T M CARR
CARR & CARR LTD
NEWBERRY MI 49868-1222

c. *Attention line (optional):* The attention line is typed a double space after the inside address. The word *attention* may or may not be followed by a colon, may be in all capital letters or initial cap, and may or may not be underlined. If both an attention line and a subject line are in the letter, the same style should be used for each.

EXAMPLES:
ATTENTION: Mrs. Amy Miles
Attention Mrs. Amy Miles
    Accounting Department
<u>Attention</u> Mrs. Amy Miles

d. *Salutation:* The greeting to whom the letter is being sent is called the *salutation* and is typed a double-space after the previous notation (either inside address or attention line). The salutation always begins with *Dear* when addressed to a person and is followed by either the person's title and last name only (formal) or just the person's first name (informal). If the letter is sent to a company, proper salutations are: *Gentlemen*, *Ladies and Gentlemen*, and *Dear* followed by use of a title within a department.

EXAMPLES:
Dear Mrs. Miles   *Dear Amy*
Ladies and Gentlemen   *Dear Sales Manager*

e. *Subject line (optional):* The subject line, if used, is typed a double-space after the salutation. The word *subject* may or may not be followed by a colon, may be all capital letters or initial caps, and may or may not be underlined. If both a subject line and an attention line are in the letter, the same style should be used for each.

EXAMPLES:
SUBJECT: *Invoice No. 9874*
Subject Invoice No. 9874
Subject Invoice No. 9874

f. *Body of the letter:* The first paragraph begins a double space after the previous notation (either salutation or subject line). Paragraphs are single spaced with double spacing between the paragraphs. A letter should have at least two paragraphs; three is the most common number of paragraphs. Paragraphs may begin at the left margin or may be indented five or more spaces.

g. *Complimentary closing:* The closing of the letter is typed a double space after the last line in the body of the letter. Only the first word of the complimentary closing is capitalized. The complimentary closing should be in agreement with the salutation (formal or informal). The most common complimentary closings are:

FORMAL
| *Yours very truly* | *Very truly yours* |
| *Cordially* | *Cordially yours* |

INFORMAL
| *Truly yours* | *Yours truly* |

FORMAL/INFORMAL
| *Sincerely* | *Sincerely yours* |

The complimentary closings *Respectfully* and *Respectfully yours* are usually used when the letter has been addressed to individuals holding important positions in government (president, governor, or legislative members), military (captain), and religious organizations (pope, pastor, or board members).

h. *Typed signature line:* The name of the person sending the letter is typed four returns (leaving 3 blank lines) after the complimentary closing. Only the writer's name need be used in the signature line. If it is difficult to identify the individual as male or female by the typed signature, a title (Mr., Mrs., Miss) should be included with the name. If a woman wishes to be addressed by her title (Mrs. or Miss), this title should be included with the name. The title can be typed before the name or after the name. Any other title which the individual holds may be included with the typed signature. A visual balance should always be maintained when titles are included with the typed signature.

EXAMPLES:
| *Mr. T. M. Johnson* | *T. M. Johnson, Miss* |
| *Miss Terry M. Johnson, CPS* | *Terrance M. Johnson* |

Preparing Communications in Final Format 369

                                                Personnel Director
T. M. Johnson (Mrs.)

i. *Reference initials:* Reference initials include the initials of the typist of the letter and may also include the writer's initials. They are typed a double space after the signature line. The most common style today is the use of the typist's initials only. If the writer's initials are used, they are typed first followed by a slash or colon; then the typist's initials are typed.

EXAMPLES:
ri (typist's initials only)
TM/ri (writer's initials with typist's initials)
TMJ:ri (writer's initials with typist's initials)

j. *Enclosure notation:* If material is enclosed with the letter, an enclosure notation should be typed a double space after the reference initials. (See Section A-1-k, Copy Notation, for proper order when both copy notation and enclosure notation are included in the letter.) The word *enclosure* may be abbreviated or typed in full.

(1) If there is only one enclosure in the letter, the notation is typed in singular form.
(2) If there are two or more enclosures in the letter, the notation is typed in plural form.
(3) The enclosure notation may be typed by itself, or it may be followed by the number of enclosures contained within the letter or a listing of the enclosures.
(4) If additional information follows the enclosure, a space, a colon, a slash, or a dash should be typed between the word *enclosure* and the additional information.

EXAMPLES:
Enc.   Encs.: 2
Enclosure/Brochure   *Encs.—Prints*
                                           Order Blank

k. *Copy notation:* This special notation is used only when a copy of the letter is being sent to another person or persons. In today's office, the copy is usually a photocopy of the original. The notation is typed a double-space after the reference initials. However, if there is also an enclosure notation, the copy notation comes before the enclosure notation if these additional people are *not* receiving the enclosure. If these additional people are also receiving a copy of the enclosure, the notation is typed a double space after the enclosure notation. The word *copy* is abbreviated to *c* in the notation and followed by a blank space, a colon, or a slash and then the individual's name and title and/or company name.

(1) When the copy is a carbon copy, the notation is typed with two *c*'s, that is, *cc*.
(2) The notation can be in lowercase or capital letters, but there are never any periods.
(3) If several people are receiving copies, the names are listed under one another, but the first name is the only one preceded by the notation.
(4) The copy notation appears on all copies: the original, the copies, and the file copy.

Before the letters are presented for signature, the copies are identified with a marking next to the name of the person who is to receive that copy. Copy markings are:

- Placing a check mark next to the name
- Underlining the name
- Highlighting the name with a marker

EXAMPLES (Copy Notation for Photocopies):
c Betty Appleton, Apex Corporation

C: Betty Appleton, Apex Corporation
  Martha Thornton, Martin Engineering

EXAMPLE:
(Check Mark Notation on Copy sent to Martha Thornton)
c/Betty Appleton, Apex Corporation
  ✓ Martha Thornton, Martin Engineering

l. *Spacing summary:* The paragraphs of the letter are single-spaced with double-spacing between. There should be a double-space between all other parts of the letter EXCEPT between the date line and inside address and between the complimentary closing and signature line where the *minimum number* of returns is four (3 blank lines). (See Letter Placement Table, Figure 11-1.)

m. *Special notations:* All special notations (*CONFIDENTIAL, PERSONAL, AIRMAIL, CERTIFIED, REGISTERED*, and *SPECIAL DELIVERY*) are typed a double space below the date line, at the left margin, and in all capital letters. The spacing between the special notation and the inside address will vary according to the length of the letter. Follow the Letter Placement Table, Figure 11-1.

EXAMPLES:
May 6, 199-   May 6, 199-

DS

CERTIFIED   CONFIDENTIAL

Minimum 4 Returns

      Mr. Terry Addams   *Honorable T. M. Carr*
      367 Wills Drive   *Carr & Carr Ltd.*
      Rockford, IL 61108-1917   *Newberry, MI 49868-1222*

2. *Letter Styles:* There are several letter styles commonly seen in business. Acceptable formats for business letters typed in different styles are outlined in the following section. In addition, each format is discussed in detail within the paragraphs of the illustration for each business letter style. Punctuation styles are also explained, and the punctuation style used for the letter illustrated is discussed within the paragraphs of the illustration. There are three letter styles used in business today: *blocked* (considered to be very efficient), *modified blocked*, and *simplified* (most efficient).

    a. *Blocked letter style:* Figure 11-2 shows an example of a business letter prepared in blocked letter style. All lines of the blocked letter begin at the left margin.

    b. *Modified blocked letter style:* Figure 11-3 shows an example of a business letter prepared in modified blocked letter style with blocked paragraphs and mixed punctuation. Figure 11-4 shows an example of a business letter also prepared in modified block letter style but with indented paragraphs and open punctuation.

        (1) The date line begins at the centerpoint of the paper or may end at the right margin.

        (2) The complimentary closing and signature line begin at the centerpoint of the paper.

        (3) Paragraphs may be blocked (beginning at the left margin) or indented (five or more spaces). When indented paragraphs are used, the letter style is referred to as *modified blocked style with indented paragraphs*.

        (4) All other parts of the letter begin at the left margin.

    c. *Simplified letter style:* Figure 11-5 shows an example of a business letter prepared in simplified letter style.

        (1) All lines of the letter begin at the left margin.

        (2) There is no salutation.

        (3) There is *always* a subject line typed in all capital letters which begins a triple space (two blank lines) after the inside address. After the subject line, there is a triple space (two blank lines) to the body of the letter.

        (4) There is no complimentary closing.

        (5) The signature line is typed in all capital letters four lines after the body of the letter.

3. *Punctuation Styles:* There are two punctuation styles used in business today: open punctuation (considered to be the most efficient) and mixed punctuation.

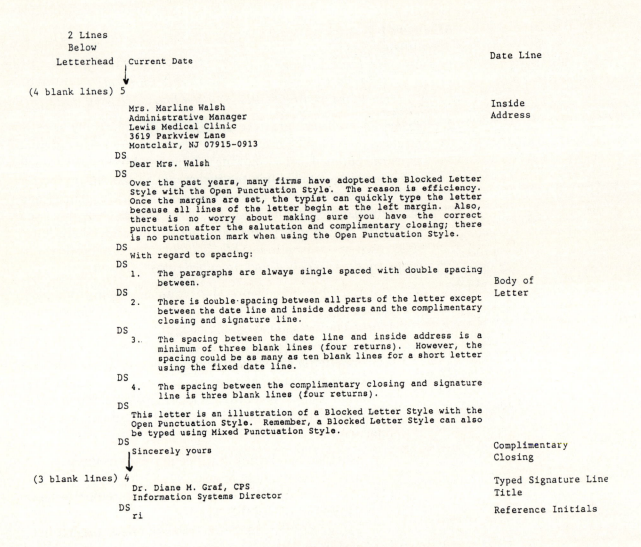

Figure 11-2
Blocked Letter Style, Open Punctuation Style

a. *Open punctuation:* No punctuation is typed after the salutation or the complimentary closing. These two notations are OPEN at the end of the line. (See Figures 11-2 and 11-4.)

b. *Mixed punctuation:* There is a colon (:) after the salutation. The colon is used in both the formal and informal salutation style. There is a comma (,) after the complimentary closing. These are the only two punctuation marks used in this style (notice that they are different—MIXED). (See Figure 11-3.)

In Figures 11-2, 11-3, 11-4, and 11-5, some of the letters have open punctuation and some have mixed. Any letter style can have any punctuation style except the simplified letter style. Since there is no salutation or complimentary closing in the simplified letter style, no punctuation style is used.

Preparing Communications in Final Format 373

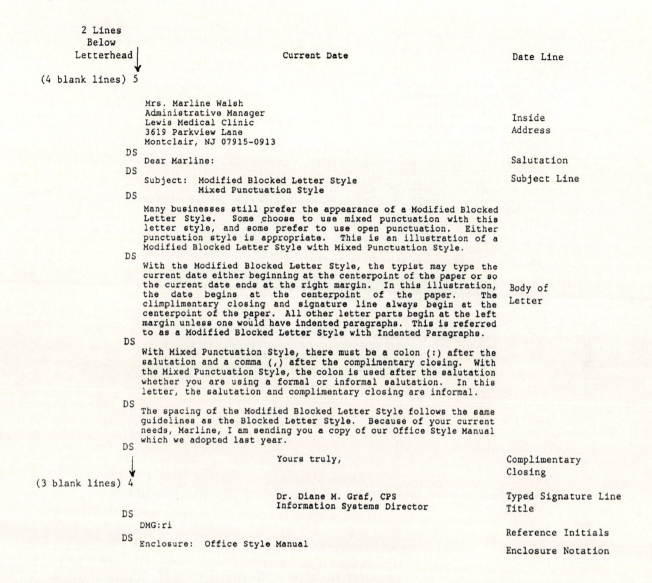

Figure 11-3
Modified Blocked Letter Style (Blocked Paragraphs and Mixed Punctuation Style)

4. *Second Page of a Letter:* The heading for the second page of a letter should include the name of the person receiving the letter, the date, and the page number. Many times a department name is included along with the person's name. If the letter is addressed to a company, the company name is used instead of the person's name. For the page number, just use the number; do not write the word *Page* and do not put parentheses or hyphens around the number.

   a. *Blocked style:* If the letter is typed in blocked style, each line of the heading begins at the left margin. The first line can begin on either line 4 or line 7. The heading is single-spaced. Triple-space after the last line of the heading to continue the letter.

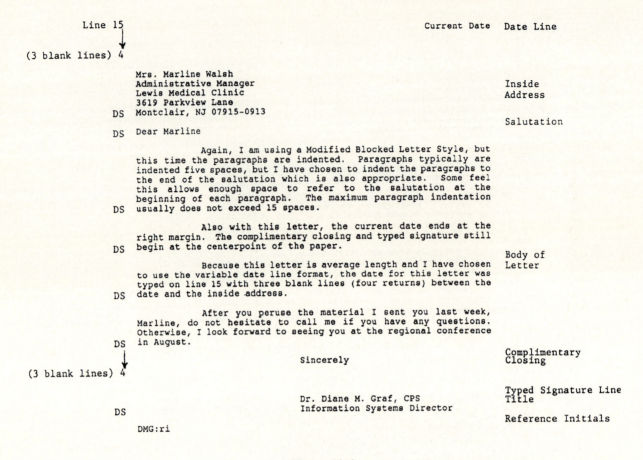

Figure 11-4
Modified Blocked Letter Style (Indented Paragraphs and Open Punctuation Style)

An example of the second-page heading using blocked letter style is shown in Figure 11-6.

 b. *Modified blocked style:* If the letter is typed in modified blocked style, the addressee's name is typed at the left margin, the date in the center, and the page number at the right margin. The heading may be typed on either line 4 or line 7. Triple-space after the heading to continue the letter. An example of the second-page heading using modified blocked letter style is shown in Figure 11-7.

 c. *Word processing headings:* Most word processing software provides a header feature. The header allows the user to key the information once for automatic placement at the top of the second and succeeding pages. The page number automatically increments when the appropriate page number code is used on the header line.

 B. **Envelopes**

The two standard envelope sizes are No. 10 (9½" x 4⅛") and No. 6¾ (6½" x 3⅝"). There are three styles used in addressing envelopes: con-

```
            Line 12  Current Date                                                    Date Line
(3 blank lines) 4

              Mrs. Marline Walsh
              Administrative Manager                                                 Inside
              Lewis Medical Clinic                                                   Address
              3619 Parkview Lane
              Montclair, NJ 07915-0913

(2 blank lines)TS
              SIMPLIFIED LETTER STYLE FORMAT                                         Subject Line
           TS
              The Simplified Letter Style was introduced in the 1950s by the
              Administrative Management Society, then known as the National
              Office Management Association.  The purpose of adopting a new
              letter style was for efficiency with a crisp, neat appearance.  The
              features of a Simplified Letter Style are:
           DS
              1.  To maintain typing efficiency, the Blocked Letter Style Format
                  of typing everything at the left margin was adopted.
           DS
              2.  The variable date line format is used; therefore, there are
                  always three blank lines (four returns) between the date and      Body of
                  inside address.                                                   Letter
           DS
              3.  To be more efficient, the salutation and complimentary closing
                  are omitted.
           DS
              4.  Immediately after the inside address a subject line is always
                  typed in all capital letters.  The spacing before and after
                  the subject line is two blank lines (three returns).
           DS
              5.  After the last paragraph, the typist leaves three blank lines
                  (four returns) and types the signature line in all capital
                  letters.
           DS
              6.  If there are enumerations within the letter, each point begins
                  at the left margin and is treated as a new paragraph.
           DS
              7.  If there is a copy notation, it begins with c/ followed by the
                  names of people who are to receive copies.
           DS
              Over the years, many businesses have adopted this letter style.
              The features of the Simplified Letter Style should be studied and
              considered as a possible style for future use.

(3 blank lines) 4
              DR. DIANE M. GRAF, CPS                                                 Typed Signature Line
           DS ri                                                                     Reference Initials
           DS c/Karl Stern, AMS                                                      Copy Notation
```

Figure 11-5
Simplified Letter Style

```
(4 or 7
 returns)
         Person's Name
         Department
         Date
         2
          3 returns
         as we had hoped before the end of the year.  Will you please let us
         know what your wishes are by Wednesday, December 3, so that we can
         proceed.
```

Figure 11-6
Second-Page Heading—Blocked Style

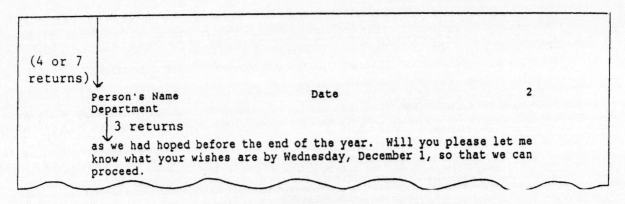

Figure 11-7
Second-Page Heading—Modified Blocked Style

ventional style, addressing for optical character recognition, and label/plate. Envelope and label addresses may also be computer generated.

1. *Conventional Style:* When typing an address on either a No. 10 or a No. 6¾ envelope, follow these procedures:

   a. Always use blocked style and single-spacing.
   b. Words should be in all capital letters for postal efficiency.
   c. There should be no punctuation marks.
   d. Type the city, state, and nine-digit ZIP code on the last line. Leave one space between the state and the ZIP code.
   e. The state should be the two-letter abbreviation for optical character recognition.
   f. The ZIP code should be the nine-digit ZIP code.
   g. Notations such as *Personal*, *Confidential*, or *Please forward* should be typed below the return address on the third line.
   h. Special mailing notations such as *Registered*, *Special Delivery*, or *Certified* should be typed in all capital letters in the upper right corner of the envelope, just under the postage block.

   Figure 11-8 shows a properly typed address on a No. 10 envelope with special mailing notations. The address begins 4 inches from the left edge of the envelope and 14 returns from the top edge. On a No. 6¾ business envelope, the address would be typed 2 inches from the left edge of the envelope and 12 returns from the top edge.

2. *OCR Requirements:* The U.S. Postal Service uses optical character recognition equipment (OCR) to process volumes of mail. The following guidelines have been developed so mail can be OCR-readable.

   a. The entire address should be located *within* an imaginary rectangle, which is the OCR-read area, formed by the following boundaries:

Preparing Communications in Final Format 377

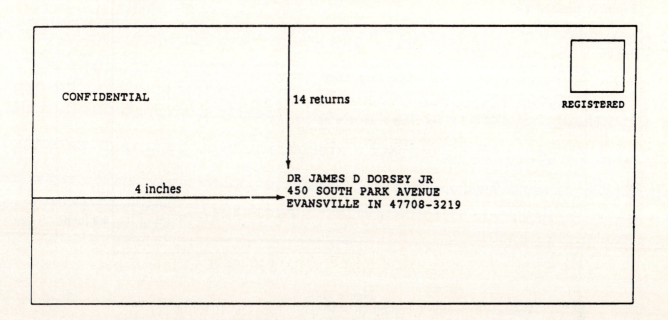

Note: On a No. 6¾ business envelope, the address would be typed 2 inches from the left edge of the envelope and down 12 returns from the top edge. Otherwise, the positioning of the special notations would be identical.

Figure 11-8
Business Envelope with Special Notations (No. 10 Envelope)

(1) One inch from the left edge.
(2) One inch from the right edge.
(3) Bottom margin of ⅝ inch.
(4) Three inches from the bottom edge.

See Figure 11-9 to see how these boundaries are formed.
b. Within the OCR-read area, the entire space below the top line of the address block should be clear of printing other than the address itself. This includes information such as boxes, advertising, computer punch holes, or other similar types of information. No printing should appear in the Bar Code read area.
c. The address should have a uniform left margin and be legible.
d. No punctuation is typed in the address.
e. The address format includes:

(1) The name of the recipient (top line)
(2) Information/attention line (second line)

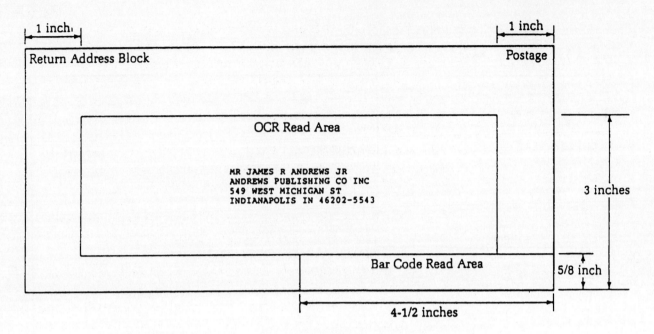

Figure 11-9
Business Envelope Typed for OCR Requirements (No. 10 Envelope)

    (3)   Delivery address (third line)
    (4)   Post office, state, ZIP code (fourth line)

The address should not exceed four lines.

- **f.** Unit, apartment, office, or suite numbers should be used in the address. This information should be placed at the end of the delivery address line.
- **g.** The standard two-letter state abbreviations and the nine-digit ZIP code should be used. The preferred location for the ZIP code is on the city, state, and ZIP code line. If this is not possible, the ZIP code may be placed at the left margin on the line immediately below the city and state.
- **h.** The entire address must always be visible. If a window envelope is used, the entire address must have at least a ¼-inch clearance between the edge of the window and all sides of the address.
- **i.** Mail addressed to a foreign country must have the full name of the city and country of the destination written in capital letters.
- **j.** Italic, artistic, Cyrillic, and scriptlike typewriting elements cannot be read by OCR equipment. Characters or numbers should not touch or overlap within a word or ZIP code.
- **k.** The use of uppercase characters is preferred but only required when the *line spacing* is 8 lines per inch. Preferred spacing is 6 lines per inch.
- **l.** The *character pitch* should be in the range of 7 to 12 characters per inch.

Preparing Communications in Final Format 379

    m.   The space between words should be one to two character spaces; however, the space between the last character of the two-letter state abbreviation and the first digit of the ZIP code can be one to five character spaces.

Additional information about OCR requirements may be obtained from the U.S. Postal Service.

3. *Label/Plate:* Addresses are sometimes prepared on labels or imprinted by means of an address plate. The amount of space for the address is confined to the label or address plate.

    a.   The maximum number of strokes you can get in one line is only 26 to 28 strokes. Therefore, some words will need to be abbreviated.

    b.   The two-letter state abbreviations help keep the address within the confined space.

    c.   All lines should be typed in all capital letters, single-spaced, and blocked at the left, with no punctuation. This adheres to postal OCR requirements.

EXAMPLE:
MS BETTY RUSSELL-WADE
DEACON RAYMOND & BROOK ATTYS
4 OAK WOOD TR SUITE 214
SAN DIEGO CA 92103-9632

    d.   The address block should be imprinted or placed (if on label) with at least a $5/8$-inch bottom margin and a left margin of at least 1 inch. Nothing should be written, typed, or printed below the address block or to the right of it.

    e.   Sometimes special information is imprinted above the address block, typically one or two lines above the name, to indicate account number, expiration date of subscription, or other descriptive words. Here is an example:

EXAMPLE:
1STK5 11622 PIN91 FEB94

B L STOCKTON
1622 PINE ST RR 3
SYCAMORE IL 60178-2136

4. *Computer Generated Addresses:* Envelope addresses or labels are often generated using computer software. The address style used could be conventional, OCR, or label/plate (see Sections B-1, B-2, and B-3 of this chapter). The most common software used for this purpose is data-base management or word processing.

When many addresses are printed, it is faster to print labels. Printers with platens use labels on strips fed by a tractor feeder. Laser printers use labels on sheets fed through the sheet feeder.

a. *Database management software:*

(1) A file must be created for all addresses. A file consists of a record for each addressee. Each addressee record will contain the necessary variable address data. Each address variable is referred to as a field. A field should reference only one variable; this provides the most flexible use of the address variables. Here is an example of addressee data (fields) for one record.

EXAMPLE:

Variable Name	Addressee Data
Title	*Mrs.*
FirstName	*Marlene*
LastName	*Kittleson*
Position	*Administrative Manager*
Department	*Word Processing Division*
Company	*Abbott Regal, Inc.*
Address	*325 Lincoln Highway*
City	*Sycamore*
State	*IL*
ZIPCode	*60178-2235*
AreaCode	*815*
WorkPhone	*895-2366*
PhoneExtension	*23*

(2) Most database management software includes a label command to print labels from the address file. Reference only those fields which you want to print in the address.

(3) To print addresses directly on the envelope eliminating the use of labels, a database command program usually needs to be written.

b. *Word processing software with mail-merge:* Most word processing software provides a mail-merge facility. The options available will depend upon the word processing software. When a mail-merge option is available:

(1) A primary file is created. This file contains the actual document that will be merged with data from the addressee files in this case, a label or envelope form.

(2) Next, a secondary file is created with data recorded for all addresses. Like database management, the file will consist of a record for each addressee which will contain the necessary variable address data (fields).

(3) Labels or envelopes can be printed using the mail-merge function, merging only selected address variables from the secondary file.

    c. *Word processing software with no mail-merge function:* If mail-merge is not available, an address code file can be created in any word processing software.

        (1) An address code file is created which contains all the paper-size, top/bottom margins, and left/right margin codes for proper address location on the envelope or label. SAVE THIS FILE FOR FUTURE USE.

        (2) The address file can then be used for printing. Immediately following the codes, type the address data. Insert a page-advance code between multiple addresses. If form-fed envelopes or labels are used, do not insert a page-advance code.

        (3) An envelope (or labels) must be inserted into the printer. Print one page at a time unless form-fed envelopes (labels) are used.

    An address-code file may be used for printing envelopes or labels whenever an individual document is mailed. It may also be used to maintain a mailing list. To maintain data integrity (accuracy), however, one should not create multiple address files. When multiple files are created, address maintenance becomes burdensome and data becomes vulnerable to inaccuracies.

C. Memoranda Format

Interoffice memorandums are used for correspondence between individuals, departments, and branch offices of the same company. Usually a heading is printed on the interoffice memorandum form, and the side margins are determined by this heading. When you do not have an interoffice memorandum form, the top and side margins must be set to produce visual appeal.

  1. *Format of Interoffice Memorandum:*

    a. *Top margin and heading:* The top margin for an interoffice memorandum varies from one to two inches. The most common is 1½ inches. The words *Interoffice Memorandum*, *Memorandum*, or *MEMO* are usually centered horizontally in all capital letters. Another variation is to type the heading in initial caps and underlined.

    b. *Side margins:* The left and right margins of the interoffice memorandum will vary depending on the length of the memorandum. The longest line of print would be one-inch left and right margins (narrowest margin). This would be used for a long memorandum. The smallest line of print would be two-inch left and right margins (widest margin). This would be used for a short memorandum. However, the left margin may be aligned with the preprinted headings on interoffice memorandum forms normally used in an office.

  c. *Notation lines:* An interoffice memorandum begins with the notation lines:

    TO:
    FROM:
  SUBJECT:
    DATE:

These lines are typed a triple-space after the heading or may be preprinted on the memorandum form. A skilled secretary would then align the variable information with the printed notation. There are always two spaces after a colon. Various styles for the notation lines are:

(1) Align notations at the left and variable data after the longest notation (subject).
(2) Align notations with the colon and key all variable data two spaces after the colon.
(3) Type in all capital letters.
or
(4) Type with initial caps only.
(5) Include titles or departments.
(6) Place the date as the fourth notation line.
or
(7) Place the date on the same line as the notation *TO*.

After the notation lines, triple-space (two blank lines) to the body of the memorandum. Paragraphs are single-spaced with double-spacing between and typed in blocked style.

EXAMPLE (with left side aligned and in all capital letters):
TO: Leon Dresser
FROM: Mary Louise Westcott
SUBJECT: Request for Professional Leave
DATE: February 4, 199-

EXAMPLE (with colon aligned and with initial caps):
    To: Leon Dresser
  From: Mary Louise Westcott
Subject: Request for Professional Leave
  Date: February 4, 199-

EXAMPLE (with left side aligned, with initial caps, and including titles):
To: Leon Dresser Date: February 4, 199-
            Personnel Director
From: Mary Louise Westcott
            Data Processing Supervisor
Subject: Request for Professional Leave

Preparing Communications in Final Format   383

EXAMPLE (with colon aligned, in all capital letters, and including titles):

    TO: Leon Dresser   SUBJECT: Request for
                Personnel   Professional
                 Director   Leave
   FROM: Mary Westcott   DATE: February 4, 199-
                 IS Supervisor

    d. *Reference initials:* Reference initials are also included on a memorandum. They are typed a double space after the last paragraph at the left margin. Formats for reference initials are included in Section A-1-i of this chapter.

2. *Style for Interoffice Memorandum:* Using the guidelines presented here for an appropriate format, an interoffice memorandum may be typed in the basic style shown in Figure 11-10.

D. **Business Report Format**

A business report is a common means of communication *within* business firms as well as *between* business firms. Figure 11-11 highlights the parts of a report. Format guidelines for reports vary in office reference manuals. However, the following guidelines are acceptable in any office.

1. *Physical Layout:* The physical layout of the format includes decisions on margins (top, bottom, right, left), how the title of the report should be typed, and the general spacing of paragraph material.

    a. *Margins:*

        (1) *Top margins:*

```
                    INTEROFFICE MEMORANDUM


TO:        Jerry Rankowski
           VP, Operations

FROM:      Darla Johnson
           VP, Personnel

SUBJECT:   August Board Meeting

DATE:      August 16, 199-


           The Board Meeting for Thursday, August 19, has been
           changed to Thursday, August 26, at one o'clock.  Please
           mark your calendar and let me know if you will still be
           available.

ri
```

Figure 11-10
Style for Interoffice Memorandum

                                    2 inches

                              KEY TO BUYMANSHIP
         TS
                 Economic theory assumes that consumers have all the informa-
            tion required about the products they buy. Can the once-every-
            three years auto buyer make an even handed deal with a sales-   1 inch
            person who sees dozens of customers a day? Can the consumer
            select the correct remedy at the best price without comparative
            prices available? The basic question still remains: "Is it
            possible to make rational decisions without information?"
         TS
            Government Regulation
         DS
                 Legislation has been proposed for regulations to have
            businesses make available price lists for their various services.
            The various services would be broken down into categories so
 1 inch   consumers could specifically see the costs of various components
            purchased. The Federal Trade Commission contends that package
            prices and refusal to advertise prices that are not required by
            law are costing consujmers more than they want to pay. The trend
            in government regulation of trade appears to be assisting consum-
            ers in the quest for information. Many "secret" pricing
            practices and "secret" formulas and ingredients are now going
            public so consumers can compare and choose based on greater fore-
            knowledge.
         DS
                 Areas of Regulation. The Federal Trade Commission has
            pushed for more price information in many areas. Thirty-four

                      1 inch

                                                             ↓ Line 4
                                                                  2
         TS
                 states have passed some form of law permitting pharmacists to
            substitute less expensive generic drugs which are chemically
            equivalent to expensive brand name prescription drugs. In 1977
            alone, more than 60 bills were introduced to Congress to bring
            more information to consumers via the food label. In the 1990s
            many more bills are expected to be introduced. Proposed
            regulations would force funeral directors to have available price
            lists for their various services.
         TS
            Critics of the Information Boom
                 There are critics of the information boom, however. A

Figure 11-11
Example of Business Report

- (a) The top margin on the first page of the report should be 2 inches when there is a title included on the page.
- (b) The top margin on the first page of the report without a title is 1½ inches.
- (c) On the second page and succeeding pages, there should be 4 returns, and then a typed page number, followed by 3 returns; then continue typing text. An alternative technique is to type the page number on the seventh line from the top followed by three returns to the continuation of the report.

(2) *Left margin:*

- (a) The left margin on an unbound report is 1 inch.
- (b) The left margin on a left-bound report is 1½ inches.

(3) *Right margin:* There should be a 1-inch right margin on all reports.

(4) *Bottom margin:* There should be at least a 1-inch bottom margin on all pages of a report.

b. *Title of report:* The title of the report is the first item typed on the first page, centered and typed in all capital letters. If the title is excessively long, it can be typed on more than one line. If the title is more than one line, single-space the title. Each successive line of the title must be shorter than the previous line.

(1) *Spacing:* Triple-space between the title and the text unless there is a subtitle.

(2) *Subtitle:* If there is a subtitle, double space after the title, type the subtitle (centered and with initial caps), and then triple-space to the text.

c. *Spacing of paragraphs:*

(1) *Spacing within text:* The text of the report is double-spaced for ease in reading. Some short reports (one page) are single-spaced, and periodically a business may decide to single-space a report to conserve on paper. However, it is advisable to double-space all reports unless otherwise instructed.

(2) *Paragraph indentions:* Because reports are double-spaced, the paragraphs must be indented *five spaces* to identify the beginning of each paragraph. If a report is single-spaced, the paragraphs may or may not be indented, but there must always be double-spacing between the paragraphs.

2. *Headings:* There can be as many as seven divisions of headings. When using headings, the number of divisions used is determined by the number of breakdowns needed under a main division.

   a. *Hierarchy of divisions:* The hierarchy of divisions, moving from the most important to the least important, is:

   (1) Centered heading in all capital letters.
   (2) Centered heading in initial caps and underlined.
   (3) Centered heading in initial caps and not underlined.
   (4) Side heading in all capital letters.
   (5) Side heading in initial caps and underlined.
   (6) Side heading in initial caps and not underlined.
   (7) Paragraph headings are always underlined and end in a period or a period and a dash.

   Headings should begin with (1), (2), or (3). Then, you may move down the hierarchy by skipping to the next level of heading you desire. Let's say you had three divisions and began with Hierarchy (2). The next division could be Hierarchy (5), and the last division could be Hierarchy (7). Heading divisions must be consistent throughout a document.

   EXAMPLE:
   <u>*Progress Report on Bradford-Brown Sale*</u>
   Preliminary Investigation of Property
   <u>*Abstract of Title.*</u>—The title to the property is in the name of Arthur J. Bradford, Jr., as shown in the deed from Thomas J. Cochran to Arthur J. Bradford, Jr., dated September 23, 1974.

   b. *Spacing for headings:*

   (1) *Centered headings:* Triple-space before a centered heading and double-space after. If a centered heading is immediately followed by a side heading, triple-space *before* the side heading.
   (2) *Side headings:* Triple-space before a side heading and double-space after.
   (3) *Paragraph headings:* A paragraph heading begins a paragraph. Therefore, there is always double-spacing before a paragraph heading. Paragraph headings are always underlined and followed by a period and two spaces or a period and a dash.

3. *Pagination:*

   a. *Numbering the first page:* When the first page has a title, there usually is no page number on that page. If a page number is used for this first page, it is typed at the bottom of the page a triple-space after the last line of text and at the center of the line of writing. This number can be typed in the one-inch margin at the bottom of the page.

When the first page does not have a title, a page number is typed in the same position as on succeeding pages.

b. *Numbering succeeding pages:* The page number is usually typed at the top of the page on the fourth line, or it can be typed on the seventh line. It can either be typed in the center of the page or at the right margin. The number is usually typed by itself without the word *page* or any notations. After the page number, there is a triple-space to the continuation of the report.

4. *Automatic Generation of Supplements:* When reports or other long documents are prepared, a table of contents; list of tables, figures, or maps (when included in the document); and bibliography (when references are used) must be included.

   Most word processing software includes a feature to create the table of contents, lists, or bibliography from the document being prepared. This automatic feature eliminates the retyping of headings for the table of contents; table, figure, or map titles; or bibliographic references. Also, as changes are made within the document, the information contained in these document supplements changes automatically. The word processing operations manual explains the steps to follow to utilize this automatic feature.

5. *Word Processing Format for Printing Reports:* When word processing software is used, the placement of codes is very important. Once a code is read by the computer system, all text following the code is formatted according to the word processing code. For this reason, final printing codes should be inserted after all editing has been completed. The life cycle of a document is: plan, create, edit, format, save/print. The function of each cycle is as follows:

   a. *Plan:* Know the purpose of the document; outline.
   b. *Create:* Compose the document according to the plan, including all tab, centering, bold, and underscore codes. For documents where extensive editing is anticipated, use double- or triple-spacing so a rough draft hard copy can be printed. SAVE often so that the information being keyed in will not be lost.
   c. *Edit:* Make changes; at the same time make grammatical corrections. Editing should be done on soft copy (reading the CRT screen). Hard copy editing is usually required for long documents or when editing is done by someone else. SAVE/Print when necessary. This step can be repeated, but do not edit more than twice.
   d. *Format:* Insert final-copy printing codes for spacing, margins, widow/orphan lines, and hyphenation. Editing is easier when

format codes (final printing codes) are not in the document. When sentences, paragraphs, or pages are moved or deleted, one does not have to be so careful about moving the appropriate codes or responding to code prompts, for example, manual hyphenation.

Figure 11-12 shows an example of final printing codes inserted at the beginning of the document so all text that follows adheres to the format code. Consult the word processing operations manual for format procedures specific to a particular software package.

e. *Save/Print:* When corrections are made, they are made only to the document which is in primary memory. If corrections are to be kept, it is important to save the document to a secondary storage medium. Diskette, hard disk, or tape are common for permanent storage.

Many times a hard copy is required. Rough-draft copies or informal in-house copies are typically printed on a dot-matrix printer. Letter-quality copies are usually printed on a laser printer or letter-quality printer.

```
Placement of Codes without Header and Page Numbering

[T/B Mar:2:,1:][W/O On] [Hyph On][L/R Mar:1",1"][Center]KEY TO
BUYMANSHIP[HRt]
[HRt]
[HRt]
[Ln Spacing:2][Tab]Economic theory assumes that consumers have
all the information required about the products they buy.  Can
the once[-]every[-]three[-]years auto buyer make an even handed
deal with a salesperson who sees dozens of customers a day?  Can
the consumer select the correct remedy at the best price without
comparative prices available?  The basic question still remains:
"Is it possible to make rational decisions without information?"
[HRt]
[Ln Spacing:1][HRt]
[UND]Government Regulation[und][Ln Spacing:2][HRt]
[Tab]Legislation has been proposed for regulations to have
businesses make available price lists for their various services.
The various . . .
```

```
Placement of Codes with Header and Page Numbering

[T/B Mar:2:,1:][W/O On] [Hyph On][L/R Mar:1",1"][Header A:Every
page;KEY TO BUYMANSHIP][Pg Numbering:Bottom
Center][Suppress:HA][Center]KEY TO BUYMANSHIP[HRt]
[HRt]
[HRt]
[Ln Spacing:2][Tab]Economic theory assumes that consumers have
all the information required about the products they buy.  Can
the once[-]every[-]three[-]years auto buyer make an even handed
deal . . .
```

Figure 11-12
Example of Placement of Word Processing Codes in Business Report

6. *Margin Guide:* When the print cannot appear in the top and bottom margin or left and right margin area, a margin guide becomes a helpful tool. Keeping print out of these margin areas is important with some legal, government, or research documents or documents prepared for publication.

   a. *Preparing the margin guide:* With a ruler, draw a straight *dark* line where the margins are set. Be careful to be accurate with the measurement of the margin area.
   b. *Using the margin guide:* Place the final hard copy on top of the margin guide. The dark ruler lines will show through the top final-copy sheet. No print on the final copy should extend beyond the ruler lines from the margin guide.

   In order to avoid a widow line at the bottom of any page or at the top of any page, you may have more than a one-inch bottom margin. A *widow line* is one line of a paragraph by itself on a page. You must always have two or more lines of a paragraph on a page. If you are using word processing software, check the manual to see whether there is a widow-line function. If so, activate the widow protection function with the appropriate code at the beginning of the document.

   Figure 11-13 illustrates a margin guide for 1-inch and 2-inch top margins, 1-inch and 1½-inch left margins, and 1-inch right and bottom margins. Measurements can be set from the outside edge of the paper.

7. *Documentation:* Preparing appropriate documentation of information contained in a report is very important in conducting both primary and secondary research. *Documentation* is defined as the creating, collecting, organizing, storing, citing, and disseminating of descriptive information. Documentation is normally in the form of reference notes (footnotes or endnotes) and bibliographic information. Footnotes or endnotes are used to cite specific information taken from other sources and used in the report. The bibliography cites all reference materials used in the preparation of the report.

   a. *Types of citations:* Reference notes or reference citations as they are sometimes called, are used to acknowledge sources of information.

      (1) *Source footnote or endnote:* This type of citation gives credit to the source for data included in a report. Footnotes are included on the page where the reference is made, whereas endnotes are used when the writer wishes all the citations to be included on a separate page at the end of the report. The first time the reference is referred to, the citation must have complete information about the source; later reference to the same work can be

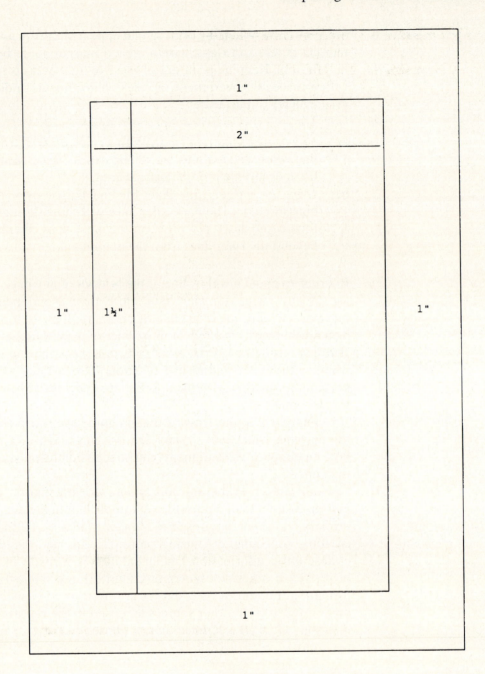

Figure 11-13
Margin Guide

abbreviated. The source information in the source footnote or endnote includes:

- Name(s) of author(s)
- Name(s) of editor(s)
- Publication title
- Publication information (name of publishing company, city, publication date)
- Page number(s) referenced

EXAMPLES:
Book with one author:
   ¹Alvin Toffler, Powershift (New York: Bantam Books, 1990), p. 11.

Book with two authors:
   ²John Naisbitt and Patricia Aburdene, Megatrends 2000: Ten New Directions for the 1990's (New York: William Morrow & Company, 1990), pp. 137-138.

Book with editor only:
   ³Lonnie Echternacht, ed., A Global Look at Business Education, National Business Education Yearbook No. 29 (Reston: National Business Education Association, 1991), p. 55.

Magazine or journal article with author given:
   ⁴Jennie Best, CPS, "The Job Search: It's More Than an Interview," The Secretary, Vol. 50, No. 6, June/July 1990, pp. 12-13.

Magazine or journal article with no author given:
   ⁵"Reports from the Ergonomic Frontiers," Office Administration and Automation, Vol. 44, No. 10, October 1983, pp. 40-41+.

Newspaper Article:
   ⁶Wilma Randle, "Women Labor to Build Experience in Skilled Trades," Chicago Tribune, October 20, 1991, Section 7, pp. 1, 8.

Interview:
   ⁷Personal interview with Mary Ann Jirak, President, Career Performance, Inc., May 29, 1990.

For additional examples of source footnotes or endnotes, refer to:
   Pearce, C. Glenn, Ross Figgons, and Steven P. Golen, Principles of Business Communication: Theory, Application, and Technology (New York: John Wiley & Sons, Inc., 1984), pp. 580-582.
   Campbell, William Giles, Stephen Vaughan Ballou, and Carole Slade, Form and Style: Theses, Reports, Term Papers, Eighth Edition (Boston: Houghton Mifflin Company), 1990.

(2) *Discussion footnote or endnote:* This type of citation gives additional information that might be related indirectly to the topic.

EXAMPLE:
   ⁸The verbs used by secretaries in submitting critical incidents were modified in order to have continuity with the Huffman et al. taxonomy of office activities.

(3) *Reference footnote or endnote:* This type of citation refers to related sources or serves as a cross reference to other parts of the report.

EXAMPLE:
⁹See Figure 11-10, "Style for Interoffice Memorandum," p. 195.

b. *Formats for citations:* The format is the way the reference actually appears on the typewritten or printed page. Numbering, indentation, and spacing are very important considerations.

(1) *Numbering:* Each reference must be numbered consecutively with arabic numerals. All footnotes within a report may be numbered consecutively; or if the report is particularly lengthy, all footnotes within a particular chapter may be numbered consecutively.

(a) Each number is a superscript, raised slightly above the writing line, within the body of the report.
(b) This number must correspond to the arabic numeral in the footnote or endnote.

(2) *Indentation:* The first line of the footnote must be indented five spaces. All other lines begin flush left.
(3) *Spacing:* References should be single-spaced with a double-space between if there are two or more citations on the same page.

c. *Later references to same citation:* Sometimes you need to footnote a particular source more than once in a report. You may shorten these references either by using traditional Latin abbreviations or by using the author's name and page number.

(1) *Traditional Latin abbreviations:*

(a) *Ibid.:* The word *ibidem* means "in the same place." This term may be used when reference is made to the immediately preceding footnote or endnote.

EXAMPLES:
¹⁰Ibid.*(Reference for same page as preceding footnote)*
¹¹Ibid., pp. 334-345. *(Citation for same reference as preceding footnote, but different page reference)*

(b) *Op. cit.:* The words *opere citato* mean "in the work cited." This term is used when reference is made to

Preparing Communications in Final Format

a previous source, but there are intervening references.

EXAMPLE:
[12]Toffler, op. cit., p. 44.

(c) *Loc. cit.:* The words *loco citato* mean "in the place cited." This term refers to the same page reference as the previous footnote.

EXAMPLE:
[13]Toffler, loc. cit.

(2) *Author's name and page number:* Another way of writing subsequent references to a previous source is to use the author's name and the page number.

EXAMPLE:
[14]Best, p. 9.

d. *Placement of citations:* References may be placed at the bottom of each report page (the "foot") or at the end of the report on a separate page (the "end").

(1) *Placement at foot of report page:* When footnotes are placed at the foot of the same page where the reference is made, the superscript numbers must appear in the text of the report as well as in the footnote.

(a) *Separation line:* A 1½-inch horizontal line should separate the body of the text from the footnotes. There should be one blank space above and below this typed line. A blank line above the underscore comes from typing the underscore; a blank line below requires a return for the blank line (double-space).
(b) *Indentation:* The first line of each footnote should be indented five spaces (or the number of spaces each paragraph in the report is indented). The remaining lines are typed flush left.
(c) *Spacing:* The footnotes should be single-spaced with one blank line between footnotes if there is more than one.

(2) *Placement at end of report:* If the reference notes are typed at the end of the report as endnotes, they should be typed in the same order as they appear in the report. When the reference is made, the superscript numbers must appear in the text of the report as well as in the endnote.

(a) *Title:* The title *Endnotes* should be typed at least 1½ inches from the top edge of the paper and centered.
(b) *Indentation:* The first line of each endnote should be indented five spaces (or the number of spaces each paragraph in the report is indented). The remaining lines in the endnote are to be typed flush left.
(c) *Spacing:* The endnotes should be single-spaced with one blank line between endnotes.

Citations give proper credit for information taken from various published sources (books, periodical articles, research reports) and unpublished sources (television programs, lectures, letters, personal interviews). The Copyright Act of 1976, which became effective January 1, 1978, influences the way in which copyrighted works are cited and used. (See *Module II—Business Law*, Chapter 6, for an explanation of copyrights.)

e. *Bibliography*: A bibliography is a list of all references consulted by the author that contributed to the content of the report. The bibliography is placed at the end of the report on a separate page.

(1) *Types of bibliographies:* There are three basic types of bibliographies that may become a part of a report: a general bibliography, a selected bibliography, and an annotated bibliography.

(a) *General bibliography:* This type of bibliography includes all references used in researching the content of the report. This is also referred to as a *working* bibliography.
(b) *Selected bibliography:* Only those references pertaining to the topic that have been cited previously in the citations will be included in the selected bibliography.
(c) *Annotated bibliography:* After each bibliographic entry, a brief paragraph comments on the content and value of the reference. The annotated bibliography gives basic information about each reference used in preparing the content of the report.

f. *Format for bibliography:* The format dictates the appearance of the bibliography. The placement of the bibliography on the page, the way the entries are typed, and the spacing required are important to an attractively prepared bibliography.

(1) *Placement on page:*

(a) The word *BIBLIOGRAPHY* should be centered two inches from the top edge of the page (line 13).

(b) There should be a triple-space after the title.
(c) The first line of each entry must be typed flush with the left margin. The second and succeeding lines are indented at least five spaces.
(d) Each entry is single-spaced with a double-space (one blank space) between entries.
(e) The second and succeeding pages of the bibliography continue the entries beginning on line 7 from the top edge (leaving a one-inch top margin).

(2) *Arrangement of entries:* The bibliographic entries may be listed in two different ways—in an alphabetic list or in categories of references.

(a) *Alphabetic list:* The entire bibliography is alphabetized and typed as a single list of references.
(b) *Reference categories:* Each reference is included in the appropriate category (books, articles, research reports, interviews, miscellaneous). Within each category, the entries are alphabetized. Side headings highlight the different categories.

(3) *Preparation of entries:* The following procedures help to standardize the way in which the bibliographic entries are typed:

(a) If the author is known, the author's surname is listed first.
(b) If the author is unknown, the title is listed first.
(c) Within the alphabetic sequences, if an author is listed for more than one reference, a one-inch line is typed instead of the author's name in the second entry.
(d) Periods, rather than commas, separate the various sections of each entry.
(e) The title of the work should be shown exactly as it appeared in the citation, that is, the name of a periodical article is typed in initial caps, lower case, and enclosed in quotation marks; the name of a book is typed in all capitals or underlined.

EXAMPLES:
Article: "Hold Technology in Your Palm"
Book: The Electronic Cottage

(f) In entries for periodical articles, the exact page numbers should be included.
(g) In entries for books or works that are used in total, the entire reference is cited rather than individual pages.

See Figure 11-14 for a sample bibliography using the citations included in the preceding section.

8. *Graphics:* The term *graphics* refers to visual representations of successive changes in the value (quantity) of one or more variables. A *graphic aid* is an illustration that is used to clarify data presented within a report.

   a. *Purposes of business graphics:* Business graphics are used for a variety of purposes. Exactly what type of graphics is desired depends upon the particular use to which it will be put.

      (1) *Presentation of ideas:* Ideas that are presented either in a written report or an oral presentation will be enhanced through the use of supplementary graphic aids. Illustrations may be used to present ideas in printed matter (company manuals, company reports) or at meetings and conferences (speeches, reports).
      (2) *Explanation of business events:* Graphics are used to explain business events that are affecting the company (the economy, sales for the month, decreasing inventories).
      (3) *Presentation of company image:* Graphics are used to project a professional image of the company to the public. Graphics included on business cards, letterheads, and company forms can help to create a company image.

BIBLIOGRAPHY

Best, Jennie, CPS. "The Job Search: It's More Than an
     Interview." The Secretary, Vol. 50, No. 6, June/July 1990,
     pp. 12-13.

Echternacht, Lonnie, ed. A Global Look at Business Education.
     National Business Education Yearbook No. 29. Reston:
     National Business Education Association, 1991.

Jirak, Mary Ann, President. Career Performance, Inc., Glen
Ellyn,
     Illinois. Personal interview, May 29, 1990.

Naisbitt, John, and Patricia Aburdene. Megatrends 2000: Ten New
     Directions for the 1990's. New York: William Morrow &
     Company, 1990.

Randle, Wilma. "Women Labor to Build Experience in Skilled
     Trades." Chicago Tribune, October 20, 1991, Section 7, pp.
     1, 8.

"Reports from the Ergonomic Frontiers." Office Administration
     and Automation, Vol. 44, No. 10, October 1983, pp. 40-41+.

Toffler, Alvin. Powershift. New York: Bantam Books, 1990.

Figure 11-14
Bibliography

Pamphlets and brochures describing the company, its products and services, and its community efforts are usually available, too.

b. *Placement of graphic illustrations within text:* Graphic illustrations included in a written report must meet five requirements: each graphic illustration must be identified, documented, introduced within the narrative, interpreted within the narrative, and placed appropriately within the text.[1]

(1) *Identifying graphic illustrations:* Graphic aids must be labeled, numbered, and entitled within a report.

   (a) *Labeling:* A common way to label these visual aids is to call them "Figure" or "Table" and assign arabic numbers to each one consecutively, for example, "Figure 1."
   (b) *Title:* The title should clearly identify the information presented in the illustration.

Once the identification is complete, the label, number, and title may be placed either above or below the illustration.

(2) *Documenting the illustration:* Proper credit must be given in the report to the source of the illustration. Three types of sources are commonly used.

   (a) *Primary source:* Data obtained through primary research may be documented by placing the words *Source: Primary* directly below the illustration; or the source note may be omitted, implying that the illustration was constructed from primary data collected during research.
   (b) *Secondary source illustration constructed from narrative:* Sometimes data contained in a secondary source, like a newspaper, is converted by the writer into an illustration. The specific citation of the secondary reference should be included in the documentation.

   EXAMPLE:
   Source: <u>Chicago Tribune</u>, November 5, 1992, p. E-2.

   (c) *Secondary source illustration presented verbatim:* When an illustration that appeared in a secondary source is presented verbatim with no change, the entire reference should be acknowledged along with the table or figure number.

---

[1] C. Glenn Pearce et al.., <u>Principles of Business Communication: Theory, Application, and Technology</u> (New York: John Wiley & Sons, Inc., 1984), pp. 248–252.

EXAMPLE:
Source: Sandra Porter with Janice DeGooyer, "What is Comparable Worth Anyway?" <u>The Secretary</u>, Vol. 43, No. 5, May 1983, p. 20.

Footnotes may be used to explain information contained in the illustration. Use a superscript of a letter or an asterisk rather than a number.

(3) *Introducing graphic illustrations:* Before presenting the illustration in the text, reference to the illustration must be made within the text to make its presence clear.

    (a) The reference should refer to the illustration by label, number, and content (possibly title).
    (b) The same procedure should be used to refer to an illustration in an appendix. The reference should indicate the label, number, and content.
    (c) The page number(s) of the table, figure, or appendix is also appropriate since this enhances the reader's ability to locate the illustration quickly.

(4) *Interpreting graphic illustrations:* Without an accurate interpretation, a graphic illustration will have little meaning in context. The purpose of the text material is to explain and emphasize ideas presented in a table or figure. The importance of the data to the overall presentation of the topic should be stressed.

(5) *Placing graphic illustrations within text:* The placement of the graphic illustration where it can best complement the text is very important. Here are a few guidelines that will help in determining where the illustration might best be placed:

    (a) If possible, the illustration needs to be placed immediately after its introduction in the text and near its interpretation.
    (b) The size of a graphic illustration should be at least one-quarter of an 8½ x 11-inch page for ease of reading.
    (c) If the size of the illustration is less than a half page, it may be placed directly after its introduction and interpretation. Thus, the illustration and introduction may often be on the same page.
    (d) If the size of the illustration is a half page or more, it should be placed on the first full page that comes after the introduction. A full-page illustration can be placed either horizontally or vertically on the page, depending upon the margins of the text.

(e) When text appears on the same page as the illustration, leave about three line spaces above and below the illustration to clearly separate the illustration from the text. Some writers prefer to place the illustration between the introduction and the interpretation.

(f) The label, number, and title of the illustration should be centered at the top of the illustration.

These five requirements for preparing graphic illustrations can be applied to the selection of appropriate types of illustrations to be included in the report.

c. *Types of graphic illustrations:* Various types of graphic illustrations are used to display detailed data in planned and ordered formats. The relationships between factors being measured are shown in order to support and clarify the content of the report. Here are some of the more common types of graphic illustrations included in reports:

(1) *Table:* A table shows text material presented in a columnar format. An orderly arrangement of the data is achieved through the use of headings, rows, and columns to structure the data. Usually a table is preferable to a chart if numerous exact figures are to be shown. (See Section D-9 in this chapter.)

(2) *Bar graph or chart:* Typically, a bar graph or chart shows a comparison from one time period to another, for example, sales for the year 1990 as compared with sales for the year 1991. The bar graph uses bars of equal width to show quantities (values) on one axis and the factor to be measured on the other axis. (See Figure 11-15.)

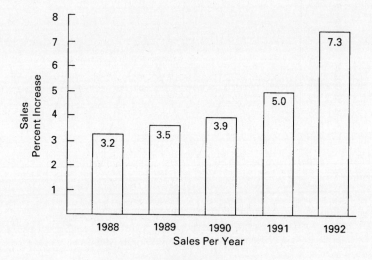

Figure 11-15
Example of Bar Graph

(3) *Line graph or chart:* The line graph consists of a series of connected lines showing a particular trend in business data for a period of time, for example, sales for each month during a particular year. The vertical axis (Y) identifies the factor and quantity being measured, and the horizontal axis (X) identifies the time period under observation. These axes form the grid upon which the data are recorded. (See Figure 11-16.)

(4) *Pie graph or chart:* The pie graph or chart represents the parts that make up a whole. The circle equals 100 percent; the sections represent parts of the whole (smaller percentages of the whole). When totaled, the smaller percentages always equal 100 percent. (See Figure 11-17.)

(5) *Pictogram:* Symbols represent the factor being measured and a specific number of units. An interpretation of the symbol is included so that the reader knows what the symbol represents and the exact quantities represented by the symbol.

(6) *Drawings:* In business there are many drawings representing the product or service of the firm. Sketches of proposed new products, engineering drawings, and product designs are a few of the types of drawings that are needed. These are all examples of business graphics.

These are only a few examples of the types of graphic illustrations that are used in the preparation of business re-

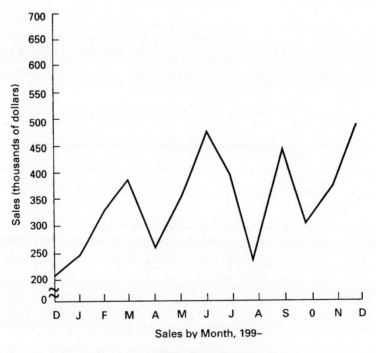

Figure 11-16
Example of Line Graph

Preparing Communications in Final Format 401

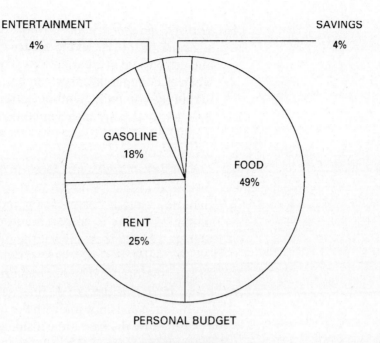

Figure 11-17
Example of Pie Graph

ports. The saying that "a picture is worth a thousand words" has much bearing on the type of graphic illustrations that will best depict business events.

d. *Preparation of graphic illustrations:* Today many graphic illustrations can be developed using computer software. In some cases, a design staff either from an in-house operation or a commercial agency is involved. In both instances, it is important to develop appropriate illustrations that will be able to be reproduced by reprographics services. The following steps are important in the design process for preparing graphic illustrations:

(1) *Computer software for generation of graphics:* Various software packages are available that are capable of generating graphic illustrations. If an appropriate software program is available, much developmental time will be saved in making appropriate use of such a program.

(2) *Original illustrations:* Drawings and sketches will have to be developed by designers. Designers need to work closely with the user department, keeping the primary purpose of the project in mind. This step would include special qualities such as lettering that might be needed as well.

(3) *Composition of typeset text:* In addition to illustrations, text may need to be written that will be converted by typesetting, composition, or desktop publishing processes to the text material needed to complement the drawings, lettering, or other illustrations being produced.

(4) *Transfer designs available:* Books with sketches and designs may be purchased to use for cutting out the designs and using them in creating copy. This is especially helpful when a commercial artist or designer is not available within the company. Symbols, letters, and lines of various sizes and styles are also available on transfer sheets and can be transferred easily from these plastic sheets to the original copy.

(5) *Original draft of design:* Once the illustrations have been prepared in black-and-white copy and the typeset text material is ready for paste up, the initial layout is prepared. The copy is prepared and pasted up so the user will get a better idea of what the final copy will look like. At this point, the user must critique the design and approve it before final layout and printing can be done.

(6) *Final layout of design:* A final layout of the design is prepared in consultation with the user; any modifications suggested by the user are considered. The text should be carefully proofread. The designer will be able to judge whether certain changes are feasible at this point, but the final approval lies with the user.

(7) *Finalizing the design:* Once any modifications suggested by the user are incorporated in the design, the completed work is ready for a final proofing. It is important at this point to read every word and look at each illustration carefully to be sure the total message is accurate.

(8) *Preparation of design for printing:* If copies are to be printed of the design copy, then a negative of the copy will need to be prepared. If the copy is more than one page, as in the case of a booklet, then a negative of each page will need to be prepared. If the original design is to be reduced, it is at this point that a photographic reduction is made. The negatives for each page are used to make plates for the printing process.

(9) *Printing of copies:* The final stage in the preparation of a graphic design is the printing of copies that are required. Most printing processes can handle almost any number of copies from 50 to 5,000 depending upon the specific requirements of the job.

9. *Statistical Data Format:* The primary technique used to present statistical data within reports is through the use of tables. A *table* is text material presented in a columnar format. A table may be placed within the text closely following its introduction in the text, or it may be placed on a separate page if it is larger than a half page.

   a. *Word processing table feature:* The purpose of the table feature in word processing software is to create and edit rows and columns of tabular data, without entering tabs or tab settings.

This feature is useful for creating forms that are formatted in tabular form. Input includes the number of columns and rows you want in the table. There is a text editing mode for editing the text you enter in the table, and there is a table editing mode that allows you to change the structure of the table. The math feature is used to perform any computations that are necessary within the table. Lines can be added by drawing vertical and horizontal lines where desired to separate column heads from text.

b. *Placement of table:* When we refer to placement of the table, we are really thinking of centering the table (horizontally and vertically) on the page.

(1) *Horizontal placement:* The horizontal placement of a table will be the same whether it is typed within the paragraphs of a document or on a page by itself. When the table function in word processing is not used, there are two methods for determining horizontal placement: the mathematical method and the backspace method.

(a) *The mathematical model:* This method requires careful arithmetic but is useful for determining the left margin and tab stops when using either a word processor or a typewriter.

- Count the number of characters and spaces in the longest line. (*Note:* The longest line consists of the characters and spaces in the longest line in each column. Remember, when you are counting the number of spaces, that also means the number of spaces between the columns.

EXAMPLE:
In this table, the longest line is underlined. Include five spaces between the columns in planning the placement of the table.

Mary Jones	<u>*1718 Jefferson Drive*</u>	<u>*Rockford, IL 61107*</u>
<u>*Thomas Smith*</u>	*321 West Avenue*	*DeKalb, IL 60115*

- Divide this total number of characters and spaces in half.
- Subtract the answer from the centerpoint for the left margin.

You need to know the center of the *paper* if the table is typed on a page by itself and the center of the *line of print* if the table is typed within a document.
Center of 8½-inch paper:
10-pitch (pica) = 42 (if left edge of paper is on 0)

10-pitch (pica) = 50 (if left edge of paper is at 8)
12-pitch (elite) = 50 or 51 (if left edge of paper is at 0)

- The tab stops are determined by adding the column spaces plus the spaces between the column to the previous position.

EXAMPLE: Using the preceding example, there are 60 total characters and spaces in the longest line. Divide 60 by 2, then subtract that answer from the centerpoint. Using 42 for the centerpoint for pica and 50 for elite, the left margin is: pica 42 - 30 = 12 and elite 50 - 30 = 20. The first tab stop would be left margin + 17 (Thomas Smith plus 5 spaces between columns): pica 12 + 17 = 29; elite 20 + 17 = 37. The second tab stop would be: pica 29 + 24 = 53; elite 37 + 24 = 61 (24 = 1718 Jefferson Drive plus 5 spaces between columns).

(b) *The backspace method:* This method is most convenient when using a conventional typewriter.

- Determine the center of the page or line of print.
- Bring your typing point to the center.
- Backspace once for every two characters and/or spaces in the longest line. (<u>Note</u>: Longest line in each column plus spaces between columns.)

When you begin backspacing from the centerpoint, you will backspace once for every combination of two characters or spaces. Using the example from the mathematical method, the longest line is:

<u>Thomas Smith</u>   <u>1718 Jefferson Drive</u>   <u>Rockford, IL 61107</u>

Backspace as follows:

Th om as space/S mi th space/space space/space space/1 71 8/space Je ff er so n/space Dr iv e/space space/space space/space Ro ck fo rd ,/space IL space/6 11 07

This totals 30 backspaces and the point where your left margin would be set for the table or the point to begin a table if it is typed within text material.

- If there should be one letter left at the very end of the longest line, this one letter is dropped. (See Example 1 in Section D-9-b(2).

(2) *Vertical placement:* The vertical placement of a table depends on whether the table is being placed within text or on a separate page.

(a) *Placement of table within text:* When centering a table vertically within a document, follow these guidelines:

- Make sure there is sufficient room for the entire table on the same page.
- Triple-space from the last line of text to the title of the table.
- Once you have typed the title, single-space and type a double underscore. When using word processing, use the double underscore code or superscript the second underscore. On a conventional typewriter, use the variable line spacer to adjust the line of print so the underscores are close together.
- After the double underscore, double-space to the column headings. (Column headings are optional. If they are omitted, double-space to the body of the table).
- Type the column headings.
- Single-space and type a single underscore.
- After the single underscore, double-space to the body of the table.
- The body of the table may be single-spaced or double-spaced.
- After you have completed the table, single-space and type a single underscore.
- Triple-space after the table to continue the document.

See Figure 11-18 for an example of correct placement of a table within the body of the report text.

(b) *Placement of table alone on page:* Use the word processing "Center on Page" command to center a table *vertically* by itself on a sheet of paper. Type the table after the command. The table will be positioned vertically. When centering a table vertically with a conventional typewriter, follow these five steps for accurate placement:

- Determine the number of lines available on the page:
  8½ x 11-inch paper:
  Full sheet = 66 lines
  Half sheet = 33 lines

  or

  If you place an odd-sized sheet of paper in the typewriter, there are *six lines to an inch*.

```
There are four main classes of auxiliary storage devices:  tape,
disk, drum, and mass storage.  Of the four, magnetic tape and
magnetic disk are the two most widely used in business today.
Typical media storage capacity and typical input/output rates are
summarized in the table.

                AUXILIARY STORAGE PERIPHERAL SUMMARY
           ═══════════════════════════════════════════════════
                                    Input/Output  Media Storage
                                       Rates         Capacity
           Device     Storage Media  (k per second) (m per unit)
           ───────────────────────────────────────────────────

           Magnetic   Cassette       .03 to 106    .3 to .7
           Tape Drive Reel           100 to 1250   15 to 60

           Magnetic   Floppy Disk    30  to 60     .25 to 1.0
           Disk Drive Disk Pack      300 to 1000   30 to 300
           ───────────────────────────────────────────────────

The input/output rate describes the speed at which characters are
moved from the . . .
```

Figure 11-18
Placement of Table Within Text

- Count the number of lines in the table. Remember that each blank line equals *one*. Therefore, if you are single-spacing, there are no blank lines. If you are double-spacing, there is one blank line between the lines. With triple-spacing, there are two blank lines between the lines.
- Subtract the number of lines in the table from the number of lines on the sheet of paper you are using. This lets you know how many blank lines are left on the sheet of paper.
- Divide the blank lines that are left by *two* (half for the top of the paper and half for the bottom of the paper).
- If you want your table to be exact, add one. This will let the typing begin on the line immediately below the exact number of blank lines required at the top of the paper.
- If you want your table in reading position, subtract 3 from your answer in the previous step. This places the table 3 lines above exact vertical placement. When using the "Center on Page" command in word processing, add 6 hard returns after the last line of the table. This places the

table 3 lines above exact vertical center when printed.

EXAMPLE 1: Let's add some more names to the horizontal placement example, and figure the vertical and horizontal placement if this material is centered on a half sheet of paper, single-spaced. The longest line is underlined for horizontal centering.

Mary Jones	<u>1718 Jefferson Drive</u>	*Rockford, IL 61107*
Thomas Smith	*321 West Avenue*	*DeKalb, IL 60115*
Sara Car	*55 Pheasant Avenue*	<u>Wilmington, IL 60481</u>
Betty Dryden	*333 Chase Avenue*	*Wenona, IL 61377*
<u>Richard Fremont</u>	*987 Campbell Drive*	*Grafton, IL 62037*

<u>Vertical Placement</u>:
Half sheet of paper = 33 lines
Lines in table = 5 lines
33 - 5 = 28 blank lines available for margins

28 blank lines divided by 2 = 14 lines for the top margin and 14 lines for the bottom margin. To print the material so it will be precisely centered vertically on the half sheet, add one to 14 and return 15 times to begin typing the first line.

To print the table in reading position, subtract 3 from 14 and begin typing the first line on line 11.

<u>Horizontal Placement</u>:
Centering the longest line horizontally with five spaces between the columns, you have one extra character at the end of the line. Do not backspace for a single character remaining at the very end of a line being centered horizontally; just drop it.

Ri ch ar d/space Fr em on t/space space/space space/space 17 18 space/J ef fe rs on space/D ri ve space/space space/space space/W il mi ng to n, space/I L/space 60 48 1(do not backspace for the 1)

EXAMPLE 2: If you were to type the same five lines on a full sheet of paper, you would end up with a remainder of ½ when you divide by 2. The remainder is dropped. Calculate the vertical placement in this way:

66   lines on a full sheet of paper
<u>- 5</u>   typed lines in table
61   blank lines available for top and bottom margins

61 divided by 2 = 30 with a remainder of 1 (to be dropped)

To have exactly 30 blank lines at the top of the paper, add 1 to 30 and begin typing the table on line 31.

To print the table in reading position, subtract 3 from 30 and begin typing the table on line 27.

The horizontal centering remains the same.

EXAMPLE 3: If the material is to be double-spaced, there would be nine lines in the problem:

5   typed lines
1   blank line between first and second line
1   blank line between second and third line
1   blank line between third and fourth line
<u>1</u>   blank line between fourth and fifth line
9   total lines

If the material is to be triple-spaced, there would be 13 lines to the problem (two blank lines between each of the typed lines).

The horizontal centering remains the same.

E.   Disk Storage Notations

In a computer environment, information is stored on a magnetic medium in a file. Today most files are stored on either a diskette, hard disk, or tape (more common in a minicomputer or mainframe computer environment).

A *file* is a collection of related information and is treated as one unit of storage. When stored, files must be named so the computer software can retrieve/restore the file. File names are also very important to the computer user (you). The file name should provide an easy reference to the contents of the file. The storage medium (diskette, disk pack, or tape) can also be named to assist the user in knowing the contents of the entire storage medium.

1.   *Naming Files:* The type of characters and the number of characters that can be used in a file name are determined by the computer software. In some cases a file name can also have an extension. In a DOS environment (Disk Operating System for IBM and IBM-compatible computers) the file name can be eight characters followed by an extension (a period plus up to three characters). Often the extension is automatically added by the software (spreadsheets, graphics, data bases) and thus is not available for the user to add to the file name in those instances. When the extension is optional (meaning the user can make use of the extra three characters), .EXT is placed in brackets when referencing the file name in the manual.

EXAMPLE: FILENAME[.EXT]

Although the exact guidelines for naming files can vary according to the software being used, there are three general guidelines. General guidelines for naming files are:

a. *Characters in file name:* The file name is one word made up of letters, numbers, and/or special characters (no blank spaces). The software manual explains which special characters and how many characters can be used.

   A general guideline is eight letters and/or numbers and the underscore as the only special character. Since the file name must be one word, never use a blank space. Also, never use the period as a special character; the period indicates an extension.

b. *File contents:* The file name should reflect the contents of the file. This is important for the computer *user* in identifying what is stored in the file. The computer reacts to any combination of letters and/or numbers as long as it is referenced in exactly the same way as it originally was stored.

c. *Unique file names within applications:* Each file name within an application and stored on the same medium must be unique.

EXAMPLE:
Word processing is one application, while spreadsheet is another application.

If the same name is assigned to a second file within an application stored on the same medium, the first file will be erased. The second file will be stored in place of the first file.

EXAMPLES:
You compose a letter to a customer about a new product, a trim saw for detail carpentry work. You also compose a memorandum to the marketing department about the same new product. You are using a word processing package for both documents. When you save the letter, you decide to reference it by the new product name—TRIMSAW. If the memorandum would also be saved under the file name TRIMSAW, the letter document would be erased. This can be avoided by using the extension option which is typically available in word processing software.

Letter file name TRIMSAW.CLI
   (indicating to client)
Memo file name TRIMSAW.MKT
   (to marketing department)

RPT is a typical extension for report, LTR for letter, and MEM for memorandum. Here are examples of two different files about the new rent increase as of October, 1992:

RENT1092.RPT (report on new rent)
RENT1092.LTR (letter on new rent)

Expanding on the new product example, a bar graph was developed on the sales of the new product in the various selling regions. *A graphics computer package was used to produce the bar graph. The file name is TRIMSAW. In graphics software, the extension is automatically used by the computer software and is* not *available to you, the user. PIC is an extension common in graphics computer software. The file name TRIMSAW is unique from the letter and memo documents; the automatic PIC extension for the graphics software package makes the file name unique.*

Note: When making revisions to a file, it is usually not important to save the old information. Using the same file name for the new information will erase the old information. This helps you manage your disk files and clean out the old ones.

2. *Naming Storage Medium:* When working with several diskettes (or when using several tapes or disk packs), it is helpful to identify the contents of the entire storage medium. Since diskettes are most common in a computer environment when a hard disk is not used, disks will be used as the storage medium reference. There are two ways to label the disk: *external label* and *disk label*. Also, disk organization plays an important role in file management.

   a. *External label:* Write the information about the contents of a disk on a label and attach it to the disk.
   b. *Disk label:* When formatting the disk for the operating system, the disk can be named. By naming the disk, the disk name can be read on the computer screen. This would be helpful if the external label was lost.
      Also, the computer disk operating system (DOS) can locate the correct disk by the disk label. This is useful in a minicomputer or mainframe computer environment.
   c. *Disk organization:* File management is as important in a computer environment as it is for conventional paper files. Think of a disk like a file drawer. Is it for a person, company, subject . . .? This becomes the disk label. Only files pertaining to that person, company, or subject are stored on that disk. Unique names for the files on that disk are then easier to manage.

   EXAMPLES:
   Using the new-product (trim saw) example and the new-rent example, two disks would be labeled, one for TRIM SAW and one for RENT. Whenever any document was created pertaining to the new product, it would be saved on the TRIM SAW disk. Whenever a document was created about rent, the RENT disk would be used.

   EXTERNAL LABEL: TRIM SAW
   FILES: CLIENT.LTR
                       MEMO1092.MKT
                       BAR.PIC

EXTERNAL LABEL: *RENT*
FILES: *REPORT89.SEP*
    LETTER89.SEP
    LINE989.PIC
    REPORT92.OCT
    LETTER92.OCT
    LINE1092.PIC

Note: *Since there is an external label and all files on the disk are only for that one subject (TRIM SAW or RENT), the file names have been changed from the previous example to more clearly reflect what is in the file. TRIM SAW files are a client letter, a memo to marketing department written October 1992, and a bar graph. RENT files are a report written in September 1989 and another in October 1992, a letter written in September 1989 and another in October 1992, and a line graph from September 1989 and another from October 1992.*

F. Other Forms of Business Communications

Communication is so important in the office, and there are many other forms in which written communication is transmitted. Only some of the most common are presented here in a brief look at the formats used for minutes, news releases, itineraries, outlines, and speeches.

1. *Minutes:* The purpose of *minutes* is to summarize the events of a meeting. The minutes become the official report of the meeting. (See Figure 11-19 for an example of minutes prepared by the secretary of an organization.) Sometimes detailed minutes are preferred; at other times only brief coverage of topics is required. All minutes, however, should be prepared in the following way:

a. *Heading:* The heading must contain the following types of information:

(1) Name of the organization (or department holding the meeting.
(2) Date of the meeting.
(3) Time of the meeting.
(4) Place of the meeting.
(5) Type of meeting (regular or special).

The heading begins 1½ to 2 inches from the top edge of the page, is either centered or arranged across the line of print, and is either typed in initial caps or in all capital letters. After the heading, triple-space to the next section.

b. *Attendance:* Information on attendance can be tabulated or incorporated into the first paragraph at the beginning of the minutes and should include:

```
                    VALLEYVIEW, INC.
                   Homeowners' Association
DS
   DATE:  March 10, 199-        LOCATION:  ValleyView Conference Room
TS
   PRESENT:  (10) Carla Albergetti, Terry Brock, Jerry Carpenter,
             Marvin Dollman, Fred Hardanger, Leroy James, Abigail
             Longsman, MaryAnn Planters, Martha Rintamaki, Sam Tillman
DS
   ABSENT:  (2)
DS
   The ValleyView Homeowners' Association monthly meeting was held on
   Wednesday, March 10, 199-, in the ValleyView Conference Room.
   President Brock called the meeting to order at 7:30 p.m.  The
   secretary circulated minutes from the February 8 meeting.  It was
   moved, seconded, and passed that the February minutes be approved.
TS
   Grounds Committee
DS
   The planting and maintenance contract was granted to BBW Lawn and
   Garden Care.  The contract is for April 1, 199-, through October
   21, 199-.  The 199- schedule is as follows:  April 1, spring flower
   beds and lawn grooming;  . . .
TS
   Recreation Committee
DS
   The spring schedule of events are April 4, Spring Showers Picnic in
   the Recreation Hall; May 10, Eagle River Boat Cruise; May 30,
   Memorial Weekend Picnic at Hopkins Park.  Abigail Longsman moved
   and Jerry Carpenter seconded that "Detailed information regarding
   the social events be included in the ValleyView Bulletin."  The
   motion passed unanimously.
DS
   No additional business was brought before the Association.  It was
   moved and seconded that the meeting be adjourned.  The President
   announced the next regular meeting (Wednesday, April 11; 7:30 p.m.;
   ValleyView Conference Room) and adjourned the meeting at 9 p.m.
DS
   Respectfully submitted,

 ↓
 4
   Leroy James, Secretary

   Note:  There are no reference initials shown here because these
   minutes were prepared by the secretary of the organization.
   Marginal notations outline the desired spacing for the minutes (DS
   = double space, TS = triple space).
```

Figure 11-19
Minutes of Meeting

(1) An alphabetical listing of those members present.
(2) An alphabetical listing of those members absent (optional).

c. *Body:* Minutes are a summary of the topics discussed at the meeting. It is helpful to follow the agenda while taking minutes at a meeting. The presentation of this summary information is usually in paragraph form. The marginal format for typing reports is followed for typing minutes. If headings are

Preparing Communications in Final Format 413

used, follow the same format as for reports. Minutes are usually single-spaced, with double-spacing between paragraphs. However, double-spacing is also appropriate.

d. *Motions:* For routine motions, it is sufficient to record, *It was moved and seconded that*... When a motion is made where the exact wording is required, the names of those making and seconding the motion are also recorded. The recording of any motion is included in the topic paragraph pertaining to the motion. Some correctly stated motions are as follows:

EXAMPLES:
Betty Caldwell moved and Julie Heartland seconded the motion that...
The motion was made by Betty Caldwell and seconded by Julia Heartland that...
It was moved and seconded that...
(This example is for routine motions only.)

e. *Closing:* The complimentary closing for minutes is *Respectfully submitted*. There are three blank lines (four returns) between the complimentary closing and the typed signature of the secretary. If you are typing the minutes for the secretary, your reference initials should follow a double space after the typed signature.

EXAMPLES:
Blocked Style
Respectfully submitted,

Martha E. Schneider
Secretary

gmd

Modified Block Style
          Respectfully submitted,

          Martha E. Schneider
          Secretary

gmd

2. *News Release:* The *news release* is an item that usually needs to be typed immediately by the secretary. The urgency of the item will depend on the date of the news. From the reader's viewpoint, news is only news if it is announcing something before the fact or immediately after it happens. If you are responsible for making sure news releases get to the press in time (whether the press is in-house or the local newspapers), you should be aware of the lead time required. This is particularly true for announcement news. Typical lead time required for a news release is ten days. To find out specifically for your local paper, contact the newspaper's City Desk. A news release should include these parts: heading, body, and closing symbols.

a. *Heading:* The heading should include the fact that it is a news release, when it should be released, the company name and address, the name of a person to contact in case there are questions, and a phone number. The heading may also include the date of the release. After the heading, there should be a break by either underscoring or typing asterisks across the line of print. (See F-2-d(5): single-space to an underscore break; double-space to an asterisk break.)

b. *Body:* The body of the news release should have a title which is indicative of what is in the news. A news release is written in the direct approach: the news is presented in the first sentence. Important facts to remember for the beginning are *who*, *what*, *where*, *when*, and *why*. The balance of the release follows up with pertinent facts. A good news release is written clearly and concisely.

c. *Closing symbols:* To indicate the conclusion of the release, printer's closing symbols are typed at the end. The symbol can be either three number symbols or a number 30 with a hyphen before and after.

EXAMPLES:
or   # #
-30-   or   - 30 -

d. *Spacing the news release:*

(1) *Top margin:* The top margin can vary from ½-inch to 2 inches depending on the length of the news release. If the news release is lengthy (although remember good news is clear and concise), the top margin should be narrower to keep the release to one page.

(2) *Side margin:* Side margins can also be adjusted to make sure the release is one page in length. Side margins should never be narrower than 1 inch, however. You must be able to judge the length of the news release and strive to have it attractively set up on one page.

(3) *Bottom margin:* A minimum of 1 inch is necessary at the bottom. However, with shorter news releases, the bottom margin could be more than 1 inch.

(4) *Heading:* Single-space data in the heading that belong together and double-space between the data. Information that should stand out should be typed in all capital letters. Using spread-typing for some of the heading information is also appropriate.

(5) *Break line:* There should appear to be a blank line between the heading and the break line. If you use the underscore, single-space to the underscore. If you use asterisks for the break line, double-space to the asterisks.

EXAMPLES OF HEADING AND BREAK LINE:

N E W S R E L E A S E   *ALFO INDUSTRIES*
                                1321 Manchester Court
                                Silver Spring, MD 20901

RELEASE IMMEDIATELY   *For Further Information*
                                Contact Sally Mitchell
                                    (301-754-3214)

****

NEWS RELEASE
RELEASE IMMEDIATELY

ALFO INDUSTRIES   *For Further Information*
1321 Manchester Court   *Contact Sally Mitchell*
Silver Spring, MD 20901   *(301) 754-3214*

****

(6) *Body:* Triple-space from the break line to the title of the news release. The title should be centered and typed in all capital letters. If the title consists of more than one line, it is to be single-spaced. Triple-space to the paragraphs. Double-space the paragraphs with five-space paragraph indentations. If block paragraphs are used, triple-space between the paragraphs.

(7) *Closing symbols:* Triple-space after the last paragraph to the closing symbol. The closing symbol is to be typed in the center of the page.

3. *Itinerary:* An *itinerary* is an executive's travel plan that specifies all details concerning business travel. Typed copies should be available prior to the trip so the office, the secretary, and the executive know the details of the trip.

    a. *Types of information:* The itinerary typically includes the following details:

        (1) Departure date, time, and place.
        (2) Type of confirmed transportation.
        (3) Arrival data, time, and place.
        (4) Hotel reservation(s) for each date or segment of the trip.
        (5) Scheduled appointments and meetings.
        (6) Complete travel information for return trip.

    b. *Parts of the itinerary:* The following guidelines will help in preparing an itinerary for the executive to share with the office, the secretary, and family. See Figure 11-20 for a sample itinerary.

ITINERARY
Marlene Bailey
January 10-12, 199-

MONDAY, JANUARY 10 (Chicago to New York City)

8:20 a.m. (CST)   Leave Chicago O'Hare Airport on United Airlines Flight 208; 747; breakfast served.

9:33 a.m. (EST)   Arrive at New York LaGuardia Airport. Take limousine to Waldorf Hotel, 2021 Second Avenue, New York (212-542-6000); guaranteed hotel reservation; confirmation in trip file.

1:00 p.m.   Meeting with Roger C. Harper, Jr., President, ACF Corporation, 994 Third Avenue, New York (212-776-1420).

7:00 p.m.   Dinner-Meeting at Stewart's Restaurant, 727 Avenue of the Americas, New York, with Joyce L. Rohrson, Consultant, American Business Systems (212-325-4692).

TUESDAY, JANUARY 11 (New York City)

9:30 a.m.   The National Office Systems Conference, City Conference Center, 1004 Central Parkway, New York (212-554-4200).

9:45 a.m.   Presentation: "The Office Environment--Networking and Today's Automated Office"

1:00 p.m.   Luncheon with Raymond L. Bernard, Vice-President and General Manager, Wilson Automation, Inc., at the Oakdale City Club, 9250 Fifth Avenue, New York (212-347-3300).

3:00 p.m.   Tour of Advanced Business Systems, Inc., 125 Seventh Avenue, New York. Contact Person: Helen Adams, Office Automation Consultant (212-774-1550).

WEDNESDAY, JANUARY 12 (New York City to Chicago)

9:45 a.m.   Leave Waldorf Hotel by limousine for John F. Kennedy Airport.

11:55 a.m. (EST)   Leave Kennedy Airport on United Flight 648, business class; lunch served.

2:10 p.m. (CST)   Arrive at Chicago O'Hare Airport. Company limousine will meet you at baggage claim.

Figure 11-20
Example of Itinerary

(1) *Headings:* The itinerary should be entitled "Itinerary for (name of business traveler)" with the dates of the trip as a subheading. These lines should be centered.

(2) *Columns of information:* Two groups of information are included on the itinerary: the dates and times of business commitments during the trip on the left and the travel and meeting information on the right.

   (a) *Dates/times:* On the left side of the itinerary, the dates and specific times of flights, meetings, ap-

pointments, and any other events must be typed. A special notation of the time in effect for each location, for example, CST for Central Standard Time, should be included so there will be no misunderstandings in regard to appointment times.
    (b) *Travel and meeting information:* In the right column, entries give detailed information regarding reservations (transportation or hotel), meetings, luncheons, conferences, or other commitments. Complete information for companies (names, addresses, telephone numbers, contact people) and any other special details should be included.

  c. *Format of itinerary:* The itinerary should be prepared in typewritten or printed form so that it can serve as an easy-to-understand reference for the executive and others to use.

    (1) *Margins:* Side margins should be at least one inch, with the top margin on the first page two inches and the bottom margin on the first page one inch. (These are minimum space allocations.)
    (2) *Spacing:* Headings should be double-spaced, with a triple-space before the body of the itinerary begins. The text material should be single-spaced with a double-space between each entry.
    (3) *Headings:* Headings should be double-spaced and centered. The main heading should be typed in all capital letters, while the subheading should be typed in uppercase and lowercase letters.
    (4) *Second-page continuation:* If the itinerary is more than one page, the second-page continuation and succeeding pages should have a page heading like this:

    ITINERARY FOR MARLENE T. BAILEY
    Page 2
    January 10-12, 199-

    This continuation-page heading should appear on line 4 from the top edge, with the text continuing on line 7.

4. *Outline:* There are times when a document must be in outline format. An *outline* consists of key words coded in descending order, using Roman numerals, numbers, and letters of the alphabet.

  a. *Coding the outline:* The Roman numeral is considered the highest in coding sequence. In descending order, the outline adheres to the following sequence:

    (1) Roman numeral, beginning with I.
    (2) Capital letters of the alphabet, A - Z.

(3) Numbers, beginning with 1.
(4) Small letters of the alphabet, a - z.
(5) Numbers in parentheses, beginning with (1).
(6) Small letters of the alphabet in parentheses, (a) - (z).

Each section starts the sequence from the beginning code, and each section should have at least two codes within the sequence. Also, when setting up the side margins for an outline, you should determine the code which will require the most space. Indent from that point so the decimal points for all codes within the sequence are aligned. All codes end with a period or parenthesis. Space twice after the period or parenthesis.

Figure 11-21 is an example of an outline format with four major divisions (identified by Roman numerals). Division IV breaks down to lowest sequencing. Notice all sequencing consists of at least two codes within that sequence.

In a word processing environment, indent (or tab) once after the period or parenthesis. If the text that follows the

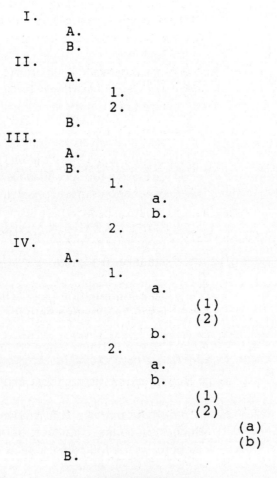

Figure 11-21
Example of Outline Format

enumeration is longer than one line, the use of the indent feature (instead of the tab) allows succeeding lines to indent and align with the text until there is a return. See Figure 11-22 (II-A in the illustration).

    b. Spacing an outline: The first consideration must be given to readability from the reader's viewpoint. Therefore, judgment on your part as to single-spacing or double-spacing the outline is important. Once spacing format has been determined, be consistent throughout the document. When a key-word phrase consists of more than one line, single-space for that code.

    (1) If the outline consists mainly of phrases that are two or more lines in length, the outline is usually double-spaced between all points.

    (2) If the key words are short in nature, you may decide to single-space within that outline.

Spacing before the main sections (those coded with Roman numerals) is always double-spacing. Spacing after the main sections may or may not be double-spaced. In Figure 11-22, double-spacing was used for readability because of the length of the typed lines. The outline still fits on one page.

5. *Speech:* When a speech must be prepared, some of the same techniques that are used to prepare a written report are used, especially

```
                    SPRING BUSINESS SHOW

   I.   Sponsored by AMS Chapter, Rockford, Illinois

        A.   Date:  April 25, 199-

        B.   Location:  Charleton Hotel

  II.   Reasons Why Abby Corporation Should Participate

        A.   Participation last year by 45 local and area

             businesses who displayed equipment and supplies

             1.   Ten of these businesses are direct competitors

             2.   Five of the businesses are those considering

                  location in Rockford

        B.   Goodwill established with participating businesses

        C.   Goodwill established with clients

             1.   Attendance last year was 10,595

             2.   Projected attendance for 199- is 15,000
```

Figure 11-22
Example of Outline

in the planning stages. The basic steps in preparing a speech include the selection of a topic, background research, organization of the material, and the actual presentation of the information. The secretary may play a very important role in assisting with the background research and organization of the material for the speech. In addition, typed copies of the outline of the speech, the actual speech (if a complete text is required), and any related handout materials will be needed.

a. *Typed outline of speech*: Many speakers use typed outlines to remind them of important points to make. The outline also has these points in sequential order so that the speaker can instantly refer to the next point without turning pages. The majority of speeches do not require a complete typed text; therefore, typed outlines (and sometimes notes) will be sufficient.

   (1) *Topical outline:* This type of outline directs the speaker from point to point with a brief listing of nouns rather than lengthy phrases. The speaker must rely heavily on memory.
   (2) *Phrase outline:* This type of outline is more extensive, with more information related to each point. Only essential words are included, however.
   (3) *Sentence outline:* Key sentences are included to prompt the speaker to expand upon these ideas. This type of outline includes the most complete information.

   No matter which type of outline is employed, details or facts that might be forgotten easily by the speaker should be noted on the outline, too.

   EXAMPLE: If the speaker highlights population trends in the United States and compares these trends with the number of employed persons in the country, perhaps it is a good idea to include these numbers on the outline as well—near the topic, phrase, or sentence used.

b. The actual speech: If the entire text of the speech needs to be typed, as is the case of a paper to be read by the speaker, the secretary will need to type for easy reading at the podium. Here are some techniques that are often used to prepare a typed speech.

   (1) *Spacing:* The speech should be double-spaced with a triple-space between paragraphs. One-inch side margins should be sufficient as well as one-inch top and bottom margins.
   (2) *Type size and style:* At least a 10-pitch type size should be used for ease of reading. A large type face such as Orator

or Orator Presenter will create typewritten images that will appear large and much easier to read from a distance. The speaker who has trouble with bifocals or lighting conditions will have an easier time reading a larger type face.

(3) *Accuracy of typing:* Be sure that there are no noticeable corrections that will distract the speaker while he/she is speaking. The typing should be neatly arranged on the page and accurately prepared.

c. *Handout materials:* The speaker may want to share some sample handout materials with the audience. In this case, the secretary should make sure that these are prepared ahead of time and arranged so the speaker can integrate these with the presentation. With speeches that are being read, the handout material may be a copy of the typewritten or printed speech; this is the case for research presentations. These copies should be available in quantity for the speaker to distribute at the close of the presentation.

d. *Visual aids:* Some speakers will require visual aids (transparencies or slides) to be prepared ahead of time to accompany the speech. The secretary should work in cooperation with the executive to determine exactly what types of visual aids to prepare. These should be ready ahead of time so that the executive can use them in practicing for the presentation.

(See Chapter 6, Conferences and Meetings, for directions on the preparation of audiovisual aids.)

Chapter 11: Review Questions

Part A: Multiple-Choice Questions

DIRECTIONS: Select the best answer from the four alternatives. Write your answer in the blank to the left of the number.

_____ 1. If the letter contains both an attention line and a subject line

  a. the attention line is typed a double-space after the inside address, with the subject line immediately following.
  b. the attention line may be underlined, while the subject line should be typed in all capitals.
  c. the attention line and the subject line should follow the same style; both all caps, initial caps, and/or underscored.
  d. the subject line is typed a double-space after the inside address, with the attention line immediately following.

_____ 2. Which of the following salutations is most appropriate for a congratulatory letter being addressed to the Norbort Corp., Sales Division, Attention Ray Johnson?

  a. Dear Mr. Johnson:
  b. Dear Sales Division Manager
  c. Dear Norbort Corp.
  d. With an attention line, the salutation is omitted.

_____ 3. The president of Mavis Corp. sent a formal letter to the new board members. The best closing for a formal letter is

  a. Cordially
  b. Sincerely
  c. Truly yours
  d. Yours

_____ 4. If material is enclosed with the letter, an enclosure notation is typed

  a. a double-space after the complimentary closing as either a full word or abbreviated.
  b. a double-space after the reference initials and typed as a full word; do not abbreviate.
  c. in all capital letters or initial caps, spelled as a full word or abbreviated, and double-spaced after the reference initials.

d. in initial caps, spelled as a full word or abbreviated, and double-spaced after the reference initials or double-spaced after the copy notation if the individuals receiving the copy also receive the enclosure.

_____ 5. Which of the following letter styles includes a subject line instead of a salutation?

   a. Blocked letter style
   b. Modified blocked letter style
   c. Open style
   d. Simplified letter style

_____ 6. Which of the following is a correctly typed second-page heading for a blocked letter style?

   a. James P. Smith, Jr.—Finance Department—Page 2
   b. James P. Smith, Jr.
      January 21, 199-
      Page 2
   c. James P. Smith, Jr.
      Finance Department
      January 21, 199-
   d. Smith—Finance—January—2

_____ 7. Where should special mailing notations, such as Registered and Certified, be typed on a business envelope?

   a. In the lower left corner.
   b. In the upper left corner, a double space after the return address.
   c. In the upper right corner, a double space under the postage block.
   d. Just above the mailing address—type the special notation, then double-space to the first line of the mailing address.

_____ 8. To process volumes of mail, the U.S. Postal Service uses

   a. magnetic ink character recognition (MICR).
   b. optical character recognition (OCR).
   c. point of sale terminal (POS).
   d. express mail.

_____ 9. When addresses are printed using database management software, the variable data are stored in

   a. a code file.
   b. a file.

c. a primary file.
d. a secondary file.

10. Your word processing software does not have a mail-merge function. The best way to address envelopes would be to

   a. create a code file to be used whenever an address needs to be printed.
   b. upgrade the word processing software to a package with a mail-merge function.
   c. use a conventional typewriter.
   d. write the addresses by hand.

11. A correspondence format specifically designed for internal use between departments and branch offices is

   a. the business letter.
   b. the interoffice memorandum.
   c. the news release.
   d. the report.

12. Which statement is correct?

   a. For an unbound report, the left margin is 1½ inches and the right margin is 1 inch.
   b. The right margin on each page of the report needs to be 1½ inches.
   c. The second page of the report can have a page number typed on the fourth or the seventh line; after the page number, however, always triple-space to the text.
   d. The top margin on the first page of a report should be 2 inches whether there is a title or no title.

13. A helpful tool for making sure text does not extend into the top or bottom margins or into the left and right margins is

   a. an automatic supplement function in word processing.
   b. a page-end guide.
   c. a margin guide.
   d. a widow function in word processing.

14. The term *Ibid.* means that reference is made to

   a. a previous source, but there are intervening references.
   b. more than one reference appearing previously in the report.
   c. the immediately preceding reference.
   d. the same page reference as a previous reference whether or not there are intervening references.

15. A reference citation that appears at the end of the report on a separate page is referred to as

    a. a bibliography.
    b. an endnote.
    c. a footnote.
    d. a note.

16. A list of all references consulted by the author that contributed to the content of the report is called

    a. an annotated bibliography.
    b. an index.
    c. a selected bibliography.
    d. a working bibliography.

17. When a graphic illustration based on primary data is used within text, the source reference

    a. is included as a part of the subtitle of the illustration.
    b. is typed immediately after the title of the illustration.
    c. may be omitted.
    d. should be included with the other reference citations.

18. An illustration that consists of a series of connected lines showing a particular business trend over a period of time is

    a. a bar graph.
    b. a line graph.
    c. a pictogram.
    d. a pie graph.

19. An illustration that depicts the parts of a whole is

    a. a bar graph.
    b. a drawing.
    c. a pictogram.
    d. a pie graph.

20. A common format for statistical representation is within a table. A table

    a. may be placed on a page with text if it can be centered on the page.
    b. may start a triple-space after text on a page if the entire table can fit on the page.

Preparing Communications in Final Format   427

c. should be placed on a page by itself because placing tables on pages with text is too cluttered.
d. should be placed on a page by itself in reading position.

_____ 21. Adhering to general guidelines for naming files, which of the following is a correct file name for disk storage of a report about a new local area network product?

a. LAN TIMER
b. NETWORKTIMER
c. REPORT.WP
d. TIMER.LAN

_____ 22. The official report of a meeting which summarizes the events of the meeting is known as

a. an agenda.
b. minutes.
c. proceedings.
d. a summary.

_____ 23. A secretary is sometimes called upon to assist with the executive's preparation for a speech. Which of the following techniques would be particularly applicable to this situation?

a. Acting as a ghostwriter for the speaker and writing the speech.
b. Gathering background research for the executive.
c. Reminding the speaker to prepare visual aids.
d. Typing a rough copy of the speech to assist with the presentation.

Part B: Matching Sets

Matching Set 1:

Match the document descriptions (24-28) with the appropriate type of business communication (A-J). Write the letter of your answer in the blank to the left of the number.

Types of Business Communication

A. Announcement
B. Blocked Letter
C. Business Report
D. Interoffice Memorandum
E. Itinerary

F. Minutes
G. Modified Block Letter
H. News Release
I. Outline
J. Summary

DOCUMENT DESCRIPTIONS

_____ 24. A detailed summary of an executive's travel plans.

_____ 25. A document containing key words and/or phrases enumerated in descending order using numerals, numbers, and letters of the alphabet.

_____ 26. An announcement sent to the local newspaper for immediate release.

_____ 27. Correspondence between individuals, departments, and branch offices of the same company.

_____ 28. The official report of a meeting.

Matching Set 2:

Look at the outline of a business letter. Match each of the items concerning letter parts and letter styles (29-39) with the appropriate term (A-S). Write the letter of your answer in the blank to the left of the number.

Terms

A. Attention Line
B. Blind Copy Notation
C. Blocked
D. Body
E. Carbon Notation
F. Closed
G. Complimentary Closing
H. Copy Notation
I. Date Line
J. Enclosure Notation

K. Inside Address
L. Mixed
M. Modified Block
N. Open
O. Reference Initials
P. Salutation
Q. Signature Line
R. Simplified
S. Subject Line

Preparing Communications in Final Format   **429**

PARTS OF LETTER/LETTER STYLES

29. _____   34. _____   38. This is an example of a _____ letter style.

30. _____   35. _____

31. _____   36. _____   39. This is an example of _____ punctuation style.

32. _____   37. _____

33. _____

Part C: Problem Situations

DIRECTIONS: For the questions relating to each of the following problem situations, select the best answer from the four alternatives. Write the letter of your answer in the blank to the left of the number.

Problem 1

As the secretary for Attorney McDunna, you manage all his correspondence files. A computer system is used to produce all correspondence; word processing, spreadsheets, graphics, and database management software are available. Attorney McDunna obtained a new client on Monday, May 21. The client, William Carter, needs legal counsel on a land development project. The following questions pertain to the management of the files (correspondence) sent to Mr. Carter.

_____ 40. A diskette was formatted for all of Mr. Carter's correspondence. The best external label for this diskette is

    a. WM. CARTER
    b. CLIENT 5-21-9-
    c. LAND DEVELOPMENT PROJECT 5-29-9-
    d. NEW CLIENT 5-21-9-

_____ 41. A cover letter and contract are always sent to new clients. The best file name for the cover letter sent to Mr. Carter on the day he became a client is
    a. CARTER.LTR
    b. LTR52192.WC
    c. NEW52192.LTR
    d. NEWCLIENT

42. On May 27, a preliminary report was sent to Mr. Carter about zoning for the area. The best file name for the zoning report is

   a. CARTER.527
   b. PRELIM.RPT
   c. REPORT.ZONE
   d. ZONE527.RPT

43. Mr. Carter requested that the land costs be broken down into percentage form. A pie graph was generated to show each cost portion to the total cost. The best file name for the pie graph is

   a. GRAPH.PIE
   b. LANDCOST.PIC
   c. LANDCOST.PIE
   d. PIECOST.PIC

44. Mr. Carter's name was added to the database address file. This requires that the secretary

   a. create a code file for Mr. Carter so labels and/or envelopes can be generated when needed.
   b. create a database file for Mr. Carter and enter the address variables.
   c. create a primary file for Mr. Carter and enter the primary data.
   d. enter the appropriate field variables for Mr. Carter into the data base.

Problem 2

EMPLOYEE SURVEY RESULTS
(SS)

(DS) NAME (SS)	DEPARTMENT	PROPOSAL
Jody Bakersmith	MIS	Agree
Karl Fisher	Marketing	Agree
Bart Hampton	Finance	Disagree
Gretta Olsen	MIS	Agree
David Routhier	Marketing	Disagree
Betty Simpson	Accounting	Agree
Lauri Thomas	Accounting	Disagree

(SS)

45. The Employee Survey Results table will be typed using word processing software. Horizontal placement is best determined by

a. beginning at column position 42 and backspacing once for every two characters/spaces.
b. beginning at column position 50 and backspacing for every character/space.
c. counting the number of characters and spaces in the longest line, divide by two, subtract the answer from the centerpoint for the left margin.
d. using the table function.

46. In using the mathematical method for determining the left margin, the longest line in the table is

   a. Jody Bakersmith   MIS   Agree
   b. David Routhier   Marketing   Disagree
   c. Lauri Thomas   Accounting   Disagree
   d. Jody Bakersmith   Accounting   Disagree

47. The table will be typed using word processing software. The body of the report is to be double-spaced. For the vertical placement on a full sheet of paper in reading position

   a. begin typing the title of the table on line 23.
   b. begin typing the title of the table on line 29.
   c. use the center-page code before typing the title of the table.
   d. use the center-page code at the beginning of the table and return 6 times after the last typed line of the table.

48. The table will be typed using a typewriter with an automatic correction feature. The body of the report is to be single-spaced. For the vertical placement on a half sheet of paper
   a. begin typing the title of the table on line 6.
   b. begin typing the title of the table on line 9.
   c. begin typing the title of the table on line 12.
   d. begin typing the title of the table on line 19.

49. The table will be typed using word processing software. The body of the report is to be single-spaced. For the vertical placement on a page following text material

   a. double-space from the last line of text to the title of the table.
   b. triple-space from the last line of text to the title of the table.
   c. triple-space from the last line of text to the title of the table; write *(Continue)* at the bottom of the page and repeat the table title followed by *(Continued)* at the top of the next page.
   d. use the center-page code before typing the title of the table.

Chapter 11: Solutions

Part A: Multiple-Choice Questions

	Answer	Refer to Chapter Section
1.	(c)	[A-1-c]
2.	(b)	[A-1-d]
3.	(a)	[A-1-g]
4.	(d)	[A-1-j and A-1-k]
5.	(d)	[A-2-c]
6.	(c)	[A-4-a and Figure 11-6]
7.	(c)	[B-1-h]
8.	(b)	[B-2]
9.	(b)	[B-4-a(1)]
10.	(a)	[B-4-c]
11.	(b)	[C]
12.	(c)	[D-1-a(1)(c) and D-3-b]
13.	(c)	[D-6]
14.	(c)	[D-7-c]
15.	(b)	[D-7-d(2)]
16.	(d)	[D-7-e(1)(a)]
17.	(c)	[D-8-b(2)(a)]
18.	(b)	[D-8-c(3)]
19.	(d)	[D-8-c(4)]
20.	(b)	[D-9-b(2)(a)]
21.	(d)	[E-1]
22.	(b)	[F-1]
23.	(b)	(F-5)

Part B: Matching Sets

Matching Set 1

24.	(E)	[F-3]
25.	(I)	[F-4]
26.	(H)	[F-2]
27.	(D)	[C]
28.	(F)	[F-1]

Matching Set 2

29.	(I)	[A-1-a]
30.	(K)	[A-1-b]
31.	(P)	[A-1-d]
32.	(S)	[A-1-e]
33.	(D)	[A-1-f]

34.	(G)	[A-1-g]
35.	(Q)	[A-1-h]
36.	(O)	[A-1-i]
37.	(H)	[A-1-k]
38.	(C)	[A-2-a]
39.	(N)	[A-3-a]

Part C: Problem Situations

40.	(a)	[E-2-a and E-2-c] The use of Mr. Carter's name would clearly identify the diskette contents.
41.	(c)	[E-1 and E-2-c] The file name NEW52192.LTR gives the most precise information for the file: NEW for new client; 52192 for date; and LTR for type of document.
42.	(d)	[E-1 and E-2-c] The file name ZONE527.RPT identifies a report concerning zoning dated 5/27.
43.	(d)	[E-1-c and E-2-c] This is the best choice because it not only tells the topic (Land Cost); it also identifies the type of graph, a pie graph. Obviously, the name could also be COST-PIE.PIC.
44.	(d)	[B-4-a(1)]
45.	(d)	[D-9-a]
46.	(d)	[D-9-b(1)(a)]
47.	(d)	[D-9-b(2)(b)]
48.	(b)	[D-9-b(2)(b)]
49.	(b)	[D-9-b(2)(a)]

GLOSSARY
Office Administration

ACTIVE RECORDS. Those records that are consulted in the current administration of the business. (4)[1]

AD HOC COMMITTEE. A small group formed to investigate a particular event or problem that has occurred within the organization; this committee has a temporary appointment and will serve until a report is presented to the executive board or committee. (6)

AGENDA. A list of items of business to be discussed or presented during the meeting. (6)

ALMANAC. A book or publication, usually published on an annual basis, that includes factual information about the events of the year. (5)

ALPHABETIC CLASSIFICATION SYSTEM. A set of filing procedures that is based on the use of the alphabet as a means of organizing the records. (4)

APERTURE CARD. A punched card that contains a slot into which a microimage (or microimages) can be inserted; text may be punched into the card or interpreted on the card. (4)

APPRAISAL OF RECORDS. The examination of company records to determine the value of the records. (4)

ARCHIVE. A facility that houses records that are being retained for research or historical value. (4) A collection of business documents of historical value maintained by a business, government agency, or university. (5)

---

[1] The number in parentheses after each entry indicates the chapter location in the text.

AUDIOCONFERENCE. A type of teleconference; only voice or sound communication takes place. (6)

AUDITRON. A device that controls use of a convenience copier through the use of a plastic card, key, or other insert device to activate the copier. (7)

AUTHOR. An executive, manager, supervisor, or other individual who originates work to be completed by professional secretaries or word processing personnel; may also be called an end user. (2)

AUTHORIZATION. The procedure implemented that permits only certain personnel to use the reprographics equipment. (7)

BIBLIOGRAPHY. A record of each reference used in researching information which includes author's name, title of book or reference, publisher, place of publication, and date of publication. (5)

BIOGRAPHICAL DIRECTORY. A publication that highlights the achievements of noted individuals who contributed to their professions, to government, or the country. (5)

BLOCK CODES. Groups of numbers reserved for records that have a common feature or characteristic. (4)

BUSINESS FORM. A record that is designed with constant information preprinted or appearing on it and space provided for variable information to be inserted later. (4)

BUSINESS REPORT. The final output of some information-gathering activity within the business, summarizing the methods, procedures, and results of a business project or research. (4)

CALENDARING. Making appropriate notations on office calendars of upcoming appointments, meetings, or other events; appointments may be entered on a computer so that a printout of appointments and meetings can be obtained each morning. (2)

CENTRALIZATION. The plan of operation that organizes support personnel in work centers with easy access to and from all departments in the company. (2)

CENTRALIZED CONTROL. The organizational pattern used to locate reprographics operations in one physical location in the organization under the direction of one manager. (7)

CHRONOLOGICAL SYSTEM. A set of filing procedures used when records are filed according to date, either most recent date first or oldest date first. (4)

CLASSIFICATION SYSTEM. A set of procedures used in a filing system based on alphabetic, numeric, or alphanumeric rules. (4)

CODING. Making notations on the record itself as to exactly how the record will be stored (under what names or numbers). (4)

COLOR CODING. An identification system that uses colored strips on the side of file folders to represent numeric or alphanumeric codes. (4)

COMMERCIAL PRINTING FIRM. An outside business organization that provides services such as artwork, graphic design, or special printing requirements through contracts with the organization. (7)

COMMERCIAL TRAVEL AGENCY. A business firm specializing in making travel arrangements for individuals and organizations requesting travel services. (1)

COMPUTER CONFERENCE. A meeting with communication between participants taking place using computer terminals to transmit information; all records produced, documents transmitted, and comments written are stored in the computer; a form of electronic mail. (6)

COMPUTER DATA BANK. An information bank to which a company may subscribe in order to have access, through the computer, to a data bank available within a particular profession or field. (5)

CONFERENCE. A formal meeting of a group of people with a common purpose; may be company-sponsored or association-sponsored meetings. (6)

CONFIRMED RESERVATION. Notification from a transportation carrier or a hotel that a reservation is being held for a given individual. (1)

CONSTANT INFORMATION. Descriptors, key words, or phrases pre-printed or appearing on a business form that remain the same on all forms of a particular kind. (4)

CONTROLLING. One of the functions of supervising that involves comparing actual productivity and results with those that were anticipated during a specific period of time. (2)

CONVENTIONAL FORMAT. A design for correspondence, business forms, or business reports that results in paper (or hard) copies. (4)

COPY QUALITY. An examination of the appearance of the copy produced to be sure that it has been prepared accurately and according to instructions. (7)

COPYRIGHT LAWS. Legislation that has been enacted to prohibit making copies of copyrighted material without the written permission of the publisher. (7)

CORRESPONDENCE. Business letters created primarily as external communication and memorandums created as internal communication. (4)

CRITICAL PATH METHOD (CPM). An outgrowth of the Gantt chart which is a more precise method of examining the breakdown of a project into procedures and an associated time plan. (3)

CROSS-REFERENCING. A notation in the file that indicates where the original document or complete file can be located; used whenever a record could possibly be filed in more than one place in the files. (4)

CROSS-TRAINING. The process of being trained on more than one job in the office. (2)

DATA. Information items that describe a person, place, event, or object. (4)

DATA BASE. An electronic method of organizing facts or data that involves the creation of one or more computer data files. (4)

DEBIT CARD. A card issued by a bank, similar to a credit card, which allows the cardholder to charge the purchases of merchandise or services and have that charge come directly out of the cardholder's bank account. (1)

DECENTRALIZATION. The plan of operation in which clerical support personnel are housed within individual departments and perform office functions needed by that department only. (2)

DECENTRALIZED CONTROL. The organizational pattern used to locate reprographics operations within the various departments where they are utilized; usually under the direction and supervision of the department manager. (7)

DEWEY DECIMAL CLASSIFICATION SYSTEM. A library cataloging system that is based on the premise that all knowledge can be classified into ten primary groupings. (5)

DIRECT-ACCESS PROCEDURES. Procedures that permit an individual to go directly to the file cabinet and locate the file, without any intermediate steps. (4)

DISPERSAL. The duplication of hard copies of documents and their storage in other locations. (4)

DOCUMENTATION. The development of written procedures that identify user requirements, functions, workflows, reports, files, and other information needed. (3)

DOMESTIC TRAVEL. Transportation services provided for travel within the boundaries of a country. (1)

DUPLEX-NUMERIC SYSTEM. Two or more sets of code numbers are assigned to files; sets of numbers are separated by a dash, comma, period, or space. (4)

EDITING. The procedure used by an author to revise the original document. (2)

ELECTRONIC BLACKBOARD. A device used with teleconferences to display business graphics on a pressure-sensitive blackboard and transmit these visuals to other meeting locations. (6)

EMPLOYEE MANUAL. A handbook that provides specific information needed to be a functional worker within the company; includes work schedules, hours, salaries, schedules for salary reviews, dress codes, vacations, benefits, and other types of employee information. (2)

FIELD. A location reserved for a specific type of information. (4)

FILE. A set of related records that are stored together or under the same file name. (4)

FILE FOLDER. An individual container used to store the documents pertaining to one correspondent, case, or account. (4)

FLOW-PROCESS CHART. The most widely used tool of procedures analysis; each step in a specific work process is identified and classified into an operation, a transportation, an inspection, a delay, or a storage step. (3)

FORMAL MEETING. A meeting that is planned in advance, usually held in a conference room or special meeting room, with a prepared agenda. (6)

FORMS MANAGEMENT. A system designed to provide an organization with forms that are both necessary and efficient and that can be produced at the lowest printing and processing costs. (4)

GANTT CHART. A bar chart developed by Henry L. Gantt in the early 1900s for scheduling work; depicts work in progress over a period of time—day, week, or month. (3)

GEOGRAPHIC FILING. A system in which records are arranged alphabetically according to geographic locations. (4)

GUIDES. Dividers for groups of records which indicate the sections of the file. (4)

HORIZONTAL COMMUNICATION. Communication from one supervisor to another supervisor or from one subordinate to another subordinate, in other words, communication on the same level. (2)

HUMAN RESOURCE PLANNING. The process of determining personnel needs for the future and developing strategies for meeting these needs. (2)

IMPORTANT RECORDS. Documents that contribute to the continued smooth operation of a company and can be replaced or duplicated (at considerable expense of time and money) if lost or destroyed in a disaster. (4)

INACTIVE RECORDS. Those records no longer referred to on a regular basis. (4)

INCIDENTAL MOTION. Motion that arises from pending question; may be introduced at any time and must be decided before the question to which it is incidental is decided. (6)

INDEX RECORD. A record containing only reference information that may be part of a relative index for files based upon either a numeric or alphanumeric classification system. (4)

INDEXING. The decision making that is necessary in deciding what names or numbers to use in filing. (4)

INDIRECT-ACCESS PROCEDURES. A filing system that requires an individual to consult a relative index in order to locate the name, subject, or number under which the file is stored. (4)

INFORMAL MEETING. A meeting with a small number of people (two to four) to discuss a particular business matter; a specific business matter has brought these people together for a meeting. (6)

IN-HOUSE MEETING. A formal meeting that is held on company premises. (6)

IN-HOUSE REPROGRAPHICS SERVICES. Those duplicating and printing services that are provided within the organization by specialized personnel trained to perform these functions. (7)

IN-HOUSE TRANSPORTATION DEPARTMENT. A department within a firm organized to provide travel services for all departments within the organization, sometimes organized as an in-house travel agency. (1)

INSPECTING. Examining a record to be sure that it has been released for filing by an appropriate authority within the firm. (4)

INTERLIBRARY LOAN. A networking system that has been established between libraries for references located in one library to be loaned to an individual through another library for a specific period of time. (5)

INTERNATIONAL TRAVEL. Transportation services provided for travel in, to, and from other countries. (1)

ITINERARY. A business traveler's plan which includes departure and arrival information, confirmed transportation and hotel/motel reservations, and scheduled appointments and meetings. (1)

JACKET. A plastic unitized record the same size as a microfiche that has single or multiple channels in which the film is inserted. (4)

JOB SHARING. The formal arrangement whereby two office employees share the same job; one full-time job is shared part time by two people on either a temporary or permanent basis. (2)

LEFFINGWELL, WILLIAM H. The father of office management; applied the principles of scientific management to office work in his book, *Scientific Office Management*, in 1917. (2)

LETTER OF CREDIT. A letter from a bank or other financial institution stating the maximum amount of money available through that bank or institution to the individual carrying the letter. (1)

LIBRARY OF CONGRESS CLASSIFICATION SYSTEM. A library cataloging system with a larger number of major classifications than the Dewey Decimal System. (5)

LOGGING FORM. The record that indicates the date/time the job is received, the number/name of the job, the name of the person for whom the work is being done, the deadline for the job, the name of the person to whom the task is assigned, and any special instructions. (2)

MAIN MOTION. A motion that states an item of business; has the lowest precedence in rank among all types of motions; must be seconded and is subject to discussion, debate, and amendment. (6)

MANAGEMENT-BY-OBJECTIVES (MBO) APPRAISAL. With the help of the supervisor/manager, the employee establishes job objectives, both for individual performance and for personal development, against which his/her performance is measured. (2)

MATRIX PLAN. The combination plan of operation which permits some office operations to be centralized and others to be decentralized, depending upon the needs of the firm. (2)

MICROFICHE. A 6" x 4" sheet of film on which microimages are placed in rows from left to right and from top to bottom; holds approximately 60 to 70 microimages. (4)

MICROFILM. The oldest type of microform; stores page images side by side on a roll of 16mm, 35mm, 70mm, and 105mm film. (4)

MICROFORM. Any record that contains reduced images on film. (4)

MICROGRAPHICS CENTER. A centralized service within a library where research studies, dissertations, and other references are stored on microforms (microfiche and microfilm); access to these materials is typically available only within the center because of the equipment involved. (5)

MIDDLE-DIGIT FILING. A numeric system that uses the middle digits of a number as the primary indexing units. (4)

MINUTES. The official record of the meeting which summarizes the business that has been transacted, reports that have been presented, and any other significant events occurring at the meeting. (6)

MNEMONIC CODE. A code used for an item that takes on additional meaning about the item. (4)

MOTION. The presentation of an item of business to the group. (6)

MOTION STUDY. The analysis of bodily motions to determine the efficiency of manual operations within certain types of office activities. (3)

NONESSENTIAL RECORDS. Records that are not necessary to the restoration of business, have no predictable value, and probably should be destroyed once their usefulness is over. (4)

NONRECORDS. Documents made for the organization's convenience or temporary need in some operation, but normally disposed of after use. (4)

NUMERIC CLASSIFICATION SYSTEM. An indirect-access filing system that consists of numeric codes assigned to names of individuals, businesses, or subjects. (4)

OFFICE LAYOUT CHART. A flow diagram that shows the flow of work through the office as an overlay on a scale drawing of the present office layout. (3)

OFFICIAL AIRLINE GUIDE (OAG). A published guide with detailed information on airline schedules and fares for both domestic and international flights. (1)

ONLINE RESERVATION SYSTEM. A computer system connecting the travel department or agency directly with the transportation companies or with the Official Airline Guide (OAG) reservation system in order to make travel reservations directly with the carriers. (1)

ORGANIZATIONAL MANUAL. An office handbook that shows the formal relationship of divisions or departments, including duties and responsibilities, within the company; includes statement of company objectives, basic philosophy, and organizational structure. (2)

ORGANIZING. The managerial function that permits the office administrator to establish specific goals that are to be accomplished through office services. (2)

OUT GUIDE. A special guide that is substituted for a folder or a record that has been temporarily removed from the file. (4)

PARLIAMENTARY PROCEDURE. A set of rules established for the appropriate conduct of business meetings. (5) The set of rules that govern the conduct of a formal meeting (*Robert's Rules of Order* is an example of such a set of rules). (6)

PASSPORT. A formal document that is proof of citizenship and identity, valid for ten years, issued by the citizen's own government granting permission to the citizen to leave the country and travel in foreign countries. (1)

PERFORMANCE STANDARDS. Criteria for evaluating the behavior, personal traits, and results of office production. (2)

PERIODIC TRANSFER. The physical movement of records from active status within a particular department or office to a centralized records center as of a specific date each year. (4)

PERPETUAL TRANSFER. The physical movement of records from active to inactive status at any time that the event has been completed or the case closed and future referral to the records will be infrequent and limited. (4)

PETITION. A formal statement, signed by individuals who are eligible to sign the statement, asking that some specific action be taken. (6)

POSTED RECORD. A card record that is used to record information to bring the record up to date; information may be updated, changed, deleted, or added to. (4)

PRIMARY GUIDE. A guide which highlights a major division or subdivision of records stored in a file drawer or on a shelf. (4)

PRIVILEGED MOTION. A motion with the highest order of precedence which affects the comfort of the members of the group that is meeting. (6)

PROCEDURE FLOW CHART. A diagram of the entire work flow in a procedure which involves more than one department in order for the procedure to be completed. (3)

PROCEDURES. Steps used to complete a given office task and governed by operations controls. (7)

PROCEDURES ANALYSIS. The study of specific office processes to determine the steps involved, the time involved in each step, the distance involved in each step, and the departments involved in the procedure. (3)

PROGRAM EVALUATION AND REVIEW TECHNIQUE (PERT). A time plan that is an outgrowth of the Gantt chart; PERT uses a time-event network so that activities needed to complete a project by a certain deadline can be presented in a flow-chart diagram. (3)

PURGING. The process of automatically deleting the contents of a record that has been electronically stored on a magnetic medium. (4)

QUORUM. The required number of voting members who must be present in order to transact business. (6)

RECORD. A document that contains information about a set of related data items. (4)

RECORDS. Official documents of the company or organization valuable enough to be retained, using a format for storing information to be used and distributed later. (4)

RECORDS CYCLE. A series of steps from the time the record is created until its final disposition. (4)

RECORDS MANAGEMENT. The systematic control of recorded information required for the operation of the business from the time of creation through the use, storage, transfer, and disposal phases of the records cycle. (4)

RECORDS TRANSFER. The physical movement of records from active status within a particular department or office to a centralized records center. (4)

RELATIVE INDEX. A card file that identifies the numeric or alphanumeric codes that have been assigned to files. (4)

REPROGRAPHICS. The office system with primary responsibility for making copies of documents needed during the operation of the business. (7)

RESOLUTION. A formal statement of an organization's appreciation, congratulations, or sympathy. (6)

RETENTION SCHEDULE. An agreement between the department creating the record, the user (if not the department of creation), and the records manager specifying how long each active record is to be held in active storage, inactive storage, and when the record may be destroyed, if ever. (4)

SECONDARY GUIDE. A special guide that is used to highlight frequently referenced sections of the records. (4)

SOURCE BOOK. A reference with specific travel information useful in making appropriate transportation, hotel, and motel reservations. (1)

STANDING COMMITTEE. A small group of members who are appointed for a definite term with specific objectives assigned for which the group is responsible during the term. (6)

STORYBOARD. A frame-by-frame plan for the preparation of an audio-visual presentation; shows the description of the picture or illustration plus any narrative that will accompany the picture. (6)

STRAIGHT-NUMERIC FILES. The arrangement of files in consecutive order, from the lowest number to the highest number; also known as sequential or serial files. (4)

SUBJECT FILING. A classification system that uses the alphabetic system as a base to arrange records by topics or categories. (4)

SUBSIDIARY MOTION. A motion that assists, modifies, or disposes of the main motion. (6)

SYSTEM. A network of interrelated procedures, personnel, and technology working together within the business environment to achieve well-defined goals. (3)

SYSTEMS ANALYSIS. The step-by-step investigation of a system in order to define what it does and determine how it can best continue to perform these operations. (3)

SYSTEMS DESIGN. The determination of the actual inputs needed in order to achieve the desired outputs. (3)

SYSTEMS PLANNING. The process of recognizing the need for a change in the present system and conducting a preliminary investigation to determine the feasibility of further development of the idea. (3)

TAB. A projection on a file folder that contains a label with a typed caption. (4)

TASK ANALYSIS. The study of all office tasks performed by an office worker in a specific assignment over a specified period of time. (3)

TELECONFERENCE. A meeting of several people, who may be in different geographical locations, that is held through telephone communications so that the individuals can speak with each other about matters of business. (6)

TERMINAL-DIGIT FILING. A numeric system that uses the last digits of a number as the primary indexing units. (4)

THESAURUS. A lexicon (dictionary) or similar book of words or information that focuses on synonyms and antonyms. (5)

TICKLER SYSTEM. A reminder system that includes project or task deadlines on a daily, weekly, and monthly basis. (2)

TRANSPARENCY. An acetate sheet that contains an image burned or drawn on it that can be projected on a screen or wall. (6)

TRAVEL ADVANCE. An amount of money received from the organization to be used for payment of out-of-pocket expenses incurred while on business travel. (1)

TRAVELERS' CHECKS. Drafts purchased through local banks, credit unions, the American Automobile Association, and savings and loan associations that can be cashed *only* by the purchaser. (1)

TRIP FILE. A folder (or series of folders) containing all business materials the business traveler needs to carry on a business trip. (1)

TURNAROUND TIME. The elapsed time between the receiving of a task and its completion; or the elapsed time that results when the author sends the task to word processing and waits for its return; or the elapsed time between the time the word processing supervisor receives the document from the author and the time it is received back from the word processing specialist. (2)

ULTRAFICHE. A 6" x 4" sheet of film on which hundreds of microimages can be stored in a similar pattern to that used on a microfiche, from left to right in rows and from top to bottom on the sheet. (4)

UNCLASSIFIED MOTION. A motion that is appropriate but cannot be classified as a main motion, a subsidiary motion, an incidental motion, or a privileged motion. (6)

USEFUL RECORDS. Records used in the operation of the organization that can be easily replaced. (4)

VARIABLE INFORMATION. Information that is inserted on the original document and will change each time the document is prepared. (4)

VERTICAL FILE SERVICE. Pamphlets, booklets, leaflets, and other loose-leaf materials stored in a file cabinet for easy access. (5)

VIDEOCONFERENCE. A formal meeting that is a type of teleconferencing; a meeting where participants who are located in different geographical locations are able to view one another on closed-circuit television (slow scan, freeze frames, or full motion) and talk in turns during the same time period. (6)

VISA. An endorsement stamped or written on a passport, showing examination by appropriate officials of a foreign country, which grants the bearer entry into that country for a specified period of time. In many foreign countries, a visa is not required. (1)

VITAL RECORDS. Records essential for the effective continuous operation of the firm. (4)

WORK DISTRIBUTION CHART. A technique used to identify the major work activities performed within a specific work group and the amount of time the work group as a whole spends on each activity. (3)

WORK SIMPLIFICATION. The process of improving work performance by finding out how people, resources, technology, time, and space can be utilized more effectively and efficiently. (3)

GLOSSARY
Communication

ABSTRACT. A summary of a document using key words from the document. (10)[1]

ABSTRACT LANGUAGE. The quality of words and thoughts where meanings can be interpreted differently by different people, even in the same situation. (8)

ACTIVE WORDS. Words that denote action on the part of the individual. (8)

ANNOTATED BIBLIOGRAPHY. A listing of all references used in the report, in alphabetical order, with a brief paragraph following each entry commenting on the content and value of the reference. (11)

ANNOTATING. Marginal notations on a document answering questions or presenting facts related to material in the document. (10)

APPENDIX. Supplementary research material included in a supplementary part of the report. (8)

BAR GRAPH OR CHART. An illustration that shows a comparison from one time period to another; uses bars of equal width to show quantities (values) on one axis and the factor to be measured on the other axis. (11)

BIBLIOGRAPHY. An alphabetical list of all information sources used for a report included at the end of the report. (8) An alphabetical list of all references consulted by the author that contributed to the content of the report; usually placed at the end of the report on a separate page. (11)

---

[1]The number in parentheses after each entry indicates the chapter location in the text.

BLOCKED LETTER STYLE. A standard letter style which begins all lines of the letter, including the opening and closing lines at the left margin. (11)

CLARITY. A criterion of effective sentence and paragraph construction that requires that any message be written in an accurate and nonconfusing manner. (8)

COHERENCE. A quality shown by writing that is consistent in style, word choice, and word usage, resulting in sentence and paragraph unity and unity of the work. (8)

COMBINATION LETTER. A message in which there is both a positive and a negative response. (8)

CONCISENESS. Writing in a brief but comprehensive manner. (8)

CONCRETE LANGUAGE. The use of words and terms that are precise in meaning; the opposite of abstract language. (8)

CONSTANT INFORMATION. Wording that will stay exactly the same on every message produced. (8)

COPY EDITING. Revising a draft of a document for consistency, conciseness, and grammatical accuracy by making revisions within the body of the document. The edited copy is returned to the author for verification. (9)

COPY NOTATION. Special notation used only when a copy of the letter is being sent to another person or persons and is typed a double-space after the reference initials. (11)

DATA BASE. A complete record of variable information. (8)

DEDUCTIVE STYLE. The direct approach to writing in which the main idea is stated first, followed by supporting details. (8)

DESCRIPTORS. Adjectives and adverbs that are used as key words to denote certain aspects or characteristics found in business writing. (8)

DOCUMENTATION. The creating, collecting, organizing, storing, citing, and disseminating of descriptive information in writing; in report writing, refers to reference notes (footnotes or endnotes) and bibliographic information. (11)

EMPATHY. An understanding of the feelings or emotions of another person. (8)

EMPHASIS. The attachment of greater importance to particular aspects of a message; placing special stress on a particular thought, word, or syllable. (8)

ENDNOTE. A reference note that appears on a separate page at the end of the report. (11)

EXPERIMENTAL RESEARCH. The conduct of a study to determine whether a change in one factor or variable causes a change in another factor or variable. (8)

EXTERNAL REPORT. Business writing which will be disseminated outside the organization. (8)

FOOTNOTE. A reference note that appears on the bottom of the page where the reference is made. (11)

FORM LETTER. Correspondence with some identical parts that may be sent to more than one person or company for a specific purpose. (8)

GLOSSARY. An alphabetical list of terms defined for the reader. (8)

GOODWILL. A positive feeling between organizations or between people working within organizations that results in positive, clear, and courteous communication. (8)

GRAPHIC AID. An illustration that is used to clarify data presented within a report. (11)

GRAPHICS. Visual representations of successive changes in the value (quantity) of one or more variables. (11)

HARD COPY. Typewritten or printed pages of a document. (9)

HORIZONTAL REPORT. Business writing that is distributed from department to department or division to division within the organization; communication at the same administrative level. (8)

IBID. Term used when reference is made to the immediately preceding footnote or endnote. (11)

INDEX. A list of names and subjects, with page references in order to find specific information contained in the report quickly; appears at end of report. (8)

INDUCTIVE STYLE. An organizational approach that implies that the writing will lead the reader to the main idea; the details and supporting information are presented first, with the main idea following. (8)

INFORMAL REPORT. Business writing used to transmit meaningful information to other people within the organization or outside the organization; usually no more than five pages at the most. (8)

INSIDE ADDRESS. The address to which the letter will be mailed. (11)

INTEROFFICE COMMUNICATION. Message transmission from one office to another within an organization. (8)

INTEROFFICE MEMORANDUM. Correspondence between individuals, departments, and branch offices of the same company; interoffice memorandum forms may be used. (11)

ITINERARY. An executive's travel plan that specifies all details concerning the business travel. (11)

JARGON. Words used in business writing which are generally understood only by others in the profession; often referred to as "slang" language in business writing. (8)

LINE GRAPH OR CHART. An illustration consisting of a series of connected lines showing a particular trend in business data for a period of time. (11)

LOC. CIT. Term which refers to the same page reference as the previous footnote. (11)

MEAN. The arithmetic average of a group of responses obtained by computing the sum of all the responses and dividing by the number of responses; a measure of central tendency. (8)

MEDIAN. The midpoint in a distribution of responses; a measure of central tendency. (8)

MEMORANDUM. The most common medium for corresponding within the firm; used for communication whenever the writer and the receiver of the message work for the same organization. (8)

MINUTES. A summary of the events of a meeting; serves as the official report of the meeting. (11)

MIXED PUNCTUATION. In business letters, there is a colon after the salutation and a comma after the complimentary closing. (11)

MODE. The response that occurs the most frequently in a distribution of responses; a measure of central tendency. (8)

MODIFIED BLOCKED LETTER STYLE. A standard letter style in which the date line begins at the centerpoint or ends at the right margin, the complimentary closing and signature line begin at the centerpoint, and paragraphs may be blocked or indented. (11)

NARRATIVE REPORT. A report that includes primarily text material (words). (8)

NEGATIVE LETTER. Correspondence that conveys a "no" response or some other form of "bad news"; an indirect approach is used to write this type of correspondence. (8)

NEWS RELEASE. A message to be disseminated to newspapers or magazines with business news about the organization. (11)

NONTECHNICAL REPORT. A report that conveys information to people who do not have backgrounds in the subject area; an effort is made to refrain from using technical language. (8)

OBSERVATIONAL RESEARCH. The conduct of a study that permits the researcher to actually see the actions or results of individual or group activity. (8)

OP. CIT. Term used when reference is made to a previous source, but there are intervening reference notes. (11)

OPEN PUNCTUATION. No punctuation is typed after the salutation or the complimentary closing in a business letter. (11)

OPTICAL CHARACTER RECOGNITION (OCR). The process used to scan characters for machine identification using light-sensitive devices; used by the U.S. Postal Service to scan addresses. (11)

OUTLINE. Key words coded in descending order, using Roman numerals, numbers, and letters of the alphabet to show the basic topics of a report or speech. (11)

PAGINATION. The number of document pages from the first page through the last page. (11)

PARALLELISM. The statement of ideas that are equal in thought in identical grammatical form. (8)

PASSIVE WORDS. Words that denote inaction or waiting for something to happen. (8)

PERSUASIVE LETTER. Correspondence that tends to be positive but complex in nature, requesting the receiver to take some action after justification for such action is presented in the letter. (8)

PIE GRAPH OR CHART. An illustration that represents the parts that make up a whole; the circle equals 100 percent, and the sections are divided off parts of the whole, or smaller percentages of the whole. (11)

POSITIVE LETTER. Favorable correspondence that says "yes" or otherwise presents good news to the receiver. (8)

PRECIS. A paraphrased summary of a document. (10)

PRIMARY MEMORY. Internal computer memory used for processing. (11)

PRIMARY RESEARCH. An investigation to gather original information to use as current data in a report. (8)

PROGRESS REPORT. A report that identifies work in process and gives the present status of a project. (8)

PROOFREADING. Checking the final copy for spelling, punctuation, and adherence to formatting guidelines. (9)

PROOFREADING MARKS. Symbols written within the margins of a typed document so the error can be viewed and corrected. (9)

RANGE. The difference between the value of the highest response and the value of the lowest response in a distribution. (8)

READING POSITION. Placement of a table three lines above exact vertical placement. (11)

REFERENCE INITIALS. The initials of the typist of the letter; may also include the writer's initials. (11)

REFERENCE NOTES. Notations used to acknowledge various sources of information; also called reference citations, footnotes, or endnotes. (11)

RELIABLE DATA. Data that are measured consistently and accurately. (8)

REPETITIVE LETTER. Form correspondence that is prepared and sent to a list of different people, each with personal name and address inserted; some small amounts of information may vary. (8)

REPORT. The result of a process whose purpose is to transmit meaningful data to an individual(s) for either information or decision-making purposes. (8)

ROUTINE LETTER. Correspondence with the primary purpose of exchanging day-to-day information; sometimes called a neutral letter. (8)

SALUTATION. The greeting to the person to whom the letter is being sent. (11)

SCHEDULED REPORT. A report that is issued at regularly stated intervals. (8)

SECONDARY RESEARCH. An investigation to gather information others have prepared to use as a supportive basis for a report. (8)

SELECTED BIBLIOGRAPHY. An alphabetical listing of those references pertaining to the topic that have been cited previously in the reference notes. (11)

SIMPLIFIED LETTER STYLE. A standard letter style in which all lines begin at the left margin, there is no salutation or complimentary closing, and a subject line is typed in all capital letters a triple space after the inside address and a triple space before the body of the letter; first introduced by the National Office Management Association, now the Administrative Management Society. (11)

SOFT COPY. The pages of a document stored on disk and viewed on a computer screen. (9)

STANDARD DEVIATION. A measure of the degree of scattering of a frequency distribution about its arithmetic mean. (8)

STATISTICAL REPORT. A report that includes primarily numerical data. (8)

SURVEY RESEARCH. A study to determine opinions, beliefs, or reactions to specific phenomena; may be administered in written (a questionnaire) or oral form (an interview). (8)

TABLE. Text material presented in a columnar format. (11)

TECHNICAL REPORT. Business writing that conveys information to professionals within the field who will understand the specialized vocabulary and terminology included in the report. (8)

TONE. The manner in which a certain attitude is expressed in writing. (8)

UNBIASED LANGUAGE. The expression of thoughts and ideas so that equal treatment is given to everyone (men and women, minority groups, and job holders). (8)

UNITY. A coherent flow of ideas throughout a written work—within sentences, within paragraphs, and between paragraphs. (8)

VALID DATA. Data that measure what they are intended to measure. (8)

VARIABLE INFORMATION. Any text material that must be inserted to complete the message; this information will change on each letter produced. (8)

VERTICAL REPORT. Business writing prepared for someone at a higher level or a lower level within the organizational structure of the company. (8)

WIDOW LINE. One line from a paragraph by itself on a page. (11)